EMOTIONS INSIDE OUT

130 Years after Darwin's
The Expression of the Emotions in Man and Animals

ANNALS OF THE NEW YORK ACADEMY OF SCIENCES
Volume 1000

EMOTIONS INSIDE OUT

130 Years after Darwin's *The Expression of the Emotions in Man and Animals*

Edited by Paul Ekman, Joseph J. Campos, Richard J. Davidson, and Frans B. M. de Waal

The New York Academy of Sciences
New York, New York
2003

Copyright © 2003 by the New York Academy of Sciences. All rights reserved. Under the provisions of the United States Copyright Act of 1976, individual readers of the Annals are permitted to make fair use of the material in them for teaching or research. Permission is granted to quote from the Annals provided that the customary acknowledgment is made of the source. Material in the Annals may be republished only by permission of the Academy. Address inquiries to the Permissions Department (editorial@nyas.org) at the New York Academy of Sciences.

Copying fees: For each copy of an article made beyond the free copying permitted under Section 107 or 108 of the 1976 Copyright Act, a fee should be paid through the Copyright Clearance Center, Inc., 222 Rosewood Drive, Danvers, MA 01923 (www.copyright.com).

⊗ The paper used in this publication meets the minimum requirements of the American National Standard for Information Sciences—Permanence of Paper for Printed Library Materials, ANSI Z39.48-1984.

Library of Congress Cataloging-in-Publication Data

Emotions inside out: 130 Years after Darwin's *The Expression of the Emotions in Man and Animals* / edited by Paul Ekman ... [et al.].
        p. cm. — (Annals of the New York Academy of Sciences ; v. 1000)
Result of a conference sponsored by the New York Academy of Sciences and held November 16–17, 2002 in New York City.
Includes bibliographical references (p.).
ISBN 1-57331-464-1 (cloth : alk. paper) — ISBN 1-57331-465-X (pbk. : alk. paper)
        1. Darwin, Charles, 1809–1882. Expression of the emotions in man and animals—Congresses. 2. Emotions—Congresses. 3. Expression—Congresses. 4. Psychology, Comparative—Congresses. I. Ekman, Paul. II. Series.
    Q11.N5 vol. 1000
    [QP410]
    500 s—dc22
    [152

                                                                2003023320

GYAT / PCP
Printed in the United States of America
ISBN 1-57331-464-1 (cloth)
ISBN 1-57331-465-X (paper)
ISSN 0077-8923

ANNALS OF THE NEW YORK ACADEMY OF SCIENCES

Volume 1000
December 2003

EMOTIONS INSIDE OUT

130 Years after Darwin's
The Expression of the Emotions in Man and Animals

Editors and Conference Organizers
PAUL EKMAN, JOSEPH J. CAMPOS, RICHARD J. DAVIDSON,
AND FRANS B. M. DE WAAL

This volume is the result of a conference entitled **Emotions Inside Out: 130 Years after Darwin's** *The Expression of the Emotions in Man and Animals*, which was sponsored by the New York Academy of Sciences and held November 16–17, 2002 in New York City.

CONTENTS

Financial assistance was received from:
• MUSHETT FAMILY FOUNDATION, INC.

The New York Academy of Sciences believes it has a responsibility to provide an open
forum for discussion of scientific questions. The positions taken by the participants in
the reported conferences are their own and not necessarily those of the Academy. The
Academy has no intent to influence legislation by providing such forums.

Introduction

PAUL EKMAN

*Department of Psychiatry, University of California, San Francisco,
San Francisco, California 94143, USA*

ABSTRACT: In *The Expression of Emotions in Man and Animals* Darwin argued that emotions are not unique to humans, but can be found in many species; that many of the same social occasions that generate emotions in humans do so in other animals. He asked why this particular expression for a particular emotion, and his answer formed part of his demonstration of the continuity of the species and was thus crucial to his evolutionary theory. Darwin was one of the first scientists to use photographs as illustrations and to use the judgment method for studying the signal value of an expression—which has become the most frequently used method in the psychology of expression. The contents of the present volume extend, support, and sometimes contradict Darwin's remarkable contribution to the field of the expression of emotions.

KEYWORDS: Charles Darwin; emotions; expression of emotions; judgment method

We celebrate the 130th anniversary of the publication of Charles Darwin's book *The Expression of Emotions in Man and Animals* in this volume. It was published 13 years after *The Origin of Species* and one year after *The Descent of Man*. He originally intended *Expression* to be a chapter in *Descent*, but it grew too long. He began keeping the notes that formed the basis of this book in the 1830s.

It is an extraordinary book, radical for his time and for today. The only evidence that he gathered directly was the answers to a series of questions he sent to world travelers asking them about the expressions they observed for different emotions. His analysis of their replies suggested that expressions are universal, which is what is to be expected if there is a common descent. In itself this evidence did not support his explanation of the origins of mankind, for if we had all descended from Adam and Eve, we would have had the same expressions. What it did do, which he pointed out quite explicitly, was chal-

Address for correspondence: Paul Ekman, Ph.D., 6515 Gwin Rd., Oakland, CA 94611.

Ann. N.Y. Acad. Sci. 1000: 1–6 (2003). © 2003 New York Academy of Sciences.
doi: 10.1196/annals.1280.002

lenge the racist theories of his day that claimed that Europeans were descended from a more advanced progenitor than the progenitors of Africans. By showing a common descent Darwin affirmed, in his words, "the unity of mankind."

Darwin argued that emotions are not unique to humans, but can be found in many species. Even bees get angry, Darwin said. It is only in recent years that those studying animal behavior have stopped shying away from the danger of anthropomorphism to recognize Darwin's wise observations that many of the same social occasions that generate emotions in humans do so in other animals.

Darwin asked a question that few before or after him have asked. Not just what expression occurs, not just when an expression occurs—although he did address these questions, he also asked why this particular expression for a particular emotion. His demonstration of the continuity of the species—that emotions are not unique to humans—which was crucial to his evolutionary theory, came from his answer to the "why this expression?" question.

He described three explanatory principles. According to the principle of *serviceable habits*, actions that originally had some usefulness would be preserved as signals. The retraction of the upper lip in a canine, exposing teeth preparatory for biting, was preserved as a display (in current terms) of the size of the weapon that might be used. In similar fashion the dog stands erect, hair on it's back upright to appear large, and thus threatening. (The concepts of *ritualization* and *intention movements* are terms current in ethology related to this principle). To explain why the dog slinks, with back down and close to the ground when affectionate or submissive, Darwin invoked his principle of *antithesis*. This stance occurs because it is the opposite of the movements for aggression. Darwin showed that these two principles applied equally to explaining the stance of an aggressive man (serviceable habits) as compared to the helpless man shrugging (antithesis) (see FIG. 1) For expressions that could not be explained by either of these two principles, Darwin invoked the principle of *direct action of the nervous system*.

His book is also a compendium of fascinating observations about the expressions of humans and other animals. We purse our lips when we concentrate on doing something, such as threading a needle. We open our mouth when listening intently. We want to touch with our faces those we love. We can bite affectionately, as do other animals. And so on, almost endlessly.

Darwin was one of the very first scientists to use photographs as illustrations, commenting in the introduction to his book how important it was to show exactly the details of expression. He was also the first scientist to use what has since become the most common method for studying the signal value of an expression—what is today called the *judgment* method. Darwin showed pictures, taken by the great French neurologist Duchenne du Boulogne[1,2] (who had published a study 10 years earlier on the anatomy of facial movement), to people and asked them what emotion was depicted.

Darwin wrote about his findings on the picture reproduced in FIGURE 2:

> One half of the face is made, by galvanizing the proper muscles, to smile; whilst
> the other half is made to begin crying. Almost all those (viz. nineteen out of
> twenty one persons) to whom I showed the smiling half of the face instantly rec-
> ognized the expression; but, with respect to the other half, only six persons out
> of twenty one recognized it—that is, if we accept such terms as grief, misery an-
> noyance as correct, whereas fifteen persons were ludicrously mistaken; some of

FIGURE 1. Darwin's illustrations of an aggressive (**A**) and a submissive (**B**) dog and
an aggressive (**C**) and a helpless man (**D**).[3]

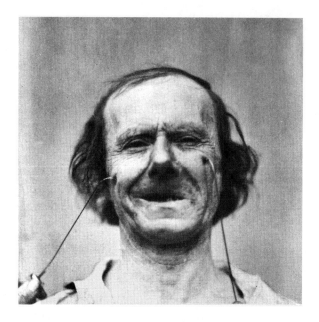

FIGURE 2. Darwin's illustration of a half-smiling, half-crying face used to elicit responses of observers.[3]

> them saying the face expressed fun, satisfaction, cunning, disgust, etc. We may infer from this there is something wrong in the expression. Some of the fifteen persons may, however, have been partly misled by not expecting to see an old man crying, and by tears not being secreted [p. 151].[3]

This method—showing pictures and studying the responses of those who observe them, the emotions they attribute to them—has become the most frequently used method in the psychology of expression.

Darwin was an extraordinarily attentive observer, and he attempted to explain every observation. For example:

> I believe ... that the depressor muscles of the angles of the mouth are less under the separate control of the will than the adjoining muscles; so that if a young child is only doubtfully inclined to cry, this muscle is generally the first to contract, and is the last to cease contracting. When older children commence crying, the muscles which run to the upper lip are often the first to contract; and this may perhaps be due to older children not having so strong a tendency to scream loudly; and consequently to keep their mouths widely open; so that the above named depressor muscles are not brought into such strong action [p. 153].[3]

This attention to description and explanation was, Darwin felt, his chief virtue. In his autobiography he wrote:

> I have no great quickness of apprehension or wit ... my power to follow a long and purely abstract train of thought is very limited ... [but] I am superior to the common run of men in noticing things which easily escape attention, and in observing them carefully [p. 141].[4]

He wrote with clarity and eloquence. Considering whether we need to learn to recognize emotions in others, or whether that ability is inborn, Darwin wrote:

> I attended to this point in my first-born, who could not have learnt anything by associating with other children, and I was convinced that he understood a smile and received pleasure from seeing one, answering it by another, at much too early an age to have learnt anything by experience. When this child was about four months old, I made in his presence many odd noises and strange grimaces, and tried to look savage; but the noise, if not too loud, as well as the grimaces, were all taken as good jokes; and I attributed this at the time to their being preceded by smiles. When five months old, he seemed to understand a compassionate expression and tone of voice. When a few days over six months old, his nurse pretended to cry, and I saw that his face instantly assumed a melancholy expression, with the corners of the mouth strongly depressed; now this child could rarely have seen any other child crying, and never a grown up person crying, and I should doubt whether at so early an age he could have reasoned on the subject [pp. 353–354].[3]

Darwin used an amazingly large array of data sources, unequalled even today. He observed humans in England and gathered observations of human expressions in other cultures from world travelers. He reported his observations of the animals in the London zoo and of domestic animals. He provided information on early development, drawing primarily on observations of his own large family. He inspected photographs supplied to him of the mentally ill. And he utilized what little was known about the nervous system and emotions to make some interesting speculations.

The contents of this volume, and the meeting on which it is based, reflect the breadth of Darwin's concern. Outstanding scientists in each of four areas report on their own work and recent work by others. First are three chapters on emotion and development, from a session organized and chaired by Joseph Campos; then three chapters on emotion in animals, from a session organized by Frans De Waal; then three chapters on expression, from a session organized by myself; and finally, three chapters on the physiology of emotion, from a session organized by Richard J. Davidson. Each of these sections is concluded by the highlights of the discussion that followed its three presentations.

This book captures the resurgence of interest in emotion. In each chapter you will read about work that extends, supports, and sometimes contradicts Darwin—each standing on the contribution made by this great man in his great book published 130 years ago.

ACKNOWLEDGMENTS

I am grateful to Rashid Shaikh, Director of Programs at the New York Academy of Sciences. When I suggested to him that there be a meeting and then a book to celebrate the 130th anniversary of the publication of Charles Darwin's *The Expression of Emotion in Man and Animals*, he was very encouraging. He endorsed my proposal that there should be four sections to represent the major areas of current research—expression, development, animal behavior, and physiology—that relate to Darwin's ideas. Throughout the planning, I received helpful advice from him about the structure of the program, which is represented in this volume.

I am also grateful for the advice and work of the three panel chairmen, whom I invited to organize the sections on development, animal behavior, and physiology—Joe Campos, Frans de Waals, and Richie Davidson, respectively. They each are leaders in their fields, and they invited for their panels outstanding scientists to cover different exciting work in their respective areas. Special thanks to Joe Campos, who managed this work while dealing with major visual problems. Each of the panel chairmen, who are coeditors of this volume, provided essential advice about the organization of the meeting and took responsibility for editing the panel discussions for their sectors.

Of course, Darwin is the man to whom we all owe a debt of gratitude. He began the field and provided lucid insights, the great majority of which have been borne out in what is reported in this book.

REFERENCES

1. DUCHENNE DE BOLOGNE, G.-B. 1862. Mécanisme de la Physionomie Humaine. Jules Renouard Libraire. Paris.
2. DUCHENNE DE BOULOGNE, G.B. 1990. The Mechanism of Human Facial Expression. A. Cuthbertson, Trans. & Ed. Cambridge Universitiy Press. New York.
3. DARWIN, C. 1998. The Expression of the Emotions in Man and Animals, 3rd edit. Harper Collins. London. (US edit.: Oxford University Press. New York.)
4. DARWIN, C. 1969. The Autobiography of Charles Darwin. W.W. Norton. New York.

Darwin's Legacy and the Study of Primate Visual Communication

FRANS B. M. DE WAAL

*Living Links, Yerkes Primate Center, and Psychology Department,
Emory University, Atlanta, Georgia 30322, USA*

ABSTRACT: After Charles Darwin's *The Expression of the Emotions in Man
and Animals,* published in 1872, we had to wait 60 years before the theme
of animal expressions was picked up by another astute observer. In 1935,
Nadezhda Ladygina-Kohts published a detailed comparison of the expressive behavior of a juvenile chimpanzee and of her own child. After Kohts,
we had to wait until the 1960s for modern ethological analyses of primate
facial and gestural communication. Again, the focus was on the chimpanzee, but ethograms on other primates appeared as well. Our understanding
of the range of expressions in other primates is at present far more advanced than that in Darwin's time. A strong social component has been
added: instead of focusing on the expressions per se, they are now often
classified according to the social situations in which they typically occur.
Initially, quantitative analyses were sequential (i.e., concerned with temporal associations between behavior patterns), and they avoided the language
of emotions. I will discuss some of this early work, including my own on the
communicative repertoire of the bonobo, a close relative of the chimpanzee
(and ourselves). I will provide concrete examples to make the point that
there is a much richer matrix of contexts possible than the common behavioral categories of aggression, sex, fear, play, and so on. Primate signaling
is a form of negotiation, and previous classifications have ignored the spe-
cifics of what animals try to achieve with their exchanges. There is also increasing evidence for signal conventionalization in primates, especially the
apes, in both captivity and the field. This process results in group-specific
or "cultural" communication patterns.

KEYWORDS: primates; facial expressions; communication; culture;
emotion

Address for correspondence: Dr. Frans B. M. de Waal, Living Links, Yerkes Primate Research
Center, Emory University, 954 N. Gatewood Road, Atlanta, GA 30322. Voice: 404-727-3695 or
404-727-7898; fax: 404-727-3270.
dewaal@emory.edu

Ann. N.Y. Acad. Sci. 1000: 7–31 (2003). © 2003 New York Academy of Sciences.
doi: 10.1196/annals.1280.003

EARLY HISTORY

Charles Darwin was the first to look at human facial expressions the way, at the time, only a biologist would—namely, as a structural albeit dynamic feature of our species that can be described and catalogued in the same way as the morphology of a plant or animal. *The Expression of Emotions in Man and Animals,* which first appeared in 1872,[1] is a masterpiece of detailed analysis and insightful conjecture. One of Darwin's main objectives was to show how human facial expressions (a) constitute a shared heritage of our species; (b) have parallels with the expressions of other animals, such as dogs, cats, and primates; and hence (c) provide one more argument—a behavioral one— for evolutionary continuity. Humans may express happiness differently than dogs; but all humans do it one way, and all dogs another way, indicating that the expression of emotions is a species-typical trait.

I will not explore this argument here in relation to the human face (see Ekman[2] for a review of the debate surrounding the universality of human facial expressions), but I do wish to stress how Darwin was an ethologist before the name even existed, giving us in human facial expressions a powerful example of what German ethologists later came to call an *Erbkoordination.* In its English translation, this concept lost the *Erb* part (i.e., "inherited") and gained in rigidity as it became known as fixed action pattern, or FAP. The central idea of the FAP is that in the same way that each species is characterized by structural features (e.g., wings, ears, digestive system), each is also endowed with stereotypical motor patterns. The insight of ethologists was that the FAP, since it occurs in recognizable form in all members of a species, must have been subject to the same laws of natural selection as any other trait.[3,4] This means that we are permitted to apply the concept of *homology* to the FAP's of different species, hence that we can trace their evolutionary origin (see below). It also implies that we can look at FAP's as adaptations— that is, assume that they have been selected for a purpose. In the case of facial expressions the obvious assumed function is visual communication: the face is the most conspicuous part of the body during face-to-face interaction.

This went further than what Darwin had proposed,[1] but Darwin's strength was that he had picked the one feature of human behavior that seems to fit most or all of the above conceptualizations. In fact, facial expressions fit the mold of inborn behavior far better than many of the behaviors now discussed as such in evolutionary psychology, such as maternal care or rape—not that these patterns cannot have a genetic component; but they are highly flexible, and their occurrence varies with learning and environment. As such, they are far removed from the complex facial muscle coordination and vocalizations, such as laughing and crying, that appear early in life and are remarkably uniform across individual humans and cultures. But not only did Darwin pick a prime candidate of innate behavior, he also recognized and carefully documented the similarity of our own facial movements with those of other primates. He suggested that of all human facial displays only blushing may be unique.

After Darwin we had to wait a long time until another scientist took up the baton of primate facial expressions. The one who did, Nadezhda Ladygina-Kohts, is little known in the US due to her having written in German, French, and most of all her native Russian. Kohts's comparison between a juvenile chimpanzee and her own son, first published in 1935, has only recently been translated into English.[5] This richly illustrated book reveals a wealth of insight into the emotional significance of primate facial expressions along with modern-sounding cognitive reflections on imitation, self-awareness, tool use, and other topics that have become fashionable only over the last few decades. It was Robert Yerkes who first drew attention to Kohts's pioneering research by reproducing excerpts and illustrations from her work in *The Great Apes*.[6]

Comparative descriptions along the lines of Darwin, but conducted in far greater detail and with a wider range of species, first reappeared in the literature with the studies of Jan van Hooff.[7,8] To illustrate the depth to which van Hooff went in cataloguing displays in an objective fashion, here is a description of the pigtail monkey's "protruded-lips face." Note the purely descriptive terminology: as an ethologist, van Hooff was careful to describe first, before assessing the possible motivation and function of a particular display:

> When a female pigtail monkey is in heat, a male which has access to this female may frequently show a most peculiar response. During the period the male may repeatedly smell at the genital region of the female, which bears large swellings. It then shows a facial posture which is mainly characterized by a protrusion of the lips. The upper lip moreover is slightly curled upwards and the lower lip is pressed against it tightly. The smelling may last a few seconds; after the male lifts its head and with the face directed slightly upwards and the eyes gazing up in an undirected way, it maintains the facial posture for a short time. In a number of cases copulation follows [pp. 56,57].[8]

Van Hooff (1967) brought to bear the concepts of ethology on facial expressions by speculating about their causal underpinnings as deduced from concomitant behavior.[8] He also tried to trace their phylogeny from its distribution over the taxonomic tree. Thus, he speculated about the origin of facial displays (e.g., lip-smacking may derive from the consumption of particles picked up during grooming) and the conflicting tendencies underlying compound displays, such as teeth-chattering, which may reflect a mixture of lip-smacking (associated with forward tendencies) and teeth-baring (associated with withdrawal in many species). Van Hooff also posited that displays that grade into each other may nevertheless have separate evolutionary origins, such as the human laugh and smile. Van Hooff's work still stands as the most comprehensive and insightful comparative analysis of nonhuman and human primate facial displays since Darwin.

Van Hooff's study was followed by Goodall's fine ethogram of wild chimpanzee behavior[9] and several reviews of primate facial expressions.[10–12] Unfortunately, some of these publications employed a rather vague or interpretative terminology. Thus, one publication labeled a certain facial expression "the threat display," which ignored that primates show a great variety of threat faces and that even the macaques studied possess more than one such display (Section 3a).[12] This author also upheld the unfortunate common name of "grimace," or "fear grimace," for what had been termed the "silent bared-teeth display."[8] According to my dictionary, a grimace is a sharp contortion of the face, hence a term that does not even begin to define the facial configuration involved. Imprecise terminology obscures the morphology that is the staple of any phylogenetic approach.

The modern study of the human face, which was initiated at around the same time as the above work, adopted from van Hooff and other ethologists the sensible habit of a strictly neutral terminology. In terms of descriptive detail, the nonhuman primate studies, which had been ahead until the 1970s, were soon left behind, however. The facial action coding system (FACS)[13] provided a more systematic muscle-by-muscle evaluation of the face. In defense of primatologists, however, it must be added that FACS requires high-quality photography of facial movements, which in naturally behaving primates is quite a bit harder to obtain than in people, who can be asked to sit still and look into a camera.

EVOLUTION OF SIGNALS

Homology and Ritualization

Darwin wrote perceptively about the facial expressions of nonhuman primates.[1] For example, he noted that the bared-teeth expression, shown in FIGURE 1 by a black Sulawesi macaque, occurs when the animal is pleased to be caressed. Retraction of the lips to expose both rows of teeth is indeed a relaxed, friendly expression in this species as opposed to the same expression in most other macaques, in which it signifies submission. How do we know this? Quantitative analysis of natural social interaction sequences among Sulawesi macaques demonstrates that the bared-teeth display predicts the onset of affinitive contact between sender and addressee, hence that it likely is associated with a positive social attitude.[14] In these macaques, teeth-baring often occurs mutually between individuals. In the better known rhesus macaque, in contrast, teeth-baring is given exclusively by subordinate to dominant individuals—hence never mutually—and is a common response to threats and intimidations (FIG. 2).[15] The colloquial term "fear grimace" for all teeth-baring expressions derives from the familiarity of researchers with the rhesus monkey—the most common laboratory primate in the West—rather than from a comprehensive look at the primate order, in which this expression has a variety of meanings.

FIGURE 1. Darwin's *The Expression of the Emotions in Man and Animals*[1] included this gravure (p. 135) of a black Sulawesi macaque, a species in which the silent bared-teeth face indeed has the affectionate meaning claimed by Darwin's sources.

It should be pointed out that the fact that identical expressions in related species may carry different meanings is never an argument against evolutionary continuity. In evolution, motivational and functional "recasting" of traits is not unusual. We apply the concept of *homology* when similar traits of different species can be traced to their common ancestor (i.e., are present in both lineages going back all the way to the ancestral type). It is not at all unusual for homologous traits to vary in function, such as in the case of a bird's wing and the human arm. Both derive from the forelimb of the common ancestor between birds and mammals, yet wings and arms serve different functions. Shared ancestry is contrasted with analogy, or convergence, when similar traits (e.g., the fish-like shape of a dolphin) are considered independent products of similar evolutionary pressures. Preuschoft and van Hooff[16] provide guidelines for the distinction between homology and analogy in relation to facial expressions.

Ritualization is another common concept used in relation to the evolution of communication. This term refers to the "evolutionary transformation of

FIGURE 2. In contrast to the Sulawesi macaque (FIG. 1), rhesus monkeys employ the silent bared-teeth face as a signal of submission. Here a juvenile reacts with the display to an approaching dominant male. (Photograph by Frans de Waal.)

nondisplay behavior into display behavior."[17] This means that evolution "takes" a normal instrumental act, such as the wiping action against a branch with which many birds clean their bills, and turns this simple act into a signal by exaggerating the movement, giving it a typical form and intensity, and repeating or emphasizing it. All of this occurs, we presume, to enhance the signal value of the behavior by making it more conspicuous and recognizable. Ethology has documented numerous examples and applies the concept of ritualization to virtually every FAP related to communication. If, on the other hand, a recognizable signal develops during individual ontogeny rather than in evolutionary time, we apply terms such as *formalization* and *conventionalization*. In humans, for example, hand-waving in greeting is often considered to be derived from times that people carried weapons and showed an empty hand before approaching a stranger. This act was turned into a signal used even when there were no weapons around. Conventionalization is a cultural process also known of nonhuman primates (discussed below in CULTURALLY LEARNED DISPLAYS).

Andrews was one of the first to speculate about the origin of ritualized facial displays, which, following in the footsteps of early of ethologists, he sought in instrumental acts termed "ancestral reflex actions."[18] Andrews speculated, for example, that frowning derives from intense attention to an object close to the face, because lowering of the eyebrows either focuses the eyes or protects them. The frown subsequently became integrated in threat displays. These first attempts at explanations of facial displays stand in contrast to Darwin's, which were often surprisingly devoid of adaptive assumptions.[19] In fact, Darwin did not always distinguish between signals as inherited characteristics or acquired habits.[1] Considering the frown, he followed an almost Lamarckian thought:

> As the effort of viewing with ease under a bright light a distant object is both difficult and irksome, and this effort has been habitually accompanied, during numberless generations, by the contraction of the eyebrows, the habit of frowning will thus have been much strengthened; although it was originally practiced during infancy from a quite different cause, namely as the first step in the protection of the eyes during screaming.[1]

Puckered eyebrows have been considered uniquely human ever since Darwin wrote that the frown may well be absent in apes.[1] He had tried to aggravate apes with an impossible, frustrating task, yet failed to get them to frown while concentrating. Only when he tickled a chimpanzee's nose with a straw did Darwin obtain a few vertical furrows between the eyebrows. Chimpanzees can and do frown at emotional moments, however; and bonobos—which have less pronounced eyebrow ridges, hence probably more flexible eyebrows—show an even stronger contraction of the *corrugators* in their so-called "tense mouth" face, in which the eyes are narrowed in a piercing expression.[20]

Laugh and Smile

Andrews also addressed the possible origin of the grin or smile, speculating that it derives from a reflex in which the teeth are bared in response to sudden, unpleasant, or noxious stimuli.[18] As an illustration, FIGURE 3 shows a baboon eating cactus with retracted lips. The spines are allowed to touch the teeth but not the vulnerable lips. This response to potentially harmful stimuli was, according to Andrews, turned into a signal by exaggerating the muscle

FIGURE 3. Ritualization refers to an evolutionary process that turns reflexes into communication signals by making them more stereotypical and conspicuous. This cactus-eating female baboon shows extreme lip retraction in reaction to noxious stimuli, the same reflex that evolution has turned into the bared-teeth display. (Photograph by Frans de Waal.)

movement and using it from a distance towards potentially harmful fellow group members. Reflexive teeth-baring thus evolved into a fearful or submissive expression.

In humans, however, the homologous expression, known as the smile, has different connotations. Not that fear is never involved (e.g., someone who smiles too much is considered nervous), yet there is also an affectionate, even happy quality to the display. It has therefore been hypothesized that smiling evolved as an indicator of cooperativeness and altruism.[21,22] In a

FIGURE 4. Van Hooff's scheme showing the evolution of the smile and laugh. Starting with a primitive insectivore and progressing through the primates, the scheme illustrates the variety of ways in which the silent teeth-baring display (**left side**) and the relaxed open-mouth display or play face (**right side**) differ and resemble each other in monkeys, apes, and humans. The human laugh stems from the play face. It resembles the chimpanzee play face not only visually, but also in its accompanying breathy vocalizations. The human smile stems from the silent bared-teeth face. These homologies do not necessarily imply exact overlap in meaning of the displays, however. (Reprinted from J.A.R.A.M. van Hooff[23] with permission.)

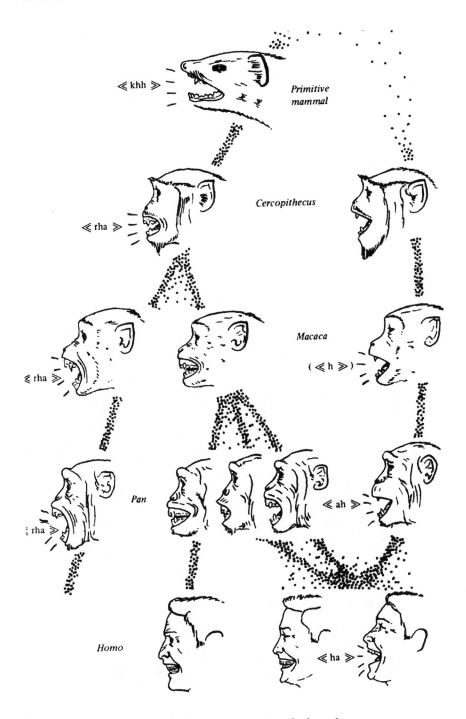

FIGURE 4. *See previous page for legend.*

phylogenetic analysis, van Hooff compared the way various primates employ the silent bared-teeth display and concluded that the appeasing and friendly qualities of the human smile are not unique.[23] In terms of appeasement. there is a clear connection with the bared-teeth display of a great variety of primates; and in terms of its friendly use, the human display connects with one of the chimpanzee's bared-teeth expressions (FIG.4). Van Hooff further proposed the "relaxed open-mouth display" of the chimpanzee and other primates as a homologue of human laughing. This expression, commonly known as the "play face," occurs especially during tickling matches and is often accompanied by sounds reminiscent of guttural, breathy human laughter.

At the time of these comparisons little was known about bonobos, inclusion of which makes an even stronger case for continuity. Bonobos—an ape species

FIGURE 5. Since bonobos bare both rows of teeth in their play face, the resemblance with human laughing is even stronger than in chimpanzees, which generally bare the lower teeth only. (Photograph by Frans de Waal.)

equally close to us as the chimpanzee—frequently bare their teeth in friendly and apparently pleasurable contexts, such as in the midst of sexual intercourse.[20] One German investigator of bonobos even spoke of an *Orgasmusgesicht* (or "orgasm face").[24] The bonobo's play face, too, bears a striking resemblance to the human laugh. Whereas the chimpanzee's play face is characterized by covered upper teeth, the bonobo's often includes full teeth-baring in which the upper teeth tend to be exposed (FIG. 5). This makes the bonobo laugh look very human-like indeed, especially if it is combined with the relatively loud laughing sounds of this species.[20]

The laughing expression of apes is clearly homologous with that of our own species: the laugh derives from a widespread mammalian play expression.[25] As we have seen, however, homology does not necessarily imply that the expression functions in the same way in all hominoids (i.e., humans and apes). In bonobos and chimpanzees laughing is closely tied to play, whereas in our own species it occurs under a much wider range of circumstances. Playful interaction is obviously included and can be considered the original laughing context, but we use the same expression also in bonding (i.e., "laughing with") and, sometimes, as a hostile signal (i.e., "laughing at"). Corresponding with this functional differentiation, laughing sounds are more variable in our species than in apes (Bachorowski, this volume).[26]

Hominoid Specialties: Grading and Gesturing

Ever since Ladygina-Kohts,[5] the chimpanzee has been the standard for comparisons between human and nonhuman facial expressions. TABLE I pro-

TABLE 1. A review of chimpanzee facial expressions and vocalizations, cross-referenced to previous descriptions in the literature[27]

Expression	Other names
Bulging-lips face	glare or compressed lips face;[9] attack face[7]
Relaxed open-mouth display	play face;[9, 30–33] relaxed open-mouth display[23]
Silent bared-teeth display	grin;[7,9,12] horizontal bared-teeth expression;[8,30] bared-teeth yelp face; silent bared-teeth display[23]
Staring bared-teeth scream face	rough scream;[34] roar, growl, scream;[35] double-tone scream[36]
Stretched pout-whimper	stretch pout-whimper;[7,8,37] whimper face, hoo-whimper, pout-moan[9]
Silent pout	pout[30]
Pant-hoot	pant-hoot;[9,37] rising hoot[30]
Pant-grunt	pant-grunts;[37] panting, bobbing pants;[9] rapid oh-oh[30]
Teeth-clacking	lip smack and teeth clack;[37] lip-smacking[30]
Splutter	splutter[30]

vides a review of the 10 main facial/vocal displays of this ape and the various labels used for these in the literature.[27] These labels do not convey the richness of context in which chimpanzees communicate, the possible meaning of their signals, and how these are combined with gestures and vocalizations. For example, there is the issue of the gradedness of signals.[28,29] What is meant by gradedness is that instead of having only signal types A and B, one also observes many types in between, such as AB and BA mixtures. Whereas this certainly is relevant to primate vocalizations, I find grading even more striking in the facial expressions of the great apes. It is easy to characterize the typical "silent pout" versus a "stretched pout whimper," but we also know that these expressions frequently grade into each other. Smooth transitions between expressions are common in apes, probably reflecting underlying shifts in emotions. Grading and intensity variations in facial expressions seem more typical of apes than monkeys, such as macaques, in which the face more often seems to freeze in a mask-like display. In the hominoids the face is continuously in motion at emotionally charged moments. It should be noted, however, that the gradedness versus discreteness of facial expressions in various species has never been the subject of systematic analysis.

It is also rarely noted in the literature that free hand gestures are limited to the hominoids. This is not a mere quantitative difference with monkeys, as with respect to the grading of signals, but a qualitative one. Facial expressions and vocalizations are common means of communication in all of the primates and beyond, but, with the exception of a single gesture to be treated below, monkeys lack ritualized hand gestures. Macaques may slap the ground with a hand when threatening another or reach back to their partner during a sexual mount, but these are the limits of their manual communication.[38] Contacts with a substrate or partner do serve a signal function but involve more than the hand. Bonobos, in contrast, wave at each other, shake their wrists when impatient, beg for food with open hand held out, flex their fingers towards themselves when inviting contact, move an arm over a subordinate in a dominance-gesture, and so on (FIG. 6). They even gesture with their feet.[20]

Like facial expressions, the free hand gestures of apes are ritualized—that is, they are stereotypical, exaggerated, and tied to specific contexts. The begging gesture, which is also universal in humans, most likely derives from a cupped hand held under the mouth of a food possessor. The origin of this gesture is visible in the only ritualized monkey gesture known to me, which is hand-cupping by capuchin monkeys. If one monkey possesses food, another will reach out a hand and hold it under the possessor's chin so as to catch dropping morsels. This seems an instrumental act, but the same gesture can also be given from a distance—for example, when two capuchin monkeys are separated by mesh and one is consuming food, as in our food-sharing experiments.[39] In those instances, the gesture is used as a distant signal, divorced from its instrumental function, similar to the way all of the great apes use it. An important difference remains, however, in that apes have generalized the

FIGURE 6. Hand gesture by a bonobo male inviting a female for sexual contact. Free hand gestures are a unique feature of ape and human communication; they are not found in the monkeys. (Photograph by Frans de Waal.)

meaning of the begging gesture to a variety of situations, whereas in capuchins the gesture is food-specific. Apes use the same begging gesture also to obtain support and help, so that in their case the precise referent needs to be read from the social context (see SIGNALS IN CONTEXT below).

Apes gesture more with the right than the left hand.[40,41] Since the right hand is left-brain controlled, this means that ape gestures share the same lateralization as human language. The highly flexible use of ritualized hand gestures, their recent appearance on the evolutionary scene (compared with other means of communication), and their culture-dependency in both humans and apes (see CULTURALLY LEARNED DISPLAYS below) should provide food for thought for any consideration of the role that gestural communication may have played in the evolution of human language.[42]

SIGNAL INTERPRETATION

Macaque Appeal-Aggression

A facial expression by itself cannot tell us if it is aggressive, fearful, or friendly. Such judgments are derived from concomitant behavior, a technique going back to classical analyses of fish and bird behavior. To give a simple illustration of such an analysis, in an earlier study we considered the agonistic displays of longtail macaques.[43] We documented the temporal associations among 31 behavior elements, ranging from the staring open-mouth face to lip-smacking and from chasing to crouching. The reasoning behind this study was that if patterns cluster together in time, the underlying motivation and functional context will be the same. Spontaneous action sequences were analyzed to arrive at a 31×31 matrix indicating the frequency with which each behavior element occurred with every other. The observed matrix was then statistically compared with one based on random association.

One might think that in macaques the two main agonistic clusters would be aggression (e.g., forward tendencies, physical attack) on the one hand and fear or submission (e.g., withdrawal, self-protection) on the other. A third cluster was found, however, which consisted of noisy threat displays combined with behavior directed at bystanders. To distinguish such behavior from exchanges with the opponent itself, de Waal spoke of side-directed behavior.

A self-confident dominant individual will give a simple stare with gaping mouth, sometimes with a few soft grunts, which is the most common form of threat in macaques. In doing so, the dominant will concentrate its attention entirely on the opponent. This pattern was labeled *straight-aggression*. A less confident individual, on the other hand, will draw attention to its confrontations with others by grunting loudly, pointing with its chin towards the opponent, presenting its behind to potential allies, such as dominant males, and "show looking" for support from bystanders with exaggerated jerky turns of the head. This was termed *appeal-aggression*, since it could be demonstrated that this form of threat (a) increases the probability of third-party support for the performer and (b) is typical of social climbers.[44] In a dramatic illustration, an alpha male who temporarily lost his position showed appeal-aggression, which he had *never* done before, during the period in which he regained his position.[45]

Macaques thus have two distinct ways of threatening an opponent: one way serves to underline existing rank positions, whereas the other serves to claim or reclaim a certain rank by recruiting third-party support. These threat displays seem adapted for their respective purposes, given that the first type is almost silent and the second type conspicuous and noisy.

Signals in Context

As opposed to a recent claim that nonhuman primates have no parallel to positively toned human expressions and generally "lack unabashedly positive facial or vocal responses"(Ref. 22, p. 154), it should be pointed out that all of the primates have a great variety of affiliative signals, ranging from contact-calls and lip-smacking in monkeys to copulation squeals, pouting, play faces, and laughing vocalizations in the apes. Well-documented examples of affiliative vocalizations are the chuck-calls of squirrel monkeys[46] and girney grunts of macaques.[47] Moreover, the teeth-baring expressions of some primates, such as Sulawesi macaques and bonobos, are similar both morphologically and functionally to the human smile (see LAUGH AND SMILE above). The ethograms of Goodall,[9] van Hooff,[30] and de Waal[20] should leave no doubt that expressions of affection, reassurance, and reconciliation are among the most common forms of communication in apes.

The interpretation of these signals derives from detailed sequential analyses. The first to apply such an analysis to great ape behavior was van Hooff,[30] who distinguished 60 behavior elements in the repertoire of chimpanzees. Fifty-three of these elements were analyzed so as to determine the frequency with which they occurred together. By feeding thousands of transitions into a cluster and factor analysis, the investigator arrived at a classification into what could be called seven motivational systems, such as play, excitement, affinitive, and aggressive systems. The analysis showed how extremely integrated the chimpanzee's behavioral repertoire is in that some behavior patterns occurred in a great variety of contexts. The interpretation of a behavioral system was given by behavior with extremely high loadings on the factor in question (e.g., grooming on the affinitive system).

A variant on the same analytical technique was applied in an analysis of the behavioral repertoire of the bonobo.[20] Forty-four behavior patterns were classified as to the behavioral context in which they occurred. The analysis compared the distribution over forty nonexclusive context types (e.g., object competition, play invitation, alarm) with the frequencies of these contexts in order to determine which associations significantly exceeded chance level. In this way, each behavior pattern could be contextually placed. As in the chimpanzee study,[30] the focus was on the most recognizable communication displays, thus ignoring variations and subtle gradations.

Whereas it is useful to assign behavior patterns to general motivational categories and contexts, to determine their exact meaning requires additional work. To return to the earlier example of macaque aggression, we are justified in calling both types of display "aggressive," but in fact the two distinct types are more accurately characterized as "assertive" versus "challenging." Thus, the highest ranking dominant rarely challenges anybody: he needs only to raise an eyebrow to get them to move away. Young social climbers, on the other hand, can successfully defeat others only if they have the backing of their family, which they actively recruit while challenging their opponent. Such distinctions in the meaning of facial/vocal displays are lost if we distinguish only aggression and fear. Fear responses, too, need to be broken down into a number of types, such as withdrawal and submission. These are entirely different modes of dealing with dominants. Submission may occur without any withdrawal or flight responses at all: some animals, such as chimpanzees and wolves, commonly express submission during actual approaches by subordinates to the dominant in a greeting ceremony.[48]

Analyses of the specific meaning of communication signals are rare, perhaps because there is no single method that can address all possible meanings. Each specific behavior requires a different approach. For example, monkey alarm calls require one methodology (Seyfarth & Cheney, this volume), recruitment screams another,[49] and contact calls yet another.[50] Different approaches are required because alarm calls deal with predators, recruitment screams are sensitive to immediate social context, and contact calls vary with the presence or absence of kin and other associates. One cannot apply a single paradigm to all of these vocalizations. Facial expresssion research is different, again, in that it requires visual presentation: one cannot do a play-back experiment as is done with calls from concealed speakers. The most controlled studies on the perception of facial stimuli and their emotional evaluation is the work by Parr (this volume).

The situation becomes even more complex if one particular signal may have multiple meanings dependent on the context. For example, a monkey may present its anogenital region so as to attract a sexual partner, but it may do the same during a reconciliation, leading to a hold-bottom or mount with the former opponent.[51] The same gesture may also be used to secure support, as with baboons, in which a female appeases a dominant male while threatening her opponent.[52] Context dependency is even more striking in the gestural communication of apes. The begging gesture, for example, has absolutely no meaning unless one can deduce its referent from the context. Obviously, if the gesture is directed at a food possessor, we assume that it relates to food; but chimpanzees also use the begging gesture as a side-directed behavior (i.e., directed at bystanders during a confrontation with another). Here the begging seems to serve recruitment of support. In a detailed video analysis of agonistic encounters, most side-directed behavior was aimed at individuals likely to support the performer, yet a few kinds are specifically directed at likely allies and protectors of the opponent. These patterns, such as kissing and embracing, probably are appeasement attempts serving to prevent disadvantageous interventions.[53]

To conclusively prove such functions is a difficult task, but I hope that the above makes it clear that the meaning of signals is incompletely captured by the general labels common in the literature, such as "aggressive" or "affinitive." Communication is a complex interplay between senders and receivers, each with their own goals and agendas. The early ethologists employed a rather mechanistic terminology that never captured this interplay and the flexible usage of sometimes-conflicting strategies. Monkeys and apes operate within a larger social context, staying in tune with multiple partners at once. To view communication as negotiation between sender and receiver about potential outcomes may prove to be a more fruitful framework than to view it in terms of general motivations and functions.[54–56]

Deictic Signals: Pointing

With regards to intentional signaling, a special place is often assigned to pointing, defined as the drawing of attention of another party to a distant object by locating it for the other in space. Given that there is no point to pointing unless one understands that the other has not seen what you have seen, "deictic" gestures, as they are known, are customarily linked to intersubjectivity and theory of mind. As a result, such gestures are sometimes considered uniquely human.[57,58]

In considering the evidence for ape pointing, the first step is to move away from anthropocentric definitions, such as the one requiring an outstretched index finger. The fact that some animals don't have arms and hands, let alone fingers, is no reason to declare a priori that pointing is beyond their abilities. We should take a broad view, one that includes whole-body points as noted in a classic study with juvenile chimpanzees.[59] The investigator would take one of the juveniles with him to hide food or a frightening object, such as a toy snake, in the grass of a large outdoor area. When the entire group was released, the others quickly understood the nature of the hidden object (attractive versus aversive) and its approximate location by watching the "knower's" body language, such as, visual orientation and posture.

A number of experiments support the view that our closest relatives, the great apes, have mastered referential signaling. For this, the hand-point has been investigated, not because it is the most natural way for apes to point, but because apes readily learn that this gesture activates humans. Investigators tested captive chimpanzees who had extensive experience with people walking, making it natural for the apes to have learned how to draw attention to items they want, such as a piece of fruit that has dropped out of their cage. Do the apes spontaneously attract attention to out-of-reach food?[60,61]

It turns out that the majority of chimpanzees will gesture to the human experimenter. They will point with the whole hand at the banana outside of their cage, and a few even point with an index finger. No one ever explicitly trained these apes to do so, and there are clear signs that they monitor the effect in exactly the same way that has been used to define intentional pointing in children. The ape first makes eye contact with the human, then points while alternating its gaze between the food and the human. One chimpanzee pointed manually at the banana and then with a finger at her mouth!

One possible criticism is that without a single exception these apes are familiar with human behavior. Would they ever have developed pointing in the absence of a species that itself points all the time and responds to it? There are two pertinent reports. One concerns my own multiple observations of more than two decades ago about how female chimpanzees may enlist the support of a male against a rival if the male has not been involved from the start, hence does not know who the opponent is in the melee of a confrontation. On such occasions, the aggressor may indicate her opponent by pointing her out to her male ally.[62]

The other report is the only one on wild apes. It concerns bonobos in dense forest that alerted their mates to hidden scientists (Ref. 63, p. 289):

> February 24th, 1989, 13:09 h. Noises are heard coming from the vegetation. A young male swings from a branch and leaps into a tree which is some 5 m away. He sits in a fork of the tree 10 m off the ground. He emits sharp calls, which are answered by other individuals who are not visible. He points—with his right arm stretched out and his hand half closed except for his index and ring fingers —to the position of the two groups of camouflaged observers who are in the undergrowth (30 m apart). At the same time he screams and turns his head to where the other members of the group are.
>
> 13:12 h. The same individual repeats the pointing and calling sequence twice. Other neighboring members of the group approach. They look towards the observers. The young male joins them.

The context of these instances of pointing strongly suggests awareness of the lack of knowledge of others (the apes pointed at objects hidden from view or hard to discern), and the behavior was accompanied by visual checking of its effects. Also, the pointing disappeared once the recipient had looked or walked in the indicated direction. Many of the same elements are present in the best controlled study of ape referential pointing with a female chimpanzee, who spontaneously and after long time intervals pointed out hidden food to humans with access to the hiding locations outside of the ape's cage. The humans did not know where the food was—they often were not even aware that food had been hidden—hence had to follow the ape's detailed instructions.[64]

CULTURALLY LEARNED DISPLAYS

Expressions of emotions appear in every member of a species in similar or identical form even if opportunities for learning have been scant. As a parallel to deaf and blind children who, despite a lack of or very limited learning opportunities, exhibit all the human facial expressions in emotionally appropriate contexts,[65] a deaf female chimpanzee at the Arnhem Zoo seemed to utter all of the varied calls of her species in the right context.[62]

It is often assumed, therefore, that the production of communication signals is little affected by learning (but see Ref. 66). The correct reading and interpretation of signals, on the other hand, seems open to many environmental influences. For example, responsiveness to communication signals varies with exposure to species-typical stimuli and opportunities for associative learning;[67] the appropriate response to vervet monkey alarm calls by juveniles of the species increases with age and experience.[68]

To the general rule that the production of communication displays is less influenced by learning than their appraisal, one important exception exists, however: the culturally transmitted communication displays of the great apes—that is, displays that individuals learn from each other. Whereas Tomasello et al. have argued against this possibility—"... imitative learning is not a major factor in the acquisition of new behaviors by chimpanzees" (Ref. 69, p. 153)—the same chimpanzee colony studied by these authors has yielded a prime example of a culturally transmitted gesture. The spread of hand-clasp grooming was followed among the chimpanzees at the Yerkes Primate Center Field Station, starting with interactions that invariably involved the same adult female.[70] Hand-clasp grooming, which is also known of a few wild chimpanzee communities,[71] occurs when two chimpanzees mutually groom each other, while one of the two takes the hand of another, lifting both of their hands high into the air. They thus sit in a perfectly symmetrical A-frame posture, each with its free hand grooming the pit of the other's lifted arm. This remarkable gesture may promote grooming reciprocity. At Yerkes, it took about one decade for the grooming hand-clasp to spread from the one female who originated it to all of the adults in the colony. The behavior ended up being commonly performed without this female's involvement, including after her temporary removal from the group.

The result of transmission through learning is that a group may develop a set of communication displays shared by all of its members but distinct from displays common in other groups. Thus, hand-clasp grooming has never been reported for any captive chimpanzee group other than the one at Yerkes. The same applies to a ritual typical of the bonobos at the San Diego Zoo, which during grooming customarily clap their hands or feet together, or tap their chests with their hands. One bonobo will sit down in front of another, clap her hands a couple of times, then start grooming the other's face in alternation with more hand-clapping. This makes the San Diego Zoo the only place in the world where one can actually *hear* apes groom. When new individuals were introduced, they picked up the habit in about two years.[72]

The same bonobos show a facial expression that may be unique for this group—it has never been reported for any other group, captive or wild, making it perhaps the only documented case of a learned facial expression in nonhuman primates. The bonobos' "duck face" is described as follows: "The lips are flattened at the mouth-corners over a greater length than in the pout face, creating a semblance to a duck bill. At the front the lips are not curled outward to the extent as in the pout face, leaving a smaller opening. No vocalizations occur with the display" (Ref. 20, p. 196). The duck face typically occurs during grooming bouts, in both groomers and groomees (FIG. 7).

Other examples of group-specific communication derive from a comparison of vocalizations across several zoo groups of chimpanzees[73] as well as from field studies on chimpanzees across Africa.[74] The latter report, while emphasizing tool use, includes several communication displays such as leaf-

FIGURE 7. One bonobo grooming another shows the duck face, an expression known only of the colony at the San Diego Zoo. This facial expression is conventionalized, meaning that it is socially transmitted, hence a cultural feature of this one group of apes. The duck face has never been reported for any other bonobos, captive or wild. Conventionalization is prominent in ape communication. (Photograph by Frans de Waal.)

clipping in courtship, the rain dance, and the aforementioned hand-clasp grooming. Recently, yet another custom was reported for wild chimpanzees, the so-called "social scratch." In this gesture, one individual rakes the hand back and forth across the body of another, usually scratching the other with the nails. It seems the typical "you scratch my back, I'll scratch yours" gesture; yet however familiar this sounds, in wild chimpanzees the social scratch is limited to a single community.[75]

Cultural communication patterns tend to be nonfacial and nonvocal. This is perhaps due to the apes' limited control over face and voice. Not that apes have absolutely no control over their facial musculature. I have documented games in bonobos that involve the repeated pulling of novel, strange faces, and described a range of deceptive tactics in chimpanzees.[62,72,76] These cases include giving false expressions or suppressing expressions when they certainly would be expected (Ekman, this volume, discusses human examples). A recent comparison of anecdotes of deception confirms that the examples are more numerous and more striking for apes than for monkeys.[77] Control over the face seems present, therefore; yet is probably incomplete at emotion-

TABLE 2. Domains of visual communication in which our closest relatives, the anthropoid apes, may differ from monkeys, suggesting that these characteristics developed recently in the primate order or only in the hominoid lineage

Domain	Apes	Monkeys
Graded signals	expressions A and B grade into each other through intermediates; the face is continuously in motion	expressions are relatively discrete
Free-hand gestures	ritualized manual gestures with free hand are common	absent
Deictic communication	intentionally directing the attention of another to the environment while monitoring the effect on the other (e.g., pointing)	absent
Conventionalized signals	certain signals spread socially; hence these signals vary across groups of the same species	rare or absent
Contextually defined meaning	the meaning of signals needs to be extracted from their specific context	less common
Emotional control	ability to suppress, modify, or call forth visual displays, such as for deceptive purposes	rare or absent

ally charged moments. This may explain why in both humans' and apes' facial expressions are less culturally variable than manual gestures.

It is perhaps due to this bias that no good examples of culturally transmitted communication exists for monkeys: one of the absolute differences between monkey and ape visual communication is the absence of free-hand gestures in monkeys (see HOMINOID SPECIALTIES: GRADING AND GESTURING above). Such differences need to be explored further, since patterns unique to apes likely tell us something about what set the visual communication of our ancestors apart. Hypothetical differences between monkey and ape communication are summarized in TABLE 2. Characteristics that we share with apes but not monkeys likely evolved recently; hence they may have provided a basis for the development of even more unique patterns, found only in humans, such as symbolic signaling.

REFERENCES

1. DARWIN, C. 1998. The Expression of the Emotions in Man and Animals, 3rd edit. P. Ekman, Ed. Oxford University Press. New York.
2. EKMAN, P. 1998. Afterword: universality of emotional expression? A personal history of the dispute. *In* The Expression of the Emotions in Man and Animals, 3rd edit. P. Ekman, Ed.: 363–393. Oxford University Press. New York.

3. TINBERGEN, N. 1953. Social Behavior in Animals. Chapman & Hall. London.
4. LORENZ, K.Z. 1981. The Foundations of Ethology. Touchstone. New York.
5. LADYGINA-KOHTS, N.N. 2002. Comparative study of ape emotions and intelligence. *In* Infant Chimpanzee and Human Child: A Classic. F.B.M. de Waal, Ed. Oxford University Press. Oxford.
6. YERKES, R.M. & A.W. YERKES. 1929. The Great Apes: A Study of Anthropoid Life. Yale University Press. New Haven, CT.
7. VAN HOOFF, J.A.R.A.M. 1962. Facial expressions in higher primates. Symp. Zool. Soc. London **8:** 97–125.
8. VAN HOOFF, J.A.R.A.M. 1967. The facial displays of the Catarrhine monkeys and apes. *In* Primate Ethology. D. Morris, Ed.: 7–68. Aldine. Chicago.
9. GOODALL, J. & H. VAN LAWICK. 1968. The behaviour of free-living chimpanzees in the Gombe Stream Reserve. Anim. Behav. Monogr. **1:** 161–311.
10. CHEVALIER-SKOLNIKOFF, S. 1973. Facial expression of emotion in nonhuman primates. *In* Darwin and Facial Expressions. P. Ekman, Ed.: 11–90. Academic Press. New York.
11. REDICAN, W.K. 1975. Facial expressions in nonhuman primates. *In* Primate Behavior. L.A. Rosenblum, Ed.: 103–194. Academic Press. New York.
12. REDICAN, W.K. 1982. An evolutionary perspective on human facial displays. *In* Emotion in the Human Face. P. Ekman, Ed.: 212–280. Cambridge University Press. Cambridge.
13. EKMAN, P. & W.V. FRIESEN. 1978. The Facial Action Coding System. Consulting Psychologists Press. Palo Alto, CA.
14. PREUSCHOFT, S. 1995. 'Laughter' and 'Smiling' in Macaques: An Evolutionary Approach. Unpublished Thesis of the University of Utrecht. Utrecht.
15. DE WAAL, F.B.M. & L.M. LUTTRELL. 1985. The formal hierarchy of rhesus monkeys: an investigation of the bared-teeth display. Am. J. Primatol. **9:** 73–85.
16. PREUSCHOFT, S. & J.A.R.A.M. VAN HOOFF. 1995. Homologizing primate facial displays: a critical review of methods. Folia Primatol. **65:** 121–137.
17. IMMELMANN, K. & C. BEER. 1989. A Dictionary of Ethology. Harvard University Press. Cambridge, MA.
18. ANDREW, R.J. 1965. The origins of facial expressions. Sci. Am. **213:** 88–94.
19. FRIDLUND, A.J. 1994. Human Facial Expressions: An Evolutionary View. Academic Press. San Diego, CA.
20. DE WAAL, F.B.M. 1988. The communicative repertoire of captive bonobos (Pan paniscus), compared to that of chimpanzees. Behaviour **106:** 183–251.
21. SCHMIDT, K.L. & J.F. COHN. 2001. Human facial expressions as adaptations: evolutionary questions in facial expression research. Yearb. Phys. Anthropol. **44:** 3–24.
22. OWREN, M.J. & J.-A. BACHOROWSKI. 2001. The evolution of emotional expression: a "selfish gene" account of smiling and laughter in early hominids and humans. *In* Emotions: Current Issues and Future Directions. T.J. Mayne & G.A. Bonanno, Eds.: 152–191. Guilford Press. New York.
23. VAN HOOFF, J.A.R.A.M. 1972. A comparative approach to the phylogeny of laughter and smiling. *In* Non-verbal Communication. R. Hinde, Ed.: 209–241. Cambridge University Press. Cambridge.
24. BECKER, C. 1984. Orang-Utans und Bonobos im Spiel. Profil Verlag. Munich.
25. FAGAN, R. 1981. Animal Play Behavior. Oxford University Press. New York.

26. BACHOROWSKI, J.-A., M. J. SMOSKI & M. J. OWREN. The acoustic features of human laughter. J. Acoust. Soc. Am. In press.
27. PARR, L.A., S. PREUSCHOFT & F.B.M. DE WAAL. 2002. Afterword: research on facial emotion in chimpanzees, 75 years since Kohts. *In* Infant Chimpanzee and Human Child. F.B.M. de Waal, Ed.: 411–452. Oxford University Press. Oxford.
28. ROWELL, T.E. 1962. Agonistic noises of the rhesus monkey. Symp. Zool. Soc. London **8**: 91–96.
29. MARLER, P. 1976. Social organization, communication and graded signals: the chimpanzee and the gorilla. *In* Growing Points in Ethology. P.P. Bateson & R. A. Hinde, Eds.: 239–279. Cambridge University Press. London.
30. VAN HOOFF, J.A.R.A.M. 1973. A structural analysis of the social behaviour of a semi-captive group of chimpanzees. In Expressive Movement and Non-verbal Communication. M. von Cranach & I. Vine, Eds.: 75–162. Academic Press. London.
31. ANDREW, R.J. 1963. The origin and evolution of the calls and facial expressions of the primates. Behaviour **20**: 1–109.
32. ANDREW, R.J. 1963. Evolution of facial expression. Science **142**: 1034–1041.
33. BOLWIG, N. 1962. Facial expression in primates with remarks on a parallel development in certain carnivores. Behaviour **22**: 167–192.
34. MARLER, P. 1969. Vocalizations of wild chimpanzees: an introduction. *In* Proceedings of the Second International Congress of Primatology. C.R. Carpenter, Ed.: 94–100. Karger. Basel.
35. REYNOLDS, V. & F. REYNOLDS. 1965. Chimpanzees of the Budongo Forest. *In* Primate Behavior. I. De Vore, Ed.: 368–424. Holt, Rhinehart, & Winston. New York.
36. YERKES, R.M. & B. LEARNED. 1925. Chimpanzee Intelligence and Its Vocal Expressions. Williams & Wilkins. Baltimore, MD.
37. MARLER, P. & R. TENAZA. 1976. Signaling behavior of apes with special reference to vocalization. *In* How Animals Communicate. T. Sebeok, Ed.: 965–1033. Indiana University Press. Bloomington, IN.
38. ALTMANN, S.A. 1962. A field study of the sociobiology of rhesus monkeys, *Macaca mulatta*. Ann. N.Y. Acad. Sci. **102**: 338–435.
39. DE WAAL, F.B.M. 1997. Food-transfers through mesh in brown capuchins. J. Comp. Psychol. **111**: 370–378.
40. HOPKINS, W.D. & F.B.M. DE WAAL. 1995. Behavioral laterality in captive bonobos (Pan paniscus): replication and extension. Int. J. Primatol. **16**: 261–276.
41. HOPKINS, W.D. & R.D. MORRIS. 1993. Handedness in great apes: a review of findings. Int. J. Primatol. **14**: 1–25.
42. CORBALLIS, M.C. 2002. From Hand to Mouth: The Origins of Language. Princeton University Press. Princeton, NJ.
43. DE WAAL, F.B.M. 1976. Straight-aggression and appeal-aggression in Macaca fascicularis. Experientia **32**: 1268–1270.
44. DE WAAL, F.B.M. 1977. The organization of agonistic relations within two captive groups of Java-monkeys (Macaca fascicularis). Z. Tierpsychol. **44**: 225–282.
45. DE WAAL, F.B.M. 1975. The wounded leader: a spontaneous temporary change in the structure of agonistic relations among captive Java-monkeys (Macaca fascicularis). Neth. J. Zool. **25**: 529–549.

46. SMITH, H.J., J.D. NEWMAN & D. SYMMES. 1982. Vocal concomitants of affiliative behavior in squirrel monkeys. *In* Primate Communication. C.T. Snowdon, C.H. Brown & M.R. Peterson, Eds.: 30–49. Cambridge University Press. Cambridge.
47. GREEN, S. 1975. Variation of vocal pattern with social situation in the Japanese monkey (Macaca fuscata): a field study. *In* Primate Behavior: Developments in Field and Laboratory Research, Vol. 4. L.A. Rosenblum, Ed.: 1–102. Academic Press. New York.
48. DE WAAL, F.B.M. 1986. Integration of dominance and social bonding in primates. Q. Rev. Biol. **61:** 459–479.
49. GOUZOULES, S., H. GOUZOULES & P. MARLER. 1984. Rhesus monkey (Macaca mulatta) screams: representational signaling in the recruitment of agonistic aid. Anim. Behav. **37:** 182–193.
50. BAUERS, K.A. & F.B.M. DE WAAL. 1991."Coo" vocalizations in stumptailed macaques: a controlled functional analysis. Behaviour **119:** 143–160.
51. DE WAAL, F.B.M. & R. REN. 1988. Comparison of the reconciliation behavior of stumptail and rhesus macaques. Ethology **78:** 129–142.
52. KUMMER, H. 1957. Soziales Verhalten einer Mantelpavian-gruppe. Huber. Bern.
53. DE WAAL, F.B.M. & J.A.R.A.M. VAN HOOFF. 1981. Side-directed communication and agonistic interactions in chimpanzees. Behaviour **77:** 164–198.
54. HINDE, R.A. 1985. Expression and negotiation. *In* The Development of Expressive Behavior: Biology-Environment Interactions. G. Zivin, Ed.: 103–116. Academic Press. Orlando, FL.
55. CHADWICK-JONES, J.K. 1991. The social contingency model and olive baboons. Int. J. Primatol. **12:** 145–161.
56. DE WAAL, F.B.M. 1996. Conflict as negotiation. *In* Great Ape Societies. W.C. McGrew, L.F. Marchant & T. Nishida, Eds.: 59–172. Cambridge University Press. Cambridge.
57. BUTTERSWORTH, G. & L. GROVER. 1988. The origins of referential communication in human infancy. *In* Thought without Language. L. Weiskrantz, Ed.: 5–24. Clarendon Press. Oxford.
58. POVINELLI, D.J. 2000. Folk Physics for Apes: The Chimpanzee's Theory of How the World Works. Oxford University Press. Oxford.
59. MENZEL, E.W. 1973. Leadership and communication in young chimpanzees. *In* Precultural Primate Behavior. E.W. Menzel, Ed.: 192–225. Karger. Basel.
60. LEAVENS, D.A. & W.D. HOPKINS. 1998. Intentional communication by chimpanzees: a cross-sectional study of the use of referential gestures. Dev. Psychol. **34:** 813–822.
61. LEAVENS, D.A. & W.D. HOPKINS. 1999. The whole-hand point: The structure and function of pointing from a comparative perspective. J. Comp. Psychol. **113:** 417–425.
62. DE WAAL, F.B.M. 1998 [1982]. Chimpanzee Politics: Power and Sex among Apes. Johns Hopkins University Press. Baltimore, MD.
63. VEÀ, J.J. & J. SABATER-PI. 1998. Spontaneous pointing behaviour in the wild pygmy chimpanzee (Pan paniscus). Folia Primatol. **69:** 289–290.
64. MENZEL, C.R. 1999. Unprompted recall and reporting of hidden objects by a chimpanzee (Pan troglodytes) after extended delays. J. Comp. Psychol. **113:** 426–434.
65. EIBL-EIBESFELDT, I. 1989. Human Ethology. Aldine. New York.

66. TAGLIALATELA, J.P., S. SAVAGE-RUMBAUGH & L.A. BAKER. 2003. Vocal production by a language-competent *Pan paniscus*. Int. J. Primatol. **24:** 1–17.
67. MASON, W.A. 1985. Experiential influences on the development of expressive behaviors in rhesus monkeys. *In* The Development of Expressive Behavior: Biology-Environment Interactions. G. Zivin, Ed.: 117–152. Academic Press. Orlando, FL.
68. CHENEY, D.L. & R.M. SEYFARTH. 1990. How Monkeys See the World. University of Chicago Press. Chicago.
69. TOMASELLO, M., J. CALL, K. NAGELL, *et al.* 1994. The learning and use of gestural signals by young chimpanzees: a trans-generational study. Primates **35:** 137–154.
70. DE WAAL, F.B.M. & M. SERES. 1997. Propagation of handclasp grooming among captive chimpanzees. Am. J. Primatol. **43:** 339–346.
71. MCGREW, W.C. & C.E.G. TUTIN. 1978. Evidence for a social custom in wild chimpanzees? Man **13:** 243–251.
72. DE WAAL, F.B.M. 1989. Peacemaking among Primates. Harvard University Press. Cambridge, MA.
73. MARSHALL, A.J., R.W. WRANGHAM & A.C. ARCADI. 1999. Does learning affect the structure of vocalizations in chimpanzees? Anim. Behav. **58:** 825–830.
74. WHITEN, A., J. GOODALL, W.C. MCGREW, *et al.* 1999. Cultures in chimpanzees. Nature **399:** 682–685.
75. NAKAMURA, M., W.C. MCGREW, L.F. MARCHANT & T. NISHIDA. 2000. Social scratch: Another custom in wild chimpanzees? Primates **41:** 237–248.
76. DE WAAL, F.B.M. 1992. Intentional deception in primates. Evol. Anthropol. 1: 86–92.
77. BYRNE, R.W. & A. WHITEN. 1990. Tactical deception in primates: the 1990 data-base. Primate Rep. **27:** 1–101.

Meaning and Emotion in Animal Vocalizations

ROBERT M. SEYFARTH AND DOROTHY L. CHENEY

*Departments of Psychology and Biology, University of Pennsylvania,
Philadelphia, Pennsylvania 19104, USA*

ABSTRACT: Historically, a dichotomy has been drawn between the semantic communication of human language and the apparently emotional calls of animals. Current research paints a more complicated picture. Just as scientists have identified elements of human speech that reflect a speaker's emotions, field experiments have shown that the calls of many animals provide listeners with information about objects and events in the environment. Like human speech, therefore, animal vocalizations simultaneously provide others with information that is both semantic and emotional. In support of this conclusion, we review the results of field experiments on the natural vocalizations of African vervet monkeys, diana monkeys, baboons, and suricates (a South African mongoose). Vervet and diana monkeys give acoustically distinct alarm calls in response to the presence of leopards, eagles, and snakes. Each alarm call type elicits a different, adaptive response from others nearby. Field experiments demonstrate that listeners compare these vocalizations not just according to their acoustic properties but also according to the information they convey. Like monkeys, suricates give acoustically distinct alarm calls in response to different predators. Within each predator class, the calls also differ acoustically according to the signaler's perception of urgency. Like speech, therefore, suricate alarm calls convey both semantic and emotional information. The vocalizations of baboons, like those of many birds and mammals, are individually distinctive. As a result, when one baboon hears a sequence of calls exchanged between two or more individuals, the listener acquires information about social events in its group. Baboons, moreover, are skilled "eavesdroppers:" their response to different call sequences provides evidence of the sophisticated information they acquire from other individuals' vocalizations. Baboon males give loud "wahoo" calls during competitive displays. Like other vocalizations, these highly emotional calls provide listeners with information about the caller's dominance rank, age, and competitive ability. Although animal vocalizations, like human speech, simultaneously encode both semantic and emotional information, they differ from language in at least

Address for correspondence: Robert M. Seyfarth, Ph.D., Department of Psychology, University of Pennsylvania, 3815 Walnut St., Philadelphia, PA 19104. Voice: 215-898-9349; fax: 215-898-7301.

seyfarth@psych.upenn.edu

Ann. N.Y. Acad. Sci. 1000: 32–55 (2003). © 2003 New York Academy of Sciences.
doi: 10.1196/annals.1280.004

one fundamental respect. Although listeners acquire rich information from a caller's vocalization, callers do not, in the human sense, intend to provide it. Listeners acquire information as an inadvertent consequence of signaler behavior.

KEYWORDS: animal communication; language; emotions

INTRODUCTION

In *The Expression of the Emotions in Animals and Man*, Darwin[1] expressed the prevailing views of his time concerning the evolution of animal vocalizations. Like his contemporaries, Darwin believed that the production of sounds by animals other than humans (hereafter "animals") had originally appeared as the involuntary consequence of other bodily movements:

> ... when the sensorium is strongly excited, the muscles of the body are generally thrown into violent action; and as a consequence, loud sounds are uttered, however silent the animal may generally be, and although the sounds may be of no use [Ref. 1, p. 83].

He noted, however, that over time the production of particular sounds had come to be associated with specific emotions, such as pain, pleasure, or rage, and as a result that many animal vocalizations had come to serve a communicative function. The roaring of lions and the growling of dogs signal these animals' rage and "thereby endeavour to strike terror into their enemies" (Ref. 1, p. 85); the incessant calling of males in the breeding season signals their "anticipation of the strongest pleasure which animals are capable of feeling" and thereby endeavours "to charm or excite the female" (Ref. 1, pp. 84–85).

In the 150 years that followed, Darwin's successors have disagreed about the "voluntary" nature of animal vocalizations but generally accepted his view that the different calls produced by nonhuman creatures are manifestations of emotion and as a result convey information only about the caller's emotional state. For example, Myers[2] states: "It remains unclear whether the nonhuman primate has developed even rudimentary mechanisms in its brain that can support any voluntary control of its face or voice." After years of field research Goodall[3] concluded that "chimpanzee calls are, for the most part, dictated by emotions;" and as recently as 1990 the linguist Bickerton[4] stated that "...[animal] vocalizations are quite automatic and impossible to suppress." By labeling animal vocalizations as exclusively emotional—in both the proximate causal mechanisms that underlie them and the information they convey—these 19th- and 20th-century scientists drew a sharp distinction between the learned, voluntary sounds that are used in human language and can convey information about external referents and the innate, reflexive sounds that are used in animal communication and can convey information only about the caller's emotions.

In retrospect, such an either/or dichotomy separating emotional from referential information is difficult to understand. Darwin himself describes many cases in which humans—through their tone of voice, for example—express an emotion like sadness or joy while they are speaking, and as a result simultaneously communicate both referential and emotional information. If the two modes of communication coexist so easily in language, why should the obvious emotional component of animal signaling be taken as proof that the referential component is absent?

Whatever the reason for this long-held bias in interpretation, one conclusion is clear: the emotional nature of animal vocalizations has never been in doubt. From their earliest description by naturalists and explorers, animal screams have been described as "distressful" and interpreted as calls for assistance;[1] their harsh, low-frequency sounds have been described as aggressive and interpreted as signs of imminent attack;[5] and their clear, high-frequency sounds have been described as submissive and interpreted as attempts to reduce the aggressiveness of opponents.[5] Given the obvious fact that animal vocalizations both communicate emotions and elicit them in others, contemporary scientists have directed their attention to the more complex question: do they communicate anything else?

AFFECTIVE AND REFERENTIAL COMMUNICATION

Premack[6] pointed out that there were circumstances in which an affective communication system—even one based entirely on emotion—could effectively become semantic. Suppose, Premack argues, you and I live in a small group and you know that more than anything else I love strawberries. And you also know that more than anything else I hate and fear snakes. Then one day, when I am out of sight behind a bush, you hear me give a great shout of joy. If you really know that I give this call only when I've found strawberries and that whenever strawberries are around I can be counted on to make this vocalization, then my cry tells you unambiguously that strawberries are present. Similarly, if you hear a scream and can be certain that I only and always give this call in response to snakes, then my scream tells you without doubt that I have seen a snake. As a result of the listener's ability to detect a pattern in another's vocalizing, a system of communication that depends entirely on the expression of emotions has effectively become one that conveys information about objects and events in the world.

The Specificity of Call Production

Was Premack correct? Throughout the animal kingdom, there are many cases in which a vocalization with specific acoustic features is elicited only by a narrow range of stimuli. Under these conditions, as Premack suggested, calls have the potential to provide listeners with very specific information. For example, the "eagle alarm call" of East African vervet monkeys (*Cercopithecus aethiops*) is elicited almost exclusively by predatory birds, or raptors.[7] Vervet eagle alarms are rarely given in response to stimuli other than raptors, and raptors rarely elicit any vocalizations other than eagle alarm calls. Under these circumstances, eagle alarm calls have the potential to provide reliable information about the presence of a specific type of predator. Through processes that may be similar to Pavlovian conditioning, listeners who have learned the predictable relation between eliciting stimulus and alarm call type can recognize immediately upon hearing an eagle alarm call that a raptor has been spotted, even if they have no other supporting contextual cues.[8–10]

Two factors determine the extent to which a vocalization can provide listeners with specific information. First is the call's *informative value*. If call type A is elicited by eagles and eagles rarely appear without eliciting call type A, then the call has the potential to provide listeners with reliable information about the presence of an eagle[10] (Rescorla[11] discusses this phenomenon as it applies to Pavlovian conditioning).

The second important variable is the breadth of stimuli that elicit a given call type, defined as the call's *referential specificity*. Some animal vocalizations are elicited by a broad array of stimuli and thus have a very low referential specificity. Both suricates (*Suricata suricatta*, a South African mongoose shown in FIG. 1) and female diana monkeys (*Cercopithecus diana*) give "alert" calls in response to many stimuli, including mammalian and avian predators, large nonpredatory animals, falling trees, and social disturbances within the group.[12–14] These general alerting signals stand in marked contrast to the more acoustically distinct calls that individuals of the same species give to specific types of predator. Suricates, for example, give one alarm call type to mammalian predators, primarily jackals (*Canis mesomelas*), a second alarm call type to avian predators, primarily the martial eagle (*Polemaetus bellicosus*), and a third alarm call type to snakes like the Cape cobra (*Naja nivea*) and to fecal, urine, or hair samples of predators and/ or foreign suricates (FIG. 2).[15] Diana monkeys give acoustically distinct alarm calls to mammalian predators like leopards (*Panthera pardus*) and to avian predators like the crowned eagle (*Stephanoetus coronatus*).[13,16] Such predator-specific alarm calls have a high referential specificity.

The strength of association between call and eliciting stimulus (informative value) plus the breadth of eliciting stimuli involved (referential specificity) interact to determine the specificity of call production—the extent to which a call has the potential to convey precise information to listeners.[10] Because they are strongly associated with a very narrow range of eliciting stimuli, some calls are highly specific and thus have the potential to transmit very precise information. Other calls are less contextually specific, and therefore

FIGURE 1. A suricate (*Suricata suricatta*) in vigilant posture. Photo by Marta Manser.

have the potential to transmit less precise information, either because the association between call and eliciting stimulus is strong but the array of stimuli for which the association holds is relatively broad, or because the association between call and eliciting stimulus is weak. Finally, the specificity of call production says nothing about whether the vocalization actually does convey specific information to listeners; it simply describes the call's potential for doing so.

Emotional and Referential Communication: Apples and Oranges

As already noted, vocal communication in animals has historically been thought to differ from human language primarily because the former is an

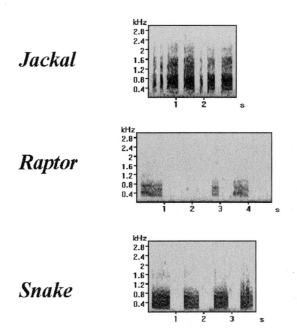

Jackal

Raptor

Snake

FIGURE 2. Sonagrams of alarm calls given by suricates to jackals, raptors, and snakes. In each case, the X axis shows time in seconds; the Y axis shows frequency in kHz.

"affective" system based on emotion, whereas the latter is a "referential" system based on the relation between words and the objects or events they represent. Following Darwin,[1] many scientists, including Scherer,[17] Bachorowski and Owren,[18] and Bachorowski (this volume) have shown that human speech conveys both referential and emotional information; however, the idea that animal calls might have a referential component remains controversial. Over the past 20 years much ink has been spilled—by ourselves and others—debating whether animal vocalizations could ever provide listeners with information about objects or events other than the vocalizer's emotions and, if so, how referential and affective signaling might interact.[7,8,19–25] Often the debate has been cast as an either/or opposition between affective and referential signaling. This dichotomy, however, is logically false.

A call's potential to serve as a referential signal depends on the specificity of call production, as defined above. The mechanisms that underlie this specificity are irrelevant. A tone that informs a rat about the imminence of a shock, an alarm call that informs a vervet about the presence of a leopard, or a scream that informs a baboon that her offspring is involved in a fight all have the potential to provide a listener with precise information because of their predictable association with a narrow range of events. The widely different mechanisms that lead to this association have no effect on the signal's potential to inform.[10]

Put slightly differently, there is no obligatory relation between referential and affective signaling. Knowing that a call is referential (that is, has the potential to convey highly specific information) tells us nothing about whether its underlying causation is affective or not. Conversely, knowing that a call's production is due entirely to the caller's affect tells us nothing about the call's potential to serve as a referential signal. Premack[6] was correct: a shout that is entirely based upon emotion can serve just as referential a function as the word "strawberries" as long as the shout is predictably elicited by strawberries and no other stimuli.

It is therefore wrong, on theoretical grounds, to treat animal signals as *either* referential *or* affective, because the two properties of a communicative event are logically distinct and independent. The first concerns a signal's relation to features of the environment, whereas the second concerns the underlying mechanisms by which that relation arises. Highly referential signals could, in principle, be caused entirely by a signaler's emotions; or their production could be relatively independent of measures of arousal. Highly affective signals could be elicited by very specific stimuli and thus function as referential calls, or they could be elicited by so many different stimuli that they provide listeners with only general information. In principle, any combination of results is possible.

The affective and referential properties of signals are also logically distinct, at least in animal communication, because the former depends on mechanisms of call production in the signaler, whereas the latter depends on the listener's ability to extract information from events in its environment.[10] Signalers and recipients, though linked in a communicative event, are nonetheless separate and distinct because the mechanisms that cause a signaler to vocalize do not in any way constrain a listener's ability to extract information from the call.

The grunts of free-ranging baboons (*Papio cynocephalus ursinus*) offer a good example. Baboons live throughout the savanna-woodlands of Africa, in groups of 30–100 individuals that contain adult males, adult females, and immatures. As they forage during the day, the baboons' most common vocalization is a low-amplitude tonal grunt. Though all grunts sound alike to inexperienced human listeners, field observations have shown that grunts in two different social contexts (FIG. 3) can be distinguished by both their mode of delivery and the responses they evoke.[26,27] *Move* grunts are typically given when the group is about to initiate a move into a new area of its range. They are given in bouts of 1–2 calls and often elicit "answering" *move* grunts from others nearby. By contrast, *infant* grunts are given during friendly social interactions—for example, as the caller approaches a mother with an infant and attempts to touch or handle her baby. *Infant* grunts are given in bouts of 5–10 calls and seldom elicit answering grunts from those nearby.[26,27] Both call

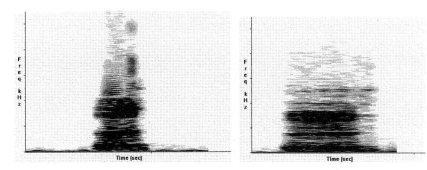

FIGURE 3. Sonagrams of representative grunts given by baboons when the group is moving ("move" grunt, **left**) and when the vocalizer is approaching a mother with infant ("infant" grunt, **right**). X axis shows time in seconds; Y axis shows frequency in kHz.

types are individually distinctive; although the two grunt types grade acoustically into one another, typical *move* grunts show subtle acoustic differences from typical *infant* grunts.[27]

Baboons seem to recognize these differences. Playback experiments conducted by Rendall *et al.*[28] examined the stimuli that elicited vocal "answers" to *move* grunts and found an effect of both call type (vocal responses were more likely when the playback stimulus was a *move* grunt than when it was an *infant* grunt) and context (grunt responses were more likely in the move than in the rest context). There was also an interaction between grunt type and context, with the majority of "answers" elicited by *move* grunts presented in a move context.

Should we describe the baboons' grunts as emotional or referential? Rendall[29] used behavioral data to code a social interaction involving *move* or *infant* grunts as one with "high" or "low" arousal. He then examined calls given in these two circumstances and found that, in each context, certain acoustic features or modes of delivery were correlated with apparent arousal. Bouts of grunting given when arousal was apparently high had more calls, a higher rate of calling, and calls with a higher fundamental frequency (F0) than bouts given when arousal was apparently low. Further analysis revealed significant variation between contexts in the same three acoustic features that varied within context. By all three measures (call number, call rate, and F0), *infant* grunts were correlated with higher arousal than were *move* grunts. *Infant* grunts also exhibited greater pitch modulation and more vocal "jitter."[29] In human speech, variation in pitch, tempo, vocal modulation, and jitter are known to provide listeners with cues about the speaker's affect or arousal[17,18] (see also Bachorowski, this volume).

It is, of course, difficult to obtain independent measures of an animal's level of arousal under natural conditions. However, similarities between human and nonhuman primates in the mechanisms of phonation[30–32] support Rendall's[29] conclusion that different levels of arousal play an important role in causing baboons to give acoustically different grunts in the *infant* and *move* contexts. Accepting this view, however, says nothing about the grunts' potential to act as referential signals that inform nearby listeners about social or ecological events taking place at the time. To understand their potential to act as functionally referential signals, we must consider grunts from a different perspective, that of the recipient.

Baboon grunts vary in their informative value and referential specificity. *Move* grunts, for example, are produced only when the group is moving, about to move, or has just begun a move from one location to another (Ref. 28, personal observation). *Move* grunts are particularly likely to be given in three circumstances: in the last few minutes of a rest period when the group is about to move and some individuals have already begun to do so; in the first few minutes after all individuals have begun to move; and as an "answering" call in the seconds immediately after another individual has produced a *move* grunt. A group's transition from resting to moving seldom occurs without at least one *move* grunt (personal observation). *Move* grunts are therefore highly informative, because they accurately predict the onset of a group move; and referentially specific, because the breadth of stimuli that elicit them is relatively narrow.

By comparison, *infant* grunts have a lower informative value than *move* grunts, for two reasons. First, when listeners hear *infant* grunts, the probability of infant handling is high, but infant handling also occurs in the absence of grunts, when the interacting individuals are silent.[26] Second, *infant* grunts are elicited in many contexts other than those that involve infant handling; for example, during friendly interactions between females without infants or as reconciliatory signals after aggression.[26,33] Compared with *move* grunts, then, *infant* grunts are less informative because they are less predictive of infant handling, and less referentially specific because the range of stimuli that elicit them is relatively broad. Infant grunts potentially provide listeners with information that a friendly social interaction is occurring, but they do not specify more than this.

The theoretical perspective outlined here differs from that adopted by Darwin,[1] largely because it examines the vocal communication of animals separately from the perspective of signaler and recipient. As a result, it is open to the possibility that a vocalization whose production is entirely emotional may nonetheless communicate to a listener information that may be described as referential. Further, it is open to the possibility that animal vocalizations may be simultaneously emotional and referential in both their underlying causation and in the information they convey to others. In the sections below we illustrate these last two points with examples from recent research on birds and nonhuman primates. We also discuss their implications for studies of animal cognition.

REFERENTIAL COMMUNICATION AND ITS IMPLICATIONS

From the Signaler's Perspective

Thus far, we have argued that a vocalization can convey referential information to listeners even in cases where the production of calls is a fixed, reflexive reaction on the part of the signaler. We now consider the mechanisms that underlie call production in greater detail.

Is the production of animal vocalizations involuntary? A variety of evidence shows clearly that it is not. In the laboratory, monkeys can learn to give different call types—or to remain silent—under different conditions;[34] in the wild, monkeys routinely vary their production of calls depending upon the identity of their social companions,[35,36] prior events,[37] and many other social or ecological factors. Captive songbirds can sing, remain silent, or modify the acoustic features of their song depending on the reward,[38] while in the wild many territorial songbirds will "match" the song of a neighbor by replying with the song type from their repertoire that most closely resembles the song type their neighbor just sang.[39] The alarm calls of birds, monkeys, and probably many other species may be given or withheld depending on the presence of an "audience."[8,40]

The existence of multiple alarm call types further weakens the argument that animal calls are involuntary, reflexive signals. When producing different alarms, animals like suricates act as if they classify other species into two broad categories, those that elicit an alarm call and those that do not, and within the former group distinguish between three predator types, presumably on the basis of their physical appearance.

In other species, the classification of predators is more complex and cannot be defined solely on the basis of shared physical features. West African diana monkeys offer a good example. Female diana monkeys respond to a male diana monkey's leopard alarm call and a leopard's growl with the same response—by giving their own, acoustically distinct, leopard alarm call. Similarly, females respond to a male diana's eagle alarm call and the sound of an eagle's shriek by giving their own eagle alarm call.[13] In habituation-dishabituation experiments, diana monkey females who first heard a male's leopard alarm call and responded to it with calls of their own were then tested, five minutes later, with the growl of a leopard coming from the same area. Under these conditions, they no longer responded to the growl. They did respond, however, if they were tested with the shriek of an eagle (they gave eagle alarms). Similarly, females who first heard a male diana's eagle alarm call did not respond, five minutes later, to the shriek of an eagle but did respond with leopard alarms if they heard the growl of a leopard.[16] Male and female diana monkey leopard alarms and the growls of a leopard are very different acoustically, as are male and female eagle alarms and the shriek of an eagle.

Nonetheless, the monkeys treated the three leopard-associated noises and the three eagle-associated noises as if they provided the same information.

One interpretation of these results argues that the mechanisms underlying call production include the formation of some internal representation about the eliciting stimulus, and this information determines whether or not a call will be produced.[16] Upon hearing a male's leopard alarm, for example, a female diana monkey stores the information that a leopard is present and this information causes her to give her own leopard-specific vocalization. Then, five minutes later, when she hears a leopard's growl coming from the same location, she compares this new information which what she already knows. Because the new information is redundant, the female does not respond to the growl as she normally would, by giving an alarm call. Instead, she remains silent. Had the growl been an eagle's shriek, however, the female would have responded by giving her own eagle-specific vocalization.

In this account, the use of terms like *mental representation* and *information* is similar to the use of a term like *memory* in other explanations of behavior. Upon hearing an auditory stimulus, a monkey is believed to store information that is specific to the stimulus. Later, this information is retrieved and exerts a causal effect on behavior. Although we cannot at present specify the neural instantiation of this stored information, we use the terms *mental representation* and *information* as hypothetical, descriptive variables that may guide further research. In this interpretation of the mechanisms underlying call production, for example, there are parallels between the processing of calls by monkeys and the processing of words by humans. Just as humans respond to words by noting both their acoustic properties (auditory processing) and their meaning (semantic processing), monkeys process calls at two levels and can, in some circumstances, treat calls with different acoustic features as providing similar information.[8,16] If this interpretation is correct, it would suggest that emotion and cognition are as inextricably entwined in the production of calls by monkeys as they are in the production of speech by humans.

In summary, if birds, ground squirrels, and monkeys gave only one "general alert" call to all of their predators, their behavior might well be consistent with the kind of uncontrolled, emotional vocalization that Darwin felt was pervasive in the animal kingdom. Clearly, however, it is not. Moreover, to explain the occurrence of acoustically different, predator-specific alarm calls *entirely* in terms of the vocalizer's emotions, we would have to assume that a suricate (for example) experiences a consistently different level of excitement whenever it sees a jackal, an eagle, or a snake and that, over evolutionary time, natural selection has acted in such a way that all suricates now "agree" on precisely what level of excitement (or fear) is associated with each type of predator. Similarly, we would have to assume that all baboons agree on the exact amount of emotion that is associated with a group move as opposed to handling another female's baby.

These assumptions may be true, but they seem unlikely, particularly given several other observations that argue against an interpretation of vocal production as exclusively emotional. We now know that when an animal sees a predator, or suddenly finds itself in a particular social situation, it does not automatically produce a vocalization; instead, in the instant before it calls it acts as if it is taking account of several other factors. What kind of predator is it? Who is nearby? Did I already respond to this same predator a few moments ago? Or, in the case of baboon grunts, what kind of social situation am I in? Who is nearby? How has the listener responded to my calls so far? At present, the most reasonable hypothesis is that vocal production is caused by both the caller's emotions and his assessment of some or all of these other factors. But while we can safely conclude that more than emotions are involved, we cannot yet specify what these other factors are, or precisely how the caller takes them into account.

From the Listener's Perspective

While the transfer of information from one individual to another is obvious in language, how can we know that it occurs in animals, where we cannot interview subjects and can assess what an individual may have learned only by observing its behavior? Early learning theorists noted that conditioning affects behavior but believed that their methods did not allow them to draw conclusions about the intervening mechanisms, which might or might not involve the acquisition of information. Some even thought that the notion of information, or knowledge, was irrelevant.[41] Applied to the study of animal communication, this view finds parallels in Owren's and Rendall's[23] suggestion that "individual primates use vocalizations to produce affective responses in conspecific receivers" (p. 307) and that "the information-based approach has failed to provide significant insight into signaling by both primates and other nonhumans."[24,42]

Other learning theorists, like Tolman,[43] took a different view, arguing that in any conditioning experiment an animal acquires knowledge and that the animal's behavior "is only an index that a given cognition has been gained."[44] Modern learning theory examines, among many other questions, whether the outcome of a conditioning experiment (the reward) serves simply to reinforce the association between antecedent events or whether the identity of the reward becomes part of the association itself. For example, if rats are trained that a lever press leads to a food pellet and a chain pull leads to sucrose, does the delivery of these rewards simply strengthen the association between certain events ("when in the experimental chamber, press the lever"), or does the reward become part of the "content of learning,"[45] strengthening the associations between the lever and food and between the chain and water? To test between these views, Colwill and Rescorla[46] selectively devalued either the food or the water. Devaluing the food diminished lever pressing but not chain pulling, whereas devaluing water had the opposite effect. For rats, learning seemed to have included the acquisition of information about the outcome of different behaviors.

In their natural habitat, where animals have the opportunity to perform a much wider variety of responses, individuals often react to vocalizations in ways that suggest they have acquired specific information. Vervet monkeys show qualitatively different responses to leopard, eagle, and snake alarm calls.[7,47] Because individuals perform these responses immediately upon hearing a call, apparently without requiring any other supporting information, their behavior strongly suggests that the call has provided them with the information about the presence of a specific predator.

Arguing against this view, Owren and Rendall[48] draw attention to the fact that vervet alarm calls, like those of many other species, consist of a rapid series of abrupt-onset, broad-band pulses with high overall amplitudes—all features designed to evoke an individual's attention and induce arousal. Such vocalizations, they argue, have evolved to "induce nervous-system responses in receivers." They conclude that the notion of information has no "value as a conceptual tool."[48]

There is no doubt that animal alarm calls have acoustic features that may make them attention getting and arousing. Owren and Rendall[48] are also correct in noting that these basic characteristics have received too little attention in studies of animal communication, and they offer a reasonable explanation of why call types with different functions, like alarm calls, distress screams, and more relaxed, within-group vocalizations, take the physical form that they do (see also Bachorowski, this volume). The acoustic features of signals are not arbitrary with respect to their function.

Acoustic features alone, however, cannot explain everything. After all, vervet monkeys, suricates, diana monkeys, baboons, and many other species of mammals and birds give acoustically different alarm calls to different classes of predator. All of these alarm call types share many of the same attention-getting, arousing features mentioned above, probably for the reasons that Owren and Rendall[48] propose. Why, then, are the various alarm calls with each species acoustically so different? Perhaps because, over evolutionary time, natural selection has favored the coevolution of signalers who warn their kin[49] using different calls for different predators and listeners who recognize the associations between call and referent, thereby acquiring, from each call, the appropriate *information*.

Upon hearing a vervet monkey's eagle alarm call, nearby animals who are on the ground look up or run into a bush. Animals in a tree look up and/or run down out of the tree and into a bush; and animals already in bushes typically do nothing.[7,8] One could, of course, argue that no information has been acquired and that the eagle alarm call has created in individuals a particular affective state whose effect on behavior differs from one microhabitat to another, thus producing different responses. A more parsimonious explanation, however, posits that calls provide listeners with specific information, and that the exact nature of an individual's response to this knowledge varies with his immediate circumstances.[8]

As another example, consider the responses shown by baboons to the sound of an aggressive interaction between two members of their group. In an experiment designed to test whether baboons recognize the calls of other group members and also associate signalers with their close genetic relatives, pairs of unrelated females were played sequences of calls that mimicked a fight between their relatives. As controls, the same females heard sequences that involved either only the more dominant female's relative or neither of the females' relatives. When call sequences involved their relatives, subjects looked towards the speaker for a longer duration than when the sequences involved nonkin. When the sequences involved the other female's relative, they also looked towards that female. Subjects did not look towards one another when call sequences involved nonkin.[50] Taken together, these results contradict the hypothesis that calls have been selected solely to induce specific emotional responses in receivers, since the same call, presented in the same context, elicits different responses in different listeners depending in part on which call it is paired with. As with alarm calls, the simplest explanation is that calls provide listeners with specific information, and each listener acts on this information depending on her particular circumstances.

The hypothesis that calls act directly on a listener's emotions to change the listener's behavior[23] and the hypothesis that calls achieve their myriad effects because they provide listeners with specific information are not mutually exclusive. More likely, as Owren and Rendall themselves suggest,[23,48] both processes are at work, and vocalizations, together with listeners' memory of past interactions, not only change listeners' affect or emotion but also provide them with information about predators, social interactions, changes in social relations, or group movements. Indeed, when we eventually arrive at an understanding of the underlying neurobiology, there may be little difference between emotional calls that affect emotions and referential calls that affect mental representations.

THE SIMULTANEOUS ENCODING OF EMOTIONAL AND REFERENTIAL INFORMATION BY BOTH SIGNALERS AND RECEIVERS

The preceding sections suggest that emotion and reference are inextricably entwined, both in the production of calls by signalers and in the perception of calls by recipients. Recent work on the vocal communication of suricates (*Suricata suricatta*) directly supports this conclusion.

Suricates are diurnal, cooperatively breeding mongooses that inhabit open semidesert areas in groups of 3 to 33 individuals. They forage for 5 to 8 hours per day, typically at a distance of 20 to 50 m from the nearest burrow or shelter.[51] Foraging animals frequently scan their surroundings for predators. Group members also alternate guarding from a raised sentinel position (FIG. 1).[52]

Guards and foraging individuals emit several acoustically different alarm calls when they spot a predator. As already noted (FIG. 2), suricates give one alarm call type to mammalian predators, primarily jackals (*Canis mesomelas*) that attack on the ground. When nearby individuals hear this call, they move rapidly toward the nearest system of burrows, looking around vigilantly. Suricates give a second, acoustically distinct alarm to avian predators, primarily martial eagles (*Polemaetus bellicosus*) and tawny eagles (*Aquia rapax*) that attack from the air. When listeners hear a suricate eagle alarm, they freeze and crouch where they are, often scanning the sky. Finally, suricates give a third alarm call type to snakes, such as the Cape cobra (*Naja nivea*) and puff adder (*Bitis arietans*). Their snake alarm call is also given to fecal, urine, or hair samples of predators and/or foreign suricates. Because alarm calls to all of these stimuli cause other animals to approach the caller, give the same alarm calls themselves, and either mob the snake or investigate the deposit, they are collectively termed *recruitment calls.*[15]

Manser[15] used discriminant function analysis to classify over 250 alarm calls according to their acoustic features. She confirmed that alarm calls to terrestrial predators, avian predators, and recruitment alarm calls were acoustically distinct (FIG. 4). In addition, within each call class the suricates appeared to give subtly different calls depending upon the imminence of the danger they faced. In any given class, the calls given to a predator that was very close (termed "high-urgency" calls) were acoustically different from those given to the same predator when it was encountered at intermediate distances or far away. The acoustic measures that accounted for variation among alarm call types were, for all but one measure, different from the acoustic measures that accounted for variation within a call type and across levels of urgency.[15] Along the dimension of urgency, changes in acoustic structure were consistent across alarm call types: low urgency calls tended to be clear and more harmonic, while high-urgency calls were harsher and noisier. This difference is illustrated in FIGURE 1, where within each call type the distinction between low- and high-urgency calls represents a shift upwards in discriminant function 1. By contrast, when level of urgency was held constant, there was no consistent rule relating acoustic features to the different predator classes.[15] The referential information about each predator type was not coded acoustically in any consistent way.

In the field, suricates were played alarm calls in the absence of actual predators, and their responses were filmed. Playback of alarm calls given in response to different predators elicited significantly different responses,

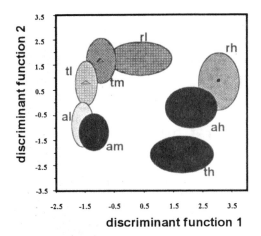

FIGURE 4. Arrangement of the alarm calls given in different predator contexts according to their values as established by discriminant function analysis of the calls' acoustic properties. *Ovals* are spanned by the mean +SD of the first two discriminant functions, with data drawn from 10 runs of the discriminant function analysis. ABBREVIATIONS: t, a, and r stand for terrestrial predator alarms, aerial predator alarms, and recruitment alarms, respectively; l, m, and h stand for low-, medium-, and high-urgency calls, respectively. Reprinted with permission from Manser *et al.*[54]

duplicating behavior seen under natural conditions. In addition to these qualitatively different responses, within each predator class subjects responded in quantitatively different ways to playback of calls that had originally been recorded in circumstances of low, medium, or high urgency. Without blurring the qualitative distinction among responses to different call types, subjects responded most strongly to playback of high-urgency calls, next most strongly to playback of medium-urgency calls, and least strongly to playback of low-urgency calls.[53]

Suricate alarm calls demonstrate clearly the separate yet intermingled role of emotion and reference in animal communication.[54] From the caller's perspective, the proximate mechanisms that underlie alarm calls may depend largely upon the caller's emotion. High- and low-urgency calls are certainly correlated with acoustic features known to be associated with fear or anxiety in both animal vocalizations and human speech[5,17,23,55] (see also Bachorowski, this volume); future research may show that the suricates' different alarm call types also reflect different levels of arousal, with one predator type eliciting the most fear, another the least, and the third intermediate. Alternatively, it may also turn out that suricates' alarms to different predators do not map easily onto acoustic correlates of arousal. Whatever the outcome, the affective basis of call production is entirely separate from the calls' ability to convey specific information to others. Regardless of the mechanisms that underlie their production, suricate listeners acquire specific information from the calls they hear—information about specific predators and about the level of danger they represent.

A FUNDAMENTAL DIFFERENCE BETWEEN ANIMAL VOCALIZATIONS AND HUMAN LANGUAGE

To this point, we have argued that emotion and reference interact to affect vocal communication in both animals and humans. There are, however, important limits to this parallel between language and animal vocalizations. The limits arise because most animals—with the possible exception of chimpanzees (*Pan troglodytes*)—cannot attribute mental states to others.[8,9,56] As a result, while signalers call in response to many stimuli, including the overt expression of emotion in others, they seem not to produce calls in response to the perception of another animal's mental state, such as knowledge or ignorance, which may not have any overt manifestation. And while listeners extract subtle information from vocalizations, they seem not to recognize that signals are reflections of the signaler's knowledge.

Goals and Intentionality in Call Production

Animal vocalizations can be elicited by an extraordinary variety of auditory, visual, or olfactory stimuli.[57] However, one class of stimuli apparently plays no role in eliciting calls from most nonhuman species. Its absence is interesting, because this class of stimuli is probably responsible for eliciting most of the vocalizations used in human conversation.

One function of language is to influence the behavior of others by changing what they know, think, believe, or desire.[58–60] For humans engaged in conversation, the perception of another individual's mental state is perhaps the most common stimulus eliciting vocalization. By contrast, there is now growing evidence that, while animal vocalizations may have evolved because they can potentially alter the behavior of listeners to the signaler's benefit, such communication is—compared with human language—inadvertent, because signalers are unaware of the means by which vocalizations exert their effects.

Several observations and experiments, mostly with nonhuman primates, have attempted to determine whether the perception of another individual's mental state ever serves as an eliciting stimulus for the production of vocalizations. In free-ranging vervet monkeys, infants often give eagle alarm calls to harmless species like pigeons. Typically, nearby adults look up, but rarely give alarm calls of their own. By contrast, when an infant is the first member of its group to give an alarm call to a genuine predator, adults often look up and give alarm calls themselves. In giving or withholding these "second alarms," however, adults do not act as if they recognize the infant's ignorance and are attempting to inform the infant that he was correct; adults give second alarms at similar rates regardless of whether the initial caller was an infant or another adult.[61]

These observations are supported by data on the production of loud calls among chimpanzees, who do not appear to adjust their calling to inform ignorant individuals about their own location or the location of food.[32,62,63] Outside the domain of vocal communication, data on the development of tool use provide a similar picture. Although chimpanzees certainly differ from monkeys in the variety and frequency of tool use,[64] there is currently no systematic evidence that knowledgeable individuals ever actively instruct others[65] or treat ignorant individuals differently from knowledgeable ones.[10,66]

In marked contrast to humans, therefore, nonhuman primates do not seem to produce vocalizations in response to their perception of another individual's ignorance or need for information (although in the domain of visual communication, evidence of spontaneous, untrained manual gestures by apes that may be intentional does exist; see de Waal, this volume). This is not to say that calls cannot inform; to the contrary, we have already reviewed many cases in which animal listeners obtain information from a vocalization. But such information comes from callers who may not, in the human sense, have intended to provide it. Many animal vocalizations whose production initially seems goal directed are not, in fact, as purposeful as they first appear.

Information That Listeners Do Not Acquire

Human listeners routinely treat words and phrases not just as semantic representations of objects and events, but also as propositions that express the speaker's disposition to think or behave toward those objects in a particular way.[59] By contrast, although nonhuman listeners acquire an extraordinary variety of information from vocal signals, there is little evidence that they also acquire information about the signaler's mental state. Evidence for a lack of mental state attribution by listeners is typically indirect; it comes in two forms. First, in most animal species no systematic observational data indicate that signalers modify their vocal production depending on the mental state of listeners, nor is there any definitive evidence that animals display mental state attribution in any other domain, such as tool use (see above). We therefore assume that it is absent in listeners.

Second, in many cases where we might be tempted to explain the behavior of listeners in terms of mental state attribution, such explanations are usually less persuasive than simpler competing arguments. Consider, for example, the reconciliatory grunts of baboons. If a dominant female grunts to a subordinate following aggression, this changes the subordinate's behavior.[37] One could conclude that the subordinate has recognized a change in the dominant's attitude toward her; that, for example, the dominant is seeking to make her former victim less anxious or afraid. Equally plausible, however, is the likelihood that the subordinate is responding on the basis of a learned contingency. Through experience and perhaps also by observing the interactions of others, she has learned that grunts are correlated with a reduced probability of attack. She therefore tolerates her opponent's approaches and even approaches her opponent with the expectation that her opponent will not attack her again.[67] Functionally, these two explanations are equivalent. The latter, however, does not require the recognition of another animal's mental state. The listener is able to extract subtle and complex information from her opponent's grunt, but this information does not require her also to attribute intentions, motives, or beliefs to her opponent.

These conclusions may not apply to chimpanzees, where the results of tests for a theory of mind are mixed. In a series of experiments, Povinelli[68] and Povinelli and Eddy[69] tested whether chimpanzees "appreciate that visual perception subjectively connects organisms to the external world." They argue that to do so the chimpanzees "would have to appreciate that seeing refers to or is 'about' something—in other words, they must interpret seeing as an intentional event."[69] Povinelli's evidence argues against such an interpretation. In a typical experiment, for example, a chimpanzee was trained to use his natural begging gesture (an outstretched hand) to request food from a human trainer. Then the chimpanzee was given the opportunity to beg from one of two trainers. One trainer was facing the subject and could plainly see him; the other trainer could not because her face was covered (or her eyes were covered, or she was facing in the opposite direction). Given this choice, chimpanzees showed no difference in their preference for one trainer over another. By contrast, three-year-old children immediately gestured selectively to the person who could see them.

In contrast, other experiments suggest that chimpanzees may have some understanding about the relation between seeing and knowing, even if this understanding is more rudimentary than that of a young child. Tomasello et al.[70] demonstrated that many nonhuman primates will reliably follow the gaze direction of a human or a member of their own species. Chimpanzees, however, do not simply orient in the appropriate direction and search randomly for something interesting. Instead, they follow gaze direction to a specific geometric location, much as human infants do.[71] More recently, tests by Hare et al.[72,73] suggest that, in at least some situations, chimpanzees know what a conspecific has or has not seen, and from this information may infer what a conspecific does or does not know. Such results do not prove that chimpanzees impute mental states like ignorance to others or that they recognize that other individuals' visual experiences may be different from their own. They do suggest, however, that some form of a theory of mind my be present in chimpanzees, even if it appears to be absent in other primates.

CONCLUSION

Since the publication of Darwin's *Expression of Emotions*, there has been little doubt that animal vocalizations reflect the emotions of the caller and that they arouse emotions in listeners. With this observation as their starting point, contemporary scientists have asked whether vocalizations reflect anything more than the emotions of caller and recipient. Specifically, they have asked whether vocalizations convey information to listeners that goes beyond the emotional state of the signaler and whether signalers intend this communication to occur.

Viewed from the signaler's perspective, animal vocalizations are unlikely to be caused exclusively by emotions because they can be given or withheld depending on many different social factors and because—in encounters with different predators, for example—animals give acoustically different calls in situations with similar emotional valence. Field playback studies demonstrate that the alarm calls of at least one mammalian species simultaneously encode information that is both emotional and referential. At present, however, we know relatively little about the precise mechanisms that underlie the production of vocalizations in animals.

Vocalizations that are predictably linked to specific external stimuli or social situations allow listeners to acquire information that is highly specific and that goes beyond information about the signaler's emotional state. In many species, the responses of listeners to different call types suggest hypotheses about the cognitive mechanisms involved and about the ways in which animals classify their social and ecological environment.

While animal vocalizations, like human language, are both emotional and referential in their causation and in the information they convey, they are also fundamentally different from language because, with the possible exception of chimpanzees, animals cannot represent the mental state of another. As a result, while signalers may vocalize to change a listener's behavior, they do not call with the specific goal of informing others or in response to the perception of ignorance in another. Similarly, while listeners extract subtle information from vocalizations, this does not include information about the signaler's knowledge. Listeners acquire information from signalers who do not, in the human sense, intend to provide it.

REFERENCES

1. DARWIN, C. 1872. The Expression of the Emotions in Animals and Man. 1896 edit. Appleton & Co. New York.
2. MYERS, R.E. 1976. Comparative neurology of vocalization and speech: proof of a dichotomy. Ann. N.Y. Acad. Sci. **280:** 745–757.
3. GOODALL, J. 1985. The Chimpanzees of Gombe. Harvard University Press. Cambridge, MA.

4. BICKERTON, D. 1990. Language and Species. University of Chicago Press. Chicago.
5. MORTON, E.S. 1977. On the occurrence and significance of motivation-structural rules in some bird and mammal sounds. Am. Nat. **111:** 855–869.
6. PREMACK, D. 1972. Concordant preferences as a precondition for affective but not for symbolic communication (or how to do experimental anthropology). Cognition **1:** 251–264.
7. SEYFARTH, R.M., D.L. CHENEY & P. MARLER. 1980. Vervet monkey alarm calls: semantic communication in a free-ranging primate. Anim. Behav. **28:** 1070–1094.
8. CHENEY, D.L. & R.M. SEYFARTH. 1990. How Monkeys See the World. University of Chicago Press. Chicago.
9. SEYFARTH, R.M. & D.L. CHENEY. 1997. Behavioral mechanisms underlying vocal communication in nonhuman primates. Anim. Learn. Behav. **25:** 249–267.
10. SEYFARTH, R.M. & D.L. CHENEY. 2003. Signalers and receivers in animal communication. Ann. Rev. Psychol. **54:** 145–173.
11. RESCORLA, R.A. 1988. Pavlovian conditioning: it's not what you think it is. Am. Psychol. **43:** 151–160.
12. GAUTIER, J.P. & A. GAUTIER. 1977. Communication in Old World monkeys. *In* How Animals Communicate. T. Sebeok, Ed.: 890–964. Indiana University Press. Bloomington, IN.
13. ZUBERBÜHLER, K., R. NOE & R.M. SEYFARTH. 1997. Diana monkey long distance calls: messages for conspecifics and predators. Anim. Behav. **53:** 589–604.
14. MANSER, M.B. 1998. The Evolution of Auditory Communication in Suricates, *Suricata suricata*. Ph.D. thesis. University of Cambridge. Cambridge.
15. MANSER, M.B. 2001. The acoustic structure of suricates' alarm calls varies with predator type and the level of response urgency. Proc. R. Soc. London B **268:** 2315–2324.
16. ZUBERBÜHLER, K., D.L. CHENEY & R.M. SEYFARTH. 1999. Conceptual semantics in a nonhuman primate. J. Comp. Psychol. **113:** 33–42.
17. SCHERER, K.R. 1989. Vocal correlates of emotion. *In* Handbook of Psychophysiology: Emotion and Social Behaviour. H. Wagner & A. Manstead, Eds.: 165–197. John Wiley & Sons. New York.
18. BACHOROWSKI, J.A. & M.J. OWREN. 1995. Vocal expression of emotion: acoustic properties of speech are associated with emotional intensity and context. Psychol. Sci. **6:** 219–224.
19. MARLER, P., C.S. EVANS & M.D. HAUSER. 1992. Animal signals: motivational, referential, or both? *In* Nonverbal Vocal Communication: Comparative and Developmental Approaches. H. Papousek, U. Jurgens & M. Papousek, Eds.: 66–86. Cambridge University Press. Cambridge.
20. HAUSER, M.D. 1996. The Evolution of Communication. MIT Press. Cambridge, MA.
21. MACEDONIA, J.M. & C.S. EVANS. 1993. Variation among mammalian alarm call systems and the problem of meaning in animal signals. Ethology **93:** 177–197.
22. EVANS, C.S. 1997. Referential signals. *In* Perspectives in Ethology, 12. D.H. Owings, M.D. Beecher & N.S. Thompson, Eds.: 99–143. Plenum Press. New York.

23. OWREN, M.J. & D. RENDALL. 1997. An affect-conditioning model of nonhuman primate vocal signaling. *In* Perspectives in Ethology, 12. D.H. Owings, M.D. Beecher & N.S. Thompson, Eds.: 299–346. Plenum Press. New York.

24. OWINGS, D.H. & E.S. MORTON. 1998. Animal Vocal Communication: A New Approach. Cambridge University Press. Cambridge, UK.

25. FISCHER, J. & K. HAMMERSCHMIDT. 2001. Functional referents and acoustic similarity revisited: the case of Barbary macaque alarm calls. Anim. Cogn. **4:** 29–35.

26. CHENEY, D.L., R.M. SEYFARTH & J.B. SILK. 1995. The role of grunts in reconciling opponents and facilitating interactions among adult female baboons. Anim. Behav. **50:** 249–257.

27. OWREN, M.J., R.M. SEYFARTH & D.L. CHENEY. 1997. The acoustic features of vowel-like grunt calls in chacma baboons (*Papio cynocephalus ursinus*): Implications for production processes and functions. J. Acoust. Soc. Am. **101:** 2951–2963.

28. RENDALL, D., R.M. SEYFARTH, D.L. CHENEY & M.J. OWREN. 1999. The meaning and function of grunt variants in baboons. Anim. Behav. **57:** 583–592.

29. RENDALL, D. 2003. The affective basis of referential grunt variants in baboons. J. Acoust. Soc. Am. **113:** 3390–3402.

30. SCHON YBARRA, M. 1995. A comparative approach to the nonhuman primate vocal tract: implications for sound production. *In* Current Topics in Primate Vocal Communication. E. Zimmerman, J.D. Newman & U. Jurgens, Eds.: 185–198. Plenum Press. New York.

31. FITCH, W.T. & M.D. HAUSER. 1995. Vocal production in nonhuman primates: acoustics, physiology, and functional constraints on "honest" advertisement. Am. J. Primatol. **37:** 191–220.

32. FITCH, W.T., J. NEUBAUER & H. HERZEL. 2002. Calls out of chaos: the adaptive significance of nonlinear phenomena in mammalian vocal production. Anim. Behav. **63:** 407–418.

33. SILK, J.B., D.L. CHENEY & R.M. SEYFARTH. 1996. The form and function of reconciliation among baboons, *Papio cynocephalus ursinus*. Anim. Behav. **52:** 259–268.

34. SUTTON, D., C. LARSON, E.M. TAYLOR & R.C. LINDEMAN. 1973. Vocalizations in rhesus monkeys: conditionability. Brain Res. **52:** 225–231.

35. SMITH, H.J., J.D. NEWMAN & D. SYMMES. 1982. Vocal concomitants of affiliative behavior in squirrel monkeys. *In* Primate Communication. C.T. Snowdon, C.H. Brown & M.R. Petersen, Eds.: 30–49. Cambridge University Press. Cambridge.

36. MITANI, J. 1996. Comparative studies of African ape vocal behavior. *In* Great Ape Societies. W.C. McGrew, L.F. Marchant & T. Nishida, Eds.: 93–145. Cambridge University Press. Cambridge.

37. CHENEY, D.L. & R.M. SEYFARTH. 1997. Reconciliatory grunts by dominant female baboons influence victims' behavior. Anim. Behav. **54:** 409–418.

38. MANABE, K., J.E.R. STADDON & J.M. CLEAVELAND. 1997. Control of vocal repertoire by reward in budgerigars (*Melopsittacus undulates*). J. Comp. Psychol. **111:** 50–62.

39. VEHRENCAMP, S.L. 2001. Is song-type matching a conventional signal of aggressive intentions? Proc. Roy. Soc. Lond. B **268:** 1637–1642.

40. GYGER, M., S.J. KARAKASHIAN, & P. MARLER. 1986. Avian alarm-calling: is there an audience effect? Anim. Behav. **34:** 1570–1572.

41. SKINNER, B.F. 1974. Verbal Behavior. Appleton-Century Crofts. New York.
42. OWREN, M.J. 2000. Standing evolution on its head: the uneasy role of evolutionary theory in comparative cognition and communication. Rev. Anthropol. **29:** 55–69.
43. TOLMAN, E.C. 1932. Purposive Behavior in Animals and Men. Appleton-Century Crofts. New York.
44. GLEITMAN. H. 1991. Psychology, 3rd edit. W.W. Norton. New York.
45. RESCORLA, R.A. 2000. Multiple mentorship: one example of Henry Gleitman's influence. *In* Perception, Cognition, and Language. B. Landau, J. Sabini, J. Jonides & E.L. Newport, Eds.: 39–48. MIT Press. Cambridge, MA.
46. COLWILL, R.M. & R.A. RESCORLA. 1985. Postconditioning devaluation of a reinforcer affects instrumental responding. J. Exp. Psychol. Anim. Behav. Proc. **11:** 120–132.
47. STRUHSAKER, T.T. 1967. Auditory communication among vervet monkeys. *In* Social Communication among Primates. S.A. Altmann, Ed.: 281–324. University of Chicago Press. Chicago.
48. OWREN, M.J. & D. RENDALL. 2001. Sound on the rebound: bringing form and function back to the forefront in understanding nonhuman primate vocal signaling. Evol. Anthropol. **10:** 58–71.
49. MAYNARD SMITH, J. 1965. The evolution of alarm calls. Am. Nat. **99:** 59–63.
50. CHENEY, D.L. & R.M. SEYFARTH. 1999. Recognition of other individuals' social relationships by female baboons. Anim. Behav. **58:** 67–75.
51. CLUTTON-BROCK, T.H., D. GAYNOR, R. KANSKY, *et al.* 1998. Costs of cooperative behaviour in suricates (*Suricata suricatta*). Proc. Roy. Soc. Lond. B **265:** 185–190.
52. CLUTTON-BROCK, T.H., M. O'RIAIN, P. BROTHERTON, *et al.* 1999. Selfish sentinels in cooperative mammals. Science **284:** 1640–1644.
53. MANSER, M.B., M.B. BELL & L. FLETCHER. 2001. The information that receivers extract from alarm calls in suricates. Proc. R. Soc. London B **268:** 2485–2491.
54. MANSER, M.B., R.M. SEYFARTH & D.L. CHENEY. 2002. Suricate alarm calls signal predator class and urgency. Trends Cogn. Sci. **6:** 55–57.
55. HAUSER, M.D. 1993. The evolution of nonhuman primate vocalizations: effects of phylogeny, body weight, and social context. Am. Nat. **142:** 528–542.
56. CHENEY, D.L. & SEYFARTH, R.M. 1998. Why monkeys don't have language. *In* The Tanner Lectures on Human Values, 19. G. Petersen, Ed.: 173–210. University of Utah Press. Salt Lake City, UT.
57. BRADBURY, J.W. & S.L. VEHRENCAMP. 1998. Principles of Animal Communication. Sinauer Associates. Sunderland, MA.
58. GRICE, H.P. 1957. Meaning. Phil. Rev. **66:** 377–388.
59. PINKER, S. 1994. The Language Instinct. W.W. Norton. New York.
60. JACKENDOFF, R. 1994. Patterns in the Mind. Basic Books. New York.
61. SEYFARTH, R.M. & D.L. CHENEY. 1986. Vocal development in vervet monkeys. Anim. Behav. **34:** 1640–1658.
62. MITANI, J. & T. NISHIDA. 1993. Contexts and social correlates of long-distance calling by male chimpanzees. Anim. Behav. **45:** 735–746.
63. CLARK, A.P. & R.W. WRANGHAM. 1994. Chimpanzee arrival pant hoots: do they signify food or status? Int. J. Primatol. **15:** 185–205.
64. MCGREW, W.C. 1994. Tools compared: the material of culture. *In* Chimpanzee Cultures. R.W. Wrangham, W.C. McGrew, F.B.M. deWaal & P.G. Heltne, Eds.: 25–40. Harvard University Press. Cambridge, MA.

65. CARO, T. & M.D. HAUSER. 1992. Is there teaching in nonhuman animals? Q. Rev. Biol. **67:** 151–174.
66. TOMASELLO, M. & J. CALL. 1987. Primate Cognition. Oxford University Press. Oxford.
67. CHENEY, D.L. & R.M. SEYFARTH. 1996. Function and intention in the calls of nonhuman primates. Proc. Brit. Acad. **88:** 59–76.
68. POVINELLI, D.J. 2000. Folk Physics for Apes. Oxford University Press. Oxford.
69. POVINELLI, D.J. & T.J. EDDY. 1996. What chimpanzees know about seeing. Monogr. Soc. Res. Child Dev. **61:** 1–152.
70. TOMASELLO, M., J. CALL & B. HARE. 1998. Five primate species follow the visual gaze of conspecifics. Anim. Behav. **55:** 1063–1069.
71. TOMASELLO, M., B. HARE & B. AGNETTA. 1999. Chimpanzees follow gaze direction geometrically. Anim. Behav. **58:** 769–777.
72. HARE, B., J. CALL, B. AGNETTA & M. TOMASELLO. 2000. Chimpanzees know what conspecifics do and do not see. Anim. Behav. **59:** 771–785.
73. HARE, B., J. CALL & M. TOMASELLO. 2001. Do chimpanzees know what conspecifics know? Anim. Behav. **61:** 139–151.

The Discrimination of Faces and Their Emotional Content by Chimpanzees (*Pan troglodytes*)

LISA A. PARR

Division of Psychobiology, Yerkes National Primate Research Center, Atlanta, Georgia 30329, USA

ABSTRACT: The ability to recognize and discriminate conspecific faces and facial expressions has played a critical role in the evolution of social communication. Darwin was one of the first to speculate that human and non-human primate facial expressions share similar mechanisms for production and functions in expressing emotion. Since his seminal publication, numerous studies have attempted to unravel the meaning of animal signals, with the most success coming from the field of vocal communication, where researchers have identified the referential and emotional nature of specific vocalizations. Studies specifically addressing nonverbal facial displays, however, have faced numerous methodological challenges, including how to objectively describe facial movements and how to study the perception and production of these signals within a social context. In this paper, I will review my studies on chimpanzee face recognition, their ability to categorize facial expressions, and the extent to which chimpanzee facial expressions may convey information about emotion. Finally, recent studies from my lab have begun to address the role of auditory and visual cues in facial expression categorization. Chimpanzees were given the task of matching expressions according to which sensory modality was more salient, the visual or auditory component. For some expressions the visual modality was preferred, while for others the auditory modality was preferred. These data suggest that different social and ecological pressures may shift attention towards one sensory modality over another, such as during long-distance communication or emotional conflict.

KEYWORDS: face recognition; communication; facial expressions; chimpanzee; social cognition; emotion

Address for correspondence: Lisa A. Parr, Division of Psychobiology, Yerkes National Primate Research Center, 954 Gatewood Rd., Atlanta, GA 30329. Voice: 404-727-3653; fax: 404-727-8470.

parr@rmy.emory.edu

Ann. N.Y. Acad. Sci. 1000: 56–78 (2003). © 2003 New York Academy of Sciences.
doi: 10.1196/annals.1280.005

Faces are highly salient social stimuli for many animal species, including sheep, primates, and birds.[1–4] In humans, faces provide viewers with rapid access to information about another individual's age, sex, individual identity, and emotional state.[5–9] The ability to use the information present in faces and respond to it discriminatively has been critical for the evolution of social communication.[10–12] In primate evolution, for example, there has been an increasing trend towards larger and more complex social groups in which individuals rely less on olfactory than visual cues, such as facial signals, for communication.[11,13] As groups became larger, the ability to acquire social knowledge by recognizing and remembering familiar individuals and their relationships with other group members became highly advantageous.[14–16] Individuals do not simply respond to specific social stimuli in fixed, invariant ways but interact within a fluid social environment that is constantly changing depending on the behavior and motivation of others and their interindividual relationships.[17] This is particularly important for chimpanzees because of their fission-fusion society, in which individuals travel in small parties that can change composition frequently and periodically come together into a larger group.[18,19] Therefore, individuals must not only be capable of flexibility in their own social interactions, but be able to monitor the relationships of others in order to survive in a constantly changing social environment.

Over the last several decades, research on the recognition of faces and affective signals has been on the rise.[6,21,22] It has even been proposed that a specific area of the brain responds selectively to faces compared to other complex visual stimuli. The fusiform gyrus, or fusiform face area (FFA)—particularly the right fusiform gyrus—is an area of the ventral temporal lobe that responds selectively to the presentation of faces, as opposed to other stimuli.[22] More recently, it has been shown that this area is particularly sensitive to stimuli for which subjects have developed considerable expertise, such as faces.[23] These studies, in particular, have led to a widespread debate over whether face processing is innate, subserved by a domain-specific neural module, as has been suggested of the FFA; or is learned through experience. The studies of Gauthier and colleagues along with recent studies in human infants provide compelling evidence for the role of learning in the development of face recognition.[24–27]

Primate evolution is also marked by an elaboration of the mimetic facial muscles used for the production of facial expressions, resulting in greater variability in the form and number of expressions that are present in more recently evolved species.[14,28] Darwin was one of the first to speculate that the facial expressions of animals and humans may have similar origins and serve similar functions. In his seminal 1872 publication, *Expression of Emotions in Man and Animal*, Darwin described the facial expressions and vocalizations of nonhuman primates in great detail, speculating about their origins as involuntary actions of the nervous system and their associated emotional content.[29]

In this volume, researchers describe the current state of expressive behavior and communication among humans and other animals. Seyfarth and Cheney neatly summarize the debate over whether animal vocalizations convey referential or emotional meaning, concluding that emotional signals can come to convey referential information depending on how reliably the signal is produced in a given context and how specific the signal is to a given referent.[30] But they also raise an important point that is often ignored in the literature on animal communication: expressive displays can be studied in terms of the immediate circumstances that provoke them and in terms of the specific physiological substrates that give them their form, such as the anatomy of the vocal cords and larynx, and the innervation of the facial musculature. These production end mechanisms were those emphasized by Darwin.[29] Expressive displays can also be analyzed in terms of their impact on other social agents, or receivers. A display may tell a receiver something about the motivational state of the sender, something about the immediate environment, or both.

Numerous studies have examined the information content of animal vocalizations, both in the wild and in captivity. Few studies, however, have focused specifically on the facial component of these signals. Ethologists have typically described facial expressions according to individual movements or specific action patterns, staying away from descriptions that imply function or emotionality. De Waal (this volume) describes the process whereby expressive displays become ritualized, divorced from their original function (Darwin's Principle I, serviceable action) to serve a new function. Through this process, displays become very stereotypical and are easily recognized by receivers to maximize their communicative message. Because of these stereotypical movements, researchers have been able to trace the presence of specific facial expressions in related species. This has led to the identification of several facial expressions in macaques and chimpanzees, particularly those that occur during play (e.g., the relaxed open-mouth face) and submission (e.g., the bared-teeth display), that appear to be homologous with the expressions of laughter and smiling in humans (de Waal, this volume).[31,32]

Additionally, de Waal describes how some nonhuman primate expressions, typically those of chimpanzees, have many different elicitors and can be used in many different contexts, unlike the referential specificity of the alarm vocalizations described by Seyfarth and Cheney. Instead, these facial signals may convey information about the motivational state of the sender, which can be similar across different contexts. Thus, the ability of chimpanzees to accurately interpret the referent for a specific gesture—for instance, the begging gesture referred to by de Waal (this volume)—requires a cognitive evaluation of the immediate social context. To accurately decode the meaning of a chimpanzee's facial expression, such as a bared-teeth display, requires a perhaps more challenging cognitive evaluation of the individual's motivation, which is, in turn, dependent on factors such as the immediate social context, the presence and identity of other individuals, the relationship of these individuals to the signaler, and the circumstances leading to the display.

Despite the importance of understanding the evolution of communication and social cognition in species closely related to humans, very few studies have taken a comparative approach to empirically examine face and affect recognition in nonhuman primates. Such an approach would be particularly beneficial because nonhuman primates share a large percentage of their genetic material with humans, they have a long period of postnatal development, have large brains relative to their body size, live in complex social environments, and exhibit advanced cognitive abilities. As stated earlier, the ability to recognize and keep track of individuals and their social relationships is critical for survival and requires early social experience.[33] Experimental studies of the meaning of primate vocalizations using playback studies both in the wild and in more controlled captive settings have focused on both the quality of the sender's signal and how it is perceived by the receiver; however, few studies have focused specifically on primate facial expressions.[15] My research concerns the perception and categorization of primate faces and facial expressions in nonhuman primates. In this paper, I will review several studies on face discrimination and facial expression categorization in chimpanzees and summarize results from a more recent study on the role of auditory and visual modalities in facial expression categorization.

FACE PROCESSING BY CHIMPANZEES

Previous studies of chimpanzee social cognition have examined subjects' ability to discriminate the faces and facial expressions of unfamiliar conspecifics from photographs. These studies employed a computerized joystick testing paradigm whereby subjects select images on a computer monitor by moving a joystick-controlled cursor. Numerous species have now been trained in this particular paradigm using software developed at the Language Research Center, Georgia State University (Atlanta, GA).[34,35] Images in our studies were presented using a matching-to-sample (MTS) format, whereby a sample image is matched to one of two comparison images. One comparison resembles the sample on some predetermined stimulus dimension, while the other does not match. Because the MTS rule does not vary—subjects are always required to select the comparison image that best matches the sample, it is possible to address additional questions by varying the dimension of stimulus similarity without the need to retrain subjects. One could, for example, match faces according to the identity, sex, or facial expression of the individual presented, which makes the MTS a very powerful and versatile paradigm for studying social cognition in nonverbal organisms.

After first being trained to control the movements of the joystick and cursor and to match abstract shapes presented in a MTS format, chimpanzees were presented with the task of discriminating between two black and white photographs of unfamiliar conspecifics. The correct pair of stimuli was identical photographs, while the nonmatching comparison stimulus was a photograph of another individual. Chimpanzees (N = 6) performed this task above chance on the very first presentation.[4] Although, they performed this task extremely well, the task itself did not specifically address whether the chimpanzees were processing the images as faces per se or whether they were simply viewing the photographs as complex grey-scale patterns and matching them accordingly. So the task was changed to address the ability of chimpanzees to discriminate specific individuals from their facial features. This task presented two different photographs of the same individual as the correct pair, while the nonmatching comparison showed a third photograph of another individual. Correct performance was now dependent on recognizing facial similarities and not similar features of the photographs themselves. With no additional training, subjects performed above chance on this task after two repetitions of each trial. So it appeared that subjects required exposure to each trial at least once before they comprehended that the dimension of matching had changed from the identity of the photograph to the identity of the individual depicted in the photograph.[4] We have performed numerous other studies to assess the specific cognitive strategies used by chimpanzees to discriminate faces. These studies have included testing whether chimpanzees show the face inversion effect, whether they recognize faces when certain facial features have been masked or manipulated,[4] and whether chimpanzee faces convey information about kinship.[36] We have also examined the way in which chimpanzees categorize their facial expressions (see below). Furthermore, we have since replicated most of these initial findings using color presentations of digitized video.[37] In these tasks, the sample stimulus is a short, five-second video clip of an unfamiliar chimpanzee, and the correct comparison image is a photograph of that individual. These and other studies have led to the firm conclusion that conspecific faces represent highly salient and discriminable stimuli for chimpanzees, despite being presented as black-and-white, static photographs; and that these are discriminated in ways that closely resemble human face recognition processes.[38–41]

FACIAL EXPRESSION PROCESSING BY CHIMPANZEES

Initially, we presented chimpanzees with the task of matching two photographs of different individuals making the same facial expression. The nonmatching comparison was a neutral portrait of a third individual. Thus, the dimension of matching in this task changed from the identity of specific individuals to the particular facial expression being made. As in previous face matching tasks, the facial expressions were black and white photographs of individuals who differed in age and sex and were shown with different head

FIGURE 1. Examples of the six chimpanzee facial expressions used in the face matching experiment. **From left to right, top to bottom:** neutral portrait, relaxed-lip face, pant-hoot, play face (relaxed open-mouth face), scream face and bared-teeth display. (Courtesy of Living Links Center, Emory University.)

orientations. An example of each of the six expression types presented in this first experiment can be seen in FIGURE 1. Because individuals differ in the quality and style of their expressions, to select the correct stimulus chimpanzees were required to generalize, within the same trial, their recognition of the type of expression presented in the sample to another individual making the same expression.

FIGURE 2 shows the data from this task graphed across the 5 testing sessions, in which 50 trials were presented per session (i.e., 50 trials represents only 2 repetitions of each of the 25 unique trials presented in the task).[42] Three of the five expressions were discriminated from the neutral portrait on the first testing session, including the bared-teeth display, the play face, and the scream. Thus, the rate of acquisition for facial expression discriminations was comparable to that found for the individual recognition task. Interestingly, the figure shows that the relaxed-lip face was never discriminated above chance from the closed-mouth neutral portrait despite the fact that the relaxed lip is a distinctive feature not present in neutral faces. Subjects did not appear to use this feature to aid them in their discrimination performance and never exceeded 50% performance even after 250 trials, or 10 repetitions.

To explore the role of distinctive features in facial expression categorization, we presented a second task that combined each of the five expression

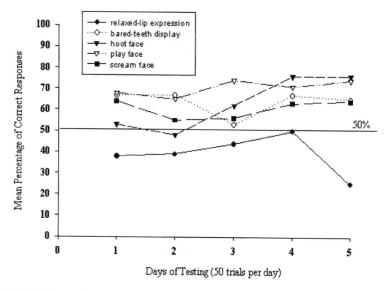

FIGURE 2. Performance of subjects over the first five expression discrimination testing sessions. Three of five expressions were discriminated from the neutral portrait on the first testing session, but the relaxed-lip face was never discriminated above chance levels from the plain neutral portrait. The *50% line* indicates chance levels.

types (we did not use the plain neutral face in this task) with every other expression, totaling 20 different expression dyads. We then selected specific facial features, such as teeth visibility, mouth shape, and eye shape, and rated whether the two expressions presented in each trial shared features in common (e.g., 3 or 4 features shared), or whether the features were distinct (e.g., <2 features shared). Ten trials of each type, similar and distinct, were identified. FIGURE 3 shows an example of each trial type. We then compared whether facial expression discriminations differed according to the number of features the two expressions shared. If chimpanzees were attending to specific salient features when discriminating facial expressions (they did not appear to be doing this in the previous task), they would be expected to perform better on the distinct trials than the similar trials. This was, in fact, the overall finding: subjects performed significantly better discriminating pairs of expressions that looked distinct than they did pairs of expressions that looked similar.[42] However, the pattern was not consistent for all of the 20 dyadic combinations of expression types. Some expressions, like the scream, were discriminated well regardless of whether they were paired with an expression that looked similar or distinct. Thus, overall it appeared as though chimpanzees were relying on something other than, or in addition to, distinctive visual features to discriminate facial expressions; or that visual features are differ-

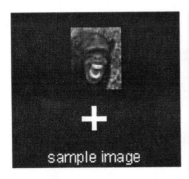
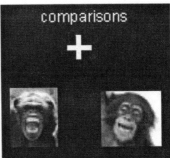
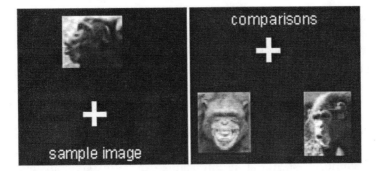

FIGURE 3. An example of two trial types used in chimpanzee facial expression categorization tasks. The **top images** show a trial that combines a scream face with a play face **(bottom right)**. These two expressions have features in common and look similar. The **bottom images** show a trial that combines a pant-hoot with a bared-teeth display **(bottom left)**. These two expressions do not share many features and look distinct.

entially salient depending on the expression type. This led us to speculate about the role of multimodal features, such as dynamic movement, vocalizations, and specific visual features in contributing to the identity and salience of chimpanzee facial expressions. These typically dynamic, affective expressions would best be presented using short video displays to capture the range of features present and would possibly help to identify the feature or features that are critical for facial expression categorization in this species.

A follow-up study presented chimpanzees with short digitized video scenes of conspecific facial expressions, approximately 5 seconds in length. These contained the vocalizations made by the subject during that display and, where possible, did not contain any conflicting signals, such as different expressions from other nearby group members. Using videos of facial expressions as the sample stimuli, we repeated the dyadic version of the facial ex-

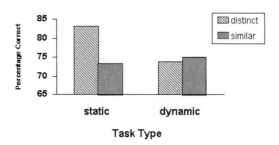

FIGURE 4. A comparison of performance on similar and distinct expression matching trials using both static and dynamic (video) sample images. Subjects performed significantly better on distinct than on similar trials in the static version of the task, but this advantage was not found when the sample images were changed to video displays.

pression categorization task described above. The sample showed a video of an unfamiliar individual's facial expression, while the correct comparison was a black-and-white photograph of a different individual making the same facial expression as shown in the sample video. The nonmatching comparison showed a different expression made by a third individual. After receiving approximately 200 trials on this task (i.e., 10 repetitions of each of the 20 novel trials), the subject's mean performance on similar versus distinct trials was statistically compared. Contrary to our previous finding, that subjects were significantly better at discriminating pairs of expressions that looked distinct than those that looked similar, no such effect was found when the sample stimulus was a video of a facial expression. FIGURE 4 shows the performance on these two trial types.[38] It seemed that presenting the sample as a video eliminated any advantage conferred from the presence of distinctive features, but without improving overall performance.

THE ROLE OF AUDITORY AND VISUAL FEATURES

A more recent direction in my laboratory has been to expand these findings by examining the salience of the auditory and visual modalities in discriminations involving facial expressions. This was done by questioning whether chimpanzees would show a preference towards one modality over the other when discriminating specific facial expressions in a multimodal version of the MTS task. Four expressions were chosen because they are typically accompanied by distinctive vocalizations.[43] These included the following vocal and visual elements: screaming and scream faces, pant-hooting and pant-hoot faces, laughter and play faces, and low-intensity screams and bared-teeth displays.

Stimuli in this experiment were combined to form one of four categories; congruent, multimodal, cross-modal, and intramodal trials. Congruent trials paired a video of a facial expression and its accompanying vocalization with a still photograph of that facial expression as the correct comparison. The congruent audiovisual combinations included those visual-auditory pairings listed above. The vocalizations used in these congruent trials were the original vocalizations that accompanied that video scene, so the audio and video tracks in the sample presentation were temporally synchronized.

Cross-modal trials paired an audio recording of the vocalization that accompanied each of the facial expressions listed above with a still photograph of that same expression (i.e., laughter paired with a photograph of a play face). While the audio clip played, the computer monitor remained black. The cross-modal trials presented a different example of the vocalization from each category than that used in the congruent trials, so there was no repetition of the vocalizations subjects heard during the congruent trials.

Intramodal trials paired a video of each facial expression, without an accompanying audio track, with a still photograph of that same expression. The intramodal trials showed the same sample videos as in the other categories, but with the audio removed. The nonmatching comparison stimuli in all categories listed above were neutral portraits. Correct responses were to select the photograph depicting the expression represented in the sample video, regardless of the modality in which it was presented. Thus, the dimension of matching in these studies, as in other expression discrimination studies, was the expression portrayed in the sample stimulus. These three categories were considered control trials because a correct response was present in each trial.

In the multimodal trials, the conditions were slightly different than for the control categories described above. For multimodal trials, the sample facial expression videos were edited so that the audio track contained a vocalization of each of the other three expression types. Hence these trials combined incongruent audio and visual tracks (i.e., a scream face paired with laughter vocal, a pant-hoot paired with screaming, etc.). These trials paired novel examples of vocalizations from each category with the original visual component of the sample videos, so there was no overlap of any of the individual vocalizations presented in this experiment. FIGURE 5 shows an illustration of a congruent trial described above and an incongruent multimodal trial.

The comparison stimuli for the multimodal trials consisted of a still photograph depicting a facial expression that matched each sensory modality presented in the sample. Thus, one comparison matched the facial expression represented visually in the sample, while the other comparison matched the facial expression represented by the vocalization. Every combination of expressions was presented, 3 possible combinations for each of the 4 expression types (i.e., scream with laughter, scream with low-intensity scream, and scream with pant-hoot) totaling 12 individual multimodal trials. Subjects were nondifferentially reinforced for the multimodal trials, meaning they

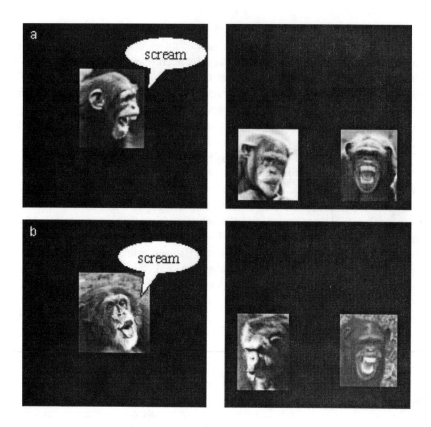

FIGURE 5. An illustration of **(a)** a congruent and **(b)** multimodal matching trial. The congruent trial shows a scream video and vocalization as the sample paired with a neutral portrait on the **left** and a scream face on the **right** (correct response). The multimodal matching trial **(b)** illustrates a pant-hoot video and scream vocalization as the sample, paired with a hoot face on the **left** (visual modality) and a scream face on the **right** (auditory modality).

were reinforced for any response they made, selecting the comparison stimulus that represented either the visual or the auditory modality presented in the sample. This enabled subjects to choose freely the modality of the sample video they preferred to match, the auditory or the visual. The modality they chose was believed to represent the most salient modality for discriminating that particular facial expression.

We hypothesized that subjects would perform best on the congruent trials, since these contained the most consistent information as to the type of expression being presented; and that they would perform well on the intramodal trials, since we knew that subjects were already competent at discriminating static photographs of facial expressions that contained no vocal information.

We hypothesized that subjects would perform above chance on the cross-modal trials; but since they had no previous experience with auditory discriminations, their performance was not expected to be as good as these as on the congruent and intramodal trials. Overall, we expected that subjects would show a preference for one modality over the other for the expressions presented in the multimodal trials. The pant-hoot, for example, is a long-distance signal; so we anticipated that the auditory modality would be more salient than the visual modality, resulting in a vocal bias for discriminations involving pant-hoots. Similarly, we anticipated that the auditory modality of laughter would be more salient than the visual signal of the play face because this latter modality is often concealed from view when animals are engaged in play wrestling. The bared-teeth display is a highly ritualized visual signal in many species.[11,44] Researchers have speculated that the silent bared-teeth expression is homologous to the human smile.[32] However, the bared-teeth display can be accompanied by a low-intensity scream or a tonal squeal, or it can be silent. Because of this, we anticipated that subjects would show a visual preference for this expression and select the bared-teeth display whenever it was shown in the sample video.

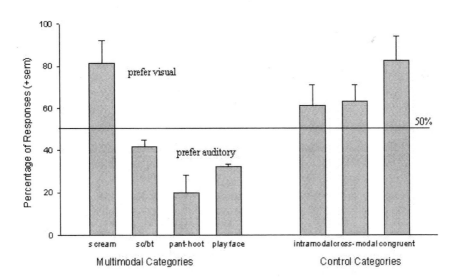

FIGURE 6. The mean performance on matching multimodal and control trials for all subjects over the five testing sessions. The *error bars* indicate the standard errors of the means. Control trials are plotted according to the percentage of correct responses—that is, selecting the comparison facial expression that matched that portrayed in the sample, regardless of sensory modality.

Finally, screams may initially appear to be an easy category to predict because they have such loud vocalizations that are easily identified. Unlike macaque screams, however, there is little evidence that chimpanzee screams convey referential information about the nature of the conflict or that they function to recruit allies during agonistic encounters.[45] Chimpanzee screams seem to be primarily affective in nature. Because the auditory component of the scream is so salient, however, we predicted that subjects would show an auditory bias for discriminations involving screams.

FIGURE 6 illustrates the performance for matching each expression type according to its visual cues, thus selecting the expression that matched the sample based on a preference for the visual modality. This shows a clear preference for the auditory modality for discriminations involving pant-hoots and play faces. Counter to our predictions, however, subjects showed a visual preference for discriminating screams, despite the fact that scream vocalizations are very loud and distinctive. Subjects showed no significant preference for the auditory or visual modality when discriminating the bared-teeth displays. These data may best be interpreted with reference to the differences between graded and discrete signals. Researchers have proposed, for example, that vocalizations given over relatively short distances, such as screams, should be graded and show more intraindividual variability than signals given over long distances.[46,47] Long-distance signals are believed to be discrete and contain little intraindividual variability compared to the more graded close-range signals. Thus, applying these hypotheses to the multimodal matching data, the auditory modality of the pant-hoot should be highly salient, while the auditory component of the scream should be highly variable, perhaps biasing discrimination preferences towards the visual modality.

MATCHING-TO-MEANING

Finally, do chimpanzee facial expressions convey emotional information, as has been demonstrated for human facial expressions?[6,48] We designed a task, named *matching to meaning*, in which subjects were presented with short emotional video scenes.[49] Subjects were then required to select one of two facial expressions that communicated a similar emotional valence, either positive or negative, as that presented in the sample video. The positive facial expression was the play face, and negative facial expressions included scream faces and bared-teeth displays. These were paired with other facial expressions, such as pant-hoot, relaxed-lip, and whimper as the nonmatching comparisons. In contrast to previous tasks—in which subjects were required to match stimuli based on their physical similarity, such as matching facial expressions—this task required subjects to match stimuli according to their emotional similarities. Five experimental scene categories and two control categories were presented. The negative experimental video categories included (1) chase = scenes of veterinarians preparing to anesthetize chimpanzees for routine medical procedures; (2) inject = scenes of chimpanzees being injected with darts and needles during these procedures; (3) dart = pictures of darts and needles; and (4) kd (knock down) = anesthetized chimpanzees. The (5) pos = (positive) experimental video category showed scenes of highly preferred items, such as bottles of grape juice and favorite toys.

The first control category (con1) showed previously learned video discriminations. These were positive and negative social scenes, such as aggression and play; they were paired with the facial expression that occurred most often in those social contexts—screams and play faces, respectively. The subjects were trained so that they performed >85% correctly prior to the matching-to-meaning experiment; this served to control for subjects' overall motivation to perform the task and conformation to the MTS rule. If, for example, subjects performed well on con1 trials but poorly on the experimental trials, then it could be concluded that they understood the goals of the task but did not see the emotional similarity between the sample and correct comparison. If, however, subjects performed poorly on both con1 and experimental trials, it may be that they were distracted, or unmotivated, during that testing session. The second control category (con2) showed scenes of chimpanzees sleeping. These were paired with facial expression that would not typically occur during sleeping (i.e., basically any expression except a neutral one). One expression was arbitrarily designated as the correct response, and subjects were rewarded if they chose that expression. Therefore, con2 controlled for performance based on subjects' history of reinforcement, because there was nothing similar between the sample and correct comparison. If subjects performed well on con2 trials in addition to the experimental trials, we could not rule out the explanation that their performance on experimental trials was not due to their history of being reinforced for selecting that expression. If, however, subjects performed well on experimental trials but poorly on the con2 trials, we could conclude that their performance was due to something other than learning based on history of reinforcement—for example, that they inferred something about the emotional similarity between the sample and correct comparison.

The performance on the MTM task can be seen in FIGURE 7.[49] Subjects performed above chance on the experimental categories after only two exposures to each trial, similar to their performance on both the individual recognition and facial expression discrimination tasks described earlier. Several categories were discriminated above chance on the very first trial. Performance on con1 trials was best, as expected, because the subjects of these trials had been previously trained to a high level of performance. The performance on con2 trials, however, never reached above chance performance after two testing sessions, nor was performance on the second testing session of con2 better than the first testing session for any experimental category. Therefore, this experiment provides evidence that the affective valence

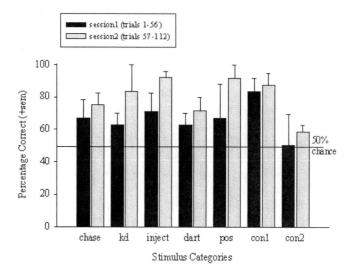

FIGURE 7. The mean performance on matching-to-meaning trials for subjects over two testing sessions. The *error bars* indicate standard errors of the means. kd = knock down; pos = positive; con = control.

of salient images may be a natural dimension by which chimpanzees can discriminate, or categorize, social stimuli. The data do not, however, go so far as to support a conscious understanding of the relationship between emotion and facial expressions. The most reasonable explanation for performance may be that because the subjects had all had experience with the situations presented in the videos, they responded to them with a form of emotional contagion, a similar state of affect to that conveyed by the images in the video.[50] This passive acquisition of emotion then biased their responses towards selecting facial expressions that shared a similar emotional content to that presented in the sample; this is similar to what has been reported in humans in tasks involving subliminal or mere exposure effects, when emotional information is acquired but not consciously perceived.[51,52] The data cannot elucidate whether subjects consciously processed the emotional information communicated by their facial expressions or whether they processed basic emotions, like anger, fear, sadness, disgust, happiness, and surprise.[6] Because of the control data and the overall design of the experiment, however, we feel confident that subjects were not using elaborate perceptual strategies to perform the task.

RECOGNITION OF FACIAL EXPRESSIONS AND THEIR EMOTIONAL CONTENT IN HUMANS

Studies of facial expression recognition in humans have had to overcome several important issues related to experimental procedures, levels of explanation, and cognitive and affective interpretation. In discussing the findings from chimpanzee facial expression studies, it would be useful to review these basic issues. First, researchers have struggled to determine the most complete and appropriate methodology for classifying human facial expressions and how these expressions are recognized by observers. What perceptual features or combination of features are important for facial expressions to be accurately identified? Additionally, what is the importance of additional contextual information that accompanies the perception of facial expressions, such as the identity of the individual making the expression, the external environment, the attitude, current mood, and personal history of the perceiver?[53]

Several lines of research have contributed significantly to overcoming most of these issues, although debate remains. This research includes methodological advancements in facial expression categorization, cognitive studies in humans, and developmental research on human infants. In order to identify facial expressions objectively and minimize the impact of contextual and subjective biases in their interpretation, Paul Ekman and colleagues developed a facial action coding system (FACS) that identifies facial expressions according to the movements of individual facial muscles.[8,48,54] The FACS has significantly advanced our understanding and identification of facial emotions, in addition to helping standardize experimental procedures in which facial expressions are used as stimuli or interpreted behaviorally.

Cognitive studies have also aided in understanding not only the relationship between facial expressions and emotion, but also how face perception may differ from the way in which facial expressions are processed. These studies have shown that facial expressions are perceived categorically, not by individual features or a configuration of physical properties.[55] Thus, while specific features and spatial orientations contribute importantly to the accuracy of facial expression recognition, this ability is not dependent on constructed bottom-up processing.[56–58] Recent studies have blended facial expressions and confirmed that facial expressions are indeed categorically perceived; but they also show important features of how categories are constituted.[49,50] Brain imaging studies have identified the contribution of different neural systems for face processing than for processing facial expressions, suggesting that facial expression recognition is not simply a subset of face processing.[61–66]

Studies of human infants have confirmed that facial expression recognition occurs in developmental stages over the first 2 years of life.[67] Infants from a very early age are able to extract certain perceptual features to discriminate some expressions over others, but it is not until after 7 months of age that infants are able to respond categorically to specific expressions.[67] Understanding the emotional significance of facial expressions may take even longer. Thus, facial expression discrimination involves more than the recognition of distinctive perceptual features. It follows a specific developmental trajectory that involves categorical processing and the recruitment of neural systems that are distinct from face processing.[66]

The recognition of facial expressions is inherently different from the recognition of perceptual patterns. Expressions are not simply perceived as mere movements, but their recognition can occur at the level of the perception of meaning.[68] Thus, integrally tied to this perceptual event is the message that the expression conveys and how individuals recognize the meaning of expressions. This is further complicated by the fact that facial expressions can convey meaning on multiple levels, including semantics, intentionality, communicative interaction, and emotion.[68] The techniques of psychophysiology, measuring subtle somatic changes in response to psychological stimuli, have contributed significantly to our understanding of how individuals respond emotionally to facial expressions. The perception of facial expressions, for example, produces a low-level motor mimicry in the perceiver that can be measured using electromyographic recordings.[69,70] These subtle movements correlate to the self-perception of emotion, suggesting an integral link between facial action and emotional experience.[71–73]

In summary, human facial expression research has identified procedures for objectively categorizing specific expressions based on muscle movements; elaborated on the neural mechanisms involved in face and facial expression processing; identified developmental stages for the discrimination, categorization, and understanding of affective facial signals; and demonstrated the integral link between facial movements and associated emotional experience. Each of these levels of analysis and explanation would be facilitated by the addition of comparative data on facial expression processing in nonhuman primate species, particularly the chimpanzees, our closest living relative. It is only through comparative efforts that we will be able to identify and understand what aspects of facial expression processing and emotional communication are indeed unique to humans and which represent older adaptations.

DISCRIMINATION OF FACIAL EXPRESSIONS AND THEIR EMOTIONAL CONTENT IN CHIMPANZEES

The data reviewed in the first half of this paper suggests that chimpanzees process facial information in ways that are similar to those of human face processing. Chimpanzees, for example, spontaneously discriminate their facial expressions when presented in an MTS task. Chimpanzees, like humans, do not automatically respond to the presentation of facial expressions with expressions of their own. This is in contrast to previous reports in monkeys, in which the presentation of photographs showing facial expressions produced emotional responses in the viewer similar to those that would occur if the presented expressions were made by a live animal.[74,75] In other words, presenting facial expressions triggered monkeys to produce facial expressions also, as though they were responding to a conspecific. The discrimination performance of chimpanzees does not appear to be dependent on the recognition of specific distinctive facial features, such as the presence of teeth in the expression, the mouth position, the eye shape, or overall head and body orientation.[42] Only a weak relationship was found for discriminations in which distinctive facial features were present, compared to discriminations in which expressions shared features in common and looked similar.[42] When facial expressions were presented as dynamic stimuli using video, subjects showed no preference for trials in which distinctive features were present. Therefore, the addition of movement, vocalizations, and context significantly changed the manner by which chimpanzees discriminated some facial expressions. Like humans, chimpanzees seemed to process conspecific facial expressions categorically. It should be noted that no studies to date have reported the successful discrimination of facial expressions in a monkey species, perhaps because they do not process facial stimuli in categorical ways and because reliance on individual facial features alone is too invariant to produce accurate results.[76]

More recent studies from my lab involving multimodal matching have furthered previous findings on facial expression processing in chimpanzees by examining the role of both auditory and visual modalities in the spontaneous categorization of conspecific facial expressions. This study demonstrated a consistent preference for one sensory modality over the other for three of the four expressions presented: for scream and scream vocalizations, visual preference; for play face and laughter, and pant-hoot and hooting, auditory preference. No significant preference was shown for either the auditory or visual modality when discriminating the bared-teeth display and low-intensity scream vocalizations. The performance of subjects was consistent across the five testing sessions, suggesting that subjects did not learn or develop these intermodal preferences over the course of repeated trials. Interestingly, the expression type that required the most training to discriminate above chance in the initial static expression matching task described above was the pant-hoot, which we found to be more salient in the vocal modality, perhaps explaining why initial performance was low for this expression type. Because their preferences were not the same for every expression type, each sensory modality appears to convey a specific salience for that expression type. Subjects did not, in general, prefer visual rather than auditory information, as has been suggested in humans.[77] This suggests that the salience for one sensory modality over another may be related to the social and ecological function of the expression types, and the salience of graded versus discrete signals.[46,47]

Finally, previous studies have demonstrated the ability of chimpanzees to match facial expressions and short emotional video scenes according to their shared emotional valence.[49] A negative video, such as a veterinary procedure, was spontaneously matched to a facial expression, such as a bared-teeth display, that represents a similar negative emotional valance to that of the video. This ability was not related to reinforcement history and seemed to be facilitated by the presence of affective information in the videos, like vocalizations. While further studies are needed to confirm or deny the presence of basic facial emotions in chimpanzees, this task provides preliminary support for the spontaneous use of emotion as a basis for discriminating naturalistic stimuli, and for the association of emotion and facial expressions in chimpanzees.[49]

Future studies are important to further understand the cognitive and perceptual processes involved in facial expression categorization in chimpanzees. Additionally, studies should continue to examine the relationship between facial expression and emotion in chimpanzees. Having a means to communicate and infer emotional information from one another would be highly adaptive, both in terms of close proximity through the use of visual signals, but also across long distance through the use of vocal signals. Studies have shown that not only can vocalizations vary according to their referential meaning, but subtle differences in acoustic parameters can convey important aspects of an individual's affective state.[44,78–80] The combination of detailed acoustic analyses and contextual categorization with controlled playback studies are necessary if we are to understand fully the complexity and potential social function of affective communication in chimpanzees.

ACKNOWLEDGMENTS

This investigation was supported by Grant RR-00165 from the NIH/NCRR to the Yerkes Regional Primate Research Center, and NSF Grant IBN-987675 to Emory University. Special thanks to Paul Ekman, Frans de Waal, and the New York Academy of Sciences; and to the Living Links Center for the use of photographic material. The Yerkes Primate Center is fully accredited by the American Association for Accreditation of Laboratory Animal Care.

REFERENCES

1. BROWN, S.D. & R.J. DOOLING. 1992. Perception of conspecific faces by budgerigars (Melopsittacus undulates): I. Natural faces. J. Comp. Psychol. **106:** 203–216.
2. BROWN, S.D. & R.J. DOOLING. 1992. Perception of conspecific faces by budgerigars (Melopsittacus undulates): II. Synthetic models. J. Comp. Psychol. **107:** 48–60.

3. KENDRICK, K. M., K. ATKINS, M.R. HINTON, *et al.* 1995. Facial and vocal discrimination in sheep. Anim. Behav. **49:** 1665–1676.
4. PARR, L.A., J.T. WINSLOW, W.D. HOPKINS & F.B.M. DE WAAL. 2000. Recognizing facial cues: individual recognition in chimpanzees (*Pan troglodytes*) and rhesus monkeys (*Macaca mulatta*). J. Comp. Psychol. **114:** 47–60.
5. BURT, D.M. & D.I. PERRETT. 1995. Perception of age in adult Caucasian male faces: computer graphic manipulation of shape and colour information. Proc. R. Soc. **259:** 137–143.
6. EKMAN, P. 1992. Facial expressions of emotion: new findings, new quesitons. Psychol. Sci. **3:** 34–38.
7. EKMAN, P. & H. OSTER. 1979. Facial expressions of emotion. Ann. Rev. Psychol. **30:** 527–554.
8. IZARD, C.E. 1971. The Face of Emotion. Appleton-Century-Crofts. New York.
9. TRANEL, D., A.R. DAMASIO & H. DAMASIO. 1988. Intact recognition of facial expression, gender, and age in patients with impaired recognition of face identity. Neurology **38:** 690–696.
10. ANDREW, R.J. 1963. The origin and evolution of the calls and facial expressions of the primates. Behaviour **20:** 1–109.
11. ANDREW, R.J. 1963. Evolution of facial expression. Science **142:** 1034–1041.
12. BROTHERS, L. 1990. The neural basis of primate social communication. Motiv. Emotion **14:** 81–91.
13. MARLER, P. 1965. Communication in monkeys and apes. *In* Primate Behavior. I. DeVore, Ed.: 544–584. Holt, Rinehart & Winston. New York.
14. ANDERSON, J.R. 1994. Valeur ethologique des visages et des mimiques chez les primates non humains. Psychol. Franc. **39:** 345–355.
15. CHENEY, D.L. & R.M. SEYFARTH. 1990. How Monkeys See the World. University of Chicago Press. Chicago.
16. HINDE, R.A. 1976. Interactions, relationships, and social structure. Man **11:** 1–17.
17. KUMMER, H. 1971. Primate Societies. Aldine. Chicago.
18. GOODALL, J. 1986. The Chimpanzees of Gombe. Cambridge University Press. London.
19. NISHIDA, T. 1979. The social structure of chimpanzees of the Mahale Mountains. *In* The Great Apes. D.A. Hamburg & E.R. McCowen, Eds.: 73–121. Benjamin-Cummings. Menlo Park, CA.
20. FRIDLUND, A.J. 1994. Human Facial Expression. Academic Press. New York.
21. RUSSELL, J.A. & J.M. FERNANDEZ-DOLS. 1997. The Psychology of Facial Expression. Cambridge University Press. Cambridge.
22. KANWISHER, N., J. MCDERMOTT & M.M. CHUN. 1997. The fusiform face area: a module in human extrastriate cortex specialized for face perception. J. Neurosci. **17:** 4302–4311.
23. GAUTHIER, I., M.J. TARR, J. MOYLAN, *et al.* 2000. The fusiform "face area" is part of a network that processes faces and the individual level. J. Cogn. Neurosci. **12:** 495–504.
24. GAUTHIER, I. & C.A. NELSON. 2001. The development of face expertise. Curr. Opin. Neurobiol. **11:** 219–224.
25. LE GRAND, R., C.J. MONDLOCH, D. MAURER & H.P. BRENT. 2001. Early visual experience and face processing. Nature **410:** 890.
26. PASCALIS, O., M. DE HAAN & C.A. NELSON. 2002. Is face processing species-specific during the first year of life? Science **296:** 1321–1323.

27. TARR, M.J. & I. GAUTHIER. 2000. FFA: a flexible fusiform area for subordinate-level visual processing automatized by expertise. Nat. Neurosci. **3:** 764–769.
28. HUBER, E. 1931. The Evolution of Facial Musculature and Facial Expression. Johns Hopkins Press. Baltimore, MD.
29. DARWIN, C. 1872. Expression of the Emotions in Man and Animals, 1955 edit. Philosophical Library. New York.
30. SEYFARTH, R.M. & CHENEY, D.L. 2003. Signalers and receivers in animal communication. Ann. Rev. Psychol. **54:** 145–173.
31. PREUSCHOFT, S. 1992. "Laughter" and "smile" in Barbary macaques (Macaca sylvanus). Ethology **91:** 220–236.
32. PREUSCHOFT, S. & J.A.R.A.M. VAN HOOFF. 1995. Homologizing primate facial displays: a critical review of methods. Folia Primatol. **65:** 121–137.
33. HARLOW, H.F. & C.E. MEARS. 1983. Emotional sequences and consequences. *In* Emotion: Theory, Research, and Experience, Vol. 2. R. Plutchik & H. Kellerman, Eds.: 171–197. Academic Press. New York.
34. RICHARDSON, W.K., D.A. WASHBURN, W.D. HOPKINS, *et al.* 1990. The NASA/LRC computerized test system. Behav. Res. Methods, Instrum. Computers **22:** 127–131.
35. WASHBURN, D.A. & D.M. RUMBAUGH. 1992. Testing primates with joystick-based automated apparatus: lessons from the Language Research Center's Computerized Test System. Behav. Res. Methods Instrum. Computers **24:** 157–164.
36. PARR, L.A. & F.B.M. DE WAAL. 1999. Visual kin recognition in chimpanzees. Nature **399:** 647–648.
37. PARR, L.A. & D. MAESTRIPIERI. Nonvocal communication in nonhuman primates. *In* Primate Psychology: The Mind and Behavior of Human and Nonhuman Primates. D. Maestripieri, Ed. Chicago University Press. Chicago. In press.
38. BAUER, H.R. & M. PHILIP. 1983. Facial and vocal individual recognition in the common chimpanzee. Psychol. Record **33:** 161–170.
39. BOYSEN, S.T. & G.G. BERNTSON. 1986. Cardiac correlates of individual recognition in the chimpanzee (Pan troglodytes). J. Comp. Psychol. **100:** 321–324.
40. BOYSEN, S.T. & G.G. BERNTSON. 1989. Conspecific recognition in the chimpanzee (Pan troglodytes): cardiac responses to significant others. J. Comp. Psychol. **103:** 215–220.
41. TOMONAGA, M., S. ITAKURA & T. MATSUZAWA. 1993. Superiority of conspecific faces and reduced inversion effect in face perception by a chimpanzee. Folia Primatol. **61:** 110–114.
42. PARR, L.A., W.D. HOPKINS & F.B.M. DE WAAL. 1998. The perception of facial expressions in chimpanzees (*Pan troglodytes*). Evol. Comm. **2:** 1–23.
43. VAN HOOFF, J.A.R.A.M. 1973. A structural analysis of the social behavior of a semi-captive group of chimpanzees. *In* Social Communication and Movement. M. von Cranach & I. Vine, Eds.: 75–162. Academic Press. London.
44. DE WAAL, F.B.M. & L.M. LUTTRELL. 1985. The formal hierarchy of rhesus macaques: an investigation of the bared-teeth display. Am. J. Primatol. **9:** 73–85.
45. GOUZOULES, S., H. GOUZOULES & P. MARLER. 1984. Rhesus monkey (Macaca mulatta) screams: representational signalling in the recruitment of agonistic aid. Anim. Behav. **32:** 182–193.
46. MARLER, P. 1976. Social organization, communication, and graded signals: the chimpanzee and the gorilla. *In.* Growing Points in Ethology. P.P.G. Bateson & R.A. Hinde, Eds.: 239–279. Cambridge University Press. London.

47. MORTON, E.S. 1982. Grading, discreteness, redundancy, and motivation-structural rules. *In* Acoustic Communication in Birds. D.E. Kroodsma, E.H. Miller & H. Ouellet, Eds.: 183–212. Academic Press. New York.
48. EKMAN, P. & W.V. FRIESEN. 1975. Unmasking the Face. Prentice Hall. Englewood Cliffs, NJ.
49. PARR, L.A. 2001. Cognitive and physiological markers of emotional awareness in chimpanzees, *Pan troglodytes*. Anim. Cogn. **4:** 223–229.
50. HATFIELD, E., J.T. CACIOPPO & R.L. RAPSON. 1994. Emotional Contagion. Cambridge University Press. Paris.
51. ESTEVES, F., F. PARRA, U. DIMBERG & A. OHMAN. 1994. Nonconscious associative learning: Pavlovian conditioning of skin conductance responses to masked fear-relevant facial stimuli. Psychophysiology **31:** 375–385.
52. MORRIS, J.S., A. OHMAN & R.J. DOLAN. 1998. Conscious and unconscious emotional learning in the human amygdala. Nature **393:** 467–470.
53. EKMAN, P. 1997. Should we call it expression or communication? Innovations Soc. Sci. Res. **10:** 333–344.
54. EKMAN, P., W.V. FRIESEN & P. ELLSWORTH. 1972. Emotion in the Human Face: Guidelines for Research and an Integration of Findings. Pergamon Press. New York.
55. ETCOFF, N.L. & J.J. MAGEE. 1992. Categorical perception of facial expressions. Cognition **44:** 227–240.
56. ARONOFF, J. & A.M. BARCLAY. 1988. The recognition of threatening facial stimuli. J. Pers. Soc. Psychol. **54:** 647–655.
57. FRANK, M.G., P. EKMAN & W.V. FRIESEN. 1993. Behavioral markers and recognizability of the smile of enjoyment. J. Pers. Soc. Psychol. **64:** 83–93.
58. KAPPAS, A., U. HESS, C.L. BARR & R.E. KLECK. 1994. Angle of regard: the effect of vertical viewing angle on the perception of facial expressions. J. Nonverbal Behav. **18:** 263–280.
59. CALDER, A.J., A.M. BURTON, P. MILLER, *et al.* 2001. A principal component analysis of facial expressions. Vision Res. **41:** 1179–1208.
60. YOUNG, A.W., D. ROWLAND, A.J. CALDER, *et al.* 1997. Facial expression megamix: tests of dimensional and category accounts of emotion recognition. Cognition **63:** 271–313.
61. HAMANN, S.B., L. STEFANACCI, L.R. SQUIRE, *et al.* 1996. Recognizing facial emotion. Nature **379:** 497.
62. KANWISHER, N., D. STANLEY & A. HARRIS. 1999. The fusiform face area is selective for faces not animals. NeuroReport **10:** 183–187.
63. KESLER-WEST, M. L., A.H. ANDERSEN, C.D. SMITH, *et al.* 2001. Neural substrates of facial emotion processing using fMRI. Cogn. Brain Res. **11:** 213–226.
64. NAKAMURA, K., R. KAWASHIMA, K. ITO, *et al.* 1999. Activation of the right inferior frontal cortex during assessment of facial emotion. J. Neurophysiol. **82:** 1610–1614.
65. SERGENT, J. & J. SIGNORET. 1992. Functional and anatomical decomposition of face processing: evidence from prosopagnosia and PET study of normal subjects. Phil. Trans. R. Soc. Lond. B **335:** 55–62.
66. HAXBY, J.V., E.A. HOFFMAN & M.I. GOBBINI. 2002. Human neural systems for face recognition and social communication. Biol. Psychiat. **51:** 59–67.
67. NELSON, C.A. 1987. The recognition of facial expressions in the first two years of life: mechanisms and development. Child Dev. **58:** 889–909.

68. FRIJDA, N.H. 1986. Facial expression processing. *In* Aspects of Face Processing. E.H.D. Ellis, M.A. Jeeves, F. Newcombe & A. Young, Eds.: 319–325. Martinus Nijhoff. Boston.
69. CACIOPPO, J.T., L.K. BUSH & L.G. TASSINARY. 1992. Microexpressive facial actions as a function of affective stimuli: replication and extension. Pers. Soc. Psychol. Bull. **18:** 515–526.
70. DIMBERG, U. 1982. Facial reactions to facial expressions. Psychophysiology **19:** 643–647.
71. DIMBERG, U. 1987. Facial reactions, autonomic activity and experienced emotion: a three component model of emotional conditioning. Biol. Psychol. **24:** 105–122.
72. HESS, U., A. KAPPAS, G.J. MCHUGO, *et al.* 1992. The facilitative effect of facial expression on the self-generation of emotion. Int. J. Psychophysiol. **12:** 251–265.
73. LANZETTA, J.T. & G.J. MCHUGO. 1989. Facial expressions and psychophysiological correlates of emotion. *In* Emotions and the Dual Brain. G. Caltagirone & C. Caltagirone, Eds.: 92–118. Springer-Verlag. New York.
74. SACKETT, G.P. 1965. Response of rhesus monkeys to social stimulation presented by means of colored slides. Percep. Mot. Skills **20:** 1027–1028.
75. SACKETT, G.P. 1966. Monkeys reared in isolation with pictures as visual input: evidence for an innate releasing mechanism. Science **154:** 1468–1473.
76. KANAZAWA, S. 1996. Recognition of facial expressions in a Japanese monkey. Primates **37:** 25–38.
77. BURNS, K.L. & E.G. BEIER. 1973. Significance of vocal and visual channels in the decoding of emotional meaning. J. Commun. **23:** 118–130.
78. BANSE, R. & K.R. SCHERER. 1996. Acoustic profiles in vocal emotion expression. J. Pers. Soc. Psychol. **70:** 614–636.
79. SEYFARTH, R.M., D.L. CHENEY & P. MARLER. 1980. Vervet monkey alarm calls: semantic communication in a free-ranging primate. Anim. Behav. **28:** 1070–1094.
80. SEYFARTH, R.M., D.L. CHENEY & P. MARLER. 1980. Monkey responses to three different alarm calls: evidence of predator classification and semantic communication. Science **210:** 801–803.

Animal Communication

Panel Discussion

FRANS B. M. DE WAAL, *Moderator*

QUESTION: Robert, you were making the point that the alarm calls of the monkeys have an emotional content, but you're not exactly sure what the content is. I wonder whether in the field you have ways of looking at this. If I were sitting high up on a tree and I saw a snake, obviously I have nothing to fear. I may be in a more emotional situation when I'm on the ground and the snake is actually nearby, and so there must be ways, maybe in your data, to make distinctions between the level of emotion involved.

ROBERT SEYFARTH (*University of Pennsylvania, Philadelphia, PA*): The study by Martha Manser on suricates is the first to systematically vary what was seen as the emotional content of a particular vocalization. We certainly have the impression that some alarm calls or grunts are more emotionally charged than others. When we first began doing work on the alarm calls, we thought we could pick out those that ought to work out pretty well in a playback experiment. But we weren't always right in picking the ones that got a response from others. We were presenting them under pretty controlled conditions, but there were some calls that were surprisingly effective in eliciting responses from others. The study that I mentioned on suricates is the only one that's taken these measures of emotion and systematically varied them. So, we're still in the infancy of this kind of work.

QUESTION: Why should there be sex differences in the acoustics of Diana monkeys' alarm calls?

SEYFARTH: In a lot of forest monkeys males have developed special structures that affect the acoustics of their vocalizations. There are some species, for example, that have resonant sacs that make the vocalizations a lot louder and make them reverberate; males have them and females don't, for reasons that probably have to do with territorial defense, male-male competition, and possibly female attraction. Sex differences in acoustic morphology that evolved for other reasons may have spilled over and led to sex differences in alarm calls, which in some cases have acoustic features that are similar to those of territorial vocalizations. This would mean the sex difference is like an accident. But even in species in which males don't have specialized structures, like vervet monkeys and baboons, the alarm calls of males and females to the

Ann. N.Y. Acad. Sci. 1000: 79–87 (2003). © 2003 New York Academy of Sciences.
doi: 10.1196/annals.1280.006

same predator are really very different. There's not an easy explanation for that.

QUESTION: A number of the speakers touched on the issue of dynamics: Dr. de Waal spoke about how unusual it is for a chimp to have a fixed expression on its face, and Dr. Parr talked about how actually providing these video clips seemed very important to help categorization. I wonder, just anecdotally perhaps, based on your experience, can you speak more about dynamics in these expressions and how they may be discriminative of different signals that are trying to be transmitted? How can you characterize these dynamics, and how do they actually discriminate between what different animal members see?

LISA PARR (*Emory University, Atlanta, GA*): My purpose in showing the dynamics stimuli was really just to give them the most appropriate sample stimulus that I could for them to match. Normally, chimpanzees don't really see facial expressions in a static way, so we just wanted to give them the most information possible, and it was a really natural way to include an auditory component in there as well. I think some of what you're asking is work that hasn't been done yet. Maybe movement in and of itself produces a lot of information about individual identity and maybe even about the type of expression that's being made. But in addition to that, maybe we made mistakes at the beginning of these experiments, not only in showing things in static ways, but in showing things that may not be the best examples of expressions.

QUESTION: Robert, you beautifully illustrated the change in the wahoo call that occurred over the course of this 10-year period and gave us an example of I believe a male whose wahoo call kind of petered out over the course of that period. Are there males whose wahoo calls don't peter out? Are those males potentially more resilient in certain ways? What do we know about the role of individual variability in this?

SEYFARTH: First, to get data on changes in acoustic structure, of vocalizations over the lifetime of a primate, requires that you do fieldwork on the same animal for 10 or 15 years and start out knowing that you're going to be doing it on vocalizations, so you start recording. We just don't have that kind of data for many species at all. So we've got this data on baboon wahoos. I don't know of any other published data on age-related changes in vocalizations in nonhuman primates. Probably the tape recordings of chimps at Gombe might reveal this, and there may be archived data elsewhere. We would love to be able to track a male's trajectory through his lifetime, because our guess is that in the case of baboons the males that are reproductively most successful are those that age in this way least rapidly. We'll probably be able to do this in the next 10 years. It's interesting that the male tenure in the alpha position in our groups of baboons is about 7 months, so we've seen males deteriorate pretty dramatically over a 5-year period.

QUESTION: I imagine that there's some cross-species appreciation of the emotional signal in, say a distress call; but is there any evidence for cross-species understanding of the semantic content—that is, you would see another species go up into a tree as opposed to crouch when you hear a particular kind of call?

SEYFARTH: If you play the starling alarm calls that I played at the beginning of my talk to vervet monkeys—and they live together in the same area throughout a lot of Africa—the vervet monkeys will respond at the starling's eagle alarm call by looking up in the air and to the starling's terrestrial predator alarm by running up a tree. This is commonly described by naturalists, but also experimentally supported.

JO-ANNE BACHOROWSKI (*Vanderbilt University, Nashville, TN*): Lisa, what are your thoughts on what the animals are doing and the preference paradigm? What would lead them to have a preference for the visual as opposed to the auditory information?

PARR: Because of how those expressions are typically used in the wild, there are preferences for one modality over the other. Thus, a long-distance vocalization is more salient in the auditory modality because they don't see the visual part with it. Screams are trickier because the auditory component is pretty salient; but maybe it's too messy, too noisy. It's not necessarily such a reliable signal. This doesn't mean that they can't use the auditory component, but that more—that is, visual—information may be needed.

At the end of that experiment, I went back through previous years of research that we had done. The very first time we showed facial expressions, the ones that they learned the fastest just by being shown photographs were the screams, and the one that took the longest was the hoot. So it seems like this is something that has been present with them for a long time.

ROBERT W. LEVENSON (*University of California, Berkeley, Berkeley, CA*): This may have been what you meant when you said that one of the next frontiers was meaning. But I suppose someone could say that by using stimulus materials that are in the experience of the animal, like the darts and the fruit juice containers, you run the risk of a kind of a learned association. It would seem that what you'd want to do is degrade those, in the sense of moving away from things of the experience and move into things of a similar kind that they had no experience with.

PARR: They do need to have some experience to know that something is bad. I have a great illustration of a father who is taking a child into the doctor for the first time. It's a young baby who has never had any injections before, so the baby looks perfectly happy with the doctor standing there with the needle; but the father is totally grimacing at the anticipated pain.

Getting my experiment to be a bit more abstract might be more convincing for some people, but I've always been a real believer in showing things as naturally as possible. There's information there that they obviously use, and that's what I'm interested in.

QUESTION: Toward the end of your talk you titillated us with the possibility that the kind of stimuli you were using might recruit emotion, and you used the phrase *emotion contagion* as a potential mechanism for enabling the animals to make the kinds of discriminations they're making. I was wondering if anyone is working on this question using pharmacological blockades or other kinds of manipulations that would allow you to essentially perturb the autonomic changes the animals may be experiencing in response to these stimuli? Do they show strong emotional reactions to these stimuli?

PARR: When you show monkeys a picture of another monkey, they usually respond as though as it's another monkey in front of them, and they respond appropriately: they'll either lip smack or threaten the monkey or withdraw or do something that's species typical for being presented with a stranger. All the photographs that I show are of unfamiliar animals, but they never, ever once made any kind of overt behavioral reaction that would lead me to think that they're responding emotionally to these pictures. If you show them a chimp with a bared-teeth face, they just sit there and do the discrimination.

QUESTION: What about the videos?

PARR: These are very short videos, about five seconds long; they're not long enough to elicit any kind of behavioral response. We have shown them much longer scenes before, and we've done things like measure temperature asymmetries to positive and negative scenes. We've seen consistent behavioral responses with the emotion that's displayed: if you show them a scene of chimpanzees fighting, the males will puff up and start to do a display similar to what they're seeing in the video; if you show them play scenes with animals, every once in a while, they'll kind of bob their head and maybe even gesture at the computer before them. This is enough to elicit some kind of similar response in itself. So we try to do the kinds of things that you're saying—not pharmacologically, but at least incorporating the physiological component.

PAUL EKMAN (*University of California, San Francisco, San Francisco, CA*): Throughout the long history of this field, from its very early days, researchers have been directly comparing what was found with chimpanzees with what was being found with their own children. Many of the studies that each of you have described would be wonderful studies to do with humans. Do you feel that's part of your obligation, to also get data on our species, so we can make those comparisons?

FRANS B. M. DE WAAL (*Emory University, Atlanta, GA*): Well, we don't want to compete with all these people who work on people. There's 100,000 people who work on people, and there's a dozen people who do the sort of stuff we do. We have our own niche.

EKMAN: You guys have such expert, wonderful designs, and you raise questions that not all the human researchers have raised; we'll have to closely attend to your work if we can't convince you to work on the easy species, us humans.

I suppose it isn't a coincidence that almost everyone on this panel and probably most of the people who are going to be speaking operate from the discrete emotions perspective. God knows why that came to be. I suppose if someone were looking at this from another perspective, they might ask, why are you trying to understand these animal phenomena in terms of the discrete emotions? Why aren't you taking more of a sequential-dimensional approach? Why aren't we considering that kind of a model, which is so powerfully represented, certainly in human research?

DE WAAL: But I think there's something different going on from what you say. I'm not sure that people who work on animals are dissecting concrete emotions. We have stayed away from the topic of emotions very carefully for a very long time, owing to the influence of the behaviorists, who at some point had to admit that humans had emotions but were never ready to admit that animals might have emotions, too. If you look at the history of the research on, for example, facial expressions or visual displays, that literature does not emphasize emotions. It emphasizes behavioral sequences, and it says in which part of the sequence we will see this particular behavior. If it occurs, for example, in an aggressive sequence, we call it aggressive behavior. If it is associated with flight responses, we call it fearful behavior. So we may label it with emotions, but it's entirely based on behavioral context, so to speak; this is the tradition of our field. To call these things emotions has almost been an afterthought.

SEYFARTH: I think Frans is right: historically we have been very shy about being accused of anthropomorphism; so field ecologists have stuck as much as possible with descriptions. You can certainly describe interactions between a male and a female baboon, for example; but you don't want to call them love or affection. I can show slides to undergraduates that they think look like love and affection, and maybe they're right; but we've been very careful not to make such assumptions. It's long been recognized that vocalizations of lots and lots of animal species are graded. Even though we can create a topology of vocalizations, descriptive according to their acoustics, there are gradations within that. Implicit in that notion is the idea that if such and such is aptly described as a threat vocalization, we could expect that there's a really strong one and a kind of diffident weak one. This can be investigated, but it hasn't been done very much experimentally. That's why we think in terms of discrete categories.

QUESTION: I had a question for Frans about the communication of play in his talk; it is a two-prong question: Could you offer something of a Darwinian explanation about the origins of the play face? Does it operate according to the principle of antithesis vis-à-vis anger or threat display? The second question is about the funny faces that you've documented in the bonobos, these sort of silly, seemingly random displays: do they have some function in addition to learning about play? What are the cognitive capacities that underlie that? I think if you look at humans, this is really complex: to be able to do something that's exaggerated requires multiple representations.

DE WAAL: There are speculations about the play face. The play face probably is derived from gnawing, a sort of biting but not really biting, which is common in all animal play. They put their teeth on someone and act as if they're biting; the covering of the teeth with the lips is maybe to blunt the bite a little. The play face is often seen more as a distance signal that derives from that movement of biting.

With regards to funny faces, I really have never thought about their function. I did speculate that the great apes sometimes suppress facial expressions or change them. For example, a male chimpanzee who is getting nervous because another male is intimidating him, may show a bared-teeth face that betrays his nervousness. He may either turn around or press his lips together with his fingers to make this grin face disappear, and so actively manipulate his face. I speculated that perhaps the facial gymnastics that the bonobos are showing has something to do with control over their face—a sort of exercise in how much can I control my face because this could be useful—not that they're thinking that, but that's maybe what they're doing.

LAURA L. CARSTENSEN (*Stanford University, Stanford, CA*): Lisa, you said you had done some work comparing, examining chimps' reactions to human facial expressions. Can you say more about that?

PARR: I gave the chimps Dr. Ekman's Japanese and Caucasian facial expressions, and they were pretty good at all of them. They're using the same kind of features they probably used for their own expressions, except for one male who couldn't get any of the Japanese faces right; I think he probably hasn't seen many Japanese people.

QUESTION: [inaudible]

SEYFARTH: Well, I'm sorry you got that impression from the talks because I had hoped what I was giving were the better examples of animals using vocalizations in a way that provides listeners with specific information about facts, objects, events, particular kinds of predators, particular sorts of social situations. We don't have—Frans is correct—any evidence from any animals, other than chimpanzees and possibly some other apes, of any sort of gestural communication that designates features of the environment. It's just not there, as far as we can tell; and so the interesting question is you do have lots of animals, birds, monkeys, mongooses, apes, that use different vocalizations in a way that conveys different information; they serve as a kind of label, to label different predators. But one would have imagined that in evolution once animals had evolved the ability to designate a couple of predators, they would start using that kind of denotative communication in all aspects of their life. So the interesting question is: we now know that monkeys have some sounds that function—I'll hedge this a bit—like words; why do they have so few? Why not lots and lots of them? But they don't, and that's a really interesting problem.

QUESTION: I wonder if you could elaborate on a couple of points about the gesture evidence that you brought up. One is a kind of topology of gestures, the way that you are looking at topologies of facial expressions or vocalizations. I know you showed a few slides of the hand begging or the folded wrist; has anybody analyzed that kind of topology? And could you elaborate on what the difference between monkeys' not having these gestures and apes' having them might mean in relation to other cognitive abilities?

DE WAAL: Unfortunately, no one has catalogued ape gestures very carefully; there are a few articles on the subject, and of course there are gestures mentioned in all the ethograms that we have of the great apes. No one has systematically looked at what primates do with their hands while they're communicating; vocalizations have received by far the most attention. One of my students, Amy Pollick, is now planning a study on the hand gestures of apes.

What it means in cognitive terms, I don't know. Of course most of the apes are also tool users; there may be a connection with having more control over the hands, because that's one of the survival skills they use. Beyond that I don't want to say much about it.

Hand gestures are context defined. Let's say you have an orange in your hand, and I hold out my hand; it's very obvious that my gesture relates to the orange. But if I have a fight with Robert and hold out my hand to you, it rather means, "Why don't you come over and support me?" If I hold out my hand after a fight with you, it means, "Shall we reconcile?" So the same hand gesture has a completely context-defined meaning, and chimpanzees seem to understand perfectly what the meaning is in each particular context. This makes gestural communication very interesting.

QUESTION: Dr. Seyfarth, I don't know if you are studying this directly, but I was wondering if you see patterns of kin selection in the alarm call behavior of monkeys?

SEYFARTH: Monkeys move around in groups containing some individuals who are closely related to the animal giving the alarm call and some who are not. At the moment there's just no way to sort out alarm calling that is selective for kin. The best evidence for that comes in species such as ground squirrels, where females will alarm-call much more readily if they have offspring in the group than if they don't.

QUESTION: The evidence for a functional shift in the silent bared-teeth face seems very convincing, but it does appear as though there's also been a morphological shift from the muscle that stretches the mouth horizontally to what looks more like a real smile in humans, the zigomatic major smile. I'm hoping that Kim Bard will have the answer to that question soon. But I was wondering if the two of you could speculate about whether such a shift, if it did occur, would have important social significance to distinguish more clearly between positive affinitive and fear signals?

PARR: Obviously if they look different, it may help disentangle the sender of the signals' intent or experience at that particular moment. But so many other things in the context probably could also, so I'm not sure that that in itself would be enough of a selection pressure to produce a different expression.

DE WAAL: The bonobo has a bared-teeth face that I call the pleasure grin, which in German is the *"Orgasmus Gesicht."* It has to do with pleasure—not just sexual pleasure, but any kind of pleasurable situation, more so than with the chimpanzee. I think that expression is different in terms of the muscles that pull the mouth; maybe it's more pulled up than in most other expressions. The problem is that when Paul Ekman developed FACS, the human literature on facial expressions became far more detailed than what we could do in primates. In order to do this kind of detailed facial analysis, you have to have very close-up detailed footage or photos, facial photos. Even though I have 50,000 negatives of primates (Lisa used a lot of my images to present to the chimpanzees), I have not nearly the detail that is necessary to get into this kind of facial cataloging. It's going to be a real challenge. With humans I can say, "look at the camera and imagine that you're scared." With chimpanzees you're running after them; they look in all directions and never do anything that you tell them to do. So it's almost impossible to get the detail that you need to answer the sort of question you raised. We will need new technologies.

QUESTION: Robert Seyfarth pointed out that expression and communication are not easily separable. This can't be just because of the association in the auditor. What brings them together? I'd like to suggest two scientifically problematic terms. The first is one you mentioned at the very beginning of your talk—*intention*; the second you mentioned at the very end of your talk—*cognition*. The reason I think these might be part of the answer is because, if I remember correctly, about 20 years ago you gave a talk about false cries of information. This involves an enormous amount of complexity, because it's not just expression, it's not just communication, it's also anticipation of how it will be heard and falsely interpreted by the auditor.

SEYFARTH: Asked like a true philosopher! I didn't discuss the issue of the communicative intent of the signaler nearly as much as I would have liked. I didn't discuss it at all, and it is a crucial element in all this. So let me give you a brief answer that says where we are on that. The question is when we look at the mechanisms that cause individuals to vocalize, can we ever say that an animal vocalizes with the intent of providing information to another, in the sense that humans routinely do in language? The answer right now is, as far as all animals except chimps are concerned, probably not. We've done a lot of experiments with really beautiful negative results with regards to the question of whether or not animals vocalize with the intent of informing individuals that don't know something. They don't seem to do so. For example, in vervet monkeys the animals give different alarm calls to different predators. They have an eagle alarm. When infant vervets first give this alarm, they make a lot of mistakes: they alarm-call in response to species like songbirds and pigeons that don't pose any danger. It's always birds, but it's never the right ones. When they do give an alarm call in response to an appropriate predator, one of these big eagles, adults alarm-call right afterwards. We thought, this is great; the adults are telling the infants, "you got it right," giving them reinforcement. But it turns out that adults are about 90% likely to give an alarm call after an infant gets it right, and they're about 90% likely to give an alarm call after an adult gets it right. So the answer is, adults give alarm calls in response to eagles but not to pigeons; they don't go out of their way to reinforce infants. I can talk about many other experiments, but that's a vivid example.

The situation may be different with chimps. At the moment there's a controversy about whether chimps have the ability to recognize the mental states of others. So setting chimps aside, this means that in animal communication we've got to be very careful to distinguish communication from the perspective of the signaler from communication from the perspective of the recipient. It's clear from our experiments that listeners are very attentive to how these vocalizations occur and are extracting a huge amount of very rich information from the vocalizations they hear. Signalers may not have intended for them to do so. And so, in some respects, a lot of monkey communication looks more like language from the listener's perspective than it does from the signaler's perspective. You're right, intention is a crucial issue.

Development of Emotional Expressions in Chimpanzees (*Pan troglodytes*)

KIM A. BARD

*Centre for the Study of Emotion, Department of Psychology,
University of Portsmouth, Portsmouth PO1 2DY, UK*

KEYWORDS: chimpanzees; *Pan troglodytes*; emotional expressions; early rearing

INTRODUCTION

Chimpanzee infants, like human infants, exhibit some emotional expressions in the first days of life, and additional expressions develop over the first months of life.[1] We know relatively little about the influence of the rearing environment on the development of emotional expression in chimpanzees (or in human infants).[2]

The specific aim of this study was to assess whether early rearing had an effect on the development of emotional expressions in chimpanzees.

METHODS

Subjects

Neonatal chimpanzees, placed in the nursery at birth owing to inadequate maternal care, participated in this study.[3] Twenty-one chimpanzees were raised in a standard care (ST) nursery in which the philosophy was that the social, emotional, and communicative needs of young chimpanzees would be met by their being raised with same-aged peers, but that humans were necessary to provide for health needs. Sixteen chimpanzees were raised in the responsive care nursery (RC), which had a different philosophy: specifically, that specially trained humans would meet the infant's emotional, social, and

Address for correspondence: Kim A. Bard, Centre for the Study of Emotions, Department of Psychology, King Henry Building, University of Portsmouth, Portsmouth PO1 2DY UK. Voice: +44 23 92 846 332; fax: +44 23 92 846 300.
kim.bard@port.ac.uk

Ann. N.Y. Acad. Sci. 1000: 88–90 (2003). © 2003 New York Academy of Sciences.
doi: 10.1196/annals.1280.018

health needs. Moreover, these adult caregivers would act to enhance the development of chimpanzee species-typical communication.[1,4]

Procedures

Emotional expressions were recorded as they occurred during the Brazelton Neonatal Behavioral Assessment Scale (NBAS) assessments.[5] NBAS assessments were conducted every other day from 2 or 3 days through 42 days of age. For each individual NBAS session, the expressions that occurred were noted, with the age of the individual. Thus, I obtained the number of individuals exhibiting each vocal and/or facial expression and the average age when each expression first occurred.

RESULTS AND DISCUSSION

Chimpanzee infants, like human infants, exhibit expressions of positive and negative emotions early in life. Moreover, many expressions are emitted in similar contexts.[1] Every chimpanzee fussed (by 4 days of age on the average), cried (by 5 days of age on average), and smiled (by 11 days of age on average). Most infants vocalized greetings (78% by 7 days of age), effort grunts (86% by 14 days of age), and laughter (81% by 37 days of age). Rearing environment significantly influenced (1) the number of individuals who exhibited anger (14% of ST versus 88% of RC expressed anger, $\chi^2(1) = 19.3$, $P < 0.01$); (2) the number of individuals who expressed greetings (67% of ST versus 94% of RC vocalized greetings, $\chi^2(1) = 3.931$, $P < 0.05$, Fischer's exact $P = 0.053$ to correct for small expected frequencies); and (3) interacted with gender in the number of smiles recorded during the NBAS test (females smiled more than males when raised in ST, but when they were raised in RC there was no gender difference, $F(1,30) = 7.33$, $P \leq 0.01$).

The chimpanzee emotional system appears to develop in interaction with the emotional responsiveness of social partners. There were significant differences in some realms of emotional expression as a function of rearing environment. It appears that a more responsive rearing environment results in a more positively expressive and less fussy infant,[6] effects which are evident even within the first weeks of life. Minimally, the study suggests that early emotional interactions are important in the development of emotional expression.

ACKNOWLEDGMENTS

Research was supported in part by NIH Grants RR-00165, RR-03591, and RR-06158 and conducted at the Yerkes Regional Primate Research Center of

Emory University. We are grateful to Kelly McDonald, Kathy Gardner, Dr. Kathy Platzman, Carolyn Fort, Dr. Patricia Hebert, Yerkes Nursery Caretakers, and many Emory University students for their invaluable assistance with assessment and daily care of the nursery chimpanzees during the study period from 1987 to 1995. Grateful appreciation is extended to Dr. David Leavens for his helpful comments.

REFERENCES

1. BARD, K.A. 1998. Social-experiential contributions to imitation and emotion in chimpanzees. *In* Intersubjective Communication and Emotion in Early Ontogeny: A Source Book. S. Braten, Ed.: 208–227. Cambridge University Press. Cambridge.
2. TREVARTHEN, C. & K.J. AITKEN. 2001. Infant intersubjectivity: research, theory, and clinical applications. J. Child Psychol. Psychiatry **42**: 3–48.
3. BARD, K.A. 1994. Evolutionary roots of intuitive parenting: maternal competence in chimpanzees. Early Dev. Parenting **3**: 19–28.
4. BARD, K.A. 1996. Responsive Care: Behavioral Intervention Program for Nursery-reared Chimpanzees. The Jane Goodall Institute. Tuscon, AZ.
5. BARD, K.A., K.A. PLATZMAN, B.M. LESTER & S.J. SUOMI. 1992. Orientation to social and nonsocial stimuli in neontal chimpanzees and humans. Infant Behav. Dev. **15**: 43–56.
6. BARD, K.A. 2000. Crying in infant primates: insights into the development of crying in chimpanzees. *In* Crying as a Sign, a Symptom, and a Signal: Developmental and Clinical Aspects of Early Crying Behavior. R. Barr, B. Hopkins & J. Green, Eds.: 157–175. MacKeith Press. London.

Response to Naturalistic Fear Stimuli in Captive Old World Monkeys

JASON E. DAVIS,[a] LISA PARR,[b] AND HAROLD GOUZOULES[a,b]

[a]*Psychology Department, Emory University, Tucker, Georgia 30084, USA*

[b]*Yerkes National Primate Research Center, Atlanta, Georgia 30322, USA*

KEYWORDS: Old World monkeys; fear stimuli; alarm response

Currently, we are exploring factors that contribute to the recognition of, and response to, naturalistic predictive stressors such as predators in Old World monkeys. We focus specifically on species differences in alarm response profiles and stimulus characteristics that may modulate these responses.

EXPERIMENT 1: RESPONSES TO LEOPARD MODEL

Groups of sooty mangabeys, pigtail macaques, and rhesus macaques were exposed to a two-dimensional model of a leopard. Three groups of each species (nine groups total) were each given two trials with the leopard model (18 trials). Each of the groups was housed in a large outdoor enclosure at the Yerkes National Primate Research Center Field Station. In each trial the horizontal model was placed outside of the enclosure. After a habituation period the model was raised into a vertical position, and remained upright for 30 seconds. Audio and video of monkeys' responses were recorded throughout the trial. Audio recordings were later digitized using the Cool Edit Pro spectrographic program developed by Syntrillium Inc. and signal analysis macros created by Brenda McCowan.[1]

On such measures as time to resume feeding, climbing, running, threatening, and vigilance, each species exhibited a unique response pattern to the predator model. Rhesus macaques displayed short-term aggression, ending soon after the model was lowered. Pigtail macaques displayed intense long-

Address for correspondence: Jason E. Davis, Psychology Department, Emory University, 323 Bentley Place, Tucker, GA 30084. Voice: 678-697-5907; fax: 404-727-8372.
Jdavis3@emory.edu

Ann. N.Y. Acad. Sci. 1000: 91–93 (2003). © 2003 New York Academy of Sciences.
doi: 10.1196/annals.1280.019

term aversion. Sooty mangabeys displayed intense short-term aversion, often resuming normal behaviors before the model was lowered. Each species also displayed a distinctive vocal profile: pigtailed macaques had high rates of alarm calling during and following the stimulus period; sooty mangabeys produced alarm calls during the approach and stimulus periods; and rhesus macaques produced almost exclusively threat barks during the stimulus period.

EXPERIMENT 2: INTERSPECIFIC ALARM PLAYBACK

Two social groups of rhesus macaques were each given two trials with each of four sets of vocal stimuli: familiar rhesus macaque alarms, unfamiliar rhesus macaque alarms, sooty mangabey alarms, and pigtail macaque alarms. The alarm calls of these species are acoustically quite different from one another. Each playback trial was composed of four bouts of alarm calls spaced across 30 seconds. Each bout was composed of four or five alarm calls. As a control, a human voice saying the alphabet was also played (relative amplitude was controlled). As before, audio and video were recorded throughout the trial and analyzed later.

Rhesus macaques responded to all vocalizations except the human voice control. However, responses were limited to short-term vigilance and cessation of feeding, and in most cases normal activity resumed before the playback session finished. A notable exception was that the responses to the alarm calls of sooty mangabeys were significantly more intense than responses to other alarm calls.

CONCLUSIONS

These findings support the idea of an innate component to predator recognition and response in some species of Old World monkeys, as well as the concept of species-level behavioral propensities. Results also show that rhesus macaques easily learn to recognize heterospecific alarm calls, even under captive situations in which danger is relatively small, and even when heterospecific alarm calls are acoustically far removed from conspecific vocalizations.

We are currently engaged in two projects designed to further explore responses to naturalistic stimuli. The first measures the responses of social groups of rhesus macaques to presentations of multiple overlapping visual and auditory stimuli. Stimuli include rhesus macaque alarm calls, coo vocalizations, the leopard model, and the control model, resulting in eight stimulus permutations.

We are also engaged in measurement of selected physiological parameters associated with exposure to naturally relevant predictive stressors and, in addition, will be investigating the role of early experience in the development of responses to these stimuli. Six mother-reared and six nursery-reared animals will be given exposure to acoustic, visual, and multimodal naturalistic stimuli in a habituation-dishabituation paradigm under controlled laboratory conditions. During these tests, heart rate, respiration, and skin temperature will be monitored continuously. We anticipate interesting and illuminating results from the final phases of this project and hope to build on our findings to further explore the neurological underpinnings of interspecific differences in unconditioned stress recognition and response.

REFERENCE

1. MCCOWAN, B. & D. REISS. 2001. The fallacy of "signature whistles" in bottlenose dolphins: a comparative perspective of "signature information" in animal vocalizations. Animal Behav. **62**(6): 1151–1162.

Visual Field Information in the Face Perception of Chimpanzees (*Pan troglodytes*)

JOSHUA PLOTNIK,*a* PETER A. NELSON,*b,c,d* AND
FRANS B. M. DE WAAL*b,c*

*a Department of Animal Science, Cornell University,
Ithaca, New York 14853, USA*

*b Living Links, Yerkes Primate Center, Emory University,
Atlanta, Georgia 30322, USA*

c Department of Psychology, Emory University, Atlanta, Georgia 30322, USA

ABSTRACT: Evidence for a visual field advantage (VFA) in the face perception of chimpanzees was investigated using a modification of a free-vision task. Four of six chimpanzee subjects previously trained on a computer joystick match-to-sample paradigm were able to distinguish between images of neutral face chimeras consisting of two left sides (LL) or right sides (RR) of the face. While an individual's ability to make this distinction would be unlikely to determine their suitability for the VFA tests, it was important to establish that distinctive information was available in test images. Data were then recorded on their choice of the LL vs. RR chimera as a match to the true, neutral image; a bias for one of these options would indicate an hemispatial visual field advantage. Results suggest that chimpanzees, unlike humans, do not exhibit a left visual field advantage. These results have important implications for studies on laterality and asymmetry in facial signals and their perception in primates.

KEYWORDS: laterality; asymmetry; face recognition

A study was conducted on the response of chimpanzees (*Pan troglodytes*) to normal and chimeric photographs of other chimpanzee faces. Morris and Hopkins found evidence of a left visual field advantage in the response of chimpanzees to images of human faces;[1] we sought to confirm their findings

Address for correspondence: Joshua Plotnik, c/o Dr. Harold Hintz, 345 Morrison Hall, Cornell University, Ithaca, NY 14853.
jmp63@cornell.edu
*d*Present address: Center for Marine Biodiversity & Conservation, Scripps Institution of Oceanography, University of California–San Diego, La Jolla, CA 92093-0202, USA.

Ann. N.Y. Acad. Sci. 1000: 94–98 (2003). © 2003 New York Academy of Sciences.
doi: 10.1196/annals.1280.020

and examined potential chimpanzee preference for a certain side of the face using conspecific images—a hemispace visual field advantage (VFA).

Recent studies of human and nonhuman primate face recognition and emotion have frequently used facial images to identify cognitive biases and brain laterality. Levy *et al.*, for example, used chimeras—compound images formed by matching half of an image with the reverse of the same half image—to test the hypotheses that humans exhibit a left hemispace VFA and that this bias correlates with handedness.[2] A left VFA would suggest that the left half of the visual field (and the right side of the subject in view) is the source of the majority of the visual information used. Fernández-Carriba *et al.* found that chimpanzee facial expressions exhibited a greater left hemimouth size, hence right-hemispheric dominance in the production of expression.[3] We tested the hypothesis that there was a similar lateral bias in chimpanzee perception of images of neutral (i.e., nonexpressive) chimpanzee faces.

Using a Canon XL-1 digital camera, we recorded video of freely interacting chimpanzees in June and July, 2002, in two social groups ($n = 18$ and 19 individuals) at the Yerkes Regional Primate Research Center field station in Lawrenceville, GA (details in Ref. 4). We used 2–3 images of each of the 37 chimpanzees chosen from video frames for clarity, lighting, subject orientation (i.e., facing the camera), and neutral expressions. All video was captured and clipped using Adobe Premiere 6.0. Suitable frames from the video were formatted using Adobe Photoshop 6.0. We cropped each image to ca. 5.1×5.1 cm and formed chimeras by pairing one half of each image with its mirror image (Fig. 1).

Using a computerized matching-to-sample (MTS) paradigm, we tested each of six chimpanzees previously trained to operate a computer joystick with the MTS program. Two experiments were performed. Recognition testing sought to determine whether the chimpanzees could distinguish between

FIGURE 1. Chimeras formed from digital photographs by pairing one half of a facial image with the mirror image of that same half.

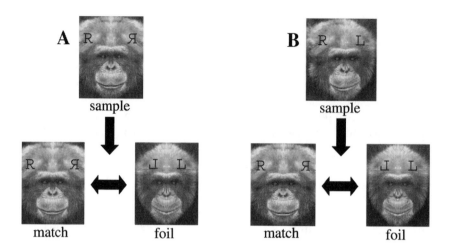

FIGURE 2. Recognition testing (**A**) required the subject to distinguish the image matching the sample from the foil. Successful matches were rewarded. Chimera testing (**B**) offered two alternatives (still "match" and "foil" by convention for the subject to pair with the sample). Selection of either alternative was rewarded.

LL and RR chimeras by requiring them to choose between LL and RR chimeric images as a match to an identical LL or RR chimera (FIG. 2A). Five of six chimpanzees responded to 12 repeats (the 6th responded to 9) of 20 trials; correct responses were rewarded. Chimera testing examined the chimpanzee's preference for either the LL or RR chimera following presentation of the unaltered image from which the chimera had been fashioned (FIG. 2B). Here, each chimpanzee responded to 6 sets of 30 trials consisting of a random arrangement of 10 LL-RR trials and 20 filler trials. In the filler trials, the subject was required to distinguish between matching and nonmatching chimpanzee faces (identity), a task (based on Parr et al.[5]) at which these subjects had previously proved themselves (de Waal, unpublished data). Thus the chimpanzees had to attend to the task in order to receive the maximal number of rewards. All data were analyzed using a heterogeneity G-test,[6] which compared observed and predicted values for individual, pooled, and total data.

Each of the six chimpanzees tested scored significantly better than 50% chance on the recognition test, indicating that there was sufficient visual information available to make this distinction (Gh = 31.9, df = 5, $P < 0.001$; Gp = 115.2, df = 1, $P < 0.001$; FIG. 3). This was the first time these chimpanzees had been presented with chimeric faces, and the high success is indicative of their strong understanding of the MTS paradigm. None of the six chimpan-

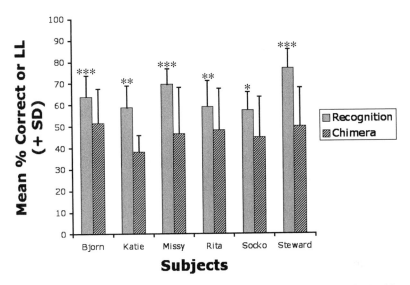

FIGURE 3. Mean percent correct (recognition testing) or percent of LL chimera choices (chimera testing). $*P < 0.05$; $**P < 0.01$; $***P < 0.001$.

zees showed an apparent hemispace VFA, choosing LL and RR chimeras with roughly equal frequency (Gh = 2.70, df = 5, $P = 0.75$; Gp = 1.60, df = 1, $P = 0.21$) in the chimera testing (FIG. 3).

Our tests show that chimpanzees can make the fine distinction between left and right sides of the same face. Using conspecific faces, they do not support the hypothesis of a visual field advantage (VFA) in face perception. Our results do not mean that chimpanzees (or other nonhuman primates) lack a hemispace visual bias. We plan additional trials using abstract images, but suggest that the application and modification of Levy's free-vision task for assessing VFAs be used cautiously.

ACKNOWLEDGMENTS

We thank R. Singer and J. Rybak for running the tests, and W. Hopkins, S. Fernández-Carriba, E. Loew, and M. Owren for advice. This research was supported by the Howard Hughes Medical Institute Undergraduate Biological Sciences award (no. 52003071) and a grant from the National Institutes of Health (RR-00165) to the Yerkes Regional Primate Research Center. The Center is fully accredited by the Association for the Assessment and Accreditation of Laboratory Animal Care International.

REFERENCES

1. MORRIS, R.D. & W.D. HOPKINS. 1993. Perception of human chimeric faces by chimpanzees: evidence for a right hemisphere advantage. Brain Cogn. **21:** 111–122.
2. LEVY, J., W. HELLER, M.T. BANICH & L.A. BURTON. 1983. Asymmetry of perception in free viewing of chimeric faces. Brain Cogn. **2:** 404–419.
3. FERNÁNDEZ-CARRIBA, S., A. LOECHES & W.D. HOPKINS. 2002. Asymmetry in facial expression of emotions by chimpanzees. Neuropsychologia **40:** 1523–1533.
4. SERES, M., F. AURELI & F.B.M. DE WAAL. 2001. Successful formation of a large chimpanzee group out of two preexisting subgroups. Zoo Biol. **20:** 501–515.
5. PARR, L.A., W.D. HOPKINS & F.B.M. DE WAAL. 1998. The perception of facial expressions by chimpanzees, *Pan troglodytes*. Evol. Commun. **2:** 1–23.
6. SOKAL, R.R. & F.J. ROHLF. 1995. Biometry. W.H. Freeman & Co. New York.

Neuroanatomical Basis of Facial Expression in Monkeys, Apes, and Humans

CHET C. SHERWOOD,[a,b,c] RALPH L. HOLLOWAY,[a,c]
PATRICK J. GANNON,[c,d] KATERINA SEMENDEFERI,[e]
JOSEPH M. ERWIN,[f] KARL ZILLES,[g] AND PATRICK R. HOF[b,c,f]

[a]Department of Anthropology, Columbia University,
New York, New York 10027, USA

[b]Kastor Neurobiology of Aging Laboratory and Fishberg Research
Center for Neurobiology, and [d]Department of Otolaryngology,
Mount Sinai School of Medicine, New York, New York 10029, USA

[c]New York Consortium in Evolutionary Primatology, New York, New York

[e]Department of Anthropology, University of California, San Diego,
La Jolla, California 92093-0532, USA

[f]Foundation for Comparative and Conservation Biology,
Needmore, Pennsylvania 17238, USA

[g]Institut für Medizin, Forschungszentrum Jülich und C.& O. Vogt-Institut für
Hirnforschung, Heinrich-Heine-Universität, Düsseldorf, Germany

KEYWORDS: facial expression; motor cortex; facial nucleus; chimpanzee;
gorilla; orangutan

INTRODUCTION

The face is a focal point for the expression of emotions and is central in mediating social exchanges among primates. Early researchers[1,2] noted phylogenetic differences in the facial expressiveness of primates. More recently, psychobiological studies have suggested that great ape and human facial expression may constitute a mode for the communication of highly nuanced nonemotional signals not present in Old World monkeys.[3] Despite these indications of phylogenetic differences in gestural communication, very little is currently known about the comparative neurobiology of facial expression.

Present address and address for correspondence: Chet C. Sherwood, Department of Anthropology and School of Biomedical Sciences, Kent State University, 226 Lowry Hall, Kent, OH 44242. Voice: 330-672-5121; fax: 330-672-2999.
csherwoo@kent.edu

Ann. N.Y. Acad. Sci. 1000: 99–103 (2003). © 2003 New York Academy of Sciences.
doi: 10.1196/annals.1280.016

Here we report data from ongoing comparative quantitative neuroanatomic studies of the brain-stem facial nucleus and primary motor cortex face area in haplorhine primates (i.e., tarsiers, New World monkeys, Old World monkeys, apes, and humans). Using these data we test the hypothesis that great apes and humans differ from other haplorhines in the neural organization of motor face representation.

IS THE FACIAL NUCLEUS ENLARGED?

We calculated the planimetric volume of the facial nucleus in 49 haplorhine individuals (including 10 great apes and 4 humans), representing 30 different species. The facial nucleus was outlined in a stack of digital micrographs of Nissl-stained sections, and total volume was obtained according to the Cavalieri principle. To test whether the facial nucleus of great apes and humans is enlarged, we calculated a prediction equation from the rest of the haplorhine data by regressing log (facial nucleus volume) against log (medulla volume). As a group, the observed values for great apes and humans were significantly larger than predicted by the haplorhine regression line (FIG. 1a; paired samples t-test: $t = 4.175$, $P = 0.001$, d.f. = 14); on average, the facial nucleus of great apes and humans is 27% larger than expected for a haplorhine of the same medulla volume. When the independent-contrasts regression line is computed and mapped back onto the original data space to generate phylogenetically informed prediction intervals,[4] however, only the orangutan point falls above the 95% prediction interval (FIG. 1b).

REORGANIZATION OF PRIMARY MOTOR CORTEX

The face area of primary motor cortex was investigated for phylogenetic differences in cytoarchitectural organization (FIG. 2a). Nissl-stained histological sections were analyzed from the region corresponding to the face representation of the right hemisphere from long-tailed macaque ($n = 3$), anubis baboon ($n = 1$), orangutan ($n = 2$), gorilla ($n = 2$), common chimpanzee ($n = 2$), and human (n = 2). Measurements of cortical layer width were performed from several locations and the percent of total cortical width represented by each layer was calculated. Compared to Old World monkeys, the motor cortex of great apes and humans has a significantly expanded layer III and a reduced layer V (FIG. 2b), although some overlap exists in the range of Old World monkey and orangutan values for layer III. Given that layer III is comprised predominantly of neurons forming corticocortical connections, this result suggests an increase in association networks in great apes and humans.

We pursued further the observation of increased thickness of layer III in great apes and humans by analyzing neuronal packing density in this layer us-

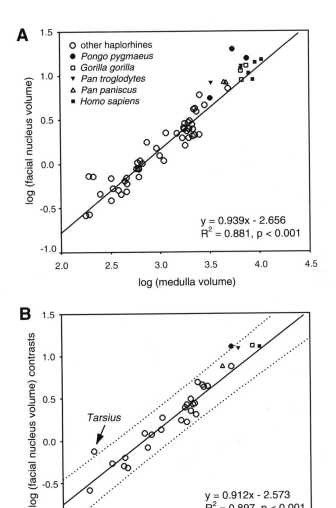

FIGURE 1. A double logarithmic scatterplot of facial nucleus volume and medulla volume is presented (**a**). The reduced major axis line was fit to the data from all haplorhines except great apes and humans. Independent contrasts of species means plotted in the original data space with 95% prediction intervals shown (**b**).

ing the optical fractionator technique (FIG. 2c). Species mean layer III neuronal density and brain weight were not correlated ($r = -0.84$, $P = 0.12$); however, we found that densities were lower in layer III of great apes and humans compared to Old World monkeys ($t = 5.31$, d.f. = 10, $P < 0.01$), revealing increased space for interconnections among neurons. Taken together with

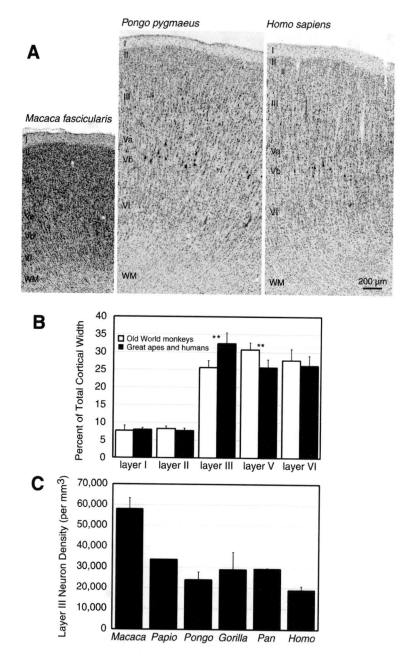

FIGURE 2. Cytoarchitecture of face area of primary motor cortex in representative catarrhine primates is shown (**a**). *Bar graphs* show phylogenetic comparisons of relative laminar widths (**b**) and neuronal densities (**c**) in primary motor cortex (mean ± 2 SEM). *Asterisks* indicate statistically significant contrasts at $P < 0.01$.

the observation that neuropil volume increases in supragranular cortical layers of primary visual cortex through primate phylogeny,[5] this suggests a general evolutionary trend in the primate cerebral cortex for increasing neuropil in supragranular cortical layers.

CONCLUSIONS

The data reported here indicate that the facial motor system of great apes and humans is evolutionarily derived in comparison to other primates. The evidence for microstructural reorganization of primary motor cortex face area may constitute a substrate for the strengthening of corticocortical integration from orbital, insular, ventral premotor, supplementary motor, cingulate motor, and parietal areas.[6] These modifications of motor face representation may underlie the evolution of flexible and subtle facial movements among humans and our close relatives, the great apes.

ACKNOWLEDGMENTS

We thank Drs. Heiko Frahm and Carol MacLeod for advice and helpful assistance. This work was supported by the Leakey Foundation, the Wenner-Gren Foundation, NSF Grant BCS0121286, and NIH Grant AG14308.

REFERENCES

1. DARWIN, C. 1872. The Expression of the Emotions in Man and Animals. John Murray. London.
2. YERKES, R.M. & A.W. YERKES. 1929. The Great Apes. Yale University Press. New Haven, CT.
3. CHEVALIER-SKOLNIKOFF, S. 1982. A cognitive analysis of facial behavior in Old World monkeys, apes, and human beings. *In* Primate Communication. C.T. Snowdon, C.H. Brown & M.R. Petersen, Eds.: 303–368. Cambridge University Press. Cambridge.
4. GARLAND, JR., T. & A.R. IVES. 2000. Using the past to predict the present: confidence intervals for regression equations in phylogenetic comparative methods. Am. Nat. **155:** 346–364.
5. ZILLES, K. *et al.* 1982. Quantitative cytoarchitectonics of the cerebral cortices of several prosimian species. *In* Primate Brain Evolution: Methods and Concepts. E. Armstrong & D. Falk, Eds.: 177–201. Plenum Press. New York.
6. TOKUNO, H. *et al.* 1997. Reevaluation of ipsilateral corticocortical inputs to the orofacial region of the primary motor cortex in the macaque monkey. J. Comp. Neurol. **389:** 34–48.

A Structural and Contextual Analysis of Chimpanzee Screams

ERIN R. SIEBERT[a] AND LISA A. PARR[b]

[a]Department of Zoology, Michigan State University,
East Lansing, Michigan 48824, USA

[b]Division of Psychobiology, Yerkes National Primate Research Center,
Atlanta, Georgia 30329, USA

KEYWORDS: chimpanzee; screams; vocalizations; emotion; social context; acoustic analysis

INTRODUCTION

Chimpanzees live in a socially and emotionally complex world where visual and vocal signals play an important role in social communication. Previous studies in monkeys have shown acoustically distinct categories of vocalizations.[1]

Acoustically distinct alarm calls in vervet monkeys convey information about predator type,[2,3] and rhesus monkey screams convey information about the status of an aggressor.[4] Far fewer studies have been done on chimpanzee vocalizations, and none of these have documented similar context-specific elements.

Chimpanzee screams are common high-amplitude vocalizations used in a variety of antagonistic contexts, and Van Hooff[5] speculated that screams may vary according to the motivational state of the caller. Contextual specificity in screams may bring about selective advantages, since screams appear to be used in part to recruit help and can be heard across long distances.

We propose that chimpanzee screams convey information about emotional state; our objective is to determine the scream structural differences that depend on the social context and motivational state of the caller.

Address for correspondence: Lisa A. Parr, Yerkes Primate Center, 954 Gatewood Rd., Atlanta, GA 30329. Voice: 404-727-3653; fax: 404-727-8993.
parr@rmy.emory.edu

Ann. N.Y. Acad. Sci. 1000: 104–109 (2003). © 2003 New York Academy of Sciences.
doi: 10.1196/annals.1280.022

9000 Hz

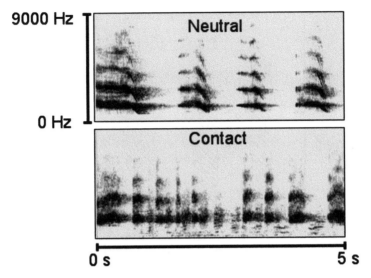

0 Hz

0 s   **5 s**

FIGURE 1. Scream spectrographs from the same individual during neutral and contact contexts.

METHODS

Screams were recorded from 12 adult chimpanzees in 2 captive groups between 1999 and 2002 using digital video recordings. Each group contained males and females, both juvenile and adult. Only naturally occurring adult screams were used in this study.

Screams were digitized at 16-bit resolution with a sampling rate of 44,100 Hz, isolated using Adobe Premiere 6.0 (Adobe Systems Inc., San Jose, CA), and saved as .wav files (see FIG. 1).

Individual screams were selected and cued by eye, using both spectral and waveform views in Cool Edit Pro (Syntrillium Software Corp., Scottsdale, AZ). No screams were used that directly overlapped with other vocalizations or other noises. A total of 355 qualified screams were collected in this study.

Four social contexts were used to categorize each scream from the video: (1) neutral: no contact or specific response by the screamer; (2) chased: the screamer was actively fleeing a chase by another individual; (3) pursue: the screamer chased the aggressor; (4) contact: aggressive contact was received by the screamer.

Individual screams were analyzed using Cool Edit Pro, and Signal Analysis.[6] Each cued scream was processed in 60 equal time segments. For each segment, the maximum amplitude was measured, and the frequency was

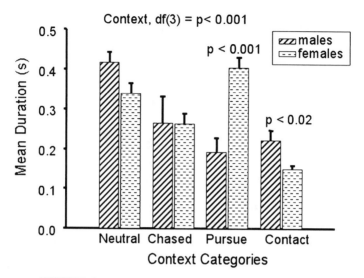

FIGURE 2. Duration of scream varies by context and sex.

measured at the time point of the maximum amplitude. No measures were made at the bout level.

These data were then analyzed for structural differences across social context and sex.

RESULTS

Mean scream duration varied across social context (FIG. 2). Screams were shorter during contact aggression compared to neutral contexts. Females screamed longer than males when pursuing their attacker, but shorter during contact aggression. Time between screams—the interscream interval—was shortest when the caller was being chased or during contact aggression (FIG. 3). Screams were spaced further apart during neutral contexts.

Screams typically decreased in frequency from start to finish (FIG. 4). Only during contact aggression was there an average pitch increase. Scream frequency was more tonal during contact aggression, and more broadband (harsh; increased coefficient of frequency modulation) during neutral contexts and pursuit (FIG. 5). Sex differences in tonality were found for all context categories except during contact aggression.

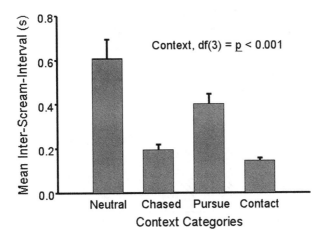

FIGURE 3. Mean interscream interval varies with context.

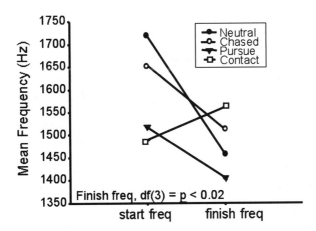

FIGURE 4. Contact aggression influences scream frequency.

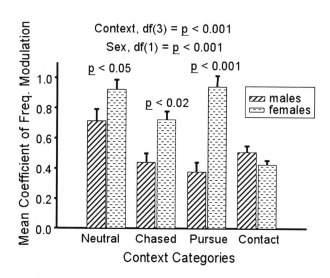

FIGURE 5. Tonal quality of screams varies with sex and context.

DISCUSSION

Chimpanzee screams varied acoustically across social context. They appear to reflect the motivational state of the caller, showing some trends in common with other animals and humans.[7,8]

Chimpanzee screams may follow Morton's Motivation-Structural Rules Model,[7] in that screams were more tonal during contact aggression, perhaps indicating increased fear (FIG. 5).

In humans, articulation rates are fastest during fear and terror.[8] Interestingly, chimpanzees showed this same pattern when being chased and during contact aggression (FIGS. 2 and 3).

In the future, a matching-to-sample joystick paradigm, similar to Parr *et al.,*[9] could be used to test chimpanzee's understanding of these different screams and their associated contexts of use.

Also, individual differences in screams could be analyzed by looking for vocal signatures, similar to what has been reported in monkeys and birds.[10–12] Chimpanzees could then be tested on their ability to match the screams of different individuals.

REFERENCES

1. GOODALL, J. 1986. The Chimpanzees of Gombe. Harvard University Press. Cambridge, MA.
2. CHENEY, D.L. & R.M. SEYFARTH. 1990. How Monkeys See the World. University of Chicago Press. Chicago.
3. SEYFARTH, R.M., D.L. CHENEY & P. MARLER. 1980. Monkey responses to three different alarm calls: evidence of predator classification and semantic communication. Science **210:** 801–803.
4. GOUZOULES, S., H. GOUZOULES & P. MARLER. 1984. Rhesus monkey (*Macaca mulatta*) screams: representational signalling in the recruitment of agonistic aid. Anim. Behav. **32:** 182–193.
5. VAN HOOFF, J.A.R.A.M. 1973. A structural analysis of the social behavior of a semi-captive groups of chimpanzees. *In* Social Communication and Movement. M. von Cranach & I. Vine, Eds.: 75–162. Academic Press. London.
6. MCCOWAN, B. 1995. A new quantitative technique for categorizing whistles using simulated signals and whistles from captive bottlenose dolphins. Ethology **100:** 177–193.
7. MORTON, E.S. 1982. Grading, discreteness, redundancy, and motivation-structural rules. *In* Acoustic Communication in Birds. D.E. Kroodsma, E.H. Miller & H. Ouellet, Eds.: 183–212. Academic Press. London.
8. SCHERER, K.R. 1986. Vocal affect expression: a review and a model for future research. Psychol. Bull. **99:** 143–165.
9. PARR, L.A., J.T. WINSLOW, W.D. HOPKINS & F.B.M. DE WAAL. 2000. Recognizing facial cues: individual recognition in chimpanzees (*Pan troglodytes*) and rhesus monkeys (*Macaca mulatta*). J. Comp. Psychol. **114:** 47–60.
10. CHENEY, D.L. & R.M. SEYFARTH. 1980. Vocal recognition in free-ranging vervet monkeys. Anim. Behav. **28:** 362-367.
11. LIND, H., T. DABELSTEEN & P.K. MCGREGOR. 1996. Female great tits can identify males by song. Anim. Behav. **52:** 667–671.
12. RENDALL, D., P.S. RODMAN & R.E. EMOND. 1996. Vocal recognition of individuals and kin in free-ranging rhesus monkeys. Anim. Behav. **52:** 1007–1015.

A Darwinian Legacy to Understanding Human Infancy

Emotional Expressions as Behavior Regulators

JOSEPH J. CAMPOS, SEINENU THEIN, AND DANIELA OWEN

Institute of Human Development, University of California–Berkeley, Berkeley, California 94720

ABSTRACT: Darwin's influence on the study of emotional responding has largely centered on the study of the production of facial movement patterns. In this paper, we present evidence on the importance of considering facial and vocal patterns as signals that powerfully regulate behavior in infancy and early childhood. We review a series of studies showing that facial expressions and vocal expressions alone can regulate the behavior of infants and, in the case of vocal expressions, do so at ages earlier than most researchers have acknowledged. We also review studies on the enduring effects of social signals, documenting that even 8.5-month-olds show minimal retention of the effects of social signals, some 10-month-olds can retain the effects of social signals for 25 minutes, and 14-month-old can do so for a period of one hour after only two trials of signal exposure. Social signals not only regulate behavior, they also are part and parcel of an important and relatively unstudied phenomenon called *affect sharing*, which is evident by 11.5 months of age. Finally, we speculate on the constitutive role of social signals, especially those linked to what Ekman has called "basic emotions" in the generation of new emotions, such as pride, shame, and guilt.

KEYWORDS: expression; emotion; behavior regulation

A DARWINIAN LEGACY TO HUMAN INFANCY: EMOTIONAL EXPRESSIONS AS BEHAVIOR REGULATORS

This paper begins where Darwin ended in *The Expression of Emotion in Man and Animals*.[1] Darwin's book has had an enormous influence on the field of emotion, as is evident in the contributions in this volume and else-

Address for correspondence: Joseph J. Campos, Ph.D., Department of Psychology, University of California–Berkeley, 3111 Tolman Hall, Berkeley, CA 94720. Voice: 510-624-2620; fax: 510-642-5292.

jcampos@socrates.berkeley.edu

Ann. N.Y. Acad. Sci. 1000: 110–134 (2003). © 2003 New York Academy of Sciences.
doi: 10.1196/annals.1280.040

where.[2,3] In research with humans, the influence of Darwin has been greatest in fostering cross-cultural research on the universality of the recognition[4] and the production of facial expressions.[5] It has also led to a number of studies concerned with how sensitively facial, vocal, and gestural patterns reflect the internal emotional state of the human.[4,6,7] It has resulted in many conceptualizations of the biological adaptive value of both individual and patterned facial movements.[8–10] And it has generated several studies designed to show that a rudimentary sensitivity and responsiveness to emotional signals are innate[11,12] or evident in infants (e.g., infant monkeys) with minimal or no social experience.[13]

In this paper, we review an aspect of the Darwinian theory that has not been so widely emphasized, yet is crucial to his theory: the role of expressions of emotions in others as regulators of the behavior of humans. We will emphasize studies of early development, because of the importance of understanding how emotional expressions work in infants with minimal socialization. We will also emphasize the role of expressions as behavior regulators to demonstrate the intrinsic functionality of such expressions as facilitators and inhibitors of the infant's behavior.

We say that we pick up where Darwin left off because it was in the next-to-the-last page of the work we commemorate here that Darwin wrote most poignantly about emotions as influences on the behavior of others, especially in infancy:

> The movements of expression in the face and body, whatever their origin may have been, are in themselves of much importance for our welfare. They serve as the first means of communication between the mother and her infant. She smiles approval and this encourages the child on the right path, or frowns disapproval. The movements and expressions give vividness and energy to our spoken words....These results follow partly from the intimate relation which exists between almost all the emotions and their outward manifestation.[1]

What follows in this paper instantiates, usually with new or not-yet-published data, the point that Darwin made in this quote. Emotional expressions of others powerfully affect the behavior of infants, in both the short and the long term. Indeed, by the early part of the second year of life, emotional expressions of others begin to have enduring impact, even after minimal exposure of the infant to such signals. This impact, we will propose, lays the basis for the generation of more complex emotions, such as pride, shame, and guilt. The emotional expressions of others are thus both regulatory and constitutive.

The literature on emotional expression and infant behavior is very complex and difficult to summarize.[14] To keep the focus of this paper manageable, we limit ourselves here to the role of emotional signals on the regulation of behavior. By regulation, we mean the process whereby the instrumental goal-oriented behaviors of the baby are changed or reinforced by the emotional expressions of others. To avoid some of the complications in the literature, we will not review studies of the development of the perception of facial or vocal expressions of emotion, and how such perception changes as the infant gets older. Studies of perception in infancy are limited by the use of paradigms, such as habituation/dishabituation, that have questionable generalizability, resulting in sharp criticism and reevaluation of what is known about the perceptual skills of the infant (see the special issue of the journal *Infancy*, Volume 1, Number 3). Also, we are interested not in the representation of emotion in the infant's perceptual world, but in how such emotion signals matter to the child. For other reasons, we will not review the scattered and not-yet-convincing literature on what has been called "affect contagion" in early life. This term refers to the emotional expressions of others eliciting similar emotional expressions in the infant.[15,16] These studies have not yet been able to differentiate superficial motor mimicry from true emotion matching across adult and baby. They also have not been replicated. Ultimately, studies of perception of expressions and contagion of expressions need to be integrated with studies of behavior regulation (or, in contemporary parlance, perception-action coupling); but the field is not yet ready for such an integration. However, the field has already begun to deal with issues of behavior regulation in infancy via emotional expressions, and such behavior regulation has more immediate functional and biological adaptive significance than does either the mere perception of emotional expression in others or expressive contagion.

The structure of what follows in this paper takes the following form: First, we review whether expression of emotion in the face alone can regulate infant behavior, and how strongly it does so. Second, we ask the same questions of the vocalic expression of emotion alone. In a third section, we review two studies dealing with the ontogeny of what might be called affective memory for facial and vocal expressions of emotion—that is, the enduring consequences of exposure of the infant to emotional signals. Finally, we will speculate on how certain emotional expressions—typically those identified as expressions of "basic emotions"—may play a role in the ontogeny of more complex emotions. Our goal in this paper is not merely to report empirical findings, even though much of what we present here is new. Rather, we want to use the findings to chart directions for future research on several topics bearing on a Darwinian approach to the functions of emotional expressions.

DO FACIAL EXPRESSIONS OF EMOTION ALONE REGULATE THE BEHAVIOR OF HUMAN INFANTS?

There is a widespread belief in the literature on infant emotion that, compared to vocal expressions, facial expressions by themselves do not regulate the behavior of infants, or do so only minimally and in restricted contexts. In part, this view stems from some investigations[17] that reported no positive findings when facial signals alone were manipulated. The bias also results from the ecological fact that the face needs to be attended to for it to register on a perceiver and influence the perceiver's behavior. The face has to be within eyeshot, and often it is not. By contrast, the voice can be imposed even on an out-of-view listener, and its message registered and rendered functional. The voice can also be made louder for effect; the face cannot, or cannot be so readily intensified, without risking inauthenticity.

Nevertheless, one might argue that emotional displays in the face are as important as those from the voice in regulating infant behavior. For instance, D'Entremont and Muir[18] have argued that the role of the voice is to help direct the infant's attention to the face. Furthermore, there is evidence[19] that infants in novel situations position themselves to be within eyeshot of the mother. Presumably, mere proximity to the mother may not be enough; the infant may have to move herself around so as to be, ideally, both close and able to read the mother's facial expressions. In this section, we present evidence that emotional expressions conveyed by the face alone do, in fact, powerfully influence the behavior of infants in the first year of life. We also propose a plausible explanation of why some studies yield strong effects of facial expressions, whereas others do not.

The strongest demonstration of the power of facial expressions of emotion alone to influence infant behavior comes from the work done on a visual cliff modified to reveal a modest dropoff (30 cm, a distance somewhat greater than the size of a stairstep).[20] This study was one of the first to investigate social referencing—the process whereby the infant (a) actively seeks out emotional information from the parent or other person to disambiguate a situation and (b) uses that information to select a course of action.[19,21]

Method and Testing Procedure

The visual cliff is a 2.5 meter–by–1.2 meter table covered in its entirety with thick transparent safety glass. On one half of the 2.5-meter side of the table, red and white checkerboard elements are placed immediately under the glass; this is called the "shallow" side. On the opposite half, similar checkerboard elements are placed at some variable distance underneath the bottom of the safety glass; this is called the "deep side." In this study, as said, the deep side consisted of a modest 30-cm drop-off, not the typical drop-off of 1.3 meters. The purpose of the change to a shorter drop was to create a context wherein the deep side was not so great as to be intimidating, yet not so shallow as to be negligible.

The testing procedure involved placing the mother at the far end of the deep side of the cliff and the infant as far as possible from the mother on the shallow side. For the infant to reach the mother, he or she had to traverse the long dimension of the table, first on the shallow side and then on the deep.

The trial began as soon as the infant was properly situated, at which time the mother was instructed through earphones to attract the infant to approach her by smiling at her infant and by placing an attractive toy ferris wheel atop the safety glass on the far deep side. There were no other signals or gestures emitted, no vocalizations or inducements aside from the mother's smile and the toy. Infants invariably left their place on the far shallow side and crawled toward their mothers under these conditions. When the infant reached the center of the table, the experimental manipulation of the study was effected: The mother (who had earlier been trained to pose facial expressions of either fear, anger, sadness, interest, or joy) was told, also by earphone, to shift from smiling to the appropriate emotional expression, each of which was modeled after facial expressions published by Ekman and Friesen[22] and Izard.[23] This study used a between-groups design, such that each infant was exposed to only one facial expression pattern.

The Findings of This Study

Results indicated that infants did reference the mother when encountering the modest dropoff, and they subsequently behaved quite differently as a function of the emotional message in the maternal facial pose they saw when they referenced her. When the infants had crawled to the point where they could see the dropoff at the center of the cliff table, the infants in all emotion conditions generally looked down at the deep side, then up to the mother, often repeating this cycle of back-and-forth looking. This is the classic information-seeking component of social referencing.[24] During this period of referencing, the mother facially posed one of the five emotions. The dependent variable of this study was the proportion of infants who crossed to the mother over the deep side. This dependent variable addressed the behavior-regulatory component of social referencing.[24]

The differential behavior-regulatory effects of the different facial expressions were very strong; they are presented in FIGURE 1. The dashed line in FIGURE 1 represents the proportion of infants in pilot work who descended onto the deep side when the mother was not available to provide any affective signal at all. Approximately half the pilot sample descended onto the deep side, and half did not under conditions of no emotional expression and no emotional communication. This dashed line provides a benchmark for assessing the effects of each facially expressed emotion.

FIGURE 1 shows that the fear face resulted in no infant of the 17 tested crossing to the mother. The anger face led to only two out of 18 infants crossing. By contrast, the joy and interest faces led to approximately 75% of infants crossing the deep. The sad-face condition led to an intermediate proportion of infants crossing to the mother (33%). Interestingly, posing a sad facial expression, which is not an emotional signal appropriate to the baby's

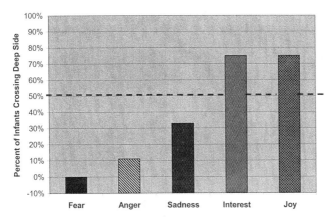

FIGURE 1. The proportion of infants crossing the modified deep side of the visual cliff to reach their mothers as a function solely of the mother's pose of a facial expression.

evaluating a drop-off, resulted in infants engaging in a considerable amount of checking to the mother, as if the infant were confused by the mother's signaling of that particular emotion.

Addressing a Potential Criticism of This Study

There was an important control condition carried out in this study that has often been lost sight of in the literature on social referencing.[14] This control was designed to assess whether infants were sensitive to the contextual appropriateness of the maternal signaling. The need for this control stemmed from the use of facial displays modeled after the actor-posed peak facial expressions used by Ekman and Izard. These poses are to some extent exaggerated. Some[14] have argued that these poses were caricatures of facial expressions and inauthentic. In short, so the argument goes, the infants' behavior on the cliff may have been arrested not because the infant registered the emotional quality of the mother's pose, but simply because the expressions were bizarre.

In the control condition, there continued to be two sides to the visual cliff, but both sides were in fact shallow. There was a change in the appearance of the side of the cliff nearer the mother, but the change did not involve depth. As in the condition with the drop-off, the mother shifted to a fear expression as soon as the infant reached the center region of the table.

The control manipulation yielded two findings. First, most infants typically did not reference the mother. Seventeen infants briefly stopped at the halfway point of the cliff, then continued on toward the mother or toy without even looking toward her. Our interpretation is that there was no need to seek information because there was no ambiguity. However, four additional infants did happen to look up to the mother at the midpoint of the cliff and did see the mother posing the prototypic, exaggerated, fear face. In contrast to the situation with the modified drop-off, in which no infant crossed while the mother was posing fear, in the dual-shallow-side condition, the facial pose of fear did not affect the crossing behavior of the subsample that referenced—they continued to cross. On the basis of these findings, we concluded that the mother's facial expression was not bizarre enough to stop a clock—or a baby! Rather, we felt that in the context of minimal or no ambiguity about a drop-off, the fear pose was not relevant for the 12-month-old, and hence not effective in regulating the infant's behavior.

We hasten to add here that the issue of the perception of authenticity in the emotional display of the parent or experimenter is an important one, and requires careful future study. Clearly, infants come to know when the mother "means it" when she is emoting, and when she does not. We have seen infants older than those tested in the visual cliff study reacting to the exaggeration of facial poses. For instance, some of the 19-month-olds in Klinnert's[25] study laughed when they saw the mother posing an exaggerated fear face. The age when infants begin to notice inauthenticity in emotional expression, and the information that enters into the perception of inauthenticity, are two important issues that await investigation.

An Interpretative Note on Biological Preparedness

Why did this study yield such clear findings when other studies, typically using toys that produce some level of uncertainty, did not? We believe that the cliff affords much more biological preparedness[26–28] for linking negative emotional signals to an environmental encounter than do cute, even if unexpected, toys (which are typically used to create a context of emotional ambiguity). If our interpretation is correct, future work should be conducted varying the biological preparedness of target stimuli (e.g., toy snakes, objects with sharp edges, events with abrupt vs. slow rate of change of movement), and testing for the rapidity and duration of the effects of emotional expressions communicated in either single or multiple modalities.[29]

DOES EMOTION EXPRESSED BY THE VOICE ALONE REGULATE INFANT BEHAVIOR TOWARDS AN OBJECT?

In the most thorough study to date on the effects of emotion in the voice on infant behavior, we manipulated exclamations of anger, fear, or joy when an infant was approaching an object and measured how the vocalizations influenced both looking to the mother and behavior toward the toy.[30,31] The study tested a total of 72 infants, 36 each at 8.5 and 11 months of age, half of whom were female. Mothers were coached to say their baby's name followed by a nonsense phrase ("tat fobble!"), expressing either joy, fear, or anger. The vocalization was done only once on each of three trials. For testing, the setting was an equilateral triangle, with the mother, the baby, and the point of emergence of a toy at the apices of the triangle, the sides of which were 2.8 meters in length. The infant was seated on the floor on one side of a room and played with toys tied to a chair leg, while the mother sat just out of eyeshot of the baby but close enough for the baby to look over to her and feel comfortable knowing she was close by. A bell rang to attract the infant's attention, heralding the appearance of a toy from behind the curtain 2.8 meters away from the infant. When the infant began to approach the toy, the mother responded once on that trial with the appropriate affective vocalization of "tat fobble," while maintaining a neutral face and body position. The trial ended one minute after the vocalization, or 10 seconds after the infant made contact with the toy, whichever came first. There was a one-minute intertrial interval, during which time the infant was placed again next to the original set of tethered toys. A different toy appeared from behind the curtain on each trial; however, the mother used the same assigned emotional expression on all three trials.

Findings on Behavior Regulation

The results of this study were extraordinarily clear: Joy vocalizations produced minimal behavioral disruption of the infant's progress toward the toy, and minimal orienting to the mother; while both anger and fear produced significant response inhibition at both ages. Moreover, there was some (though minimal) indication that infants were able to retain the effect of the social signal across the brief (one-minute) span of time it took to go from one trial to the next. On the other hand, although there was clear evidence that both fear and anger inhibited behavior, there was very little evidence that the infants' behavior following fear was different from that following anger. In this study, the behavior regulation was a function only of the hedonic tone of the signal.

The first reaction any infant gives to exposure to an unexpected sound (in this case, the mother's vocalizing "tat fobble") is an orienting response marked by behavioral arrest. This happened in all three groups, but the duration of the behavioral arrest differed across the different vocalic signaling conditions in meaningful ways. Orienting was very brief (2 seconds) in the joy group, much longer (9 seconds) in the fear group, and an intermediate amount (6 seconds) in the anger group—a highly significant effect for vocalic emotion ($P < 0.004$). On trials 2 and 3, the cessation of movement following the joy vocalization was found to be significantly briefer than either the fear ($P < 0.01$) or the anger condition ($P < 0.01$). (On trial 1, only the contrast be-

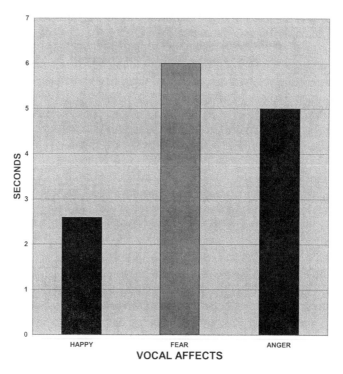

FIGURE 2. Duration of looking to the mother as a function of maternal vocalic signaling of a discrete emotion.

tween joy and fear was significant). There were no age differences. Both ages responded similarly across all three trials.

In this study, we found that the vocalic signal was not sufficiently strong to maintain behavioral arrest for the remainder of the trial. After orienting to the mother, infants in all three groups eventually resumed locomoting toward the toy. However, the resumption of locomotion also reflected the effects of the mother's vocalic signal. For example, the speed of locomotion of infants toward the toy was fastest in the joy condition, and significantly slower in the two negative conditions. These findings are presented in FIGURE 2, which shows the similarity of the performance of infants at the two ages. This similarity is important to note; many reviews of the literature on emotional communication assume that infants do not show behavior regulatory effects to emotional expressions until 10 months or later. Moreover, chi-square tests further revealed that significantly fewer infants touched the toy in the fear and anger conditions than in the joy condition—a finding that applied at both ages tested.

So, for both 8.5- and 11-month-old infants, the different qualities of maternal utterance resulted in differences in duration of behavioral arrest, latency to resume locomotion, speed of locomotion toward the toy, and likelihood of touching the toy. On each of these dependent variables, the negative emotional vocalizations produced greater inhibition of behavior than did the joy signal. Moreover, the intensity of the mother's vocalization played no role in this study. Within the limits of acoustic intensity of the emotional vocalizations that we measured, there was no correlation between the infant's behavior and the acoustic intensity of the mother's vocalization as measured on a sound pressure meter at the level of the infant's starting point. We conclude that the fear and anger vocalizations inhibited behavior more than joy for reasons other than loudness.

Results on Enduring Effects of Vocalizations

An important issue in the study of behavior regulation by way of emotion signals is that of enduring effects. In this study, it was possible to tap into whether the infants' behaviors on subsequent trials were affected by what took place a short time earlier on prior trials. For example, on trials 2 and 3, there were differences in the infants' tendency to look toward the mother as a function of emotion condition even prior to initiating locomotion toward the toy (see FIG. 3). A similar relation was found with the infants' latencies to eventually initiate locomotion toward the toy after its emergence (but before

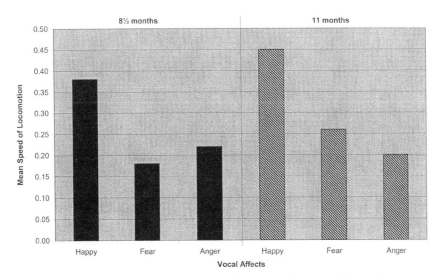

FIGURE 3. Speed of locomotion toward the toy as a function of the mother's prior vocalic expression of fear, anger, or joy.

the mother again vocalized the "tat fobble" command). Here, too, there was evidence for a carryover effect from earlier trials at both ages.

The evidence for the carryover effect was nevertheless minimal at these ages, and more evident in looking at the mother than in latency to resume locomotion toward the toy. Because in this study any carryover effect involved a delay of only a minute, it seems unlikely that single vocalizations of emotion will have enduring consequences across lengthy periods of time at these ages.

(Lack of space precludes reporting a number of interactions between emotion and gender in some of these effects. The interested reader is referred to Svejda[31] for a thorough presentation of these interactions and their implications.)

Interpretative Comments

This study has major implications for the literature on triadic emotional communication. Contrary to widespread conclusions,[14] this study on vocalic communication shows that behavior regulation to emotional signals can take place in triadic contexts well before 11 months of age. Indeed, for many reasons, we believe that expressive regulatory effects should be evident earlier than most researchers cite. For example, there is evidence for a shift at nine months from what has been called "primary intersubjectivity" (meaning dyadic communication) to "secondary intersubjectivity" (a two-person communication about a third event).[32,33] The study we have just described has the characteristics required for inferring secondary intersubjectivity and tested infants close to the age when secondary intersubjectivity is believed to become effective.

The shift from primary to secondary intersubjectivity may be paced by experiences related to crawling or self-produced locomotion (which typically begins at 7.5 months of age or so). There are two reasons for raising this possibility: First, our own research using 8.5-month-old infants found that infants who had locomotor experience (either from crawling or from the use of walker devices) showed evidence of triadic communication (i.e., the ability to follow the point and gaze of another), whereas infants of the same age but with no locomotor experience did not.[34] Since all of the infants in this study were self-mobile, presumably their level of locomotor experience was enough to mediate triadic communication. Second, a study by Campos, Kermoian, and Zumbahlen[35] reported that mothers of newly locomoting infants began to attribute responsibility to their infants, and sharply increased their distal vocalic communications to their infants as they "got into everything." Crawling, thus, is a setting event for distal affective communication from the parents. These factors suggest a study comparing locomotor and prelocomotor infants on a paradigm such as this one. We would expect that infants with locomotor experience will register and use the emotional information from the mother to a greater extent that prelocomotor ones.

There is nothing to preclude such an investigation. Because the great majority of infants do not crawl or locomote much before 8 months of age, the paradigm used here cannot be extended downward in age without restricting generalizations to infants who are precocious in locomotion. However, there exists an alternative to a paradigm that relies on crawling. We suggest that the infant's reaching response provides such an alternative. Reaching for objects is reasonably well established by 4.5 to 5 months of age. If vocalic communication is effective in triadic contexts even prior to crawling onset, a study using reaching responses should yield positive findings. If an increase in exposure of the infant to vocalic signals following locomotor experience is crucial, then reaching should be affected by the emotional envelope of a maternal communication only following the onset of crawling. We propose that a study extending downward in age the paradigm reported on here is relevant to understanding the process by which emotional signals become functionalized (i.e., effective), and will help untangle some of the processes that result in the shift from primary to secondary intersubjectivity.

A major finding in this study is that the two rather different emotional signals of fear and anger did not produce reliable differences in emotional behavior on the part of the infant. We had expected them to do so, at least at the older age. However, the mother's fear signals did not lead the infant to seek her proximity, and her anger signals did not lead to the infant's moving away from her or avoiding her. The behavior-regulatory findings discussed above also showed no systematic effects differentiating the two negative emotions. It is possible that during this age period in the last quarter of the first year of life, behavior is too undifferentiated to permit evidence of differential control of behavior by different negative emotions. It is thus important to follow up this work with studies of much older infants in an attempt to demonstrate at what ages different negative emotions result in different behavioral outcomes. We know of no studies on this crucial issue as of this writing.

WHAT ARE THE ENDURING CONSEQUENCES OF EMOTIONAL SIGNALS DIRECTED AT INFANTS?

Study One: Enduring Consequences of Anger vs. Disgust

We have conducted two studies to determine if there are developmental changes in the enduring consequences of the emotional signals uttered by an experimenter. In the first of these studies, carried out as a doctoral dissertation by Bradshaw,[36] 10- and 15-month-old infants were tested ($n = 47$ in the former group, and 48 in the latter). Participants were randomly assigned to one of three emotional expression conditions—anger, disgust, and bland. A female experimenter signaled the desired emotion using both the face and voice simultaneously. (An experimenter was used rather than the mother for improved experimental control of affect poses.) There were three phases in this study: an emotion-communication phase, a time-out phase, and a retest phase some 25 minutes after the end of the first phase.

Method of Testing

Testing began when the mother and the experimenter were seated diagonally on opposite sides of a room, with the baby stationed on the ground in front of the mother. Two very different–looking target objects were located between the mother and the experimenter and were placed sufficiently apart to be in different visual fields of the baby. The target objects were highly decorative, and designed to look different from toys that the baby might have at home. The mother did no explicit signaling in this study. She was instructed to maintain neutral affect and to fill out a questionnaire, minimizing interaction with her infant. Testing began when the infant approached one of the objects. Once the baby moved towards one of the target objects, the experimenter said the baby's name, then vocalized a nonsense phrase ("tat fobble"), with both the face and the voice posed so as to convey the same emotion. The body was also slightly tensed in the two negative conditions. After 6 seconds of holding the facial expression, the experimenter repeated the phrase, and after 6 more seconds relaxed her face and body into a neutral, nonexpressive position for the remainder of the 3-minute trial. The experimenter signaled to the infant only when the baby approached one and the same toy. No signaling was associated with approach to the second toy, but the baby was free to choose which toy to approach.

After the 3 minutes of signal imposition, there was a 25-minute break during which the mother, baby, and experimenter moved into a different room, had a snack, and played with toys. During the break the experimenter tried to keep the baby occupied without eliciting much of an emotional reaction from the baby. After 25 minutes mother, baby, and experimenter returned to the original testing room, where all the participants were stationed as in the first part of the experiment, except that the experimenter's back was to the baby and she did not vocalize at all. The posttest phase, which lasted three minutes, began when the baby was placed on the floor in front of the mother.

Results during the Emotion Communication Phase

During the exposure period, the emotional signals significantly affected the infants' behavior toward the toy. The indices were speed of withdrawing the hand following the signal, latency to resume touching the toy, and duration of touching the toy. These indices were also combined into a composite

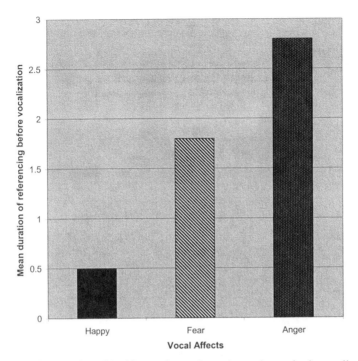

FIGURE 4. Duration of looking to the mother prior to the mother's vocalization of emotion as a function of the specific emotion vocalized on earlier trials.

score, which yielded a significant effect of emotion. The results, which can be seen in FIGURE 4, show the pattern of inhibited touching pooled over both ages and sexes for the composite index. Anger produced the greatest inhibition, followed by disgust, with bland showing the least inhibition. Posthoc analyses revealed that the two negative conditions produced significantly more inhibition than did the bland expression. Interestingly, there were no significant effects of age in the exposure period: both 10- and 15-month-olds behaved similarly in response to the experimenter's signals during this phase of the study.

Results during the Retest Period

During the retest period, there were trends, such that both the anger and disgust condition produced slightly more inhibited behaviors than did the bland condition. There was also a trend, evident in FIGURE 4, suggesting an effect of age, such that a carryover effect appeared to be present in the older, but not the younger, infants. However, neither of these trends reached significance. Over the entire set of infants, then, this study failed to document re-

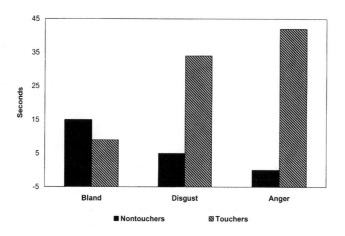

FIGURE 5. Duration of touching an object as a function of the mother's vocalization 25 minutes earlier in infants who had either touched, or not touched at all, that same object on the emotion exposure period.

tention of the effects of the emotion signals over the 25-minute delay at either age.

However, an individual-difference analysis did reveal a carryover effect, though the effect of age could not be assessed due to the constrained sample size. In the exposure period, some 30 infants (10 at 10 months of age, and 20 at 15 months) did not touch the toy at all following the experimenter's signals. This effect of not touching the toy occurred significantly more for both the anger and the disgust condition than for the bland condition, although a few infants in the bland condition also failed to touch the toy.

When the behavior of these nontouchers in the exposure condition was contrasted with the behavior of touchers, a major and highly significant effect was obtained, as seen in FIGURE 5. There was a highly significant effect of retention of the signal over the 25-minute delay when nontouchers were compared to touchers. For instance, the duration of touching the target toy in the group who did touch the toy 25 minutes earlier was 42 seconds in the anger condition, 34 seconds in the disgust condition, and 12 seconds in the bland; by contrast, the duration of touching the toy by infants who did not touch the toy in the exposure period was 0 seconds when they had previously heard and seen the experimenter's anger, 5 seconds when they were exposed to disgust, and 13 seconds in the bland condition. The fact that infants in both the toucher and nontoucher groups behaved similarly in the bland condition suggests that temperamental inhibition of touching was not the mediator of this effect. The results appear to have been due to the different qualities of the emotion signals posed by the experimenter, and are significantly so as revealed by Mann-Whitney tests comparing each emotion condition to the bland one.

In sum, then, the results of this study revealed that (1) the emotional signals of an experimenter did regulate the behavior of both 10- and 15-month-old infants; (2) the carryover effect of these signals over a 25-minute period was weak and not significant; but (3) subsets of infants (those whose behavior revealed complete inhibition of touching the toy following the signal in the exposure period) did show a significant carryover effect that was mediated by the two negative affective signals. For more details, the reader is referred to Bradshaw.[36]

Study 2: Enduring Consequences of Disgust Compared to Positive Emotion

The link found between touching and not touching the toy during the exposure period on the one hand, and enduring effects of the emotional signaling on the other, suggested an important approach to the study of the retention of emotional signals in infancy. If infants are allowed to touch a toy that had previously received a proscriptive signal, and such touching receives no further proscription from the experimenter, the inconsistency of such messages over time may communicate that it is ultimately acceptable to approach and touch the toy. This line of reasoning suggested the need for a paradigm that would allow the infant to perceive a link between an emotional signal and a toy, but not be allowed to touch that toy, or any other toy, during the exposure period.

Just such a paradigm was developed by Hertenstein[37] and reported in Hertenstein and Campos.[38] The objective of this study was to assess the lasting regulatory effects of an adult's emotional displays on infant behavior in 11- and 14-month-olds. Two studies looked at the lasting consequences of emotional signals—one study across a one-hour period, and a second study across a much shorter period of three minutes. A male experimenter posed two emotional signals—joy and disgust. Joy was manipulated in this study instead of bland emotion in order to create a larger difference between levels of the independent variable of the study. (A bland emotional signal can increase error variance in the performance of infants because bland expression may be perceived as ambiguous—mildly positive or mildly negative, depending on context.) As in the prior study, two very unusual toys were used—toys that were also very different from those an infant is likely to encounter in the home. The toys were presented to the infant sufficiently far from each other that the infant could readily discern to which of the two toys the experimenter's emotional signals were directed.

The major questions addressed in this study centered on presentation of the emotion signals in such a manner that the infant could see the potential target of the signal, but not touch the object during the exposure period. Only during the posttest period were the objects within reach and grasp of the baby.

Method

There were 64 infants tested in each study, 32 at each age, with half being exposed to the joy signal and half to the disgust. The mother sat next to the infant, but her face was not in view of the child. (She was completing a questionnaire.) The design involved the same three phases of testing (exposure, time out, and posttest) as in the prior study, but in this investigation, the exposure period involved two discrete emotional communication trials, each 15 seconds in duration.

In the exposure phase, two target objects (a yellow bird-like object and a blue animal-like object), initially out of the infant's sight, were lowered from the ceiling onto the table, both landing within sight but out of reach of the infant. As soon as the toy made contact with the table, the experimenter emoted either the pleasure/joy signal or the disgust emotion, using vocal, facial, and postural signals. The experimenter also looked at, and pointed to, one of the target objects. To vocally express emotion, the experimenter used the nonsense phrase "tat fobble" and other vocal cues such as "euuuh" and "ahhh." After 15 seconds of emotional display, the objects were raised to the ceiling, out of sight of the infant, and the mother was allowed to interact with her infant. The second trial used exactly the same procedure, except that the positions of the two objects were reversed. The experimenter posed the same emotion and pointed to the same object exactly as in the first trial.

During the time-out period, the mother and infant moved to another room or went outside the building for a walk for the one-hour delay period. After the hour, the posttest began. The baby was placed back in the high chair for the final trial and the mother returned to her same position as in the first two trials. The experimenter was absent from the room during the posttest. The target objects were now positioned to descend within reach of the infant for the first time. Once the objects descended, the infant was free to interact with the two objects for one minute. At the end of the minute the testing was completed.

Results, which are presented only for the posttests in both studies, were analyzed across five variables: number of infants who touched the target toy, duration of touching the target, latency to touch the target, whole-hand touch of the target, a scale of negative facial/vocal expression, and a scale of positive expression. We will restrict discussion here to the two variables most like those in prior work—latency and duration.

Enduring Effects over a One-Hour Delay

Because infants were not allowed to touch the toy during the exposure period in this study, there are no data to report on this phase of the study (in con-

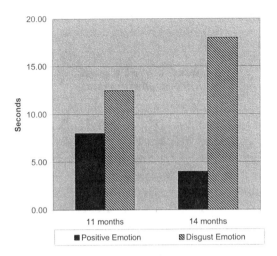

FIGURE 6. Latency to touch the target object as a function of age and a one-hour delay between exposure to the targeted emotional expression and test period.

trast to the study described above). Data are presented only for the posttest phase, where the results were extremely clear: enduring effects were found in this study, but only at 14 months of age. One hour after being exposed to the emotional signals, significantly more subjects at 14 months touched the target object than the distractor in the joy condition; by contrast, fewer infants touched the target object than the distractor toy in the disgust condition. However, 11-month-olds touched both targets equally after the one-hour delay.

The duration of touch also significantly differed in the two conditions at 14 months of age, but did not differ significantly at 11 months of age (see FIG. 6). The 14-month-olds waited four times longer to touch the target object in the disgust condition than in the joy condition, while the 11-month-olds did not show a significant difference in the latency to touch either object. Thus, 14-month-olds had a much greater retention than did 11-month-olds of the quality of the adult's affective signals and reacted accordingly even one hour after the affective signals were presented. These findings are particularly striking in light of the minimal affective information (just two trials) imparted during the exposure period.

Enduring Effects across a Three-Minute Delay

The second study was conducted to determine whether 11-month-olds would show any evidence of a differential effect of the two emotional signals even when the delay between exposure and posttest was extremely brief. In short, the study was designed to rule out the possibility that the enduring effects seen at 14 months merely reflected the effectiveness of the emotional signaling in the exposure period at that age, and the lack of effectiveness of signaling in the exposure period at 11 months.

To address this issue, yet keep all methodological factors constant across studies, the second study had a very brief time-out of only three minutes instead of one hour; but in that time-out, the infant was removed from the seat used in the exposure trials. Only 11-month-olds participated in study 2.

The 11-month-olds showed emotion-appropriate behavior regulation after the three-minute delay between exposure and posttest. Hence, the retention shown at 14 months of age was not an artifact of the paradigm. Infants at 14 months can retain the emotional meaning of the experimenter's social signals over a one-hour time period. By contrast, 11-month-olds are able to retain the emotional impact of social signals after a brief delay, but may not be able to do so over an hour, at least not with so few exposure trials and with emotions such as disgust and joy. The results of the Hertenstein and Campos study also suggest an important methodological point: to demonstrate enduring effects of emotional signals, it may be important not to give implicit mixed messages to the infant by allowing infants at these ages to touch a toy that had previously received a prohibitory message.

Explaining the Improvement with Age in Retention of the Effects of Emotional Signaling

Why should infants begin to demonstrate retention of the consequences of emotional signals between 11 and 14 months of age? We believe that a number of factors play a role. First, there is a marked improvement in memory by the infant at around the first year of life.[39] This improvement may well go hand in glove with general improvements in the symbolic processing by the infant that is emerging during the same time period. We expect that infants may show much better retention of not just of emotional signals targeted at toys, but also of nonemotional information as a function of age before and after about 12 months.

We also believe that parents sharply increase the frequency and intensity of vocalic and facial communication as the child becomes older. The child thus learns a general skill—not unlike a learning set[40]—wherein few trials are needed for learning to be effective precisely because of the transfer of training from previous problems that the animal or child has solved. By acquiring such a hypothetical emotional learning set, infants at 14 months may require only a few exposures to an emotional signal targeted at an object to learn to approach or avoid it, and to retain the learning over a reasonably enduring period of time.

Between 11 and 14 months, the child shows a marked improvement in his or her ability to read the intentional state of the other person.[32] Therefore, the child may better link the emotional communication of an adult to specific objects and events in the environment. By understanding the much greater specificity of the intentional state of the other, the infant may be more effective at "tagging" an emotional meaning to an environmental event, and, on the assumption that what is better understood is better retained, remember that tag over periods of increasing duration.

We are not proposing that infants younger than 14 months are incapable of retaining the consequences of emotional signals over a reasonably long period of time. Presumably, a child who receives multiple emotional expressions transmitted with great intensity willl show retention effects at much earlier ages than we have demonstrated in these studies. The study of affective memory in infancy is ripe for investigation; the research that we have presented here merely documents the ages at which retention of emotional communications have been shown with relatively few trials and relatively modest signals.

The Future of Studies on Triadic Emotional Communication: Social Signals as Constitutive of New Emotions

The studies we have been describing involve a triangular arrangement wherein the mother or experimenter plays a role as provider of emotional information; a toy or event (such as the approach of a stranger, insect, or animal, or a drop-off) provides the target for the emotional information; and the infant observes the emotion as well as its targeting and changes his or her behavior appropriately.

This simple triadic setting for emotional communication actually provides a number of important and as-yet-unstudied variations of the power of emotion in the construction of emotional meaning in early life. Consider a situation wherein the infant is the one that provides the emotional information about an event, and the mother becomes the target of the communication. This phenomenon is a powerful one, called *affect sharing*, and constitutes one of the most profound alternatives to the use of security as a means of measuring attachment. Infants beyond a certain age, not yet identified or traced developmentally, will look to the mother upon seeing something affectively noteworthy, either point or look at the event, then at the mother, then back to the event, as if to attract the mother's attention. Although infants will show affective sharing with other figures than their parents, in general we suspect that the parents are the typical targets of such emotional communication. Indeed, when clinicians talk about emotional availability as an important factor in early mother–infant interaction, they imply not only that the mother gives the child security, but also that she provides crucial functions of affective acknowledgment and social feedback to her baby. Such emotional affirmation, we propose, is a crucial component of the development of the early self.

Why has affective sharing been studied so sparingly? We believe that the same factors that have held back the study of emotional expressions as powerful regulators of the behavior of the infant are involved in the neglect of the study of affective sharing. An important study on the development of the social-cognitive component of affective sharing has been conducted by Rachel Conrad[41] in 9-, 11.5-, and 14-month-old infants. In this study, infants were exposed to a growling gorilla stimulus while the mother was either available to receive emotional signals from her child, or had her back to the child and hence was unavailable. Conrad's study did not extend to the "flip side" of social referencing, in the sense that she did not manipulate the quality of the infant's affect to see how it affected the mother's behavior. However, she did measure the extent to which the infant communicated to the mother in the two conditions of availability. She found clear developmental trends, such that 11.5- and 14-month-olds communicated to the mother about the gorilla when she was available, but not when she had her back to the child. By implication, this study suggests that at the end of the first year of life, infants are attempting to influence the mother by bringing affective events to her attention.

There are other variations possible on the triadic emotional communication theme—variations that have equally profound implications for the development of the child's emotions. Consider the triadic situation in which the mother's targeting of the emotion is directed not so much at the third object or event, but at the child who is interacting with the event. This type of triadic communication constitutes the canonical means by which infants learn how their actions on the world are received by significant others. When significant others direct their positive emotions to the child who has engaged in an act on the world, such as a successful problem solution, the child's registration of the parent's positive emotion enhances the intrinsic positive emotions resulting from success with a task. We would expect the emotion of pride to emerge from this kind of triadic interaction.

The same type of triadic interaction wherein the mother targets the child's engagement in the world in a negative manner is the setting by which the emotion of shame begins to be constructed from the reception by the child of negative emotional signals in the context of the child's engaging in negative behavior.

The cognitive, perceptual, and social factors that enter into the type of triadic communications that we are proposing help bring pride and shame about should be available to the infant at about the same time as the skills that enter into social referencing and the regulation of behavior by imposition of emotional signals directed at a toy or event. If so, it should be possible to create an experimental context for generating in laboratory settings the emotions of pride and shame. To our knowledge, no one has yet embarked on such a set of empirical investigations.

There is still another possible variation in the theme of triadic emotional communication that we believe has not yet been investigated: it is the situation in which there is no necessary targeting of emotion by the person who is with the child, but in which the child notices the effects of his or her behavior on the emotions of the other person. For example, the child might break a prized possession of the parent, who then shows sadness, pain, or distress. We believe that when the child notices these emotions, and links them to his actions on the object, the conditions are met by which the emotion of guilt is generated, at least in rudimentary form. As with the situation of affect sharing in the generation of pride and shame, the emotion of guilt, viewed in this triadic communicational manner, can be involved in the creation of new and more complex emotions.

For years, emotion theorists have speculated on the ways by which emotional reactions become "blended" to produce emotions such as shame, pride, and guilt. These theories have often been referred to as "palette theories" to convey the sense that the various complex emotions are constituted from responses of simpler emotions.

What we are proposing here is a very different palette view of the generation of complex emotions. The palette comes from the meaning of the specific basic emotions (in Ekman's way of construing basic emotions) that are conveyed in the triadic context of child, event, and other person. We do not stress the constitutive role of basic emotional *responses* in the generation of complex emotions, but rather the *social signaling* role of such emotional responses. The responses that emerge from being the target of parental disapproval are unique, involving withdrawal from social intercourse and speech; they are not behavioral mirrorings of parental anger, sadness, or scorn. The same holds true for pride. The swelling up of the chest, the heightened elevation of the body, and the other responses manifested when one is proud are not exclusively or primarily behavioral mirrorings of the joyful responses of the applauding parents, though on occasion there may be evidence of such response similarity. The clearest differentiation between palette theories that concern responses and those that stress social signaling comes from guilt. The behaviors one observes in a person in a state of guilt are typically undoing, reparation of the damage caused, and contrition. None of these behaviors is morphologically similar to the behaviors seen when a person is sad, hurt, or disappointed as a result of the actions of the guilty party. We believe these considerations place the social signaling role of Ekman's basic emotions into high profile for future studies.

Mention of Ekman's ideas on basic emotions raises an issue relevant to contemporary treatments of his approach to emotions. The recent emphasis on appraisals and action tendencies has broadened the concept of what a "basic" emotion is to a very great extent. As a result, Ekman's approach to basic emotions has been given an increasingly secondary role in emotion theory, as reflecting a subset (and a minor subset at that) of the pantheon of fundamental emotions.

If our speculations on the origins of pride, shame, and guilt are correct, Ekman's theory of basic emotions is again placed onto central stage. We say so because we do not believe that it is possible to explain the generation of, for example, pride versus guilt without taking Ekman's basic emotions into account as primary determinants of what is communicated to the child and eventually internalized as shame and guilt. Consider that shame is elicited by the Ekman basic emotions of scorn, anger, and sadness; but fear in our conceptualization probably plays no role in generating shame in the other.

By contrast, guilt is produced when sadness, disappointment, suffering, pain, and other emotions such as fear and worry are observed in the aggrieved person. If the aggrieved shows anger, scorn, or contempt, the person committing the offending action is not likely to experience guilt. Indeed, quite the contrary: the person may accentuate the behaviors that produced the hurt in the target individual.

In sum, discrete emotions such as those Ekman has stressed in his many theoretical writings are, indeed, central ones in the manner by which we construe the development of complex emotions. We also believe that the many different ways by which triadic emotional communication can be manipulated in the developmental laboratory make this technique well suited to incisive naturalistic observation of the infant and young child, and precise quantification of outcomes.

We are disappointed that we have little to report in the world's literature on these approaches to triadic communication, but we hope that this paper plays a role in fostering the study of the new and important phenomena we have described in the conclusion of this paper.

REFERENCES

1. DARWIN, C. [1872] 1998. The Expression of the Emotions in Man and Animals, 3rd edit. P. Ekman, Ed. Harper Collins. London. (US edit.: Oxford Press. New York.)
2. EKMAN, P., Ed. 1973. Darwin and Facial Expression. Academic Press. New York.
3. COSMIDES, L. & J. TOOBY. 2000. Evolutionary psychology and the emotions. *In* Handbook of Emotions, 2nd edit. M.A.H.-J. Lewis, Ed.: 91–155. Guilford. New York.
4. EKMAN, P. 1998. Afterword. *In* The Expression of the Emotions in Man and Animals. P. Ekman, Ed.: 363–394. Oxford. New York.
5. CAMRAS, L., H. OSTER, J.J. CAMPOS & R. BAKEMAN. 2003. Emotional facial expressions in European-American, Japanese, and Chinese infants. Ann. N.Y. Acad. Sci. **1000:** this volume.
6. IZARD, C.E. 1977. Human Emotions. Plenum Press. New York.
7. IZARD, C.E. 1991. The Psychology of Emotions. Plenum Press. New York.
8. FOGEL, A., E. NWOKAH, J. DEDO, *et al.* 1992. Social process theory of emotion: a dynamic systems approach. Soc. Dev. **1:** 122–142.
9. FRIJDA, N.H. 1986. The Emotions. Cambridge University Press. Cambridge, MA.

10. STENBERG, C. R. & J.J. CAMPOS. 1990. The development of anger expressions in infancy. *In* Psychological and Biological Approaches to Emotion. N.L. Stein, B. Leventhal & T. Trabasso, Eds.: 247–282. Lawrence Erlbaum Associates. Hillsdale, NJ.

11. MARTIN, G. B. & R.D. CLARK. 1982. Distress crying in neonates: species and peer specificity. Dev. Psychol. **18:** 3–9.

12. SAGI, A. & M.L. HOFFMAN. 1976. Empathic distress in the newborn. Dev. Psychol. **12:** 175–176.

13. KENNEY, M.D., W.A. MASON & S.D. HILL. 1979. Effects of age, objects, and visual experience on affective responses of rhesus monkeys to strangers. Dev. Psychol. **15:** 176–184.

14. SAARNI, C., D. MUMME & J. CAMPOS. 1998. Emotional development: action, communication, and understanding. *In* Social, Emotional, and Personality Development, Vol. 3. Handbook of Child Psychology. N. Eisenberg, Vol. Ed.: 237–310. Wiley. New York.

15. HAVILAND, J.M. & M. LELWICA. 1987. The induced affect response: 10-week-old infants' responses to three emotion expressions. Dev. Psychol. **23:** 97–104.

16. FIELD, T.M., R. WOODSON, R. GREENBERG & D. COHEN. 1982. Discrimination and imitation of facial expressions by neonates. Science **218:** 179–181.

17. MUMME, D.L., A. FERNALD & C. HERRERA. 1996. Infants' responses to facial and vocal emotional signals in a social referencing paradigm. Child Dev. **67:** 3219–3237.

18. D'ENTREMONT, B. & D. MUIR. 1999. Infant responses to adult happy and sad vocal and facial expressions during face-to-face interaction. Infant Behav. Dev. **22:** 527–539.

19. KLINNERT, M.D., J.J. CAMPOS, J.F. SORCE, *et al.* 1983. Emotions as beahvior regulators: social referencing in infancy. *In* Emotion: Theory, Research, and Experience. R. Plutchik & H. Kellerman, Eds.: 57–86. Academic Press. New York.

20. SORCE, J.F., R.N. EMDE, J.J. CAMPOS & M.D. KLINNERT. 1985. Maternal emotional signaling: its effect on the visual cliff behavior of 1-year-olds. Dev. Psychol. **21:** 195–200.

21. CAMPOS, J.J. & C.R. STENBERG. 1981. Perception, appraisal, and emotion: the onset of social referencing. *In* Infant Social Cognition: Empirical and Theoretical Considerations. M.E. Lamb & L.R. Sherrod, Eds.: 273–314. Erlbaum. Hillsdale, NJ.

22. EKMAN, P. & W.V. FRIESEN. 1976. Emotion in the Human Face: A Guide to Recognizing Emotions from Facial Clues. Prentice-Hall. Englewood Cliffs, NJ.

23. IZARD, C.E. 1971. The Face of Emotion. Appleton-Century-Crofts. New York.

24. CAMPOS, J.J. 1983. The importance of affective communication in social referencing: a commentary on Feinman. Merrill-Palmer Q. **29:** 83–87.

25. KLINNERT, M.D. 1984. The regulation of infant behavior by maternal facial expression. Infant Behav. Dev. **7:** 447–465.

26. VALENTINE, C.W. 1930. The innate bases of fear. J. Genet. Psychol. **37:** 394–420.

27. SELIGMAN, M.E. 1970. On the generality of the laws of learning. Psychol. Rev. **77:** 406–418.

28. COOK, M. & S. MINEKA. 1990. Selective associations in the observational conditioning of fear in rhesus monkeys. J. Exp. Psychol. Anim. Behav. Processes **16:** 372–389.

29. WALDEN, T. & C. PASSARETTTI. 1996. "I don't care what you say. I'm not touching that snake." Biologically-relevant fear and social referencing. Presented at the International Conference on Infant Studies, Providence, RI.

30. SVEJDA, M. & J.J. CAMPOS. 1982. Vocal expressions of emotions as behavior regulators in infancy. Presented at the meeting of the International Society for Infant Studies, Austin, TX.

31. SVEJDA, M. 1981. Infant sensitivity to mother's voice messages. Unpublished doctoral dissertation. University of Denver. Denver, CO.

32. CARPENTER, M. K. NAGELL & M. TOMASELLO. 1998. Social cognition, joint attention, and communicative competencies from nine to fifteen months of age. Monogr. Soc. Res. Child Dev. **63**(4).

33. TREVARTHEN, C. & P. HUBLEY. 1978. Secondary intersubjectivity: confidence, confiders, and acts of meaning in the first year of life. *In* Action, Gesture, and Symbol: The Emergence of Language. A. Lock, Ed.: 183–229. Academic Press. New York.

34. CAMPOS, J.J., D.I. ANDERSON, M.A. BARBU-ROTH, *et al.* 2000. Travel broadens the mind. Infancy **1:** 149–220.

35. CAMPOS, J.J., R. KERMOIAN & M. ZUMBAHLEN. 1992. Socioemotional transformations in the family system following infant crawling onset. *In* New Directions for Child Development: Emotion and its Regulation in Early Development, Vol. 55. N. Eisenberg & R.A. Fabes, Eds.: 25–40. Jossey-Bass. San Francisco.

36. BRADSHAW, D. 1986. Immediate and prolonged effectiveness of negative emotion expressions in inhibiting infant's actions. Unpublished doctoral dissertation. University of Denver. Denver, CO.

37. HERTENSTEIN, M.J. 2002. The lasting regulatory effects of an adult's emotional displays on infant behavior. Unpublished doctoral dissertation. University of California–Berkeley. Berkeley, CA.

38. HERTENSTEIN, M.J. & J.J. CAMPOS. Tracing the duration of retention of the regulatory effects of emotional displays on infant behavior. Submitted for publication.

39. BAUER, P.J., J.A. WENNER, P.L. DROPIK & S.S. WEWERKA. 2000. Parameters of remembering and forgetting in the transition from infancy to early childhood. Monogr. Soc. Res. Child Dev. **65**.

40. HARLOW, H. 1949. The formation of learning sets. Psychol. Rev. **56:** 51–65.

41. CONRAD, R. 1994. Infant Affect Sharing and Its Relation to Maternal Availability. Doctoral dissertation. University of California–Berkely. Berkely, CA.

Emotional Facial Expressions in European-American, Japanese, and Chinese Infants

LINDA A. CAMRAS,[a] HARRIET OSTER,[b] JOSEPH J. CAMPOS,[c] AND ROGER BAKEMAN[d]

[a]Department of Psychology, DePaul University, Chicago, Illinois 60614, USA

[b]Department of Surgery, New York University School of Medicine, New York, New York 10016, USA

[c]Department of Psychology, University of California, Berkeley, Berkeley, California 94720, USA

[d]Department of Psychology, Georgia State University, Atlanta, Georgia 30303, USA

ABSTRACT: Charles Darwin was among the first to recognize the important contribution that infant studies could make to our understanding of human emotional expression. Noting that infants come to exhibit many emotions, he also observed that at first their repertoire of expression is highly restricted. Today, considerable controversy exists regarding the question of whether infants experience and express discrete emotions. According to one position, discrete emotions emerge during infancy along with their prototypic facial expressions. These expressions closely resemble adult emotional expressions and are invariantly concordant with their corresponding emotions. In contrast, we propose that the relation between expression and emotion during infancy is more complex. Some infant emotions and emotional expressions may not be invariantly concordant. Furthermore, infant emotional expressions may be less differentiated than previously proposed. Together with past developmental studies, recent cross-cultural research supports this view and suggests that negative emotional expression in particular is only partly differentiated towards the end of the first year.

KEYWORDS: emotional facial expressions; infants; culture; emotion

Address for correspondence: Linda A. Camras, Ph.D., Department of Psychology, De Paul University, 2219 N. Kenmore Ave., Chicago, IL 60614. Voice: 773-325-4261; fax: 773-325-7888.

lcamras@depaul.edu

Ann. N.Y. Acad. Sci. 1000: 135–151 (2003). © 2003 New York Academy of Sciences.

doi: 10.1196/annals.1280.007

Charles Darwin was among the first to recognize the important contribution that infant studies could make to our understanding of human emotion expression. As one of the first infant diarists, Darwin kept extensive notes on his own children's emotional expressions.[1,2] He included descriptions of them along with other infants' emotions in his *The Expression of Emotions in Man and Animals*, together with a number of photographs and drawings.[3] Like his theoretical adversary, Sir Charles Bell, Darwin believed that infants display emotions "with extraordinary force" and that their expressions reflect a "pure and simple source" rather than the intervening effects of emotion socialization processes.[3] However, he also suggested that initially infants' expression repertoire may be highly restricted, as indicated in the following incisive observation:

> The earliest and almost sole expression seen during the first days of infancy…
> is that displayed during the act of screaming; and screaming is excited, both at
> first and for some time afterwards, by every distressing or displeasing sensation
> and emotion—by hunger, pain, anger, jealousy, fear, etc.[3]

Today there is considerable controversy about the nature of infant facial expressions and their relation to emotions. Do very young infants experience and express discrete emotions, or is emotional expression less differentiated during the first months of life? Much—but not all—of this debate centers on whether in early infancy negative emotions differ from one another in their expression. However, there are also a number of other controversies regarding the relation between expression and emotion in infants.

According to one popular theory (the *differential emotion theory*, or DET)[4,5] discrete basic emotions emerge during infancy according to a maturational timetable. Each emotion has its corresponding prototypic facial expression as described in the MAX[6] and AFFEX[7] coding systems. These expressions resemble, but are not always identical to, adult prototypic emotional expressions. In its original formulation, the differential emotions theory also asserted that there is a one-to-one correspondence between these expressions and discrete emotions such that: (a) whenever an infant experiences an emotion, she produces the corresponding expression, and (b) she never produces these expressions in any other circumstances. The theory thus has been particularly appealing because it promises both researchers and parents a "fool-proof" way to read infants' true feelings. Although older children and adults may sometimes modify their genuine, spontaneous expressive behavior in accord with social display rules,[8,9] such modification is not thought to occur during the infant's first year. More recently, Izard has begun to acknowledge the possibility that infant facial expressions and infant emotions may not be uniquely related.[10] However, many developmentalists have been loathe to relinquish the principle of invariant concordance, probably because it offers a simple solution to the problem of understanding the feelings of infants.

Nonetheless, considerable research exists that is inconsistent with this principle, strongly suggesting instead that there is not invariably a one-to-one correspondence between infant facial expressions and infant emotions (see Camras[11] and Camras, Malatesta & Izard[12] for reviews of the early literature). A number of studies have demonstrated that configurations identified as invariant expressions of emotion often occur when the corresponding emotion is unlikely to be experienced. For example, facial configurations of surprise are regularly observed when infants bring a familiar object towards the mouth for oral exploration.[13] DET-specified expressions of physical pain/discomfort occur during mother-infant face-to-face interaction, a situation in which pain is not likely to be experienced.[14] The raised brow (a variant of the interest expression as described within DET) is associated with infants' lifting their heads and/or gaze, and these physical actions have been proposed to be synergistically linked as a coordinative motor structure.[15] Conversely, other studies have shown that infants do not typically produce the predicted emotional facial expression in a situation commonly believed to elicit the corresponding emotion. For example, infants generally do not show prototypic fear expressions during some acknowledged fear situations, such as the visual cliff procedure studied extensively by Campos.[16] Similarly, the prototypic surprise expression is not generally observed in infants during expectancy-violating procedures, such as a covert toy switch.[17,18]

In addition, Darwin's early observations about "screaming"[3] have been essentially replicated, and they, too, are relevant to the debate about the relation between expression and emotion in infancy. As articulated a number of years ago by Hiatt, Campos, and Emde, if facial expressions do invariantly correspond to discrete emotions, one should be able to demonstrate both their intersituational and intrasituational specificity.[16] For example, one should see anger expressions occurring in anger situations but not fear situations (intersituational specificity); and in unblended anger situations one should see expressions only of anger and not any other negative emotion (intrasituational specificity). However, as Darwin noted, young infants actually show similar facial expressions during a wide variety of negative emotion situations. In particular, the DET-described facial expressions for sadness, anger, and discomfort/pain are seen together in a range of situations, including medical inoculations, presentation of unusual masks, separation from mother, tasting a sour vitamin, being bathed, and having one's pacifier taken away.[19,11,12] Furthermore, infants often appear to cycle among these facial expressions within a single bout of crying.[19] These observations suggest that intersituational and intrasituational specificity do not exist for the anger, sadness, and pain expressions.

The results of several judgment studies also challenge the view of infant facial expressions presented within the differential emotions theory. In a set of well-designed procedures involving adults' ratings of infants' emotions, Oster, Hegley, and Nagel showed that adults do not spontaneously interpret the DET-described expressions for anger, sadness, fear, and disgust as indicating discrete negative emotion states.[20] Instead, adults appear to judge these expressions as reflecting either blends of several negative emotions or a more generalized state of distress. Similar results have been obtained in more recent studies involving judgments of both facial and nonfacial actions.[21,22] Thus at least some of the DET-described facial configurations may be more reasonably interpreted as expressions of qualitatively undifferentiated distress rather than discrete negative emotions.[19,20,22–25]

Taken together, this research strongly suggests that the relation between expression and emotion during infancy is more complex than that described in the differential emotions theory. With respect to negative emotion in particular, infant facial expressions may be relatively undifferentiated. That is, infants may begin with a set of negative facial expressions that they use to express negative emotion—but there may not be a one-to-one correspondence between specific expressions and specific discrete negative emotions. Instead, different negative configurations may reflect different intensities of more generalized distress or attempts to regulate distress, or may result from nonemotional factors that can influence facial behavior (e.g., direction of gaze). Campos, Oster, and Camras have each discussed this elsewhere in the context of distinct but related theoretical perspectives (i.e., differentiation theories;[23,24] dynamical systems approaches;[11,19,17] and functionalist approaches.[26–28] However, there are several limitations to the previous research on which our proposal is based. For example, most previous studies have not addressed the differentiation question by examining the same group of infants in more than one negative emotion situation. Even those studies that have included several negative emotions have used only one eliciting situation for each emotion. In addition, almost all infant studies of negative emotion have been restricted to a European-American sample. In our international collaborative study, we have sought to remedy these problems.

In our collaborative project,[29–31] we are examining both facial expressions and nonfacial behavior produced by 11-month-old Chinese, Japanese, and European-American infants in laboratory situations designed to elicit several different emotions. The two procedures that have been most thoroughly analyzed thus far are nonpainful arm restraint (designed to elicit frustration and/or anger) and growling gorilla presentation (designed to elicit fear). During both procedures, each infant was seated in a high chair while its mother was seated in a chair facing perpendicular to the infant. The mothers remained passive during the stimulus presentation. In the arm restraint procedure, a female experimenter gently grasped the infant's wrists and held them immobile on the tray table for up to 3 minutes. The experimenter was instructed to release the infant's wrists before the time limit if the infant showed 7 seconds of continuous crying. In the growling gorilla procedure, the experimenter placed a toy gorilla head on the table approximately 120 cm from the infant. After 10 seconds, the gorilla was remotely activated and emitted six loud growls (lasting approximately 15 seconds). The experimenter then moved the silent gorilla head 15 cm closer to the infant. This sequence was repeated up to three times but was terminated if the baby cried for more than 7 seconds. Both procedures were videotaped by two cameras, one focused on the infant's face and one showing a wide-angle view of the infant's body and the experimental context.

Observer judgments of the infants' nonfacial emotional reactions were collected in order to assess whether the European-American, Japanese, and Chinese infants were responding to each procedure with the predicted emotion.[29] These data would be potentially useful in interpreting any differences that might be found in their facial behavior. Edited versions of the wide-angle videotapes were created in which the infant's face was electronically deleted. These tapes were viewed (and heard) by American undergraduate students, who rated each baby for nine emotions: frustration, anger, fear, distress, disgust, sadness, surprise, interest, and happiness. For the arm restraint procedure, the ratings for frustration were significantly higher than the ratings for all other emotions. These were followed by the distress and anger ratings, which were both significantly higher than the ratings for the remaining six emotions. The only cultural difference obtained was for the distress ratings, with the American infants being rated significantly higher than the Chinese infants. For the gorilla procedure, fear was rated significantly higher than all other emotions, and there were no significant cultural differences. Comparing across procedures, the arm restraint and growling gorilla presentation each generated significantly higher ratings for its own predicted emotion than did the other procedure. Thus, overall the ratings suggested that the two procedures differentially evoked their intended target emotions in infants from all three cultures. An additional finding was that distress was rated higher during arm restraint than during the growling gorilla presentation. The findings for distress will be further discussed below in relation to the data on facial expression.

The infants' nonfacial behavior was also objectively scored to obtain further evidence that they were responding to each procedure with the predicted emotion. A variety of body movements were examined, including several we thought might be situationally appropriate manifestations of emotion. These were: increased respiration, stilling, withdrawal, struggling, turning toward mother, hiding face, squirming, self-stimulation, looking toward mother, pointing at object, double take, and banging on the tray table. Because behavioral coding is very labor intensive, the procedures were not scored in their entirety. Instead, a baseline interval and a stimulus interval for each procedure were designated for coding. The baseline episode was the 10 seconds immediately preceding the onset of the negative stimulus (i.e., grasping the infant's wrists, growling by the gorilla); the stimulus episode was the first 20 seconds after stimulus onset.

During the arm restraint procedure, significantly more babies struggled, leaned away (i.e., moderate withdrawal) and turned toward mother during the stimulus episode than during the baseline episode. For the growling gorilla procedure, more babies showed increased respiration and bodily stilling during the stimulus episode than during baseline. No significant differences were found between the European-American infants and the Japanese or Chinese infants. Struggling (and possibly leaning away) can be plausibly interpreted as reflecting anger/frustration in the arm restraint situation while bodily stilling and increased respiration can be plausibly interpreted as reflecting fear during the growling gorilla procedure. Thus these findings again suggest that these two procedures differentially evoked anger/frustration and fear in the infants.

The infants' facial expressions were coded using Oster's Facial Action Coding System for Infants and Young Children (BabyFACS).[25] BabyFACs is an infant-appropriate version of Ekman, Friesen, and Hager's anatomically based Facial Action Coding System.[32] In both FACS and BabyFACS, the basic coding units are minimally distinguishable actions of the facial muscles (termed *action units*, or AUs). However, BabyFACS' description of these action units includes consideration of several significant differences between adults' and infants' facial morphology. For example, infant faces have more subcutaneous fat than adult faces, and the relative proportions of cheek, forehead, and chin differ. Thus the same facial muscle movement may look somewhat different in infants and adults.

In recent years, the anatomically based systems FACS and BabyFACS have virtually replaced previous methodologies, in which observers directly applied emotion-based labels to facial behavior, thus recording the subject as producing, for instance, a "happy" or "sad" expression. Such labeling techniques can gloss over individual, situational, and cultural differences in the morphology of such "happy" or "sad" expressions. In addition, such labeling precludes any objective empirical examination of the relationship between an emotion and a particular facial configuration. This is because emotion-based categories embody the assumption that such an invariant relationship exists. Thus, using an objective anatomically based system is important in the study of infants' emotional expressions across both situations and cultures.

Although the maximal detail provided by a raw BabyFACS coding is sometimes desirable, in the current investigation a preliminary clustering of facial actions was performed in order to increase data manageability.[31] Thus some facial actions were grouped together if they often co-occurred or were difficult to visually distinguish and related to the same emotion. In addition, some facial action combinations that occurred infrequently were grouped with combinations that occurred more frequently and are believed to be related to the same emotion. For example, AU 1+3, AU 1+4, and AU 1+3+4 were grouped together because they all produce an oblique brow shape accompanied by brow contraction, and they can all serve as the brow component for the adult prototypic expression of sadness.[32,33] Importantly, distinctions that previous researchers have related to different discrete emotions were retained in the preliminary clustering.

An initial data analysis was performed, focusing simply on the magnitude of the infants' expressive behavior in response to the two procedures.[30] That is, did the infants produce more expressive behavior in response to the arm restraint or the growling gorilla procedure? In addition, were the babies from some cultures more expressive than others? The analysis showed that the amount of time that infants produced some form of facial behavior (i.e., their facial movement time) did not significantly differ across procedures. However, there were cultural differences in that the Chinese infants were less expressive overall than both the American and Japanese infants.

Similar cultural differences were found for two other variables representing infants' overall positive and negative reactions to our procedures—that is, latency to cry mouth and Duchenne-smiling. Chinese infants became upset less quickly than American infants, with the Japanese infants falling in between. This pattern of cultural differences mirrors the pattern of cultural differences found for observers' ratings of distress in the arm restraint situation. Thus observers were perhaps interpreting the infants' crying during arm restraint as an indication of distress. Chinese infants also produced significantly fewer Duchenne-smiles than both the American and Japanese infants. Duchenne-smiles are considered to be smiles of genuine enjoyment in adults.[34,35]

Thus, overall, the American infants were found to be more expressive than the Chinese infants. Furthermore, the Japanese infants tended to react more like American babies than Chinese infants. This pattern of similarities and differences across cultures is noteworthy because it violates stereotypic notions regarding Westerners' vs. Asians' expressive behavior.[36–38] The results showed that there can be significant differences between two Asian cultures (i.e., the Japanese and Chinese infants) as well as similarities between American and Asian groups (i.e., the American and Japanese babies). These observations suggest that scholars should be wary of the current propensity to lump all Asian cultures together using broadly general concepts such as collectivism[39] and that assumptions regarding general East-West differences should be reexamined.

Previous studies have also found that Chinese babies are less emotionally expressive than American infants. Both biological and environmental factors have been proposed to explain these differences. For example, Freedman reported that Chinese-American neonates showed less reactivity and distress during standardized infant testing procedures than did European-American infants.[40] Freedman attributed these findings to innate differences between the ethnic groups. More recently, Kagan *et al.* found similar differences between four-month-old European-American and Chinese infants from Beijing.[41] Like Freedman, Kagan has taken the position that there are inherent ethnic differences in emotional arousal and reactivity.[42]

Differences in expressiveness between Chinese and European-Americans may also be influenced by culture and socialization. Over 30 years ago, Ek-

man described cultural differences in expressive behavior that are due to cul-
ture-specific displays rules—that is, social norms that dictate how and when
a person should display emotions.[8,9] Because humans have voluntary control
over many of the facial muscles, an individual may override his or her spontaneous facial expression and instead inhibit, minimize, exaggerate, or even
falsify an emotional response (e.g., one can smile at funerals). Most psychologists who have studied display rules have focused on children's and adults'
behavior. However, display-rule socialization may start much earlier, perhaps
even during infancy. Cultures are known to differ greatly in their infant-care
practices.[43] In particular, American and Chinese mothers differ in attitudes
and behaviors that might well be expected to affect their infants' expressiveness. For example, American mothers value and encourage emotional expression much more than Chinese mothers.[44,45] Thus the cultural differences in
the amount of expressive behavior found in this investigation may be the result of socialization. One strategy for investigating the relative influences of
biology and environment on emotional expression might involve the study of
ethnic Chinese children raised within European-American families. Towards
this end, a study of emotional expressivity in adopted Chinese children is currently under way.[46]

To return to the differentiation question, the infants' production of facial
expressions was compared across the frustration/anger vs. fear situations.
The initial comparisons involved a subset of the facial action codes generally
acknowledged to indicate negative affect. As indicated earlier, investigators
often differ in terms of what type of negative emotion they associate with a
particular facial expression component when it is displayed by a young infant
(e.g., anger vs. distress for a lowered brow). However, there is widespread
agreement about the set of facial actions that share a negative valence. In this
investigation, the set of negative facial action codes included: (a) brow lowered, (b) brow oblique and contracted, (c) brow raised and contracted, (d)
nose wrinkle and/or upper lip raise (with or without nasolabial fold deepen),
(e) nasolabial fold deepen (without nose wrinkle or upper lip raise), (f) mild-
to-intense cry mouth, (g) horizontal cry mouth or lip stretch, (h) lip corners
depressed with or without chin raise, and (i) modulated negative mouth. Regarding the relation of these movements to adult expression prototypes,[32,33]
brow lowered can occur as a component of the adult prototypic anger expression, whereas brow raised and contracted can be a component of the prototypic fear expression, and brow oblique can be a component of the prototypic
sad expression. Nose wrinkle can be a component of the disgust expression,
whereas nasolabial fold deepen can be a component of sadness. The horizontal cry mouth resembles the mouth component of the fear expression, while
lip corners depressed is a component of sadness. The mild-to-intense cry
mouth configuration would be coded as an "anger" mouth according to the
AFFEX system[7] based on the differential emotions theory. However, while
this mouth configuration resembles a component of the adult anger prototype,

TABLE 1. Difference across procedures in use of negative facial codes (intersituational specificity

Arm Restraint > Growling Gorilla Procedure		Growling Gorilla = Arm Restraint Procedure	
Negative Facial Code	Related Emotion	Negative Facial Code	Related Emotion
Brow lower	anger	modulated negative mouth	distress regulation
Brow oblique, contracted	sadness		
Nose wrinkle	disgust		
Nasolabial fold	sadness		
Lip corners down, chin raise	sadness		
Mild-to-intense cry mouth	anger		
Horizontal cry mouth	fear		
Brow raised, contracted	fear		

it does not include the lip tightening that has been described for adults. Modulated negative mouth includes a set of facial actions that Oster has proposed to reflect the infant's attempt to regulate his or her negative emotion.[25]

In order to address the issue of intersituational specificity, infants' use of each negative code was compared across the arm restraint vs. growling gorilla stimulus episodes (see TABLE 1). Eight of the nine negative movements were produced by more infants during the arm restraint than during the growling gorilla procedure. These included the two fear-related movements (brow raised and contracted, and horizontal cry mouth) as well as the two anger-related movements (brow lowered and mild-to-intense cry mouth). One movement (modulated negative mouth) was produced by the same number of infants in both procedures.

In order to address the issue of intrasituational specificity, infants' use of the several negative codes was also compared within each situation (see TABLE 2). Contrary to expectation, in the anger/frustration situation (arm restraint), brow lower (the anger-related brow) was produced by fewer infants than brow raised and contracted (the fear-related brow) or brow oblique (the sad-related brow). Similarly, more infants produced the fear-related horizontal cry mouth than the anger-related mild-to-intense cry mouth. In the fear procedure (growling gorilla), brows raised and contracted (the fear-related brow) was indeed produced by more infants than the other two brow configurations. However, fewer infants produced the fear-related horizontal cry mouth than the anger-related mild-to-intense cry mouth.

Clearly, these data are not consistent with the proposal that negative emotional facial expression is differentiated in 11-month-old infants as it is believed to be in adults. Although some differentiation across situations did

TABLE 2. Rankings within procedures in use of negative facial codes (intrasituational specificity)

	Arm Restraint Procedure			Growling Gorilla Procedure	
Rank	Negative Facial Code	Related Emotion	Rank	Negative Facial Code	Related Emotion
1	nose wrinkle	disgust	1	brow raised, contracted	fear
2.5	horizontal cry mouth	fear	2	mild-to-intense cry mouth	anger
2.5	brow raised, contracted	fear	3.5	brow oblique, contracted	sadness
4	brow oblique, contracted	sadness	3.5	nose wrinkle	disgust
5.5	brow lower	anger	5	horizontal cry mouth	fear
5.5	mild-to-intense cry mouth	anger	6	nasolabial fold	sadness
7	nasolabial fold	sadness	7.5	brow lower	anger
8	modulated negative mouth	distress regulation	7.5	modulated negative mouth	distress regulation
9	lip corner down, chin raise	sadness	9	lip corner down, chin raise	sadness

NOTE: Identical ranks represent ties.

occur, it occurred for nonpredicted codes as often as for predicted codes. Furthermore, infants did not show preferential use of anger-related brow and mouth movements during arm restraint and of fear-related mouth movements during the growling gorilla procedure.

Because the emotion interpretation of isolated individual movements is sometimes ambiguous,[47] examining facial configurations involving co-occurring movements is important in the analysis of emotional expression. In the present study, brow and cry mouth codes were most distinctly identified with the emotions intended to be elicited by the two procedures and were produced frequently enough for meaningful analysis. Therefore, combinations of the three negative brow codes and the two cry mouth codes were examined with particular focus on those configurations characteristic of the prototypic anger expression (brow lower and mild-to-intense cry mouth) and the prototypic fear expression (brow raised and contracted and horizontal cry mouth). With respect to intersituational specificity (see TABLE 3), more infants produced five out of the six brow and mouth configurations during the arm restraint procedure than during the growling gorilla procedure. These included both the anger-related brow and mouth combination (brow lowered and mild-to-intense cry mouth) and the four combinations that included one anger-related component (either brow lowered or mild-to-intense cry mouth). The

TABLE 3. Differences across procedures in use of negative brow-mouth configurations (intersituational specificity)

Arm Restraint > Growling Gorilla Procedure	Growling Gorilla = Arm Restraint Procedure
Brow lower + mild-to-intense cry mouth (anger-related brow + anger-related mouth)	Brow raised, contracted + horizontal cry mouth (fear-related brow + fear-related mouth)
Brow lower + horizontal cry mouth (anger-related brow + fear-related mouth)	
Brow raised, contracted + mild-to-intense cry mouth (fear-related brow + anger-related mouth)	
Brow oblique, contracted + mild-to-intense cry mouth (sad-related brow + anger-related mouth)	
Brow oblique, contracted + horizontal cry mouth (sad-related brow + fear-related mouth)	

configuration involving both the fear-related brow and the fear-related mouth (brow raised and contracted and horizontal cry mouth) was produced by the same number of babies in both procedures.

In order to address the issue of intrasituational specificity, infants' use of the six possible brow-mouth combinations was also compared within each situation (see TABLE 4). In the arm restraint situation, the anger-related configuration (brow lower and mild-to-intense cry mouth) was indeed produced by the greatest number of infants. However, in the gorilla situation, the configuration produced most often was also the anger-related combination. This was followed by one of the fear-anger "blends" (brow raised and contracted and mild-to-intense cry mouth) and then the fear-related brow-mouth configuration.

Again, these data suggest that these negative brow–cry mouth configurations are not fully differentiated in 11-month-old infants, as they are believed to be in adults. In fact, several findings are also consistent with the proposal that at least some of these configurations may represent more generalized distress rather than discrete emotions. For example, five of the six configurations were used by more infants during arm restraint, the procedure that was rated higher for distress than the gorilla procedure. Furthermore, the anger-related brow-mouth combination was the most frequent combination produced during both the arm restraint and growling gorilla procedures. This combination has also been found to occur most often in a wide variety of other negative emotional situations.[12]

Turning to the question of culture, for our individual codes the proportion of infants producing each code differed somewhat across cultures. In the arm

TABLE 4. Rankings within procedures in use of negative brow–cry mouth configurations (intrasituational specificity)

Arm Restraint Procedure		Growling Gorilla Procedure	
Rank	Negative Configuration	Rank	Negative Configuration
1	Brow lower + mild-to-intense cry mouth (anger-related brow + anger-related mouth)	1	Brow lower + mild-to-intense cry mouth (anger-related brow + anger-related mouth)
2	Brow raised, contracted + mild-to-intense cry mouth (fear-related brow + anger-related mouth	2	Brow raised, contracted + mild-to-intense cry mouth (fear-related brow + anger-related mouth
3	Brow oblique, contracted + mild-to-intense cry mouth (sadness-related brow + anger-related mouth)	3	Brow raised, contracted + horizontal cry mouth (fear-related brow + fear-related mouth)
4	Brow oblique, contracted + horizontal cry mouth (sadness-related brow + fear-related mouth)	4	Brow oblique, contracted + mild-to-intense cry mouth (sadness-related brow + anger-related mouth)
5.5	Brow raised, contracted + horizontal cry mouth (fear-related brow + fear-related mouth)	5	Brow oblique, contracted + horizontal cry mouth (sadness-related brow + fear-related mouth)
5.5	Brow lower + horizontal cry mouth (anger-related brow + fear-related mouth)	6	Brow lower + horizontal cry mouth (anger-related brow + fear-related mouth)

NOTE: Identical ranks represent ties.

restraint procedure, 27 comparisons were made (three pairwise cultural comparisons for each of the nine negative facial components). The average difference between cultures was 19%. In the growling gorilla procedure, the average difference between cultures was 12%. For the comparisons involving the six brow-mouth code combinations, cultural differences in the proportion of infants who showed each combination averaged 12% for the arm restraint situation and 18% for the gorilla procedure.

Do these data suggest that infant emotional expression is not universal but instead differs from culture to culture? Such a conclusion would be unwarranted at the present time. One reason for this avowal is based in part on the observation that infants showed many nonpredicted facial movements as well as predicted facial movements during the experimental procedures. For example, many infants showed brow oblique, a sadness-related movement, and nose wrinkle, a disgust-related movement. Yet the emotions of sadness and disgust were not intended to be elicited, and indeed both emotions were rated extremely low by observers in the judgment study. These apparently disparate findings may possibly be reconciled by considering them in light of previous research on nonemotion factors that can influence facial movement. For example, Michel, Camras, and Sullivan have shown that brow raising systematically occurs when young infants lift their head and/or gaze.[15] This raises the possibility that head and gaze direction may have played a role in producing some of the negative brow movements observed in the present study. The three negative brow codes (brow lower, brow oblique, and brow raised and contracted) all include brow knitting, a form of horizontal contraction produced by the action of the corrugator muscle. However, two of the movements (brow oblique and brow raised and contracted) also involve a brow raise component. Thus cultural differences found for the production of the three negative brow codes may be due to differences in the infants' head and gaze activity, rather than qualitative differences in their negative emotional reactions. More generally, some of the differences in facial movement observed across procedures, cultures, and individuals may be related to a range of nonemotion factors that interact with emotion to determine the specific morphology of infant facial behavior. However, the relations between these factors and infants' facial movements may indeed be universal.

One theoretical framework that can accommodate observations of variability in infant emotional expression is the dynamical systems perspective.[11,19,48–50] According to this view, emotional expressions (and indeed emotional reactions more generally) may be viewed as self-organizing systems in which control is distributed between central influences (emotion) and noncentral factors (e.g., various elements of the context). A distinct but related theoretical perspective is the functionalist approach advanced by Campos and his colleagues.[26–28] According to this approach, emotions are processes that operate in the service of achieving one's desired relational goals with respect to the environment. Therefore, emotional responses may vary depending upon what will serve to achieve these goals in a particular situation. A third perspective, compatible with, but different from, the previous two views, is the differentiation perspective.[20,24,51,52] According to this view, specific discrete emotions and their facial expressions gradually evolve from global, undifferentiated emotional reactions in early infancy. Thus infant emotional expression may be less differentiated at first because their emotional experience is less differentiated. Which negative configuration infants show may be partly determined by the intensity of their more generalized distress response.[19,25] In addition, Oster has proposed that some infant expressive components may be related to the modulation of distress (i.e., the modulated negative mouth components).[53,54]

The findings from this collaborative study raise an interesting question about the problem of understanding infant emotions. If there is not a one-to-one relationship between discrete emotions and specific facial expressions in infants, how can we reliably determine what babies are feeling? Fortunately, this lack of invariant concordance between emotion and expression would not be an insurmountable impediment to understanding emotion. Observers could still accurately read infants' emotions by interpreting their facial and nonfacial behaviors together within a particular situational context. For example, observers might discount some anomalous facial movements (e.g., sad-related brows in a nonsad situation) just as they discount nongenuine adult emotional expressions that are produced in response to known social display rules. Such discounting does not imply that facial expressions are unimportant in the judgment of emotion. Instead, facial expressions may be seen as critically important components within a larger pattern of emotion cues that observers perceive and integrate in the process of making an emotion judgment. Human beings are in essence pattern-processing organisms, exquisitely tuned to the complex patterning of their environment and easily capable of accurately responding to a multiply determined behavioral output system such as emotional expression.[55]

In conclusion, the current study suggests that the relationship between infant emotion and infant facial expression is more complex than previously proposed. More important, there does not seem to be an invariant relationship between specific discrete emotions and specific facial configurations, at least within the first year of life. In addition, negative emotional expressions are not fully differentiated, at least within the first year. Several alternative theoretical approaches are being explored that can accommodate the data. In addition, several directions for further research may also be identified. As part of the project described here, future coding and analyses will determine whether the patterns of situational and cultural differences found for the arm restraint and growling gorilla procedures are replicated when the second anger procedure (toy removal) and the second fear procedure (stranger approach) are examined. In addition, systematic relationships between infants' facial movements and both emotion and nonemotion factors will be sought. In this way, a more complete understanding of infant emotional expression will eventually be achieved.

REFERENCES

1. DARWIN, C. 1877. A biographical sketch of an infant. Mind **1**: 285–294.
2. DARWIN, C. 1887. The Autobiography of Charles Darwin. John Murray. London.
3. DARWIN, C. [1872] 1998. The Expression of the Emotions in Man and Animals. Reprinted with introduction, afterword, and commentary by P. Ekman. John Murray. London.
4. IZARD, C. 1991. The Psychology of Emotions. Plenum. New York.
5. IZARD, C. & C. MALATESTA. 1987. Perspectives on emotional development I: differential emotions theory of early emotional development. *In* Handbook of Infant Development. J.D. Osofsky, Ed.: 494–554. Wiley. New York.
6. IZARD, C. 1979. The maximally discriminative facial movement coding system (MAX). University of Delaware, Instructional Resources Center. Newark, DE.

7. IZARD, C., L. DOUGHERTY & E. HEMBREE. 1983. A system for identifying affect expressions by holistic judgments (AFFEX). Instructional Resources Center, University of Delaware. Newark, DE.

8. EKMAN, P. 1972. Universals and cultural differences in facial expressions of emotion. *In* Nebraska Symposium on Motivation, 1971: Vol 19: Current Theory and Research in Motivation. J. Cole, Ed.: 207–283. University of Nebraska Press. Lincoln, NE.

9. EKMAN, P. & W.V. FRIESEN. 1969. The repertoire of nonverbal behavior: categories, origins, usage, and coding. Semiotica **1:** 49–98.

10. IZARD, C. 1997. Emotions and facial expressions: a perspective from differential emotions theory. *In* The Psychology of Facial Expression. J. Russell & J. M. Fernandez-Dols, Eds.: 57–77. Cambridge University Press. Cambridge.

11. CAMRAS, L.A. 1991. Conceptualizing early infant affect: view II and reply. *In* International Review of Studies on Emotion. K. Strongman, Ed.: 16–28, 33–36. John Wiley. New York.

12. CAMRAS, L.A., C. MALATESTA & C. IZARD. 1991. The development of facial expressions in infancy. *In* Fundamentals of Nonverbal Behavior. R. Feldman & B. Rime, Eds.: 73–105. Cambridge. Cambridge University Press.

13. CAMRAS, L.A., L. LAMBRECHT & G. MICHEL. 1996. Infant "surprise" expressions as coordinative motor structures. J. Nonverb. Behav. **20:** 183–195.

14. MATIAS, R. & J. COHN. 1993. Are MAX-specified infant facial expressions during face-to-face interaction consistent with differential emotions theory? Dev. Psychol. **29:** 524–531.

15. MICHEL, G., L. CAMRAS & J. SULLIVAN. 1992. Infant interest expressions as coordinative motor structures. Infant Behav. Dev. **15:** 347–358.

16. HIATT, S., J. CAMPOS & R. EMDE. 1979. Facial patterning and infant emotional expression: happiness, surprise, and fear. Child Dev. **50:** 1020–1035.

17. CAMRAS, L.A. 2000. Surprise!: facial expressions can be coordinative motor structures. *In* Emotion, Development and Self-Organization. M. Lewis & I. Granic, Eds.: 100–124. Cambridge University Press. New York.

18. CAMRAS, L.A., Z. MENG, T. UJIIE, *et al.* 2002. Observing emotion in infants: facial expression, body behavior, and rater judgments of responses to an expectancy-violating event. Emotion **2:** 179–193.

19. CAMRAS, L.A. 1992. Expressive development and basic emotions. Cogn. Emotion **6:** 269–284.

20. OSTER, H., D. HEGLEY & L. NAGEL. 1992. Adult judgments and fine-grained analysis of infant facial expressions: testing the validity of *a priori* coding formulas. Dev. Psych. **28:** 1115–1131.

21. CAMRAS, L.A., J. SULLIVAN & G. MICHEL. 1993. Do infants express discrete emotions? Adult judgments of facial, vocal, and body actions. J. Nonverb. Behav. **17:** 171–186.

22. SULLIVAN, J. 2002. Adult Perceptions of Infant Facial Expressions and Behavior. Unpublished doctoral dissertation.

23. FRIDLUND, A., P. EKMAN & H. OSTER. 1987. Facial expressions of emotion: review of literature. *In* Nonverbal Behavior and Communications. A. Siegman & S. Feldstein, Eds.: 143–224. Lawrence Erlbaum Associates. Hillsdale, NJ.

24. OSTER, H. 1997. Facial expression as a window on sensory experience and affect in newborn infants. *In* What the Face Reveals: Basic and Applied Stud-

ies of Spontaneous Expression using the Facial Action Coding System (FACS). P. Ekman & E. Rosenberg, Eds.: 320–327. Oxford University Press. New York.

25. OSTER, H. 2002. Baby FACS: Facial Action Coding System for Infants and Young Children. Unpublished monograph and coding manual. New York University. New York.

26. BARRETT, K. & J. CAMPOS. 1987. Perspectives on emotional development II: a functionalist approach to emotions. *In* Handbook of Infant Development. J. Osofsky, Ed.: 555–578. Wiley. New York.

27. CAMPOS, J., D. MUMME, R. KERMOIAN & R. CAMPOS. 1994. A functionalist perspective on the nature of emotion. The development of emotion regulation. Monogr. Soc. Res. Child Dev. **59:** 284–303.

28. SAARNI, C., D. MUMME & J. CAMPOS. 1998. Emotional development: action, communication, and understanding. *In* Handbook of Child Psychology: Vol. 3. Social, Emotional, and Personality Development. W. Damon & N. Eisenberg, Eds.: 237–310. Wiley. New York.

29. CAMRAS, L.A., H. OSTER, J. CAMPOS, *et al.* 1997. Observer judgments of emotion in American, Japanese, and Chinese infants. *In* New Directions in Child Development: No. 4. The Communication of Emotion. W. Damon & K. Barrett, Eds.: 89–105. Jossey-Bass. San Francisco.

30. CAMRAS, L.A., H. OSTER, J. CAMPOS, *et al.* 1998. Production of emotional facial expressions in American, Japanese, and Chinese infants. Dev. Psychol. **34:** 616–628.

31. CAMRAS, L.A., H. OSTER, R. BAKEMAN, *et al.* 2002. Chinese, Japanese, and European-American infants' facial expressions in two negative emotion situations. In preparation.

32. EKMAN, P., W.V. FRIESEN & J. HAGER. 2002. Facial Action Coding System (FACS). Network Information Research Corporation. Salt Lake City, UT.

33. EKMAN, P. & W.V. FRIESEN. 1975. Unmasking the Face. Prentice Hall. Englewood Cliffs, NJ.

34. EKMAN, P., R. DAVIDSON & W.V. FRIESEN. 1990. The Duchenne-smile: emotional expression and brain physiology: II. J. Pers. Soc. Psychol. **58:** 342–353.

35. FRANK, M., P. EKMAN, & W. FRIESEN. 1993. Behavioral markers and recognizability of the smile of enjoyment. J. Pers. Soc. Psych. **64:** 83–93.

36. KLINEBERG, O. 1938. Emotional expression in Chinese literature. J. Abnorm. Soc. Psychol. **33:** 517–520.

37. MATSUMOTO, D. 1996. Unmasking Japan. Stanford University Press. Stanford, CA.

38. MATSUMOTO, D. 2001. Culture and emotion. *In* Handbook of Culture and Psychology. D. Matsumoto, Ed.: 171–194. Oxford University Press. New York.

39. TRIANDIS, H.C. 1975. Individualism and Collectivism. Westview Press. Boulder, CO.

40. FREEDMAN, D.G. 1974. Human Infancy: An Evolutionary Perspective. Halsted Press. New York.

41. KAGAN, J., D. ARCUS, N. SNIDMAN, *et al.* 1994. Reactivity in infants: a cross-national comparison. Dev. Psychol. **30:** 342–345.

42. KAGAN, J. 1998. Biology and the child. *In* Handbook of Child Psychology: Vol. 3. Social, Emotional and Personality Development. W. Damon & N. Eisenberg, Eds.: 177–235. Wiley. New York.

43. HARKNESS, S. & C. SUPER. 2002. Culture and parenting. *In* Handbook of Parenting. Vol. 2. Biology and Ecology of Parenting. M. Bornstein, Ed.: 353–380. Erlbaum. Mahwah, NJ.
44. KAGAN, J., R. KEARSLEY & P. ZELAZO. 1978. Infancy: Its Place in Human Development. Harvard University Press. Cambridge, MA.
45. KUCHNER, J. 1989. Chinese-American and European-American mothers and infants: cultural influences in the first three months of life. Paper presented at the Meeting of the Society for Research in Child Development, Kansas City, MO.
46. CAMRAS, L.A., Y. CHEN, K. NORRIS, *et al.* 2002. Emotional expression in adopted Chinese, Chinese-American, European-American, and Chinese children. In preparation.
47. EKMAN, P. 1979. About brows: emotional and conversational signals. *In* Human Ethology. M. von Cranach, K. Foppa, W. Lepenies & D. Ploog, Eds.: 169–202. Cambridge University Press. Cambridge.
48. CAMRAS, L.A. 1994. Two aspects of emotional development: expression and elicitation. *In* The Nature of Emotion. P. Ekman & R. Davidson, Eds.: 347–351. New York. Oxford University Press.
49. FOGEL, A. & E. THELEN. 1987. The development of early expressive and communicative action. Dev. Psychol. **23:** 747–761.
50. FOGEL, A., E. NWOKAH, J. DEDO, *et al.* 1992. Social process theory of emotion: a dynamic systems approach. Soc. Dev. **1:** 122–142.
51. BRIDGES, K.M.B. 1932. Emotional development in early infancy. Child Dev. **3:** 324–341.
52. SROUFE, L.A. 1996. Emotional Development. Cambridge University Press. New York.
53. Oster, H. 1982. Pouts and horseshoe-mouth faces: their determinants, affective meaning and signal value in infants. Paper presented at the International Conference on Infant Studies, Austin, TX.
54. OSTER, H. & P. EKMAN. 1978. Facial behavior in child development. *In* Minnesota Symposia on Child Psychology, Vol. 11. A. Collins, Ed.: 231–276. Erlbaum. Hillsdale, NJ.
55. ANDERSON, J. 2000. Cognitive Psychology and Its Implications. Worth Publishers. New York.

Aging, Emotion, and Evolution

The Bigger Picture

LAURA L. CARSTENSEN AND CORINNA E. LÖCKENHOFF

Department of Psychology, Stanford University, Stanford, California 94305, USA

ABSTRACT: Ample empirical evidence shows that basic cognitive processes integral to learning and memory suffer with age. Explanations for age-related loss typically cite the absence of evolutionary selection pressures during the postreproductive years, which consequently failed to optimize functioning during old age. In this paper, we suggest that evolutionary pressures did operate at older ages and that an evolutionary account is entirely consistent with the pattern of findings currently available in the psychological literature on aging. Cognitive loss is limited primarily to new learning, yet integrated world knowledge increases with age. In addition, socioemotional regulation improves with age, which is associated with increased investment in emotionally meaningful others (most notably kin). In this chapter, we argue that this profile of late-life characteristics contributes to the reproductive success of kin. We consider how the uniquely human ability to monitor place in the life cycle and the consequent motivational shifts that occur when boundaries in time are perceived contribute to the adaptive value of long life. Finally, we suggest that joint consideration of evolutionary theory and life-span psychology can lead to fruitful advances in the understanding of human aging.

KEYWORDS: aging; evolutionary theory; cognitive loss; socioemotional regulation; socioemotional selectivity theory

INTRODUCTION

Aging is generally conceptualized as a process of decline. Much psychological research supports this view.[a] Over the course of decades, findings

---

[a]Old age generally refers to the period in life that begins at 65 years. Although this custom obscures changes that occur throughout old age, we adhere to the practice in this chapter because the main focus of our argument about inclusive fitness is the phenomenon of survival beyond menopause and not age differences within older age groups. We acknowledge, however, that the young-old differ notably from the old-old, and positive outcomes in old age are less strong in the very old.

Address for correspondence: Laura L. Carstensen, Department of Psychology, Stanford University, Jordan Hall, Building 420, 450 Serra Mall, Stanford, CA 94305. Voice: 650-723-3102; 650-725-5699.

llc@psych.stanford.edu

Ann. N.Y. Acad. Sci. 1000: 152–179 (2003). © 2003 New York Academy of Sciences.
doi: 10.1196/annals.1280.008

from cognitive psychology have shown that basic cognitive processes integral to learning and memory suffer with age. Working memory—namely, the ability to keep multiple pieces of information in mind while acting on them—declines with age.[1] Speed of information processing slows as well, and the ability to inhibit certain kinds of information while one directs attention elsewhere also deteriorates.[2,3] Although experience-based knowledge continues to increase over time, processing new information takes longer and in certain circumstances is somewhat degraded in quality. These changes are highly reliable, occur gradually and steadily across adulthood, and are seen in virtually everyone, regardless of sex, race, or educational background.[4] Evidence suggests that, in all likelihood, these effects are accounted for by normative age-related changes in the efficiency of neurotransmission.[5]

As bad as this news is, important qualifications are necessary. First, on the basis of a broad review of research findings in this area, a National Research Council committee recently concluded that performance on purely cognitive processes, as measured in the laboratory, does not map perfectly (or arguably even well) onto performance in everyday life.[6] In other words, individual differences on tests administered in the laboratory, while predicting how well people will perform on very similar laboratory tasks, do not predict very well how individuals fare generally in daily life. Most likely, some of the discrepancy occurs because by later adulthood people engage in well-practiced activities of daily routines. Second, although new learning is no longer central, it can be accomplished with sufficient practice. A now-classic study reported by Baltes and Kliegel[7] (see also Kliegel & Baltes[8]) showed that older people's memory performance benefited from practice so much that after relatively few practice sessions, older people performed as well as younger people who had not practiced. Research also shows that in areas where older people have considerable expertise (e.g., life planning and life management), age-related decline is minimal into the 80s.[9] Hence, it is primarily new learning and speed of processing that suffer with age, while everyday functioning and previously acquired knowledge are maintained.

Moreover, social and emotional functioning appear to *improve* with age.[10] Subjective well-being is as good, if not better, in older people as in their younger counterparts. Negative emotions are experienced less frequently and positive emotional experiences are as frequent,[11] if not more frequent,[12] in the old as in the young. Importantly, older people are more satisfied with their social relationships than younger people, especially regarding relationships with their children and younger relatives.[13–15]

Generally speaking, psychologists have considered the juxtaposition of emotional improvements with physical and cognitive decline in the later years as perplexing. How can people fare as well as they do given well-documented declines? The phrase "paradox of aging" has been coined to refer to the pattern of relatively high life satisfaction coupled with physical and cognitive decline. Considerable research attention has focused on possible psychological mechanisms that could account for the ostensible paradox. Phenomena such as the lowering of expectations,[16] downward social comparison,[17] and outright denial[18] are among those that have been empirically investigated. In other words, there is widespread suspicion among social scientists that the apparent socioemotional gains in later life actually reflect forms of coping with loss.[19]

Such reasoning occurs against a backdrop of assumptions in psychology that evolution failed to act on the postreproductive years. Schulz and Heckhausen[20] ground their developmental theory of primary and secondary control in evolutionary principles, asserting that decline in later adulthood reflects the fact that "there are no selection mechanisms available for altering the program during postreproductive years"(p. 246).[21] Reasoning on similar grounds about the "incomplete architecture of human ontogeny," Baltes concludes that "any theory of life span development that were to posit general positive advances across broad domains of functioning in later adulthood can be judged to be false" (p. 369).[22]

We contend that widely held beliefs that evolutionary selection acted minimally on old age are based on two erroneous presumptions. One, they overlook the fact that although average life expectancy at birth throughout most of our evolutionary history was only about 27 years, high rates of infant mortality greatly skewed the age distribution in the population. Even among modern-day hunter-gatherers such as the !Kung in Southern Africa, only about 60% of children reach adulthood.[23] Yet, life expectancy in adulthood is quite a different matter. Paleodemographic estimates of our ancestors' life expectancies[24] and estimates of present-day hunter and gatherer societies are quite similar, with about 30% of adult females living beyond menopause and a remaining life expectancy of 30 to 35 years at the age of 20.[23,25,26] Thus, a significant minority of postreproductive adults lived among our ancestors.

Second, the presence of even small numbers of older people—if systematically linked to gene survival—could have important implications for evolution. As Darwin wrote in the *On the Origin of Species*, "Can we doubt (remembering that many more individuals are born than can possibly survive) that individuals having any advantage, however slight, over others would have the best chance of surviving and procreating over other kinds?" (pp. 80–81).[27] To the extent that older people have been invested in the welfare of younger offspring, their presence could have contributed powerfully to the inclusive fitness of their genes. These ideas are not new in the anthropological literature, where grandparents, especially grandmothers, are presumed to have played an essential role in the support of young children throughout our ancestral history.[26,28–30] However, these ideas have not filtered into the literature on life span development. In this chapter, we revisit possible evolutionary influences on the postreproductive years and argue that the broad pattern of psychological findings about later life is not paradoxical, but rather offers a notably coherent profile of findings. Essentially, we contend that evolution may not have acted on *new* learning in late life—that is, the area where age-related decline is widely documented—not because evolution failed *broadly* to act on older ages, but rather because the relatively stable environments in which our ancestors evolved presented little demand for new learning in the fifth and sixth decades of life and beyond. By contrast, evolutionary selection should have *favored* skills that help older people help others. From this perspective, findings that old age is characterized both by large stores of knowledge about the world and everyday life, and social and emotional investment in younger kin, are hardly paradoxical. Postreproductive adults would be expected to increase their descendants' chances of survival if they were emotionally balanced, knowledgeable about social relationships and the world in general, and invested in social cohesion.

Hence, we argue that the paradox of aging is not a paradox at all, and from this starting point we turn to a consideration of life span theory of motivation. In evolutionary terms, older adults hold adaptive value only if they contribute to the reproductive success of younger kin. In short, older people have to selectively "care." Before proceeding, we should acknowledge that higher-order cognition need not be invoked to explain evolutionary advantages of older kin. Benefits of grandparents in other long-lived species have been well documented. In colonies of vervet monkeys, for example, the presence of a grandmother in a group increases reproductive success.[31,32] Also, fossil evidence suggests that the adaptive shift towards grandmothering occurred long before substantial increases in hominid brain size.[26] Thus, even in the absence of higher-order cognition grandparental investment may benefit younger offspring. However, in humans, grandparenting involves the use and transmission of specialized world knowledge and requires higher-level cognitive skills. We argue that the cognitive mechanisms and psychological processes associated with human grandparenting likely reflect evolutionary selection.[33]

On the one hand, human grandparenting behavior, like most other human behavior, is highly variable, responsive to subtle environmental changes and marked by great flexibility. Indeed, the absence of strictly determined scripts is the hallmark of human behavior.[34] On the other hand, the readiness to provide support to grandchild offspring has been remarkably consistent throughout our ancestral history, suggesting that there may be a built-in preparedness or readiness to act on the behalf of younger relatives. In this chapter we consider what age-linked, heritable psychological mechanisms may promote actions that enhance the welfare of others as people age. Consistent with Kaplan's life history theory,[35,36] we suggest that higher-order cognitive processes such as the ability to monitor time coevolved with increased life expectancy in humans and function as universal triggers that influence motivation. Specifically, we propose that when people perceive constraints on time left in life, motivation shifts from goals related to personal advancement to goals that benefit others.

Below we describe socioemotional selectivity theory, a life span theory of motivation premised on the uniquely human ability to monitor place in the life cycle, and suggest that it may contribute answers to questions about why older people care. After reviewing empirical evidence that supports the essential postulates of the theory, we return to the broader profile of findings about human ontogeny and consider them from the vantage point of evolutionary theory.

SOCIOEMOTIONAL SELECTIVITY THEORY

Socioemotional selectivity theory[37–39] asserts that goals are always set within temporal contexts, and that goal selection depends fundamentally on the perception of time. The monitoring of time is so basic to human functioning that it was likely instrumental in the evolution of human thought and cognition.[40] Markings engraved in ancestral bones dating back to the Ice Age reflect systematic recordings of a lunar calendar,[41] and the sophistication of Aztec sundials reveals that time has been interwoven into the social and political fabrics of societies for centuries. People are always aware of time—not only of clock and calendar time, but also of lifetime.[42] Biologist John Medina writes,

> When contemplating life we inevitably assume the presence of an internal clock. Wound to zero at birth, it incessantly and inherently ticks away during our entire terrestrial tenure. So solid are these concepts in our mind that we have coined the term, "life span" to denote its boundaries [p. 9].[43]

When time is perceived as largely open-ended, goals that prepare the individual for a long and nebulous future are prioritized, such as expanding horizons, meeting new people, and being drawn to novel information. When boundaries on time are perceived, goal hierarchies are reorganized such that emotionally meaningful goals in the present moment are prioritized over goals that aim to shape the future. In the absence of a long future, goals that are realized in their very pursuit, such as the goal of feeling satisfied, gain in importance. For most people, such goals are realized in the context of social relationships with highly familiar and emotionally significant social partners.

Socioemotional selectivity theory categorizes goals into two main clusters. One concerns goals related to expanding horizons, such as acquiring knowledge or making new social contacts. The second comprises goals related to emotional meaning, including feeling states or sensing that one is needed by others.[b] Theoretically, in situations where goals compete with one

---

[b]We acknowledge that the emotion system is inherent in all goal-directed behavior whether goals involve seeking novel information or meaning in life. Approach and avoidance always involve the affective system.[44] Subsequently, classifying some social motives as "emotionally meaningful" and others as "knowledge-related" is, in some ways, artificial, but the distinction is intended heuristically to distinguish between goals that are pursued because of the accompanying feelings that ensue and goals that are pursued to obtain novel information or experience.

another, a principal mechanism involved in goal selection is time perspective. When time is perceived as open-ended, expansive goals are pursued. When boundaries on time are perceived, emotionally meaningful goals are pursued, presumably because the payoff is in the process of goal pursuit itself, not promised at some nebulous time in the future.[c] Because of the inextricable association between time left in life and chronological age, age-related patterns in motivation emerge. Older adults generally foresee a relatively limited future, whereas younger adults envision a relatively expansive one.[45] Importantly, the theory contends and empirical evidence suggests that time perspective, not age *per se*, influences goal selection. Changes in goal hierarchies can be produced at any age in adulthood when stimuli that prime endings are encountered. Hence, to a degree, time perspective is malleable. However, because age is strongly correlated with time perspective,[45,46] the theory posits clear developmental trajectories for psychological goals. Early in life, time is typically perceived as expansive, and people are motivated to prepare for a long and unknown future. Because of this future orientation, developing organisms allocate considerable resources to obtaining knowledge and developing new skills. Because knowledge striving is so important from late adolescence to middle adulthood, it is pursued relentlessly even at the cost of emotional satisfaction. In contrast, older people see fewer opportunities awaiting them and perceive less time available to benefit from purely knowledge-related goals. Developmentally, the knowledge trajectory starts high during the early years of life and declines gradually over the life course as knowledge accrues and the future for which it is banked grows ever shorter.

Phenomenologically speaking, as people move through life they become increasingly aware that time is in some sense "running out." New social contacts come to feel superficial—even trivial—in contrast to the ever-deepening ties of existing close relationships. It becomes more important to make the "right" choices in life and not to waste time on gradually diminishing future payoffs. Increasingly, emotionally meaningful goals that are satisfied by the resulting feeling state itself are pursued because they are experienced immediately, a valuable commodity in the face of limited time. For the vast majority of people, such goals are achieved in the context of close social relationships, usually with kin. As people realize that they are gradually approaching the end of life—something only humans can do—they care more about experiencing meaningful social ties and less about expanding their horizons. This motivational shift leads to a greater investment in the quality of important social relationships and a generally enhanced appreciation of life.

---

[c]When goals do not compete—for example, when working on a personally meaningful research project—the theory predicts only that motivation for the behavior would be very high at any age.

EMPIRICAL SUPPORT FOR SOCIOEMOTIONAL SELECTIVITY THEORY

Socioemotional selectivity theory generates three central postulates: (1) goals are causally influenced by future time perspective; (2) emotionally salient goals favor attention and memory for material that promotes current well-being; and (3) pursuing emotional meaning in the present benefits psychological well-being and the effective regulation of social relationships. In this section we review empirical evidence for each of these postulates.

Perceived Time and Social Choices

Our research team has conducted a series of studies examining age differences in social goals, based on participants from diverse cultures, including the United States,[47] Hong Kong (ref. 48, studies 2 & 4), Taiwan, and Mainland China.[46] In each of these studies, participants were asked to imagine that they had half an hour of free time with no pressing commitments and to choose one from among three potential social partners. Options were: (1) a member of your immediate family; (2) the author of a book you have read; or (3) an acquaintance with whom you seem to have much in common.[d] These three prospective social partners were selected because they service different goals related, respectively, to deriving emotional meaning, gaining information, and expanding social horizons. In every one of these studies, when simply asked about their preferences, older adults, but not their younger counterparts, showed a strong preference for spending time with familiar social partners.

Important exceptions occurred when time perspective was altered, in both hypothetical and real-life situations. When asked to imagine a recent medical advance virtually insuring an active life 20 years beyond their expectations, older adults showed an increased preference for novel social partners.[47] And younger adults, asked to imagine an impending geographical move, shifted preferences, such that they displayed the same preferences for familiar partners observed in older adults.[48] Outside of the laboratory, this phenomenon has been observed in more ecologically valid paradigms. Even macrolevel sociopolitical endings instigate shifts in social goals. When Hong Kong was returned from British rule to the People's Republic of China in 1997, there was a widely held view among the people of Hong Kong that the return represented the end to Hong Kong as they knew it. Calendars that marked the number

---

[d]An alternate set of social partner options, featuring "an old friend," "a friendly new roommate/housemate," "a famous person you admire," shows the same pattern of results.

of days until the transition were popular, and political commentaries featured cartoons suggesting the end of Hong Kong. One year prior to the handover, Hong Kong citizens were asked to choose among three potential social partners. The same age differences that were observed in the United States emerged. Older people showed a strong preference for emotionally close social partners, but younger people did not. Two months prior to the handover, as the ending approached, younger adults exhibited the same bias for well-known social partners as older adults. Interestingly, age differences reappeared after the peaceful handover had occurred, which one woman characterized as the "rebirth of Hong Kong."[48] There is considerable anecdotal evidence that in the United States and elsewhere September 11, 2001 functioned as a powerful "endings" prime and that people's goals changed such that emotionally close social partners were preferred and emotionally meaningful goals were more likely to be pursued. Fung[49] documented this shift empirically in a sample of Hong Kong citizens shortly after September 11, 2001. In summary, there is a robust and reliable preference for spending time with familiar social partners when endings are primed. This is the case when time perspective is limited experimentally or when political or traumatic events in life prime endings.

Goals Influence Cognitive Processing

Socioemotional selectivity theory posits that the age-associated motivational shift towards emotional goals extends beyond conscious preferences. Goals also influence subconscious processes by directing attentional and encoding processes. As Zajonc[44] has argued, even basic cognitive processes such as categorization reflect dimensions of life that *matter*. Following such logic, Fredrickson and Carstensen[47] studied mental representations of social partners in older and younger adults. Of interest were the dimensions that people used to categorize others and the relative weight placed on these dimensions by younger and older adults. Research participants, who ranged from adolescents to octogenarians, categorized a set of 18 prospective social partners according to how similarly they would feel interacting with them. Three general dimensions were revealed by the sorts: an emotional or "like/dislike" dimension, an informational dimension, and a dimension characterized by future possibilities. Older people weighted the emotional dimension most heavily, followed by middle-aged and younger people. In a subsequent study, a sample of young men were examined.[50] All of the men were gay, some were HIV negative, some HIV positive but asymptomatic, and some HIV positive and symptomatic. The men who were HIV positive and symptomatic—actuarially closest to the end of their lives—weighted the emotional dimension most heavily and performed the card sorts indistinguishably from older people. Once again, these findings suggest that closeness to the end of life, not chronological age, leads to the motivational shift posited in socioemotional selectivity theory, even as reflected in areas that are under less conscious control, such as cognitive categorization.

Further, when emotional goals are prioritized, emotional material is weighted more heavily—attended to more readily, processed more deeply, and better remembered—than nonemotional material. Although rarely conceptualized as a self-regulatory process, the events, people, and places that individuals retrieve from memory clearly influence well-being. And, of course, memory itself is not simply a process of retrieval, but an elaborative process by which current goals influence constructions of the past.[51]

An age-associated focus on emotional information has been found on a number of memory tasks. Using an incidental memory paradigm, people aged 20–83 years read a narrative drawn from a popular novel and were later asked to recall as much as they could from the passage. Of what people remembered, the proportion of emotional information, as opposed to neutral information, increased with each successively older age group.[52] Moreover, in a study asking people to describe a past vacation, older couples provided more information on the subjective aspects, such as descriptions of people, and less information on the factual aspects, such as itineraries, than younger couples.[53] Similarly, younger people recalled more sensory and perceptual details about imagined and real experiences, but older adults recalled a greater number of feelings and evaluative statements.[54] When memory for music was examined, older adults rated songs from their youth as more emotional and remembered those songs better than younger adults.[55] Older people were also more likely to remember advertisements with emotional slogans, like "Capture those special moments" than information-related slogans, like "Capture the unexplored world." They also preferred the emotional framing of the advertisements more than younger adults.[56]

Because decline in attention and working memory have been well established in older adults, it is conceivable that decreased cognitive control[57] and/or disinhibition[3] play a role in age differences. That is, emotional disinhibition could interfere with the retrieval of other types of information. Emotional memories may flood output, not because they are more highly prioritized, but because they cannot be inhibited. Memory difficulties could also lead people to rely more heavily on gist memory, which tends to be more affectively laden (e.g., remembering it was a good party, but few of the details of the party). However, a general disinhibition hypothesis cannot account for well-preserved memory in specific circumstances. In a recent study of source memory, age differences disappeared when the source was emotionally significant.[58] Source memory refers to the ability to remember in what context an event or item was learned or experienced. For example, if I know I heard the movie was good, but I can't recall who told me, I experience a failure of source memory. There is considerable evidence that older people have poorer source memory than younger people and recall fewer contextual details than younger adults.[59,60] Rahhal and her colleagues tested the hypothesis that some sources are more relevant than others and that a person's character may be particularly important to older adults. In one condition, participants were required to source a series of statements associated with the name John or Mary. In another condition, they were required to source a series of statements made by an honest or a dishonest person. As predicted, age differences were evident when the source was simply a name, but disappeared when the source concerned character.[58]

Moreover, disinhibition cannot explain why the type of emotional information recalled by older adults is disproportionately positive. When recalling previously presented positive, negative, and neutral images, the proportion of correctly recognized and recalled negative images declines linearly with age across younger, middle aged, and older adults.[61] The age difference extends to autobiographical memory as well. Older age is related to a tendency to underestimate the intensity of sadness experienced in the past.[62] In addition, when asked to recall the single most important experience in their moral development, older adults are more likely to cite a positive episode than are adolescents and young adults.[63] In a longitudinal study, asking people to recall their childhood at different points in their lives, memories became increasingly positive with age.[64] This reduced emphasis on negative events and increased emphasis on positive events may be one reason why reminiscence—the process of recalling personal memories—is experienced more positively for older than younger adults.[65] Such memory patterns are likely to optimize emotional experience by reducing regret and increasing satisfaction with past decisions.

One recent study documents age differences in attention as well.[66] Older and younger participants were presented with a pair of faces on a computer screen. One of the faces was neutral, and the other was happy, sad, or angry. The faces were presented for 500 ms, then they disappeared, and a dot probe appeared on either side of the screen. Participants were required to press a key indicating on which side of the screen the dot probe had appeared. Differential response speeds to emotional and neutral faces indicated that the participants were systematically attending to one type of facial expression. As hypothesized, older adults responded fastest to happy faces, suggesting that older people are drawn to the positive faces, whereas younger adults did not show a systematic preference for one face type. Participants in this study were given a memory task for the faces as well, and older participants disproportionately remembered the positive faces.

In short, age differences in goals are associated with age differences in categorization, attention, and memory, with older adults placing greater emphasis on emotionally meaningful and positively valenced material. Socioemotional selectivity theory further suggests that selecting emotionally relevant goals should benefit mental health, a point to which we turn below.

The Pursuit of Emotionally Meaningful Goals Is Good for Psychological Well-Being and Social Relations

Early models of emotion and aging so strongly presumed the same downward course that is observed in cognitive and biological aging that empirical investigation was nearly absent. However, population-based studies of psychiatric disorders have revealed lower rates of depression and anxiety in older adults than in their younger counterparts.[67–69] Moreover, national and international studies of well-being and satisfaction with life have found that older people are at least as satisfied with life as younger people.[70,71] As longitudinal studies have come of age, they, too, show in multiple cohorts that the frequency of negative affect decreases over time while positive affect remains markedly stable.[72] Older people express fewer worries about finances and social events,[73] experience less anger,[74] and have lower levels of emotional distress after natural disasters.[75]

Asked directly about emotion regulation, older people representing diverse groups—including African and European Americans, Chinese Americans, Norwegians, and American nuns—consistently report better control of negative emotions than their younger counterparts.[76] One study that sampled emotional experiences in day-to-day life found that *negative* emotions decline steadily until approximately age 60 (at which point they level off), but that age is unrelated to the frequency and intensity of *positive* emotions.[11] Another study found modest increases in positive emotion from middle adulthood to early old age.[12] Thus, the overall ratio of positive to negative emotions improves over the life span.

Studies of emotion regulation under more naturalistic conditions provide additional evidence for age-associated improvements. Findings from the experience sampling study mentioned above indicate that the intensity of experienced negative emotion is similar across different age groups. However, once a negative mood state is experienced, older adults are quicker to return to more positive states than are younger people.[11] An observational study of older married couples sheds some light on possible emotion-regulatory strategies older people may use to reduce negative experience. When discussing a conflict in their relationship, older couples, as compared to their middle-aged counterparts, exhibit less physiological reactivity[77] and express less anger, belligerence, and disgust and more affection for one another.[78] This is true for happily and unhappily married couples, and the effect remains even after controlling for severity of the conflict discussed. These findings are consistent with the age-related increase in agreeableness,[79] a characteristic that holds considerable social value.[80] Thus, older people not only prioritize emotionally meaningful goals, such as maintaining high-quality relationships; they also appear more skilled at managing emotionally charged interactions.

The sense that time is limited, particularly in the context of social relationships, may also explain why emotion regulation among older adults is not characterized by hedonism, but rather by a complex mix of positive and negative emotions. A sense that each good-bye kiss may be the last creates more complex, poignant, and deeply gratifying emotional experiences. Even a happy event, such as attending a family reunion, may become bittersweet by the realization that it may be the last one. Under conditions where social endings are made salient, younger adults also experience mixed emotions, but because age is highly correlated with time perspective, older adults are more likely to experience these mixed emotions than younger adults. Indeed, the experience sampling study mentioned above shows that older ages are increasingly associated with greater emotional complexity, as indexed by the simultaneous experience of both positive and negative emotions.[11]

Consistent with age-related changes in social partner preferences, social network size decreases as people get older. Age-related changes appear to reflect selective pruning; that is, reduced size is due primarily to a systematic reduction in peripheral social partners. The numbers of emotionally significant social partners in a given network remain reasonably stable across adulthood and into advanced old age. Consequently, the networks of older people are comprised disproportionately of well-known, emotionally close social partners, most of whom are kin.[81] Importantly, the majority of such changes result from active interventions of the individual and are not due to uncontrollable factors such as the death of network members. In a prospective longitudinal study in which participants' networks were assessed over time and changes in networks examined, Lang[82] found that, in most cases, people who disappeared from older peoples' networks had been actively excluded. A longitudinal analysis focused on early and middle age found a similar pattern. Interactions with acquaintances dropped from 18 to 50 years of age, whereas interactions with family were maintained.[37] Importantly, people reported satisfaction with these age-graded social patterns. Moreover, older people report greater satisfaction with their social networks than younger people, suggesting that highly selected social networks may benefit emotional and psychological well-being.[81,83,84]

To summarize, empirical support for socioemotional selectivity theory suggests that as people move through life, they adjust their goal hierarchies. They become less interested in novel social partners, less drawn to exploration. Instead, they prefer familiar social partners, who are often but not exclusively kin, and structure their social worlds around them. People focus their attention on the positive and forget the negative. Relatedly, self-regulatory skills improve, emotions are better controlled, and social relations better modulated. We suggest that this profile of findings is precisely the profile that would benefit inclusive fitness and propose that temporal monitoring, with its implications for goal reorganization, may represent the psychological mechanism that triggers a shift away from motivation for individual striving and toward greater investment in the care of younger kin.

THE BIGGER PICTURE

Socioemotional selectivity theory did not arise from considerations of evolutionary theory. However, findings generated by the former theory, and indeed its essential postulates, could have been derived just as well to account for the reliable contributions that older people make to younger offspring. Taking the approach advocated by Cosmides and Tooby,[33] which urges consideration of evolutionary principles in conceptualizing the human mind, we now integrate findings generated by systematic hypothesis testing based on socioemotional selectivity theory and findings from the broader literature on cognitive and social aging with anthropological evidence for the adaptive value of grandparents. Our aim is to illustrate how social and cognitive changes associated with aging could represent successful adaptations shaped by evolutionary pressures.

As mentioned above, knowledge about the world and about social relations as well as emotion-regulatory skills clearly increase with age. In order for these qualities to contribute to inclusive fitness, postreproductive adults have to use them to benefit younger kin. We suggest that motivational shifts primed by perceived endings trigger investment in younger kin. As described above, awareness of one's place in the life cycle (and approaching endings) reorganizes goal hierarchies. When endings are perceived, goals directed toward emotionally meaningful contact with familiar social partners are prioritized over goals aimed at individual advancement. In older adults, this leads to increased intergenerational contact and provides a context in which helping one's younger relatives is facilitated and becomes emotionally rewarding. Initially, the awareness of one's own limited time in life may have been a byproduct of improved short-term planning skills. However, gradually it could have acquired selective benefits through its association with effective grandparenting behavior.

In the next section of this chapter, we support our arguments by considering findings about intergenerational support in prehistoric and modern-day hunter-gatherers. After discussing the benefits of late-life motivational changes for inclusive fitness in the ancestral environment, we illustrate how analogous mechanisms are still at work in today's postindustrial societies. In doing so, we note parallels between the elders of today and those of yesteryear. We organize our review into three sections. The first concerns instrumental aid to familiar social partners, the second concerns knowledge transmission, and the third deals with social coherence and conflict resolution.

Intergenerational Aid to Familiar Social Partners, or the "Grandmother Hypothesis"

As discussed above, evolutionary selection should have favored late-life changes that provide older people with both the skills and the motivation to help others. In support of this claim, older adults in both hunter-gatherer and postindustrial societies were found to provide a range of services to younger generations.

The most obvious way in which older relatives in ancestral times contributed to the reproductive success of their offspring was through food provision. The grandmother hypothesis offered by Hawkes and her colleagues states that postreproductive generations hold evolutionary significance when weaning occurs before the infant can feed itself. In such circumstances, a sizable proportion of children's caloric intake is dependent on older people's gathering efforts. Hawkes and her colleagues[26,28–30] posit that grandparenting first emerged in *Homo erectus* about 1.8 million years ago. At that time, environmental changes increased the reliance on food sources that could not be easily exploited by children. Similarly, Kaplan[85] argues that the main dietary difference between hunter-gatherers and nonhuman primates is the human reliance on nutrient-dense and difficult-to-acquire food resources such as tubers, roots, or meat. Under these conditions, selective pressures should have favored higher vitality in postreproductive individuals who contribute to caring for the young. Consistent with this prediction, older individuals' help in food provision was shown to affect infant nutritional status and mortality across a range of traditional societies.

Hawkes and colleagues[29] examined the influence of grandmothering on infants' nutritional status in a small community of modern-day Hazda hunter-gatherers in northern Tanzania. In a long-term observational study, they collected daily logs of activities as well as records of infants' body weights. For each of the observed grandmother-mother dyads, mothers' gathering efforts affected children's body weight. Overall, mothers' gathering efforts were lowest when they were nursing newborn babies. Grandmothers provided compensatory increases in gathering at these times. Grandmothers' gathering affected children's body weight—particularly after weaning. A similar dependence on the gathering efforts of postreproductive women was observed among Hiwi and Ache foragers in South America.[86]

Differences in nutritional status ultimately affect childhood mortality. Sear and her colleagues investigated the influence of maternal grandmothers on grandchildren's nutritional status and childhood mortality among a farming population in rural Gambia.[87] They found that children were better nourished if the maternal grandmother was alive. Also, childhood mortality was lower if children had a maternal grandmother or elder sister. The positive influence of grandmothers on nutritional status and mortality rates increased in importance at about 18 months of age, when the mothers started to focus their attention on younger siblings.

However, positive effects of grandparenting are not limited to support from maternal grandmothers. Hawkes and her colleagues[29] found that only 25% of the postmenopausal females who supported nursing mothers were maternal grandmothers; the others were paternal grandmothers or aunts. Nor is grandparenting behavior limited to older females. There is growing evidence that support for younger generations is provided by older men and women alike. Comparing several hunter-gatherer societies in South America, Kaplan[88] found that both grandfathers and grandmothers contributed significantly to the nutritional welfare of their grandchildren.

In spite of their radically different societal structures and life contexts, modern Western societies show a reliance on intergenerational support similar to that of ancestral societies. Of course, there is a considerable range in the roles that grandparents assume.[89] Today, food provision has been replaced by other forms of intergenerational support such as the transfer of wealth from older to younger generations[90] and assistance in child rearing. When grandparents live in reasonable proximity to grandchildren, they typically play integral roles in family life. In the rural south of the United States, 60% of grandparents have frequent contact with their grandchildren and provide a number of services for them, from giving advice to child care.[91] In the event that family crises arise, the grandparent generation often serves as arbitrator, and in times of extreme crises, many assume primary caretaking responsibilities for their grandchildren.[92,93] In the U.S., 1 in 10 grandparents assumes primary care for a grandchild for a period of at least six months,[94] a number not far from the 16% of children among Machiguenga hunter-gatherers who live with their grandmothers instead of their parents.[85] Hagestad[95] likened elders in the family to the National Guard—well-trained, ready reinforcements in times of need, who lay silent most other times.

Overall, these findings suggest that instrumental support from older relatives contributes to the welfare and survival of younger generations in ancestral and modern-day societies alike. However, support from older individuals does not come only from maternal grandmothers, who can be relatively confident of direct genetic ties to the children they support, but also from aunts, grandfathers, and non-kin.[29,85] Thus, grandparenting behavior cannot be reduced to exclusive support for one's direct relatives. Also, there are no reports of specific societal pressures on older people in hunter-gatherer societies to provide for younger generations. Thus, two puzzling questions remain: why do older individuals care for younger generations at all, and whom do they select to care for?

We argue that the proposed association between time perspective and goal reorganization can help to answer these questions. As discussed above, limitations on time perspective shift the focus from personal advancement to emotional well-being in the moment. Instead of preparing for their own future, older individuals derive increasing pleasure from providing help to familiar social partners. Thus, we suggest that older adults selectively care for younger individuals to whom they perceive strong social ties because such care elicits immediately gratifying social interactions. In traditional hunter-gatherer societies, where biological kinship is often uncertain, familiarity is a good proxy for biological relatedness. As a result, older adults for whom the association between limited time perspective and selective care for familiar individuals was stronger would have contributed more to the fitness of their descendants.

Knowledge Transmission

Support from older generations is not limited to instrumental support. Older adults may also contribute their expertise and world knowledge to benefit younger kin. As discussed above, age-related cognitive changes are circumscribed. While there are considerable declines in speeded tasks and the ability to process new information, expert knowledge remains stable until very old age. This profile of skills benefits inclusive fitness if it is combined with the ability to successfully transfer knowledge to younger generations. We argue that knowledge transmission is aided by the socioemotionally selective changes in older adults' cognition that we have outlined above. Specifically, older people's emphasis on emotionally salient and positively valenced information may make the information they provide more memorable and meaningful. Further, age-related preferences for familiar social partners foster close interactions in small groups that form ideal settings for the exchange of information. Thus, selection pressures may not only have favored maintenance of acquired knowledge, but also characteristics that facilitate the transmission of knowledge from one generation to another.

Indeed, a number of authors argue that human brain development is specifically geared to optimize the storage and transfer of accumulated world knowledge. For example, Skoyles[96] claims that the primary benefit of larger brain size in hominids is not related to fluid intelligence, but rather to storage capacity for accumulated knowledge. Life history theory[35,36,85,88] posits trade-offs among cognitive development, physical growth, and reproductive success in a given species. Large body and brain size are associated with an increased need for nutrient-rich foods and a prolonged period of support from experienced adults. Thus, the evolution of the large human brain increased the capacity for learning and insight, but it is also linked to an extended period of juvenile dependency. Intellectual advances, according to Kaplan, co-evolved along with the need to procure energy-dense food. Therefore, long-lived, knowledgeable relatives are valuable commodities in a species where juveniles demand prolonged and intensive care. Consistent with these claims, Finch and Sapolsky[97] argue that long juvenile dependency and the need for knowledge preservation may explain why age-related neurodegeneration has a later onset in humans as compared to other primates.

Mergler and Goldstein[98] go one step further and suggest that older individuals are also equipped with a unique set of skills that allows them to effectively transfer their expertise. They argue that evolutionary pressures geared older adults to become "unique information processors"(ref. 99, p. 77), who possess a stable memory system, the ability to interpret new material in the light of previous experiences, and the ability to communicate knowledge—often through storytelling—to others. Building on this claim, we suggest that a preference for contact with familiar social partners and for emotionally meaningful activity contribute to the inclination to share knowledge with younger kin. At the same time, emphasis on emotionally salient material optimizes the memorability of the information that is shared. Empirical evidence suggests that this pattern of abilities and preferences is present among older individuals in both hunter-gatherer and postindustrial societies.

Anthropological research on expertise among hunter-gatherers reveals that successful food provision requires extended periods of learning but remains stable into old age. Lee[100] reported that among !Kung, the most successful hunters were middle-aged and older individuals. Of 127 hunters, 25% were older than 49 years, and they accounted for a disproportionate number (33%) of kills. Arguably, expertise may be even more important than physical prowess. Knowing where to find prey and how to successfully stalk it are the most challenging aspects of hunts. Hill and Kaplan[101] reported that Ache and Hiwi hunters do not reach maximal daily production until 25 to 30 years of age. Once acquired, hunting skills remain stable until late midlife. Similarly, gathering skills in women remain stable well into the postreproductive years. Thus, in present-day hunter-gatherer societies, expertise in crucial areas of life is well maintained.

Older hunter-gatherers also share their knowledge with younger kin. Lee[100] reported anecdotal evidence suggesting that older and younger hunters frequently cooperate, with older hunters providing tracking skills and younger hunters pursuing the prey. Birdsell[102] recounts the example of an old Australian Aborigine who led his group to a remote waterhole during a drought. The old man accomplished this by tracing back a trip he had taken with his guardian during his initiation ceremony decades earlier. In addition, he supplemented his memory by recalling the appropriate place names from traditional song cycles. This illustrates how the transmission of culturally relevant knowledge between generations may also have provided mnemonics to help descendants deal with environmental challenges. Throughout their evolutionary history, humans were faced with extreme environmental variations that may have resulted in the sudden loss of resources.[103] In such instances, the accumulated experience of older adults could have provided important clues about how to respond effectively.

Once again, empirical findings based on modern Western populations show many parallels. Laboratory research on age-related changes in cognitive abilities provides solid evidence that the "crystallized" aspects of intelligence (i.e., acquired knowledge and abilities) increase across the life span as a function of cumulative experience and expertise.[104–106] Also, although there is an age-related decrease in the "fluid" aspects of intelligence—the acquisition and processing of new information—age-related losses are limited and everyday functioning is largely preserved.[107]

Moreover, older adults seem to have the necessary skills to successfully share their knowledge with others. Research suggests that older people are very effective storytellers. For one thing, stories read by older adults are more memorable. Mergler, Faust, and Goldstein[99] recorded older, middle-aged, and younger adults as they read several stories aloud. Readers were encouraged to use their own intonation and pacing style. Next, the recordings were played to younger adults. In an incidental memory paradigm, younger adults recalled more story units when an older person as compared to a younger person had read the story. Interestingly, these effects occurred only for oral recall, not written. Thus, the benefits of older adults' story presentation were limited to the type of recall that is typical for preliterate ancestral societies. Moreover, older adults are especially good at telling stories when the listener is a child, which would be consistent with an emphasis on intergenerational transfer. Adams and colleagues[108] asked adults of different ages to learn a story with the goal to tell it either to a child or to an adult experimenter. When telling the story to another adult, older adults recalled less than younger adults. However, there were no age differences in recall when the listener was a child. Compared to younger adults, older adults also made greater adjustments of story complexity to accommodate the age of their listener. This suggests that older people's story telling performance depends on the specific social context. In particular, older individuals seem to be more motivated to share knowledge with a child than with an adult listener, which would foster intergenerational transfer. Stories told by older people may be also more pleasant to listen to, because older storytellers highlight positive emotional content. Pasupathi and her colleagues asked older and younger women to tell stories to young girls. Next, stories were coded for their emotional content. As expected, older women were found to modulate the emotional material to a greater extent and to emphasize positive over negative emotions.[109]

In summary, older adults across different societies maintain high levels of expertise until late life and are well equipped to transmit their knowledge to younger generations. Age-related changes in social motivation and increased emphasis on the emotional aspects of stories add to the selective advantage of these characteristics. For one, knowledge transmission has the greatest impact on the inclusive fitness of one's genes if information is shared with direct kin instead of nonrelated individuals, and age-related changes in social partner preferences selectively prioritize contact with close relatives. In addition, older people's focus on emotionally toned information and their preference for positive content make their stories more engaging, especially for children.

Social Coherence and Conflict Resolution

Even if sufficient instrumental support and a solid knowledge base are available, younger generations will not thrive if social conflict disturbs peace and stability within the close-knit groups common to the hunter-gathering lifestyle. Socioemotional selectivity theory predicts that as they approach the end of their life, older people place greater emphasis on intimate social interactions and on emotionally salient information. In the long run, this focus on one's emotions and social relations translates into superior social problem solving and emotion-regulatory abilities. We argue that these skills lead to a selective advantage if they are used to support coherence and resolve conflict among older people's circle of kin. We further suggest that because older adults prioritize socioemotional well-being, they should be motivated to avoid the negative emotions that are typically associated with social conflict. Once again, findings support the theory and are remarkably consistent across different types of societies and research methods.

In hunter-gatherer societies, older adults are often responsible for the social stability of the group. For example, among the Ju/'Hoansi hunter-gatherers in Botswana, older adults control the complicated kinship system. They decide about people's relative positions within the system, and use their accumulated experience to negotiate good matches among families or to resolve interpersonal conflicts.[110] Also, older Ju/'Hoansi sometimes assume positions as powerful healers who are respected for their spiritual knowledge.[110]

Again, research on current Western populations is consistent. Empirical findings suggest that the ability to solve everyday social problems is maintained or improves with age (for a review see Blanchard-Fields[111]). In particular, older adults place greater emphasis on the emotional meaning and the interpersonal consequences of different problems. Sinnott,[112] for example, reported that when asked to interpret various problems, older adults are more likely than younger adults to focus on possible interpersonal implications. Also, with age, people seem to get better at considering multiple perspectives with regard to a single problem situation.[113,114] These age-related improvements in perspective taking and the assessment of interpersonal implications are highly relevant when mediating among the different parties in a conflict.

In addition, older adults seem to be better at assessing the specific type of intervention that is needed to solve a given problem. Blanchard-Fields and her colleagues[115] investigated age differences in strategy use for instrumental and social domains of problem solving. Compared to younger adults, older adults were more flexible in their use of different strategies. They were more likely to use problem-focused strategies when dealing with instrumental problems and more likely to avoid emotional reactivity when dealing with interpersonal conflict. Similarly, Blanchard-Fields and her colleagues[116] asked young, middle-aged, and older adults to write essays on how they would resolve each of 15 problem situations. When the situation was emotionally salient, older adults were more likely to use emotion-regulatory problem solving strategies than younger adults. However, if the situation was not emotional, no age differences were visible. Thus, older adults seem to flexibly adjust their problem-focused and emotion-focused problem solving strategies depending on the specific requirements of the situation. Moreover, older people seem to intentionally avoid strong emotional reactions to interpersonal problems—in close-knit hunter-gatherer groups this skill would have been very helpful in negotiating interpersonal conflict and promoting group stability.

In short, as they get older, humans seem to acquire advanced interpersonal skills that make them successful negotiators. They are able to appreciate different perspectives, assess complex interpersonal implications, and decide which course of action is most promising. Moreover, older adults' emphasis on well-being in the moment may motivate them to use their skills to reduce social conflict in order to minimize the ensuing negative emotions.

SUMMARY AND CONCLUSIONS

In this paper, we have argued that human evolution did act on the post-reproductive years. Converging evidence drawn across multiple disciplines—paleodemography, anthropology, psychology, and sociology—suggests that older people were an integral part of the ancestral environment in which we evolved. Across the millennia, older kin likely contributed to the welfare of younger individuals by providing instrumental support, knowledge, social expertise, and conflict resolution.

Importantly, older adults not only have the skills to contribute to inclusive fitness, but, there is good reason to think, they also were motivated to use these skills. As proposed by socioemotional selectivity theory, constraints on time trigger heightened emphasis on emotional well-being and close social relationships. We suggest that over the millennia, the genes of older adults who were knowledgeable and invested in kin were more likely to have survived in the gene pool.

With socioemotional selectivity theory, we outlined a theoretical framework that assumes that selective pressures acted across the human life span, not just during the early years. Hence, we understand age-related changes in late life as specific adaptations that were selected for because they maximized the inclusive fitness of older adults and their offspring in the environment of evolutionary adaptedness—prehistoric hunter-gatherer societies. While this approach builds upon ideas proposed by other disciplines—most notably anthropology and biology—it is relatively new in the field of psychology, where research agendas are still dominated by the assumption that evolutionary pressures failed to act on later years. As a result, positive developments in old age may be overlooked or misinterpreted as coping with inevitable decline.[19,117]

We suggest that careful consideration of evolutionary trajectories may inform alternative research agendas that acknowledge the possibility of life-long growth and optimize the use of older people's unique profile of skills while meeting their specific needs.

An evolutionary perspective may also help us to better understand the challenges and opportunities associated with an aging population. The proportion of older adults in today's societies is steadily rising, and across the world the "oldest old" (i.e., individuals aged 85 and beyond) are now the fastest growing age group (UN Population Division, 1998[118]). If older people's competencies evolved to serve the specific needs of younger relatives, there are now many more people who fit this job description. Postindustrial societies present challenges: the rapid pace of change demands new learning throughout life, and increased mobility means that older people often live far away from younger kin.

In contrast to prehistoric times, when there was little change in relevant world knowledge across an individual human life span, technological advances have been growing exponentially since the beginning of the 17th century.[119] Hence, our evolutionary past may have left us somewhat ill-prepared for the ensuing need for lifelong learning. It can be argued that these technological advances have rendered older people less useful because it is more reliable to store information in computers than in human brains. On the other hand, older adults' social skills have not lost any of their relevance. In fact, social coherence may be needed more than ever. Today's children are born into families with multiple generations of adults invested in their economic and socioemotional well-being. Distances no longer present the barriers they did in the past. Improved transportation and enhanced computer technology enable older generations to maintain ties with their grandchildren and great-grandchildren despite geographic dispersion. In this best-case scenario, older generations can provide the stabilizing force in young children's lives that balances social disruptions caused by divorce, remarriage, and increased mobility.

Thus, a joint consideration of the strengths and weaknesses that old age entails is needed.[120] Some age-related changes that would have been highly adaptive in the ancestral environment may be at odds with the contingencies of current postindustrial lifestyles, while others retained their benefits across the millennia. We argue that an evolutionary perspective can address the challenges of aging populations in a changing world by suggesting new ways to utilize older people's specialized skills and by pointing out new directions for research on previously neglected resources that older adults may use to adapt to new environments.

ACKNOWLEDGMENTS

We are deeply grateful to Professor Robert Seyfarth (University of Pennsylvania) and Professor Richard Klein (Stanford University) for steering us to animal and anthropological literatures, respectively; and to Professors

Caleb Finch (University of Southern California) and Karen Fingerman (Purdue University) for their comments on earlier drafts of this chapter.

REFERENCES

1. BADDELEY, A. 1999. Essentials of Human Memory. Psychology Press, Taylor and Francis. Hove, England.
2. SALTHOUSE, T. 1996. The processing–speed theory of adult age differences in cognition. Psychol. Rev. **103**: 403–428.
3. HASHER, J., R.T. ZACKS & C.P. MAY. 1999. Inhibitory control, circadian arousal, and age. *In* Attention and Performance XVII. Cognitive Regulation of Performance. Interaction of Theory and Application. D. Gopher & A. Koriat, Eds.: 653–675. MIT Press. Cambridge, MA.
4. PARK, D., G. LAUTENSCHLAGER & L. HEDDEN. 2002. Models of visuospatial and verbal memory across the adult life span. Psychol. Aging **17**: 299–320.
5. LI, S.C. 2002. Connecting the many levels and facets of cognitive aging. Curr. Dir. Psychol. Sci. **11**: 38–43.
6. NATIONAL RESEARCH COUNCIL. 2000. The Aging Mind: Directions in Cognitive Aging Research. P. Stern & L.L. Carstensen, Eds. National Academies of Sciences Press. Washington, DC.
7. BALTES, P.B. & R. KLIEGL. 1992. Further testing of limits of cognitive plasticity: negative age differences in mnemonic skills are robust. Dev. Psychol. **28**: 121–125.
8. KLIEGL, R. & P.B. BALTES. 1991. Testing the limits kognitiver Entwicklungskapazität in einer Gedächtnisleistung. Z. Psychol. Suppl. **11**: 84–92.
9. STAUDINGER, U.M. 1999. Older and wiser? Integrating results on the relationship between age and wisdom-related performance. Int. J. Behav. Dev. **23**: 641–664.
10. CARSTENSEN, L.L. & S.T. CHARLES. 1998. Emotion in the second half of life. Curr. Dir. Psychol. Sci. 7(5): 144–149.
11. CARSTENSEN, L.L., M. PASUPATHI, U. MAYR & J. NESSELROADE. 2000. Emotional experience in the daily lives of older and younger adults. J. Pers. Soc. Psychol. **79**: 1–12.
12. MROCZEK, D.K. & C.M. KOLARZ. 1998. The effect of age on positive and negative affect: a developmental perspective on happiness. J. Pers. Soc. Psychol. **75**: 1333–1349.
13. FINGERMAN, K.L. & E.L. HAY. Intergenerational ambivalence in the context of the larger social network. *In* Intergenerational Ambivalence. K. Luescher & K. Pillemer, Eds. Elsevier/JAI Press. Belgium. In press.
14. FINGERMAN, K.L. 2001. Aging Mothers and Their Adult Daughters: a Study in Mixed Emotions. Springer Publishers. New York.
15. FINGERMAN, K.L. 2000. "We had a nice little chat": age and generational differences in mothers' and daughters' descriptions of enjoyable visits. J. Gerontol. Psychol. Sci. **55**: 95–106.
16. BRANDTSTÄDTER, J. & W. GREVE. 1994. The aging self: stabilizing and protective processes. Dev. Rev. **14**(1): 52–80.

17. HECKHAUSEN, J. & J. KRÜGER. 1993. Developmental expectations for the self and most other people: age grading in three functions of social comparison. Dev. Psychol. **29:** 539–548.

18. CUMMING, E. & W.H. HENRY. 1961. Growing Old: The Process of Disengagement. Basic Books. New York.

19. LÖCKENHOFF, C.E. & L.L. CARSTENSEN. 2002. Is the life-span theory of control a theory of development or a theory of coping? *In* Personal Control in Social and Life Contexts. S. Zarit, L. Pearlin & K.W. Schaie, Eds.: 263–280. Springer Publishing. New York.

20. SCHULZ, R. & J. HECKHAUSEN. 1996. A life-span model of successful aging. Am. Psychol. **51**(7): 702–714.

21. SCHULZ, R., C. WROSCH & J. HECKHAUSEN. 2002. The life-span theory of control: issues and evidence. *In* Personal Control in Social and Life Course Contexts. S.H. Zarit & L.I. Pearlin & K.W. Schaie, Eds.: 233–262. Springer Publishing Company. New York.

22. BALTES, P.B. 1997. On the incomplete architecture of human ontogeny: selection, optimization, and compensation as foundation of developmental theory. Am. Psychol. **52:** 366–380.

23. HOWELL, N. 2000. Demography of the Dobe !Kung. De Gruyter. Hawthorne, NY.

24. BOCQUET-APPEL, J. & J.N. BACRO. 1997. Estimates of some demographic parameters in a neolithic rock-cut chamber (approximately 2000 BC) using iterative techniques for aging and demographic estimators. Am. J. Phys. Anthropol. **102:** 569–575.

25. GAGE, T.B., J.M. MCCULLOUGH, J.A. WEITZ, *et al.* 1989. Demographic studies and human population biology. *In* Human Population Biology. M.A. Little & J.D. Haas, Eds. Oxford University Press. New York.

26. HAWKES, K., J.F. O'CONNELL & B.N.G. JONES. 2003. Human life histories: primate tradeoffs, grandmothering, socioecology, and the fossil record. *In* Primate Life Histories & Socioecology. P. Kappeler & M. Pereira, Eds.: 204–227. University of Chicago Press. Chicago.

27. DARWIN, C. 1964. On the Origin of Species. Harvard University Press. Cambridge, MA.

28. HAWKES, K., J.F. O'CONNELL, B.N.G. JONES, *et al.* 1998. Grandmothering, menopause, and the evolution of human life histories. Proc. Natl. Acad. Sci. USA **95:** 1336–1339.

29. HAWKES, K., J.F. O'CONNELL & B.N.G. JONES. 1997. Hadza women's time allocation, offspring provisioning, and the evolution of long postmenopausal life spans. Curr. Anthropol. **38**(4): 551–577.

30. HAWKES, K. 2003. Grandmothers and the evolution of human longevity. Am. J. Hum. Biol. **15:** 1–21.

31. FAIRBANKS, L.A. 1988. Vervet monkey grandmothers: interactions with infant grandoffspring. Int. J. Primatol. **9:** 425–441.

32. FAIRBANKS, L.A. & M.T. MCGUIRE. 1986. Age, reproductive value, and dominance-related behaviour in vervet monkey females: cross-generational influences on social relationships and reproduction. Anim. Behav. **34:** 1710–1721.

33. COSMIDES, L. & J. TOOBY. 1994. Beyond intuition and instinct blindness: the case for an evolutionarily rigorous cognitive science. Cognition **50:** 41–77.

34. TOOBY, J. & L. COSMIDES. 1992. The psychological foundations of culture. *In* The Adapted Mind: Evolutionary Psychology and the Generation of Culture.

J.H. Barkow, L. Cosmides & J. Tooby, Eds: 19–136. Oxford University Press. New York.

35. KAPLAN, H. & A.J. ROBSON. 2002. The emergence of humans: the coevolution of intelligence and longevity with intergenerational transfers. Proc. Natl. Acad. Sci. USA **99:** 10221–10226.

36. KAPLAN, H., K. HILL, J. LANCASTER & M.A. HURTADO. 2002. A theory of human life history evolution: diet, intelligence, and longevity. Evol. Anthropol. **9:** 156–184.

37. CARSTENSEN, L.L. 1992. Social and emotional patterns in adulthood: support for socioemotional selectivity theory. Psychol. Aging **9:** 259–264.

38. CARSTENSEN, L.L. 1993. Motivation for social contact across the life span: a theory of socioemotional selectivity. *In* Nebraska Symposium on Motivation. J.E Jacobs, Ed. Dev. Persp. Motiv. **40:** 209–254.

39. CARSTENSEN, LL., D.M. ISAACOWITZ & S.T. CHARLES. 1999. Taking time seriously: a theory of socioemotional selectivity. Am. Psychol. **54**(3): 165–181.

40. SUDDENDORF, T. & M.C. CORBALLIS. 1997. Mental time travel and the evolution of the human mind. Genet. Soc. Gen. Psychol. Monogr. **123:** 133–167.

41. MARSHACK, A. 1972. The Roots of Civilization. McGraw Hill. New York.

42. AVENI, A.F. 1995. Ancient Astronomers. Smithsonian. Washington, DC.

43. AVENI, A.F. 1995. Empire of Time: Calendars, Clocks, and Cultures. Kodansha America. New York.

44. ZAJONC, R. 1984. On the primacy of affect. Am. Psychol. **39**(2): 117–123.

45. LANG, F.R. & L.L. CARSTENSEN. 2002. Time counts: future time perspective, goals, and social relationships. Psychol. Aging **17:** 125–139.

46. FUNG, H.H., P. LAI & R. NG. 2001. Age differences in social preferences among Taiwanese and Mainland Chinese: the role of perceived time. Psychol. Aging **16:** 351–356.

47. FREDRICKSON, B.L. & L.L. CARSTENSEN. 1990. Choosing social partners: how age and anticipated endings make people more selective. Psychol. Aging **5:** 335–347.

48. FUNG, H.H., L.L. CARSTENSEN & M.A. LUTZ. 1999. Influence of time on social preferences: implications for life-span development. Psychol. Aging **14:** 595–604.

49. FUNG, H.H. 2002. Emotional reactions from afar: age differences in Hong Kong Chinese's emotional reactions toward the 9-11 attacks on America. Paper presented at the Annual Meeting of the Gerontological Society of America. Boston, MA.

50. CARSTENSEN, L.L. & B. FREDRICKSON. 1998. Influence of HIV status and age on cognitive representations of others. Health Psychol. **17:** 494–503.

51. JOHNSON, M.K. & S.J. SHERMAN. 1990. Constructing and reconstructing the past and the future in the present. *In* Handbook of Motivation and Cognition: Foundations of Social Behavior. E.T. Higgins & R.M. Sorrentino, Eds.: 482–526. Guilford Press. New York.

52. CARSTENSEN, L.L. & S. TURK-CHARLES. 1994. The salience of emotion across the adult life span. Psychol. Aging **9:** 259–264.

53. GOULD, O.N. & R.A. DIXON. 1993. How we spent our vacation: collaborative storytelling by young and older adults. Psychol. Aging **6:** 93–99.

54. HASHTROUDI, S., M.K. JOHNSON & L.D. CHROSNIAK. 1990. Aging and qualitative characteristics of memories for perceived and imagined complex events. Psychol. Aging **5:** 119–126.

55. SCHULKIND, M.D., L.K. HENNIS & D.C. RUBIN. 1999. Music, emotion, and autobiographical memory: they're playing your song. Mem. Cognit. **27**: 948–955.
56. FUNG, H.H. & L.L. CARSTENSEN. 2003. Sending memorable messages to the old: age differences in preferences and memory for emotionally meaningful advertisements. J. Pers. Soc. Psychol. **85**(1): 163–178.
57. JENNINGS, J.M. & L.L. JACOBY. 1993. Automatic versus intentional uses of memory: aging, attention, and control. Psychol. Aging **8**: 283–293.
58. RAHHAL, T., C.P. MAY & L. HASHER. 2002. Truth and character: sources that adults can remember. Psychol. Sci. **13**: 101–105.
59. HASHTROUDI, S., M.K. JOHNSON, N. VNEK & S.A. FERGUSON. 1994. Aging and the effects of affective and factual focus on source monitoring and recall. Psychol. Aging **9**(1): 160–170.
60. HENKEL, L.A., M.K. JOHNSON, D.M. DE LEONARDIS. 1998. Aging and source monitoring: cognitive processing and neuropsychological correlates. J. Exp. Psychol. Gen. **127**: 251–268.
61. CHARLES, S.T., M. MATHER & L.L. CARSTENSEN. 2003. Aging and emotional memory: the forgettable nature of negative images for older adults. J. Exp. Psychol. Gen. **132**(2): 310–324.
62. LEVINE, L.J. & S. BLUCK. 1997. Experienced and remembered emotional intensity in older adults. Psychol. Aging **12**: 514–523.
63. QUACKENBUSH, S.W. & M.A. BARNETT. 2001. Recollection and evaluation of critical experiences in moral development: a cross-sectional examination. Basic Appl. Soc. Psychol. **23**: 55–64.
64. FIELD, D. 1981. Retrospective reports by healthy intelligent elderly people of personal events of their adult lives. Int. J. Behav. Dev. **4**: 77–97.
65. PASUPATHI, M. & L.L. CARSTENSEN. 2003. Age and emotional experience during mutual reminiscing. Psychol Aging **18**: 430–442.
66. MATHER, M. & L.L. CARSTENSEN. 2003. Aging and attentional biases for emotional faces. Psychol. Sci. **14**(5): 409–415.
67. GEORGE, L.K., D.F. BLAZER, I. WINFIELD-LAIRD, *et al.* 1988. Psychiatric disorders and mental health service use in later life: evidence from the Epidemiologic Catchment Area Program. *In* Epidemiology and Aging. J. Brody & G. Maddox, Eds.: 189–219. Springer. New York.
68. REGIER, D.A., H.J. BOYD, J.D. BURKE, *et al.* 1988. One-month prevalence of mental disorders in the United States. Arch. Gen. Psychiatry **45**: 977–986.
69. WEISSMAN, M., P.J. LEAF, M.L. BRUCE & L.P. FLORIO. 1988. The epidemiology of dysthymia in five communities: rates, risks, comorbidity, and treatment. Am. J. Psychol. **145**: 815–819.
70. DIENER, E. & R.E. LUCAS. 1999. Personality and subjective well-being. *In* Well-being: The Foundations of Hedonic Psychology. D. Kahneman, E. Diener & N. Schwarz, Eds.: 213–229. Russell Sage Foundation. New York.
71. DIENER, E. & E. SUH. 1997. Measuring quality of life: economic, social, and subjective indicators. Soc. Indic. Res. **40**: 189–216.
72. CHARLES, S.T., C.A. REYNOLDS & M. GATZ. 2001. Age-related differences and change in positive and negative affect over 23 years. J. Pers. Soc. Psychol. **80**: 136–151.
73. POWERS, C.B., P.A. WISOCKI & S.K. WHITBOURNE. 1992. Age differences and correlates of worrying in youth and elderly adults. Gerontologist **32**: 82–88.
74. SCHIEMAN, S. 1999. Age and anger. J. Health Soc. Behav. **40**: 273–289.

75. Bolin, R. & D.J. Klenow. 1982-1983. Response of the elderly in disaster: an age-stratified analysis. J. Aging Hum. Dev. **16:** 283–296.
76. Gross, J.J., L.L. Carstensen, M. Pasupathi, et al. 1997. Emotion and aging: experience, expression, and control. Psychol. Aging **12:** 590–599.
77. Levenson, R.W., L.L. Carstensen & J.M. Gottman. 1994. Influence of age and gender on affect, physiology, and their interrelations: a study of long-term marriages. J. Pers. Soc. Psychol. **67:** 56–68.
78. Carstensen, L.L., J.M. Gottman & R.W. Levenson. 1995. Emotional behavior in long-term marriage. Psychol. Aging **10:** 140–149.
79. Field, D. & R.E. Millsap. 1991. Personality in advanced old age: continuity or change? J. Gerontol.: Psychol. Sci. **46:** 299–308.
80. Graziano, W.G. & N. Eisenberg. 1997. Agreeableness: dimension of personality. In Handbook of Personality Psychology. R. Hogan, J. Johnson & S. Briggs, Eds.: 795–828. Academic Press. San Diego, CA.
81. Lansford, J.E., A.M. Sherman & T.C. Antonucci. 1998. Satisfaction with social networks: an examination of socioemotional selectivity theory across cohorts. Psychol. Aging **13:** 544–552.
82. Lang, F.R. 2000. Endings and continuity of social relationships: maximizing intrinsic benefits within personal networks when feeling near to death? J. Soc. Pers. Relation. **17:** 157–184.
83. Lang, F.R. & L.L. Carstensen. 1994. Close emotional relationships in late life: further support for proactive aging in the social domain. Psychol. Aging **9:** 315-324.
84. Lang, F.R., U.M. Staudinger & L.L. Carstensen. 1998. Perspectives on socioemotional selectivity in late life: how personality and social context do (and do not) make a difference. J. Gerontol. Psychol. Sci. **53:** 21–30.
85. Kaplan, H. 1987. The evolution of the human life course. In Between Zeus and the Salmon: The Biodemography of Longevity. K.W. Wachter & C.E. Finch, Eds.: 175–211. National Academy Press. Washington, DC.
86. Hurtado, A., K. Hill, H. Kaplan & I. Hurtado. 1992. Tradeoffs between female food acquistion and child care among Hiwi and Ache foragers. Hum. Nat. **3**(3): 185–216.
87. Sear, R., F. Steele, I.A. McGregor & R. Mace. 2002. The effects of kin on child mortality in rural Gambia. Demography **39**(1): 43–63.
88. Kaplan, H. 1994. Evolutionary and wealth flow theories of fertility: empirical tests and new models. Pop. Dev. Rev. **20**(4): 753–791.
89. Becker, G., Y. Beyene, E. Newsom & N. Mayen. 2003. Creating continuity through mutual assistance: intergenerational reciprocity in four ethnic groups. J. Gerontol. Soc. Sci. **58B:** s151–s159.
90. McGarry, K. & R.F. Schoeni. 1995. Transfer behavior in the Health and Retirement Study: mesurement and the redistribution of resources within the family. J. Hum. Res. **30:** S184–S226.
91. Spence, S.A. S.R. Black, J.P. Adams & M.R. Crowther. 2001. Grandparents and grandparenting in a rural southern state: a study of demographic characteristics, roles, and relationships. J. Fam. Issues **22**(4): 523–534.
92. Minkler, M. & K.M. Roe. 1993. Grandmothers as Caregivers: Raising Children of the Crack Cocaine Epidemic. Sage Publications. Thousand Oaks, CA.
93. Goodman, C.C. & M. Silverstein. 2001. Grandmothers who parent their grandchildren: an exploratory study of close relations across three generations. J. Fam. Issues **22**(5): 557–578.

94. FULLER-THOMSON, E., M. MINKLER & D. DRIVER. 1997. A profile of grandparents raising grandchildren in the United States. Gerontologist 37(3): 406–411.
95. HAGESTAD, G.O. 1988. Able elderly in the family context: changes, chances, and challenges. *In* Retirement Reconsidered: Economic and Social Roles for Older People. R. Morris & S.A. Bass, Eds.: 171–184. Springer Publishing Co. New York.
96. SKOYLES, J.R. 1999. Human evolution expanded brains to increase expertise capacity, not IQ. Psycoloquy 10: np.
97. FINCH, C.E. & R. SAPOLSKY. 1999. The evolution of Alzheimers disease, the reproductive schedule, and ApoE isoforms. Neurobiol. Aging 20(4): 407–428.
98. MERGLER, N.L. & M.D. GOLDSTEIN. 1983. Why are there old people? Senescence as biological and cultural preparedness for the transmission of information. Hum. Dev. 26(2): 72–90.
99. MERGLER, N.L., M. FAUST & M.D. GOLDSTEIN. 1984. Storytelling as an age-dependent skill: oral recall of orally presented stories. Int. J. Aging Hum Dev. 20(3): 205–228.
100. LEE, R. 1979. The !Kung San: Men, Women, and Work in a Foraging Society. Cambridge University Press. New York.
101. HILL, K. & H. KAPLAN. 1999. Life history traits in humans: theory and empirical studies. Ann. Rev. Anthropol. 28: 397–430.
102. BIRDSELL, J. 1979. Ecological influences on Australian aboriginal social organization. *In* Primate Ecology and Human Origins. I.S. Bernstein & E.O. Smith, Eds. Garland. New York.
103. ALLMAN, J. & A. HASENSTAUB. 1999. Brains, maturation times, and parenting. Neurobiol. Aging 20(4): 447–454.
104. HORN, J.L. & R.B. CATTELL. 1967. Age differences in fluid and crystallized intelligence. Acta Psychol. 26(2): 107–129.
105. HORN, J.L. & G. DONALDSON. 1976. On the myth of intellectual decline in adulthood. Am. Psychol. 31(10): 701–719.
106. BOSWORTH, H.B. & K.W. SCHAIE. 1999. Survival effects in cognitive function, cognitive style and sociodemographic variables in the Seattle longitudinal study. Exp. Aging Res. 25: 121–139.
107. CERELLA, J., J.M. RYBASH, W. HOYER & M.L. COMMONS, EDS. 1993. Adult Information Processing: Limits on Loss. Academic Press. San Diego, CA.
108. ADAMS, C., M.C. SMITH, M. PASUPATHI & L. VITOLO. 2002. Social context effects on story recall in older and younger women: does the listener make a difference? J. Gerontol.: Series B: Psychol. Sci. Soc. Sci. 57B(1): P28–P40.
109. PASUPATHI, M., M. HENRY & L.L. CARSTENSEN. 2002. Age and ethnicity differences in storytelling to young children: emotionality, relationality, and socialization. Psychol. Aging 17(4): 610–621.
110. LEE, R. 2003. The Dobe Ju/'hoansi. Wadsworth, Thomson Learning. Florence, KY.
111. BLANCHARD-FIELDS, F. 1996. Emotion and everyday problem solving in adult development. *In* Handbook of Emotion, Adult Development, and Aging. C. Magai & S.H. McFadden, Eds.: 149–165. Academic Press. San Diego, CA.
112. SINNOTT, J.D. 1989. Life-span relativistic postformal thought: methodology and data from everyday problem-solving studies. *In* Adult Development,

Vol. 1: Comparisons and Applications of Developmental Models. M.L. Commons and J.D. Sinnott, Eds.: 239–278. Praeger Publishers. New York.

113. BLANCHARD-FIELDS, F. 1986. Reasoning on social dilemmas varying in emotional saliency: an adult developmental perspective. Psychol. Aging 1(4); 325–333.

114. BLANCHARD-FIELDS, F. 1994. Age differences in causal attributions from an adult developmental perspective. J. Gerontol. 49(2): P43–P51.

115. BLANCHARD-FIELDS, F., Y. CHEN & L. NORRIS. 1997. Everyday problem solving across the adult life span: influence of domain specificity and cognitive appraisal. Psychol. Aging 12(4): 684–693.

116. BLANCHARD-FIELDS, F., H.C. JAHNKE & C. CAMP. 1995. Age differences in problem-solving style: the role of emotional salience. Psychol. Aging 10(2): 173–180.

117. SCHAIE, K.W. 1988. Ageism in psychological research. Am. Psychol. 43: 179–183.

118. UNITED NATIONS POPULATION DIVISION. 1998. The Sex and Age Distribution of the World Populations. United Nations Secretariat. New York.

119. MENARD, H.W. 1971. Science: Growth and Change. Harvard University Press. Cambridge, MA.

120. BALTES, P.B. 1987. Theoretical propositions of life-span developmental psychology: on the dynamics between growth and decline. Dev. Psychol. 23(5): 611–626.

Development

Panel Discussion

JOSEPH J. CAMPOS, *Moderator*

QUESTION: At what age can children appreciate their place in the life cycle—that is, when can children acquire the cognitive appreciation of mortality? Is that known?

LAURA L. CARSTENSEN (*Stanford University, Stanford, CA*): There is a whole literature on children's understanding of death, the finality of death, and how very young children don't have any knowledge about it. But I think you're asking something a little different, about your place in the time line. I think that by adolescence that capability is present, but whether it's in the forefront of consciousness at that age is, I think, fairly doubtful. But, certainly, adolescents would be capable of that understanding.

QUESTION: You didn't show us the two faces. Can you explain this paradigm?

CARSTENSEN: This is a paradigm to study attentional differences. We present two faces at the same time: one is always neutral, and the other shows a positive or negative emotion. They're presented for 500 milliseconds; then they disappear, and a dot appears on the screen. The participant is required to press a key on the right or left side of the keyboard, indicating the side of the screen on which the dot appeared. We were interested in differential attention to positive or negative faces. What we got in that study is increased speed in responding when the dot appears behind the positive face. They're faster to the positive and slower to the negative. Older people are relatively faster, which suggests that they're already looking at the positive face when the faces disappear.

QUESTION: In the evolutionary aspect of your talk you placed a great deal of emphasis on human awareness that the end is coming. But I'm sure you know there's a branch of evolutionary biology called life history theory that argues, with lots of data to support it, that natural selection doesn't select for a single strategy—for example, a reproductive strategy, a parental strategy—in long-lived animals. It selects for a particular life history strategy—a different deployment of investment in children or grandchildren at different points during a life. Though no biologist has ever given the kind of cognitive gloss to this

Ann. N.Y. Acad. Sci. 1000: 180–192 (2003). © 2003 New York Academy of Sciences.
doi: 10.1196/annals.1280.009

that you have today, there's really no difference between what you are saying about changes in behavioral strategies in humans as they age and what biologists say about many animals' changes in behavioral strategies as they age. That would argue against the view that a conscious awareness that the end is coming is the driving force. This may be simply another very complex example to what life history biologists have been finding in everything from guppies to elephants.

CARSTENSEN: You would know this better than I, but my understanding is that human grandparenting behavior is very different from that of any other species, with much greater investment. Would you agree with that?

QUESTION: Yes. It's a common joke among all of us who know about kin selection theory: we say to our colleagues when they're first going to have kids, be ready. Grandparents are completely off the line. Humans are the only species, or one of the few species, in which individuals live long beyond their reproductive lifetime, particularly human females. It may be that humans are different simply because most mammalian females reproduce for 90% of their usual life, so we don't see them when they're nonreproductive.

CARSTENSEN: One of the things we've been thinking about this is that the approach-of-endings effect may be driving investment throughout the life course at different times, in different contexts, which would actually be consistent with what you're saying. That is, we don't find this just in old people; we can get it to appear in younger people with remarkably simple kinds of instructional, contextual shifts. We think we might be onto a cognitive mechanism that could play along with other kinds of influences. This could be a mechanism that helps to activate differing levels of investment in kin, but it could be activated in early life as well.

QUESTION: Can I ask about sex differences in your findings? I'm assuming that maybe you don't have any, or you would have already talked about them. But I know that there are really prominent sex differences in all the Lang slides. How does that interact with aging?

CARSTENSEN: We have looked at sex differences, and essentially there are no interaction effects with age. So in the emotional experience studies and the Lang studies, we get what you would expect—the main effects, but nothing that accounts for the age effects. And by the way, we have equal amounts of males and females in our studies.

QUESTION: I'm interested in the studies on children having lots of facial expressions that don't seem appropriate for the context or that don't fit the emotions that we think are normally behind the expressions. Does this sort itself out at some point, when the children grows older, so that expressions become more closely attached to particular situations and emotions? Do you think this is true for all our facial expressions and not just for young children?

LINDA A. CAMRAS (*DePaul University, Chicago, IL*): The empirical data aren't really in yet. We are interested in following this effect over time, but we haven't even finished with our six procedures for infants; so I can't really do much more than speculate. I would not be surprised if we found that things straightened themselves out as you're saying, to some extent, but not 100% of the time; because I think we adult humans are used to dealing with vast arrays of cues that interact in very complex ways in all sorts of domains that don't have to do with understanding emotion or reading emotion cues. If it turned out that we do that for children's facial expressions and maybe sometimes for adult facial expressions also, it wouldn't surprise me very much.

But in saying that kind of thing, I don't in any way mean to detract from the importance of facial expression as a cue to emotion. I think historically there's been an oppositional tendency to try to create a false dichotomy and ask whether people go for context or vocalization or facial expression. I think we may get ourselves into trouble if we keep trying to make broad generalizations that apply across contexts. It's going to differ from context to context, and I think the whole literature and the whole theory behind display rules tells us that already. We already know that as adults we sometimes discount facial expressions for very good reasons. At a funeral, for instance, we know that people are very unhappy but may nonetheless feel that they need to smile at you. We know that we do that as adults, and we may do it in more cases than we acknowledge. But I always get nervous when I say this because I'm worried that people might think I'm minimizing the important role of facial expressions in emotion interpretation and recognition. I want to emphasize that I think facial expressions are critically important, but they're not the only thing.

RICHARD J. DAVIDSON (*University of Wisconsin–Madison, Madison, WI*): It seems that the inferences you're making about facial expression are at least in part based upon the assumption that we know what emotions should be expressed in response to the particular contexts or situations that you described. How do we know that?

CAMRAS: I think it's a fascinating question because people have been looking for decades for the gold standard for emotion identification. If we can't use facial expression as the gold standard for emotion identification, what do we have left? I'm not sure I can provide a satisfactory answer because I'm not sure there is a gold standard yet. One of the reasons we're trying to use multiple methods is to bolster that assumption; that's why we used observer judgment and nonfacial behaviors, although I admit that all of those are imperfect.

QUESTION: When you ask people to describe in their own terms the most intense experience of fear that they could imagine anyone in the world would have, and then ask them to do it for anger, and then vary the order, you get the same situation. The torture and death of loved ones is the most intense fear and also the most intense anger, so the assumption that important situations are single-emotion situations is questionable. You have to do a follow-up. Do you?

CAMRAS: That was in part where I was leading: it seems to me that the future in this area is going to depend on these multimodal assessments. The other issue is the extent to which the kind of facial behavior that you reported is characteristic of the majority of children or infants at that particular age, because the facial behavior patterns can arise as a consequence of some infants showing one particular pattern and others showing the other pattern. A related question is the extent to which these patterns that do not conform to any of these prototypes are really consistent across the vast majority of infants in those particular situations.

COMMENT: I think identifying the factors and then showing that you can get the relationships when you look at individuals and not just groups would be an important next demonstrative step.

CAMRAS: To me there are three criteria. Number one: one could predict that with arm restraint or the removal of a cookie or toy there would be frustration, which should result in something more anger-like than fear-like. The approach of a stranger clearly falls into the category of threat, not frustration. There's no goal being frustrated per se. The goal that's being activated is that of security. Second, one has a rich array of instrumental behaviors in infants, and these behaviors are quite clear in differentiating the situations. The third factor that enters into play is the use of converging research operations. For example, in Stenberg and Campos's study of the effects of arm restraint, there was a huge array of converging evidence, other than in the face, indicating that the infant's behavior was anger-like. There was a report of flushing of the face; the vocalizations that the child made, when analyzed blindly, sounded anger-like to parents and experimenters. It was phenomena like that that led us to believe that some of the instigating circumstances that we used were likely to produce the desired outcome.

Now these are bootstrapping processes. You have to start somewhere. We have a lot more of a consensus about what the affective valence of a slide should be than we do about how to produce an emotion in the child. Frankly, I think the fact that we have a consensus about the affective valence of the slide does not take us very far in understanding emotion, becuase the affective valance could be purely a judgment, cold and cognitive, and not necessarily something that affects the adaptation of the child or the person to his or her world. So I agree with the implicit question that you raised about how we know what we're eliciting. You have to start somewhere. I think these paradigms that we've tried out are reasonable starting points.

JOSEPH J. CAMPOS (*University of California–Berkeley, Berkeley, CA*): I would like to see a study done with anybody at any age. I think what you see are components; what you see is the aggregation by the human brain of an average, expectable set of facial movements. The prototype may not be observed in nature very often. The prototype constitutes what Paul has studied; it may not be evident in nature in quite the clear way that Paul has studied in connection with facial recognition. We have to keep that possibility in mind.

PAUL EKMAN (*University of California–San Francisco, San Francisco, CA*): I guess I can't not respond. Actually 90% of the work I've done is measuring facial behavior, not facial recognition, because recognition is a rather limited method. But it depends on where you look in nature. If you look at John Gotman's videotapes of interactions between violent husbands and their wives, you see a lot of prototypes. If you look at Mardi Horowitz's videotapes of spouses discussing a spouse who has recently died, you see lots of prototypes. If you look at most social interactions that occur in universities, you don't see as many prototypes. It just depends on where in nature you look. Most psychologists don't look at highly charged emotional situations.

ROBERT W. LEVENSON (*University of California–Berkeley, Berkeley, CA*): I thought it was really interesting that fear was so potent as a facial expression compared to anger. I suppose if you asked someone who didn't know the social referencing literature what's the most potent emotion to communicate to a child to stop his behavior in his tracks, that person would probably say an angry expression, thinking perhaps that anger might induce fear in the child, and the child might freeze. Certainly, we don't use fear very much. That kind of vicarious fear is a way of shaping children's behaviors. In this situation the expression of fear requires at some level this transformation: the child has to say, "Oh, my mom is afraid; maybe it has something to do with something I'm doing. What am I doing?" There's a whole lot of operations at some primitive level that have to take place, because fear is not an emotion that says stop like anger does. I guess the question is, how do you think about this? Was it a surprise that anger was not the most potent baby-stopping emotion? Or is there a big flaw in this analysis?

CAMPOS: The data that you saw showed 100% of babies tested—that is 19, out of 19 failed to cross the modified deep side of the cliff with fear, and 18 of the 19 failed to cross with anger; so you're talking about an N of 1 difference. Let me go beyond that and suppose we had 1000 or 10,000 babies. I think fear is still contextually appropriate.

I mentioned something about biological preparedness. I know of one study in the social referencing literature—and it's a terrible study—that deals with biological preparedness. I happen to believe that of the signals that the baby is likely to get, the one that is most biologically suitable is fear; because there is a threat there, and the mother wants to communicate that threat. Anger communicates something different.

I would argue that the fear signal is the biologically appropriate one. Incidentally, I should mention, for the sake of clarifying, that a lot of people have said that the reason why we got the data on the visual cliff that we got was that the fear signal that you saw displayed in the video clip would be such as to stop a clock. We did a situation where there was no deep side. There was a shift from a shallow side to a different shallow side. It was the same side as the deep side, except the deep side was moved all the way up to the bottom of the glass. The mother posed the fear face, and what the kids did is: first of all, there was very little referencing, there was no need for referencing; and second, those kids that did reference to the mother when they crossed that white strip at the center and saw her posing that fear face, looked at her, seemed puzzled, and then just continued crossing. In other words, the issue of contextual appropriateness, I think, is very important. I think that in some contexts anger would be the emotion for cessation of a child's behavior; in other situations it would be fear. In this case, statistically there's no difference, but I do believe that fear is more appropriate.

LEVENSON: Except that over time fear comes to beget a range of responses, including support. If I see fear in someone, one possibility is that whatever is making them afraid is really dangerous, let's get out of here. But the another possible response is to comfort them, so I think that fear moves in two directions.

HARRIET OSTER (*New York University, New York, NY*): I think the reason the apparent disassociation between expression and emotion in infants appears is that the dissociation is based on the use of Carroll Izard's coding system for measuring discrete emotions in infants. Babies don't show adult-like prototypes when you expect them to; they show different emotions, but I think they have different prototypes. If you look at the infant expressions in that way, then it appears as though they really are expressing emotion. I'm not saying that babies don't experience fear and anger by 11 months, because they do, as is obvious from other kinds of behavior. But their facial expressions don't fit the adult prototypes, and there are reasons why you would not expect them to. If an infant is frightened, the baby can't escape or defend itself. It needs to signal somebody to come and help; that's a distress signal. I think infants' expressions are less differentiated than adults', and from the evolutionary perspective that makes sense: babies need help from other people to accomplish their goals.

QUESTION: Dr. Carstensen, as you were listing the differences between a look to the future and a look to the present, I was reminded of some of Barbara Fredrickson's work with the broaden-and-build theory: a look towards the future looked very much more broadening and building, expanding horizons; but it may be the opposite. Are older folks already broadened and already built?

CARSTENSEN: I guess that is what I would say, that they already are broadened and built. I hadn't thought about the relationship of this to the broaden-and-build kind of model. But as I understand the theory, it's not necessarily broadening and building to learn a lot of new things, take new chances, take risks; it's being open and able to experience life. So I think qualitatively they're slightly different.

QUESTION: I'm wondering if the expression of emotion isn't really more complex than just what's on the face, and that perhaps there are other elements that we might not be thinking about. For example, what about the element of body animation. Is a smile in a person conveying the same thing as a smile in a picture? I think body dynamics, energy, auras, and other kinds of elements come through beyond just the pursing of the lips. Do you take that into consideration in your research?

CAMRAS: Yes, I think we're all pretty much in agreement that those are aspects of the context of a still face. What I'm really interested in doing is broadening that context as far as possible, being as inclusive as possible of the various factors that influence or interact with the morphology of the facial expression itself in terms of influencing our interpretation.

QUESTION: What I'm suggesting is that in Dr. Campos's experiment about the child looking at his mother's different expressions, if that were just from the neck up, would it be the same as it would be if he's looking at the entire body? I can't be positive from what I have heard that it is purely the facial expression that's being related to.

CAMPOS: In the visual cliff, the mother is standing behind a table, and the child is in an ecological setting in which he couldn't possibly see the rest of her body; hence, I would say it's ecologically appropriate.

In another setting, where the mother's total body is visible but only the face is manipulated, you have an impoverished stimulus; a very different kind of message is given to the child. It will have an effect on the child that will be measurable; it may even be statistically significant. But in terms of showing maximal relationship to behavior, I would argue, no, you have essentially cut the heart out of the gestalt. The evidence I would bring to bear, as I mentioned in the presentation, is that in the study in which only the voice was manipulated and the mother was instructed to keep her face neutral, the baby did look to the mother; and it struck us that the baby was trying to get confirmation from the mother's face and sometimes also from the mother's getting up, picking the child up, and getting him away from the toy. Lacking that, the child gave the vocalization from the mother somewhat less weight than it otherwise would have had.

So the study definitely showed that the voice regulated the baby's behavior. No question about that; the results are very, very powerful in that regard. Are they as powerful as they could be in the real world? By manipulating these other factors that you described, and that I agree exist, I think you would get maximal behavior regulation.

QUESTION: Dr. Campos, I'm interested in individual differences, and I suspect that there are a lot of individual differences in some of the data that you saw. I'm wondering whether there might be learned differences, as between a mother spending a lot of time during the day with an infant and, at the opposite extreme, other siblings or the father spending a lot of time there, with less interaction with the mother. And perhaps there might also be more inborn reasons for the individual differences, related to other maturational milestones.

CAMPOS: Just as there's a concept called temperament, having to do with individual differences in the expressivity of emotion, Karen Barrett and I were convinced that there are individual differences in the susceptibility to emotional signals and that these individual differences, we would bet our bottom dollar, would be shown to be closer in monozygotic than dizygotic twins, for example. We were not able to find much in the way of literature at the time to allow us to flesh out that story, and since then I have seen very little more. Nevertheless, my own personal belief—and this is just an expression of belief—is that there is something called *temp-percept*, in which there are individual differences—no question about them, absolutely no question.

And do you know what else enters into individual differences? It is something I was going to mention in the talk but didn't: the emotional climate in the home. If the emotional climate in the home is one in which certain kinds of emotional signals, such as the anger voice, is emitted 10–20 times an hour, it's going to have a different impact on the child than if it's very unusual for the child. There are some data about this in our studies. We did exactly the same study that I described to you—the one with the triangular arrangement with the mother's voice—in Japan and in the United States. In America, we never found differences between anger and fear, in terms of the behavior regulation of the child. We found differences between anger and joy, fear and joy, but not between anger and fear. In Japan, anger was way off the chart. We attributed it not to the fact that the Japanese babies were innately more sensitive to anger, but to the fact that in the typical ecology of the Japanese child, the mother–child interaction does not expose a child to anger; so for the Japanese child, it is an extremely disruptive event. That's why in the Japanese version of the social referencing study we got such enormous differences between fear and anger.

So my answer is, yes: I do think there are factors in the mother–child relationship that enter into individual differences. Beyond that, the emotional climate of the house creates, as it were, an adaptation level. For instance, if you have a particular experience with the temperature of water, something a little bit warmer will seem hot to you, and something a little bit colder than that adaptation level will seem cold. You can change the adaptation level and make that which seems cold at one time now seem warm. The same thing can happen in terms of the emotional reaction to these signals, and I think that is a very significant factor. That is an example of what we need to investigate in order to understand contextual factors.

QUESTION: Are there any biological milestones to which some of these differences might be related? It's really all the nature-nurture question. I'm interested in what happens to these children when they grow up. If the environment causes changes in their behavior, how does that look when they become adolescents, for example?

CAMPOS: One of the advantages of doing studies using a basic emotions perspective is that it goes well beyond attachment theory. Attachment theory has attracted the question you asked in general terms. A very significant factor in the formation of secure "attachment" is sensitivity by the parent to the social signals of the child and appropriate responsiveness in the form of social signaling by the parent to the behaviors of the child. When you start thinking about more specific emotions, I think one might be able to make more specific predictions about the future of the child.

QUESTION: Dr. Campos, you found that in the child's recognition of mother's emotional signals, something happens between age 8 1/2 and 14 months, and then you identified that as the development of motor functions. The development of motor functions coincides with the myelinization of motor pathways. That's generally true of many functions. A newborn infant is almost helpless because most of the major nerve tracks are not myelinated; the process proceeds slowly, gradually, and coincides with critical periods. This happens to the motor functions at the time you mentioned. Now, what do you know about myelinization of the emotional pathways involved? They have to connect to the motor functions, but they're not necessarily the same as the motor functions.

CAMPOS: I'm sorry to say that I don't have any specific data on the issue of myelinization, and I'd like to make a clarification about the motor issue. The motor issue is specific to the assessment of joint attention, that something that coordinates with the sensitivity to the emotional signal per se to regulate the child's behavior towards an object. I was limiting the motor development to only this particular joint attention, not to emotion itself.

QUESTION: I understand that; it has to be an enabling condition. But then you don't know when the emotional pathways are myelinated?

My second question is about interspecies emotional connections. Without such connections, the domestication of animals would not have been possible, and we wouldn't have human civilization as we know it. Yet, I don't see anyone mentioning it. We have plenty of people who are in contact with other species—herders, many pet owners. They have deep emotional connections. The human emotion of mourning is almost universal among mammals; combined with wishful thinking, this emotion is probably responsible for the concept of the soul. In primitive societies when somebody dies, the survivors are very sad about it; they see him in their dream, and then somebody says, yeah, there's a place where he went to. From such thinking you get the soul. Almost every primitive society has that. That emotion is what ties pets to pet owners. Consideration of this kind of connection is left to animal rights enthusiasts; no one is doing any serious study on it.

ANSWER: This is an interesting topic, but we haven't studied it. I don't have a good theoretical reason for excluding it.

QUESTION: My concern is about the positive bias in the elderly. It strikes me that there's a downside to that development: that being sensitive to negative—for example, the negative face, the angry face in the crowd—is a benefit to all people; and that somehow the elderly are more vulnerable. Would you comment on that?

CARSTENSEN: We have some studies going on right now where we're trying to address some of the pitfalls of positivity bias in memory, though not specifically in the way that you're suggesting. What we're doing is more a matter of giving people information about a choice—for example, a health care plan. Then you ask them to remember it, and we see this kind of positivity bias in the memory of the health care plan they chose. One of the things we're wondering is if this kind of choice supportiveness might have a negative consequence in the future—for instance, if you forget that your health care plan doesn't provide coverage for the new hip that you need. So, we think there may well be some negative consequences to this, as well as positive consequences probably relating to emotional well being and regulation.

QUESTION: My question is primarily for Dr. Carstensen. All of you talked about changes in emotional development relative to some sort of life event—for instance, the development of social referencing with respect to the onset of crawling behavior. But when you talked about changes in emotional regulation in the second half of life, the reference point is in the future. It's the end time, and so it's very easy to turn those effects off. And you talked about a number of different aspects of emotional regulation: the increased reliance on spending time with family as a way of providing positive emotion, the increased salience of positive events, whether social or otherwise. I wonder if you have a sense that any of those might have past time points as well, if there are life experiences that trigger some of those in a way that can't be turned off easily or freely?

CARSTENSEN: That's an interesting question. Is a positivity bias evidenced in autobiographical memory, in what people remember about their personal past? That literature is very interesting. Even when you take extreme negative events, like the Holocaust, when people are asked about those events, at, say, 10-year intervals, they become increasingly less negative. Now, in that case they never become positive, but they're less negative over time. So we do see evidence for this, even when people are drawing on past significant events; it's not all about what may happen in the future. And I don't think it's so much that people are thinking about the future more as they get older. I think they're relieved of concerns about the future, so the future becomes irrelevant. It's when the future is relevant and everything seems to matter—all the "what if this happens or that happens"—that, I think, a lot of negative emotion is felt in younger adults. This tends to be alleviated with age.

QUESTION: My question is also for Laura Carstensen: I like the picture you painted of aging, and I suspect I'll like it more with each year.

CARSTENSEN: Yes, everybody likes my research better as they get older.

QUESTION: But I was wondering to what extent the picture you paint is one of normal, normative aging or potentially one of healthier or even hyper-healthy aging. I'm sure you wrestle with finding a community sample that is some- how representative of the aging population; and you tend you get people who are mobile, motivated, probably healthy. Could you address that?

CARSTENSEN: Sure, we do have healthy samples. I won't belabor this point; but I do think that when studying aging populations, we want to study healthy people, so we're not studying disease. Illness makes people unhappy regard- less of age, although, I think, less unhappy as they get older. So if you study older cancer patients compared to younger cancer patients, the older ones are doing better emotionally. Still, health is an important issue. What I would like to say about samples is that we use a survey research firm to recruit our them; about 1/3 are blue collar, half are African-American, and half are European American. We stratify across class and race throughout the sample. So we do have healthy samples, but they're not just the superagers, they're not just those people who are healthy, and wealthy, and wise.

QUESTION: Professor Carstensen, the driving motor in your analysis is that people become conscious of their life span, and we see the results are changes in emotional salience and emotional life. One way to test that theory is to go to nonhuman primates, which—let us assume—are not conscious of their time span. Is there a way to operationalize and test that in nonhuman pri- mates, to see if there is a changing emotional component? Because your the- ory suggests that there should not be such a change along the life span of nonhuman primates.

CARSTENSEN: Right. Truly, I wouldn't expect to see a positivity bias, for ex- ample, in nonhuman primates. I don't know. But it's interesting—a wonder- ful topic for study.

QUESTION: Is the proportion of positive expressions in primates very much smaller than that of negative expressions?

CARSTENSEN: First of all, primates have tons of positive expressions—facial expressions, vocalizations. There are nice studies on chimp sounds and squirrel monkeys and stuff like that. Chuck sounds they're called. So there's lots of positive affect expressed in the nonhuman primates. This relates a little bit to comments earlier that there is a life span effect anyway, regardless of the cognition that may or may not be involved. For example, an older male chimpanzee who has all the dominance battles behind him because he's now 40 plays only political games, not power games. The way he will play with, for example, an infant is totally different from a young male who's in the middle of these battles, because a young male has no time for infants and tickling games and running around with kids, like grandfathers do in our society also. So I think you get a general mellowing of the male—for example, his lower testosterone. You also get a different role for the female in many primate societies when her offspring are having offspring. Sometimes in captivity females survive beyond the reproductive age and start to behave quite differently in the matrilineal system in which they live.

QUESTION: So a lot of the effects you are talking about probably have parallels in nonhuman primates, but without any of the awareness of mortality that humans have. All the things that are happening because of changing hormone levels and other things that change with aging make it impossible to say with assurance that these effects are due to our awareness of mortality.

CARSTENSEN: I couldn't agree more. Clearly there are developmental changes, age-related changes, that influence people's behavior independently of the perspective of time. I'm not trying to say the cognitive findings explain and cause everything that we're seeing. I'm saying that they are consistent with an effect in which people can appreciate time and can shift gears. The fact that we can experimentally change people's goals by giving them two sentences of instructions suggests that something can shift motivation. That's not to say that is the only reason for the changes we see with age.

COMMENT: Those findings are very instructive—the ones where you tell people they have 20 more years to live and they change their attitudes.

CARSTENSEN: Right.

COMMENT: That's very interesting and instructive, and certainly relates to the hypothesis that you have, but there are plenty of other changes going on at the same time.

CARSTENSEN: I agree.

COMMENT: What you're describing now is dependent upon the extent to which the species relies on cooperative behavior. You're much more likely to see these positive-affect expressions in the bonobos and chimps than you are in species that aren't cooperative with each other over longer periods of time.

COMMENT: Yes, but almost all the primates we worked with spent less than 5% of their time in antagonistic situations, as we call them—fighting and threatening and stuff like that. They probably spent easily 20% of their time in affiliative situations. So the positive, cooperative side of primate societies is, in terms of time budget, far more conspicuous than the antagonistic or dominance-related side; in general, there are very high levels of cooperation in almost all the primate societies that we study.

Latency and Intensity of Discrete Emotions

Are Discrete Emotions Differentiated by Latency and/or Intensity of Expression?

MARTA E. LOSONCZY[a] AND LINDA J. BRANDT[b]

Salisbury University, Psychology Department, Salisbury, Maryland 21801, USA

Psychology Department, The George Washington University, Washington, DC 20052, USA

KEYWORDS: latency; intensity; discrete emotions; emotional expressions; infants

According to some developmental theorists, emotions are undifferentiated at birth and become more differentiated with development.[1–3] While these theorists acknowledge that the nervous system has a role in emotional expression, they do not elaborate on that relationship. Another view of emotional development posits that emotions result from specific neural circuits that are associated with specific facial expressions.[4–8] This theory, *differential emotions theory*, identifies the basic emotions of joy, anger, fear, surprise, disgust, sadness, interest, and contempt as discrete and differentiated from each other. According to differential emotions theory, neural mechanisms influence latency because neural mechanisms are responsible for the activation of emotions and emotion thresholds.[9] Neural mechanisms influence the intensity of expressions since they play a role in the amplification and attenuation of emotional expressions.[6] If specific neural mechanisms are responsible for specific emotions, then one would expect to be able to differentiate these emotions along the parameters of latency and intensity. The purpose of this study was to examine whether or not basic emotions can be differentiated in terms of latency and intensity of emotional expression. To

Address for correspondence: Marta E. Losonczy, Salisbury University, Psychology Department, 1101 Camden Avenue, Salisbury, MD 21801. Voice: 410-543-6444, fax: 410-548-2056.
melosonczy@salisbury.edu

Ann. N.Y. Acad. Sci. 1000: 193–196 (2003). © 2003 New York Academy of Sciences.
doi: 10.1196/annals.1280.023

minimize the effects of socialization on emotional expressions, infants, aged 7 through 13 months, were used as subjects. One hundred and fourteen infants were screened for normal development; only 82 infants with an APGAR score of 7 or above, and who received an "N" (normal) on the Denver II (a standard pediatric screening tool) were used in the study. In a laboratory situation, infants' emotional expressions to 12 different stimuli, presented in randomized order, were videotaped using a time code generator, which encoded the time in minutes, seconds, and frames (1/30 of a second). Videotapes were analyzed, and discrete emotions were identified using the Maximally Discriminative Facial Movement Coding System (MAX).[10] Latency was the time between the onset of stimulus presentation and onset of facial expression. Intensity was measured as a composite score of facial, vocal and bodily expression using a newly constructed scale. The facial portion of the scale incorporated codes from MAX (with permission of the author). The vocal items were derived (with permission) from the Laboratory Temperament Assessment Battery (Lab-Tab, version 3.1).[11] The bodily expression portion of the scale was based on an inventory of bodily movements and postures, some of which were derived (with permission) from Lab-Tab.

University students who were trained and obtained proficiency in coding using both MAX and the new measure analyzed videotapes. Each subject was analyzed on each of the 12 stimuli, which resulted in 984 coded observations (82 subjects × 12 stimuli). Reliability was assessed for the newly constructed intensity measure by having each subject analyzed by two independent raters. Reliability was measured by how well the two raters agreed on what emotion was being exhibited by a particular subject for a particular stimulus on each of the 983 observations (1 lost datum). A Cronbach's alpha revealed an alpha score of 0.8204, $N = 983$. Interrater reliability for the intensity of expression was examined for the constructed scale by comparing the total intensity score by each of the two raters for each subject for each stimulus. The total intensity score was the sum of facial intensity (scale of 0–3), vocal intensity (scale of 0–3), and bodily intensity (scale of 0–17). Chronbach's alpha was 0.7196, $N = 983$.

Criterion validity was assessed by comparing the facial portion of the constructed measure to a well-established measure, MAX. Each subject was coded by the same rater at different times using MAX and the constructed measure. Ratings were compared on whether or not they agreed on the emotion that was displayed by a particular subject in response to a particular stimulus. The emotion identified for each observation was compared between both measurement systems. Cronbach's alpha was 0.8955, $N = 983$.

It was hypothesized that basic emotions could be differentiated on the basis of latency. Observations with zero latency time and observations in which there were no emotional responses were excluded from this analysis, resulting in 765 observations. As hypothesized, a Kruskal-Wallis Test revealed that differences in latency between various emotions were statistically significant,

χ^2 (6, $N = 765$) = 13.38, $P < 0.05$. Nonparametric statistics were used since the sample failed Bartlett's Box F Test and Cochran's C test for homogeneity of variances. A series of Mann Whitney U Tests revealed the following differences in terms of latency (significant at $P < 0.05$ or less): sadness could be differentiated from joy, interest, surprise, anger, and pain; joy could be differentiated from interest.

It was also hypothesized that basic emotions could be differentiated on the basis of intensity. Observations with zero intensity and observations in which there were no emotional responses were excluded from this analysis, resulting in 765 observations. As hypothesized, a Kruskal-Wallis Test revealed that differences in intensity between various emotions were statistically significant, χ^2 (6, $N = 765$) = 132.68, $P < 0.0001$. Nonparametric statistics were used because intensity was measured using an ordinal scale. A series of Mann Whitney U Tests revealed the following differences in terms of intensity (significant at $P < 0.05$ or less): anger was found to be different from joy, interest, surprise, fear, sadness, and pain; sadness was different from joy and interest. Although the study was not trying to induce pain, the pain expression appeared and was found to be different from joy, interest, surprise, fear, anger, and sadness in terms of intensity.

In conclusion, as hypothesized, it was found that certain emotional expressions could be differentiated on the basis of latency and intensity. These results are consistent with the idea that emotions are discrete and lend support to the position taken by differential emotions theory that specific neural circuits may be associated with specific emotional expressions.

REFERENCES

1. BRIDGES, K.M.B. 1932. Emotional development in early infancy. Child Dev. **3:** 324–341.
2. LEWIS, M.D. & L. MICHALSON. 1983. Children's Emotions and Moods: Developmental Theory and Measurement. Plenum Press. New York.
3. SROUFE, A.L. 1979. Socioemotional development. *In* Handbook of Infant Development. J.D. Osofsky, Ed.: 462–516. Wiley. New York.
4. IZARD, C. E. 1991. The Psychology of Emotions. Plenum Press. New York.
5. IZARD, C.E. 1994. Innate and universal facial expressions: evidence from developmental and cross-cultural research. Psychol. Bull. **115:** 288–299.
6. IZARD, C.E. & C. MALATESTA. 1987. Perspectives on emotional development I: differential emotions theory of early emotional development. *In* Handbook of Infant Development, 2nd edit. J.D. Osofsky, Ed.: 494–554. Wiley. New York.
7. TOMKINS, S. 1962. Affect, Imagery and Consciousness: Vol. 1. The Positive Affects. Springer. New York.
8. TOMKINS, S. 1963. Affect, Imagery and Consciousness: Vol. 2. The Negative Affects. Springer. New York.

9. IZARD, C.E. 1993. Four systems for emotion activation: cognitive and noncognitive processes. Psychol. Rev. **100:** 68–90.
10. IZARD, C.E. 1995. The Maximally Discriminative Facial Movement Coding System. University of Delaware.
11. GOLDSMITH, H.H. & M.K. ROTHBART. 1999. Laboratory Temperament Assessment Battery; prelocomotor version 3.1. University of Wisconsin and University of Oregon.

Emotion in the Infant's Face

Insights from the Study of Infants with Facial Anomalies

HARRIET OSTER

McGhee Division, School of Continuing and Professional Studies, New York University, and Institute of Reconstructive Plastic Surgery, New York University School of Medicine, New York, New York 10012-1165, USA

ABSTRACT: Darwin viewed "experiments in nature" as an important strategy for elucidating the evolutionary bases of human emotional expressions. Infants with craniofacial anomalies are of special interest because morphological abnormalities and resulting distortions or deficits in their facial expressions could make it more difficult for caregivers to read and accurately interpret their signals. As part of a larger study on the effects of craniofacial anomalies on infant facial expression and parent-infant interaction, infants with different types of craniofacial conditions and comparison infants were videotaped interacting with their mothers at 3 and 6 months. The infants' facial expressions were coded with Baby FACS. Thirty-seven slides of 16 infants displaying 4 distinctive infant expressions (cry face, negative face, interest, and smile) were rated by 38 naïve observers on a 7-point scale ranging from intense distress to intense happiness. Their ratings were significantly correlated with ratings based on objective Baby FACS criteria ($r > 0.9$ in all infant groups). A 4 (infant group) × 4 (expression category) ANOVA showed a significant main effect for expression category, $F(3) = 71.9$, $P = 0.000$, but no significant effect for infant group or group × expression interaction. The observers' ratings were thus highly "accurate" in terms of *a priori* Baby FACS criteria, even in the case of infants with severely disfiguring facial conditions. These findings demonstrate that the signal value of infant facial expressions is remarkably robust, suggesting that the capacity to read emotional meaning in infants' facial expressions may have a biological basis.

KEYWORDS: facial expression; emotion; infancy; craniofacial anomalies; smiling; negative affect; observer judgments

Address for correspondence: Harriet Oster, Ph.D., McGhee Division, School of Continuing and Professional Studies, New York University, 50 W. 4th Street, Suite 225, New York, NY 10012-1165. Voice: 212-998-9143; fax: 212-995-4666.

harriet.oster@nyu.edu

Ann. N.Y. Acad. Sci. 1000: 197–204 (2003). © 2003 New York Academy of Sciences.
doi: 10.1196/annals.1280.024

Darwin[1] viewed "experiments in nature" as an important strategy for eluci-dating the evolutionary bases of human emotional expressions. Infants with craniofacial anomalies are of special interest because morphological abnor-malities can result in ambiguities, distortions, or deficits in their facial ex-pressions, which could make it more difficult for caretakers (and researchers) to read and accurately interpret their signals. Earlier researchers reported that infants with craniofacial anomalies smile less, are less socially responsive, and show less clear-cut signaling than unaffected infants and that their moth-ers show less contingent responsiveness and warmth toward their infants.[2–5] However, the infant's facial expressions were not coded with explicit, objec-tive criteria in these studies. Therefore, it is not clear whether infants showed objectively definable abnormalities or deficits in facial expression, whether the mothers had difficulty reading and accurately interpreting their infants' signals, or both. The well-established "attractiveness halo effect"[6] could be an additional source of bias in mothers' and other observers' judgments of fa-cial expressions in infants with facial abnormalities.

As part of a longitudinal study on the effects of craniofacial anomalies on infant facial expression and mother-infant interaction, infants with a variety of craniofacial conditions and comparison infants were videotaped interact-ing with their mothers at 3 and 6 months. The infants' facial expressions were coded with Baby FACS (Facial Action Coding System for Infants and Chil-dren),[7] a fine-grained, anatomically based coding system adapted for infants' faces from Ekman and Friesen's[8] Facial Action Coding System. Baby FACS does not attempt to label infant facial expressions in terms of prototypical adult expressions of discrete emotions but rather describes typical infant fa-cial configurations in terms of their component facial actions. Baby FACS also provides explicit guidelines for coding intensities and variants of infant smiles and cry-face expressions.

Baby FACS coding is based on multiple and redundant cues to each facial action and takes individual variations in facial morphology into account. Thus, the facial muscle actions of infants with craniofacial anomalies can be identified and reliably coded despite morphological abnormalities, and defi-cits or ambiguities in the surface appearance of their facial expressions can be objectively specified. Objective coding with Baby FACS has revealed that the basic repertoire of infant facial expressions, including the capacity to sig-nal gradations of positive and negative emotion, is largely preserved even in infants with severe facial anomalies.[9,10]

The question raised in the study reported here is whether visible abnormal-ities in the facial expressions of infants with facial anomalies affect the social signal value of their expressions. Handler and Oster[11] found that moth-ers'spontaneous attributions of emotion to their infants' expressions during face-to-face social interaction were largely accurate. However, nonfacial cues were also available from the infants' vocalizations and body movements. The study reported here was a more stringent test of the social signal value of the infants' facial expressions: the ability of untrained judges unfamiliar with the infants to decode the hedonic valence and intensity of the emotion communicated in infants' facial expressions, without additional nonverbal or contextual cues.

METHOD

Stimulus Slides

The 37 slides used in the study showed close-up facial expressions of 16 3- to 6-month-old infants (18 male, 19 female) from the larger sample, each infant showing two or three different expressions. There were four infants in each of four groups: uncomplicated cleft lip with or without cleft palate (CLP); craniofacial anomalies (CFA) involving deformities of the skull and/ or soft tissue of the face and in some cases partial facial paralysis; facial hemangiomas (HEM), vascular anomalies that could mask one or more facial features; and unaffected comparison infants (COMP). The infants in the three facial anomaly groups represented a range of severity and disfigurement. There were no significant group differences in infant gender and no gender differences in observers' emotion ratings. Therefore, gender was not examined in further statistical analyses.

The slides were selected by the investigator from a larger pool of slides to fit four basic categories of infant facial expression: cry face, negative face, interest, and smile. Smiles were further coded as small, medium, or big smiles according to the Baby FACS matrix for coding smile intensity[12] and were rated on a 7-point scale ranging from (1) intense cry face to (7) intense smile, with interest expressions rated as 4 points. A second coder trained in Baby FACS used explicit facial action criteria to classify the infant expressions (95% agreement, *Kappa* = 0.927, *P* = 0.000) and to rate the slides on the 7-point scale ($r = 0.97$, $P = 0.000$).

The 37 slides included two examples of cry face, negative face, and interest expressions in infants in each of the four infant groups and one example of a small, medium, and big smile from infants in each group. One additional big smile from the CFA group was included because of the heterogeneity of facial conditions within this diagnostic group. Each infant was shown with two or three of the four basic expressions (cry face, negative face, interest, and smile). Although the stimulus expressions were selected to be unambiguous in terms of their component facial muscle actions, their appearance in infants with facial anomalies was unusual in ways that could affect observers' emotion ratings. Examples of four infants showing medium-intensity smiles, rated 6 on the *a priori* scale, are shown in FIGURE 1. (Additional details on the coding and classification criteria can be obtained from the author.)

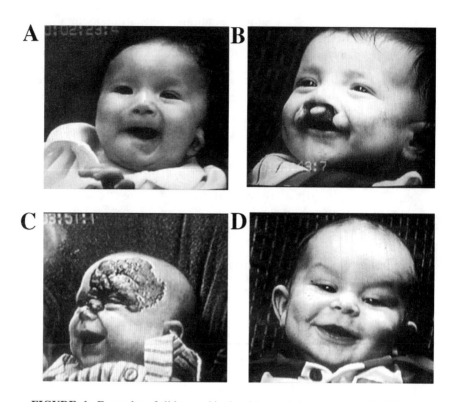

FIGURE 1. Examples of slides used in the observer judgment study. All slides were classified as smiles and were rated 6 on the 7-point intensity scale by objective Baby FACS criteria. The numbers following each infant's group and diagnostic category are the mean ratings and (in parentheses) standard deviations across 38 naïve judges on the 7-point emotion rating scale. (**A**) Goldenhar's syndrome (CFA), 5.71 (0.649); (**B**) bilateral cleft lip (CLP), 5.89 (0.863); (**C**) hemangioma (HEM), 5.89 (1.25); (**D**) comparison (COMP), 5.97 (0.563).

Judges

Thirty-eight undergraduates enrolled in a laboratory course in developmental psychology served as subjects. They had no training in facial coding and were unfamiliar with facial anomalies. They were informed that we were interested in the extent to which different observers agree in rating the facial expressions and appearance of infants, including infants who have conditions that affect their facial appearance. The first six slides shown were practice slides to familiarize subjects with a range of different facial conditions and expressions. The 37 test slides were presented one at a time for 10 seconds. Subjects rated the emotion shown in the infants' faces on a 7-point scale ranging from (1) extremely unhappy/distressed to (7) extremely happy, with 4 marking the midpoint. The slides were then shown a second time, and subjects rated the attractiveness of the infants on a 7-point scale ranging from (1) extremely unattractive to (7) extremely attractive. The results of the attractiveness ratings will be reported separately. However, as a manipulation check, we conducted an ANOVA for infant group differences in attractiveness. The results showed that the mean attractiveness ratings of the infants in the three facial anomaly groups were not significantly different from each other (CLP = 2.8, CFA = 3.1, HEM = 2.7), while all three were significantly lower than the mean ratings of the comparison infants (5.4), F (3) = 29.7, $P = 0.000$.

RESULTS

The naïve observers' emotion ratings were significantly correlated with ratings based on objective Baby FACS criteria ($r > 0.95$ for all four infant groups, $P = 0.000$). A 4 (infant group) × 4 (expression category) ANOVA with mean observer emotion ratings as the dependent variable was highly significant, F (15) = 14.9, $P = 0.000$. There was a significant main effect for expression category, $F(3) = 71.9$, $P = 0.000$, but no significant effect for infant group or group × expression interaction. *Post hoc* analyses showed that mean ratings of slides in each of the expression categories differed significantly

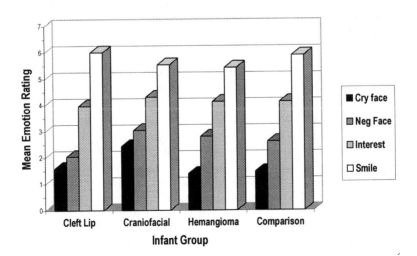

FIGURE 2. Mean emotion ratings of slides showing four Baby FACS–specified infant facial expressions (cry face, negative face, interest, and smile) produced by four groups of infants. $N = 38$ untrained judges.

(< 0.05) from those in each of the other categories. Ratings of slides in the four *a priori* expression categories in each of the four infant groups are shown in FIGURE 2. The observers' ratings were thus highly "accurate" in terms of *a priori* Baby FACS criteria, even in the case of infants with severely disfiguring facial conditions.

Finally, in order to find out whether observers' hedonic ratings differentiated slides showing different expressions in the same infant (3 slides for 5 infants, 2 slides for 11 infants), we conducted 25-paired samples *t*-tests on the 38 judges' ratings of each pair of slides showing the same infant. There were significant differences (< 0.0001) in all but one of the 25 pairs, all in the expected direction (higher ratings for more positive expressions). The one exception was for an interest expression and small smile in an infant with a severe craniofacial anomaly and partial facial paralysis.

DISCUSSION

The findings of this study demonstrate that the signal value of infant facial expressions is remarkably robust. Despite visible deficits or ambiguities in the surface appearance of the facial muscle actions in infants with facial conditions, the judges were able to extract information about the hedonic valence and intensity of their facial expressions. This finding indicates that information about emotion is based on multiple cues in different regions of the face, so that distortions or ambiguities in the cues produced by their facial muscle actions do not make it impossible to read the infants' emotional signals. Emotion is not specified by a single facial cue (e.g., upturned lip corners or lowered brows). Although the infants in all three craniofacial anomaly groups were rated as significantly less attractive than infants in the comparison group, we found no evidence that the observers' judgments were biased by a negative halo effect. Infants with facial disfigurement were not judged as showing more negative emotion, as might be expected by research demonstrating the powerful influence of attractiveness on social judgments and behavior.[6] Although we specifically asked the judges to rate the emotion shown in the infants' faces, we did not predict that they would be able to do so as accurately as they did. The findings are consistent with the view that infant facial expressions are biologically based adaptations that are crucial for the survival and normal development of infants.[1,13–15] They also support the idea that the capacity to read and respond intuitively to infants' facial expressions may also have a biological basis.[14,16]

The findings also have important clinical implications. With the exception of those with total or extensive facial paralysis, infants with craniofacial anomalies are capable of producing a wide range of facial expressions. To the extent that their caregivers are sensitive to their signals, they should not be inexpressive or lacking in positive expressions, as reported in some earlier studies. At the same time, there is considerable individual variability in infants' facial expressiveness. In infants with craniofacial anomalies, the frequency and intensity of smiling and negative affect expressions shown during mother-infant interactions are affected by the mothers' psychological adjustment and sensitivity to the infant's signals and not just by the infant's facial condition.[10] Thus, the results of this observer judgment study show that the *potential* for effective emotional communication is present in infants with facial anomalies.

ACKNOWLEDGMENTS

A preliminary report of the data reported here was presented at a symposium, Cues to "Intuitive" Responses to Infant Signals: Converging Evidence from Adults' Attributions and Detailed Coding, conducted at the Meeting of the Society for Research in Child Development, Minneapolis, April 2001. The longitudinal study was supported in part by grants to Dr. Oster from the National Foundation for Facial Reconstruction, the March of Dimes Birth Defects Foundation, and the American Cleft Palate-Craniofacial Foundation. I gratefully acknowledge the cooperation and support of the faculty and staff of the Institute of Reconstructive Plastic Surgery at New York University School of Medicine (most notably Drs. Joseph G. McCarthy, Court B. Cutting, Barry Grayson, and Francine Blei; and Patricia Chibbaro, R.N.). I also thank the mothers and infants who participated in the study and the research assistants who contributed to data collection, reliability coding, and data analyses (Shilpa Taufique, Ilya Vinnick, Sarah Kamens, and Lynn Prosperi)

REFERENCES

1. DARWIN, C. [1872] 1998. The Expression of the Emotions in Man and Animals, 3rd edit. P. Ekman, Ed. Oxford University Press. New York.
2. BARDEN, R.C., M.E. FORD, A.G. JENSEN, *et al.* 1989. Effects of craniofacial deformity in infancy on the quality of mother-infant interactions. Child Dev. **60:** 819–824.
3. FIELD, T.M. & N. VEGA-LAHR. 1984. Early interactions between infants with cranio-facial anomalies and their mothers. Infant Behav. Dev. **7:** 527–530.
4. SPELTZ, M.L., E.W. GOODELL, M.C. ENDRIGA & S.K. CLARREN. 1994. Feeding interactions of infants with unrepaired cleft lip and/or palate. Infant Behav. Dev. **17:** 131–139.
5. WASSERMAN, G. 1986. Affective expression in normal and physically handicapped infants: situational and developmental effects. J. Am. Acad. Child Psychiatry **25:** 393–399.
6. LANGLOIS, J.H., J.M., RITTER, R.J. CASEY & D.B. SAWIN. 1995. Infant attractiveness predicts maternal behaviors and attitudes. Dev. Psychol. **31:** 464–472.

7. OSTER, H. 2003. Baby FACS: Facial Action Coding System for Infants and Young Children. Unpublished monograph and coding manual. New York University.

8. EKMAN, P. & W.V. FRIESEN. 1978. Facial Action Coding System. Consulting Psychologists Press. Palo Alto, CA.

9. OSTER, H. 2001. The repertoire of infant facial expressions: universal configurations and individual differences. Presented at a conference on Regulation in Typical and Impaired Emotional Development, May 27–29, Hôpital de la Salpetrière, Paris, France.

10. OSTER, H., S. TAUFIQUE & A. GRINBERG. 2000. Mothers and infants at play: the effects of infant facial anomalies and maternal depressive symptoms on affective communication. Presented at the XVIth Biennial Meetings of the International Society for the Study of Behavioral Development, July 11–14, Beijing, China.

11. HANDLER, M.K. & H. OSTER. 2001. Mothers' spontaneous attributions of emotion to infants' expressions: effects of craniofacial anomalies and maternal depression. Presented at a symposium, Cues to "Intuitive" Responses to Infant Signals: Converging Evidence from Adults' Attributions and Detailed Coding Conducted at the Meeting of the Society for Research in Child Development, Minneapolis, MN.

12. SEGAL, L., H. OSTER, M. COHEN, et al. 1995. Smiling and fussing in seven-month-old preterm and full-term Black infants in the Still-Face situation. Child Dev. **66:** 1829–1843.

13. BOWLBY, J. 1969. Attachment and Loss, Vol. 1. Attachment. Basic Books. New York.

14. HINDE, R. 1974. Biological bases of human social behavior. McGraw Hill. New York.

15. OSTER, H. 1997. Facial expression as a window on sensory experience and affect in newborn infants. *In* What the Face Reveals: Basic and Applied Studies of Spontaneous Expression Using the Facial Action Coding System (FACS). P. Ekman & E. Rosenberg, Eds.: 320-327. Oxford University Press. New York.

16. PAPOUSEK, H. & M. PAPOUSEK. 1983. Interactional failures: their origins and significance in infant psychiatry. *In* Frontiers of Infant Psychiatry. J.D. Call, E. Gallenson & R.L. Tyson, Eds. Basic Books. New York.

Darwin, Deception, and Facial Expression

PAUL EKMAN

*Department of Psychiatry, University of California, San Francisco,
San Francisco, California 94143, USA*

ABSTRACT: Darwin did not focus on deception. Only a few sentences in his book mentioned the issue. One of them raised the very interesting question of whether it is difficult to voluntarily inhibit the emotional expressions that are most difficult to voluntarily fabricate. Another suggestion was that it would be possible to unmask a fabricated expression by the absence of the difficult-to-voluntarily-generate facial actions. Still another was that during emotion body movements could be more easily suppressed than facial expression. Research relevant to each of Darwin's suggestions is reviewed, as is other research on deception that Darwin did not foresee.

KEYWORDS: Darwin; deception; facial expression; lies; lying; emotion; inhibition; smile; leakage; micro-facial-expressions; Facial Action Coding System; illustrators; pitch; Duchenne; asymmetry

The scientific study of the facial expression of emotion began with Charles Darwin's *The Expression of Emotions in Man and Animals*, first published in 1872.[1] Among his many extraordinary contributions Darwin gathered evidence that some emotions have a universal facial expression, cited examples and published pictures suggesting that emotions are evident in other animals, and proposed principles explaining why particular expressions occur for particular emotions—principles that, he maintained, applied to the expressions of all animals. But Darwin did not consider at any length when, how, and why emotional expressions are reliable or misleading.

Neither *deception* nor *lies* (or *lying*) appears in the index to his book. In the 19-page conclusion there is only one sentence that refers to this: "They [the movements of expression] reveal the thoughts and intentions of others more truly than do words, which may be falsified" (p 359). A bit too simple; for surely we know—and research has documented[2,3]—that some facial expressions can be very misleading. In brief comments elsewhere Darwin provides a more complex view, suggesting how true feelings may be shown despite efforts to conceal emotions and also how false expressions, which display emo-

Address for correspondence: Paul Ekman, 6515 Gwin Rd. Oakland, CA 94611.

Ann. N.Y. Acad. Sci. 1000: 205–221 (2003). © 2003 New York Academy of Sciences.
doi: 10.1196/annals.1280.010

tions not felt, may be betrayed. Much research has supported and sometimes qualified his comments.[a]

Darwin suggested that muscles that are difficult to voluntarily activate might escape efforts to inhibit or mask expression, revealing true feelings. "[W]hen movements, associated through habit with certain states of the mind, are partially repressed by the will, the strictly involuntary muscles, as well as those which are least under the separate control of the will, are liable still to act; and their action is often highly expressive (p. 54)." The same idea in somewhat different words: "A man when moderately angry, or even when enraged, may command the movements of his body, but . . . those muscles of the face which are least obedient to the will, will sometimes alone betray a slight and passing emotion" (p. 79).

INHIBITING EXPRESSION

Two very interesting ideas are contained in these brief quotations. The first is Darwin's suggestion that if you cannot make an action voluntarily, then you will not be able to prevent it when involuntary processes such as emotion instigate it. I am going to refer to this as the *inhibition hypothesis* to distinguish it from another idea contained in this quotation that I will get to later. Darwin does not explain why this might be so, but it is well known that the facial nucleus, which transmits impulses to the specific muscles to contract or relax, receives impulses from many different parts of the brain. The motor cortex is the source of the impulses resulting from voluntary efforts to make a facial expression. Other lower areas of the brain send impulses to the facial nucleus when emotions are aroused involuntarily. Clinical reports about certain neurological disorders[4–7] support the distinction between voluntary and involuntary facial actions, between facial movements that are easy and hard to make deliberately.

Each type of expression may depend upon different potentially independent neural pathways. Lesions in the pyramidal systems impair the ability to perform a facial movement on request, such as the ability to smile when asked to do so; yet they may leave emotional expressions intact, so that the patient might smile if amused by a joke. Lesions in the nonpyramidal systems may

---

[a]I considered in this chapter all the research I have found comparing voluntary and involuntary facial expressions, but I have excluded most of the research on deception and demeanor for the following reasons: most of it did not actually meaasure facial expression—or, if it did, the measurement was very crude; most dealt with trivial lies, where the rewards were of little consequence, and if there was any punishment, it was slight; most did not threaten punishment to anyone considered to be lying, regardless of whether the person actually was being truthful; most did not allow their subjects to choose whether to lie or tell the truth. In short, with few exceptions, the research on interpersonal deception carried out by other than our own group has had no ethological validity.

produce the reverse pattern; so, for example, a patient could smile on request but might not do so spontaneously.

But Darwin's inhibition hypothesis goes beyond simply distinguishing between voluntary and involuntary facial muscular actions. He said that if you cannot voluntarily activate a muscle, then you will not be able to voluntarily inhibit its involuntary activation in a spontaneous emotional expression. This sounds reasonable, but what would be the neural mechanism responsible for such a defect in inhibition? I asked a research neurologist, Bruce Miller, who studies emotion in various neurological disorders, if we could assume that those actions that are difficult to perform voluntarily must have poor representation in the motor cortex; and if that is so, would such poor representation in the motor cortex be responsible for the failure of voluntary efforts to inhibit those actions when they are directed by nonpyramidal systems. He said: "I don't know if there is any data on what part of the brain is involved in the voluntary inhibition of a smile, but I don't think that it necessarily involves the motor cortex. It is possible that there is a system involved with the inhibition of the smile that is still intact in a patient who cannot voluntarily smile. In fact, that is my guess" (personal communication October 2002).

It is remarkable that we do not know the answer; but now that we have focused on the question, I hope others will pursue it in studies of neurological patients. However, it is not necessary to know the neural substrates involved in order to check through behavioral observation Darwin's inhibition hypothesis. To determine whether Darwin was correct in proposing that if you cannot deliberately contract a muscle, you will not be able to deliberately prevent that muscle from contracting when it is activated involuntarily we must first identify which facial actions are difficult to make deliberately. We did that more than 20 years ago.[8] TABLE 1 shows the actions that fewer than 25% of our subjects could deliberately produce. If Darwin is correct, then these movements should provide what we have called *leakage* of felt emotions,[9] betraying how a person feels even when the person attempts to conceal that

TABLE 1. Action units

Latin Name	Name in FACS	Associated Emotion
Orbicularis oris	24: lip pressor	anger
Triangularis	15: lip corner depressor	sadness
Depressor labii inferioris	16: lower lip depressor	disgust, sadness
Frontalis, pars medialis	1: inner brow raiser	sadness
Frontalis, pars lateralis	2: outer brow	—
(Corrugator = AU 4)	1+4	sadness
	1+2+4	fear
Risorius	20: lip stretcher	fear
Orbicularis oculi, pars lateralis	6: raises cheeks, narrows eyes	enjoyment, sadness

information. Examining videotapes of people lying and telling the truth, we have seen, again and again, instances in which the activity of these muscles are not inhibited—not in all people, but in many. I have called the actions listed in TABLE 1 the *reliable* facial muscles.[10] I am embarrassed to confess that because it seemed so obvious, we never quantitatively tested Darwin's inhibition hypothesis.

WHICH IS MORE RELIABLE, THE FACE OR THE BODY?

The second idea contained in those brief quotations from Darwin is that people can "command" the movements of the body when angry (and presumably in any other emotion), and therefore bodily movement, unlike the reliable facial muscles, should be easy to conceal. This I have called the *face>body leakage hypothesis*. The evidence does not support Darwin's hypothesis. It is a more complex matter than one source, the face or the body, being a better source of leakage than the other.

We have proposed that, although bodily movements of the hands and feet would be easy to inhibit, consistent with Darwin's reasoning in the face>body leakage hypothesis, most people do not bother to censor their body movements.[9] Because most of us do not get much feedback from others about what our body movements are revealing, we do not learn the need to monitor these actions; and so, we hypothesized, when people lie, they usually do not fine-tune their body actions. If we are right, the body will be a good source of deception clues—exactly the opposite of what Darwin predicted.

Since people generally receive more comments on their facial expression, we predicted that people would focus their deceptive efforts on managing this, and thus the face would be a less useful source than the body of information about lying versus truthfulness. Our theorizing was only partly supported by the experiments we then conducted; it was a more complex matter than we anticipated.

In our first study we showed groups of observers videotapes of women who had either lied or told the truth about whether they were experiencing enjoyment induced from watching nature films.[2] Half of them were actually watching gory films, claiming falsely that they were feeling positively about watching nature films. The observers saw either the face or the body of the subjects when they were being interviewed about how they felt. The words spoken were not provided. The judgments made by the observers were more accurate when made from the body than from the face. This was so only in judging the deceptive videos, and only when the observers were also shown a sample of the subjects' behavior in a baseline, nonstressful condition.

Another finding was consistent with the reasoning underlying our proposal that the body provides more leakage than the face. The women who had been videotaped lying and telling the truth about what film they were seeing and how they felt were asked after the experiment what aspects of their behavior they had focused on controlling when they lied. Nearly all mentioned the need to manage their facial expressions; only a few referred to the need to manage their body movements.

Now let us consider another finding, which partially contradicted our proposal that the body is a better source of information than the face and is consistent instead with Darwin's face>body leakage hypothesis. Darwin is only partially supported by the finding I next describe because the face, it turned out, was an accurate source of information, but for only a limited number of special people. Before describing this and subsequent findings, I must first explain a subtlety in facial expression that we uncovered.

In the late 1960s before we did this experiment we discovered *micro facial expressions* when examining our films of psychiatric patients who had lied during a clinical interview, concealing either plans to commit suicide or hallucinations. We defined *micro expressions* as being

> ... so brief that they are barely perceptible to the untrained observer. Micro displays may be fragments of a squelched, neutralized or masked display. Micro displays may also show the full muscular movements associated with macro affect display, but may be greatly reduced in time. We have found that such micro displays when shown in slow motion do convey emotional information to observers, and that expert clinical observers can see micro displays and read the emotional information without the benefit of slow motion projection [p. 27].[9,b]

In our first paper on deception we proposed that

> ... the face is equipped to lie the most and leak the most, and thus can be a very confusing source of information during deception. ... [A person] can get away with and best perpetrate deception through his face. Although he must monitor quickly and work continually to inhibit this fast responsive system, he has most awareness of his facial display and is usually well practiced in the display rules for modulating facial affects. ... [T]he face is the major site for lies of commission [through macro expressions, which are large in scope and of sufficient duration to be readily seen]. ... [Most people will ignore or disregard such] important sources of information as micro displays and the rough edges on the simulated display. ... [O]ne would expect the usual observer of the face typically to be misled. One would expect the keen observer, on the other hand, to receive contradictory information from facial cues: simulated messages, micro leakage of information which contradicts the simulations, and deception clues of squelched displays and improperly performed simulations [pp. 98–99].[9]

---

[b]A few years earlier Haggard and Isaacs described having seen what they called "micromomentary expressions."[50] They thought these expressions are not detectable without slow-motion viewing. We know that is not so, that some people can detect them at real time. They also said micro expressions are the result of repression, revealing information about which the person is unaware. We have no reason to doubt that does occur, and in a few clinical case studies we found support for their contention; but micro expressions also occur with deliberate concealment.

By this reasoning people who are highly trained in observing facial movement might have made accurate judgments when they saw the videotapes of the subjects who had lied or told the truth about the emotions they felt. We showed the face-only videotapes to four associates who had been using our first technique for measuring the face[11] for more than a year. Each of these four people achieved an accuracy score of 80% or higher. So the face does contain accurate information, as well as misinformation, when people lie. Most people respond to the macro expressions and are misled, while a few keen observers detect the micro expressions and other imperfections in the macro displays and are correctly informed.

Let me summarize where we are in the argument and the evidence before proceeding. Although Darwin was correct—the skeletal muscles that generate body movements are easy to "command" and on that basis should not leak—we were correct in noticing that most people do not censor their body movements when they lie because they have not found that the targets seem to notice what they do with their body. This reasoning was supported by the finding in the experiment in which observers who saw the body were more accurate than those who saw only the face. While facial expression should be a fertile source of leakage because, as Darwin pointed out, it involves muscles most people cannot inhibit (the reliable muscles), our reasoning suggested that because people pay so much attention to each others' facial expressions, most people will attempt to tune their facial expressions when they lie. So, contrary to Darwin's prediction, the face should not be as good a source for observers as the body. An exception—an important one—is that micro expressions do leak information, but only keen observers can perceive it.

Now let us look at this matter from a different perspective, examining not what others can see (which is what the experiment described above did), but what is revealed when we use fine-grained measurements of how people behaved when they lied. Putting together Darwin's proposal and our elaboration, we should find micro expressions, squelched expressions, masked expressions, as well as leakage in body movements when the women lied.[c]

We measured the behavior shown in the videotapes of the women who had lied or been truthful about the emotions they were feeling.[3] The facial movements were measured with our Facial Action Coding System (FACS),[12,13] which identifies each and every facial muscular movement. We measured only one type of body movement, what we have termed *illustrators*[14]—hand movements that emphasize and otherwise illustrate simultaneous speech. The pitch of the voice was measured. Those who made these measurements of face, body, and voice did not know whether the interviews they scored were honest or deceptive and were unfamiliar with the purpose of the experiment.

---

[c]The relationship between these two approaches to assessing the information contained in expression is discussed at more length in ref. 51, chap. 2.

When the women attempted to conceal negative emotions, claiming to feel enjoyment, they showed more masking smiles—in which a smile (*zygomatic major* or AU 12 in FACS scoring) is superimposed over muscular actions associated with fear, sadness, or disgust—than they showed when they had truthfully described enjoyable feelings. Just the reverse was found with the type of smile that other evidence (described below) has identified as a sign of enjoyment (*zygomatic major* and *orbicularis oculi, pars lateralis* or 6+12). This type of smile was shown more often when the subjects honestly described enjoyable feelings than when they falsely claimed to have such feelings.[15] We did find micro expressions when some of the subjects lied, but only about a quarter of them showed these expressions. In later research studying other types of lies[16] we again found micro expressions, but only in some of our subjects.

Hand movements that illustrate speech decreased, as had been predicted; but the difference was only a trend, not reaching accepted levels of statistical significance. We noted that another type of body movement occurred only when people were lying—a fragment of a shrug gesture—but only by a third of our subjects. As with micro expressions, many of the signs of lying that we have identified are not shown by everyone. Their absence does not mean a person is truthful; but their presence, especially when there are multiple different types of signs (e.g., a fragment of a shrug and micro expressions), is suggestive. We also found that voice pitch became higher when the subjects lied.

Instead of only analyzing the average difference found across the entire group, we also considered how many of the subjects could be correctly identified by the behavioral measures. For illustrators it was possible to tell whether 38% were lying or truthful, 26% were misidentified, and it was not possible to classify 35%. Combining two smiling measures, we found that 48% were correctly identified, 16% were misidentified, and 35% could not be classified. The pitch measure accurately identified whether 59% of the subjects were lying or truthful, 16% were misidentified, and 31% could not be classified. Combining the facial measures and pitch slightly improved the discriminations: 61% correct, 10% incorrect, and 29% unclassified. Adding the illustrator measurement did improve accuracy.

It is too simple to say that there is more leakage in either the face or body. When people lie, there are both misleading signals and signals that betray the lie in both face and body. I will wait until the end of this chapter, after we have considered other types of facial behavior and other kinds of lying, to summarize which are the more reliable signals.

IDENTIFYING THE SMILE OF ENJOYMENT

The idea that actions that are difficult to make voluntarily will leak otherwise-concealed emotions (Darwin's inhibition hypothesis) is logically relat-

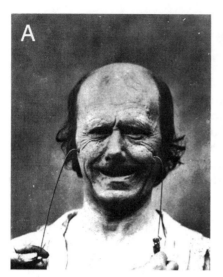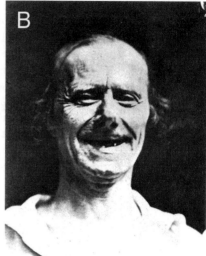

FIGURE 1. Photographs by Duchenne included in Darwin's *The Expression of the Emotions in Man and Animals.* (A) Smile produced when zygomatic major muscle was electrically stimulated. (B) Smile generated when subject was told a joke. The orbicularis oculi muscle was stimulated in addition to the zygomatic major.

ed to Duchenne's proposal about how to distinguish a smile of enjoyment from nonenjoyment smiling.[17] Duchenne compared the smile produced when he electrically stimulated the zygomatic major muscle (FIG. 1A) with a smile generated when he told the man a joke (FIG. 1B). The smile in response to a joke included not just the zygomatic major, but also the orbicularis oculi muscle (which orbits the eye, pulling the cheeks up, producing crow's feet, and slightly lowering the brows). Without orbicularis oculi, Duchenne said, "... no joy could be painted on the face truthfully ... it is only brought into play by a genuinely agreeable emotion. Its inertia in smiling unmasks a false friend [p. 72]."[18] In agreement with Duchenne we found that most people cannot voluntarily make this action. Those who can do it usually cannot do so on both sides of their face simultaneously; although once they have produced it on each side of their face, they can hold the contraction on both sides.

Darwin included in his book the Duchenne photographs that appear in FIGURE 1. Darwin noted that the best sign that the muscle is not active is the failure of the eyebrows to lower slightly. This implies what we have found: that it is not the entire orbicularis oculi whose absence unmasks the false friend, only the outer portion of this muscle—what is called the orbicularis oculi, pars lateralis (AU 6).

In discussing the smile that lacks the orbicularis oculi, Duchenne said: "You cannot always exaggerate the significance of this kind of smile, which often is only a simple smile of politeness, just as it can cover a treason. ...We

... politely smile with our lips at the same time as being malcontented or when the soul is sad" (pp. 127–128).[18] Darwin tested Duchenne's proposal by showing FIGURE 1 to observers. He reported that only FIGURE 1B, which includes the orbicularis oculi, was said to show happiness. In his honor I suggested that we call smiles incorporating the orbicularis oculi, pars lateralis *Duchenne's smile.*[19]

The failure to use Duchenne's distinction between smiles with and without the orbicularis oculi led to the mistaken conclusion that smiling is unrelated to emotion.[20–25] Even in recent years some investigators have failed to take the trouble to distinguish between Duchenne and non-Duchenne smiling. For example, Fridlund reported no relationship between smiling and self-reported happiness.[26] Yet we had reported earlier that Duchenne smiles were related to self-reported happiness, but total amount of smiling (Fridlund's measure) was not.[27] We also found that Duchenne smiles occurred more often when people watched amusing films as compared to gory films. Consistent with those findings Ekman, Davidson, and Friesen found that only Duchenne smiles distinguished which of two positive experiences subjects reported enjoying more.[19]

Currently, all those who studied deception (apart from our group) have continued to ignore Duchenne's distinction and have mistakenly concluded that smiling is unrelated to truthfulness. We were able to duplicate their failure when we used only a simple measure of total smiling; but, as I reported earlier in this chapter, when we separated Duchenne's smile from all other smiling, we were able to identify whether people were concealing strong negative emotions with a smile or actually enjoying themselves.[3,15]

In the last decade a number of studies have supported Duchenne's distinction. Fox and Davidson found more Duchenne smiles in 10-month-old infants when they were approached by their mother and more other forms of smiling when the infants were approached by a stranger.[28] When they combined Duchenne and non-Duchenne smiles, the differences between approach by mother and stranger disappeared. They also reported that only Duchenne smiles were associated with left frontal EEG activation, the pattern of cerebral activity repeatedly found in positive affect. This EEG pattern of cerebral activity was found in adults watching amusing films only when they simultaneously showed Duchenne smiles.[19] And when Ekman and Davidson selected subjects who could voluntarily contract the orbicularis oculi, pars lateralis (a minority of people) and asked them to make a Duchenne smile and a non-Duchenne smile, the EEG pattern of cerebral activity associated with enjoyment was generated only by their Duchenne smiles.[29] Many other studies by investigators in a number of countries have also found differences between the two forms of smiling (many are reported in Ekman & Rosenberg[30]).

Clearly, the distinction between Duchenne smiles and other forms of smiling based simply on the presence or absence of a muscle that most people cannot activate voluntarily (the orbicularis oculi, pars medialis) is powerful. But, as I explained earlier, the fact that measurements reveal a difference does not tell us whether observers can see that difference when viewing expressions in real time. Frank, Ekman, and Friesen addressed this matter by asking observers to judge whether each smile they saw was a true, genuine expression of enjoyment or a false or social expression.[31] The smiles were drawn from two prior experiments, the one described earlier in which women lied or told the truth about how they felt[2] and a study in which subjects sat alone watching amusing or unpleasant films.[32] When the observers saw each smile one at a time, they were correct only 56% of the time, somewhat better than chance (t(39) = 2.97, P < 0.01). When they were shown two smiles of each person, one a Duchenne smile and one which was not, accuracy was significantly (P < 0.0001) higher, with a mean accuracy of 74% (t(39) = 12.47, P < 0.001). Neither condition—judging single smiles or judging pairs of smiles—very closely resembles real-life contexts, in which smiles are seen embedded in other behaviors, including speech, voice, and gesture. Nevertheless, this experiment does substantiate that Duchenne smiling can be recognized in real time.

The same video was used in another experiment, in which new groups of observers were asked not to say which smile was more genuine, but instead to fill out rating scales describing their impression of the persons they saw: for example, outgoing-inhibited, expressive-unexpressive, natural-awkward, likeable-unlikable. Frank et al.[31] combined the ratings on 15 such scales into an overall positive score. The ratings on this scale were more positive when the observers saw segments that contained a Duchenne smile as compared to segments that contained a non-Duchenne smile. This study shows that the type of smile observed influences global impressions even when attention is not directed to focus on smiling.

I believe these findings about the Duchenne smile can be extended to a wider set of emotional facial expressions. When emotional expressions lack a muscular movement that is difficult to make voluntarily, that expression should be less reliable; and those expressions that contain the reliable muscle should be more likely to be trustworthy. TABLE 1 shows that there is such a reliable muscle for sadness (Aus 1, 1+4 and 15), fear (Aus 1+2+4 and 20), and anger (AU 23) in addition to enjoyment. The research to check my proposal has yet to be done.

MICRO FACIAL EXPRESSIONS

Let us return to consider what we have learned about individual differences in the ability to identify a micro facial expression. We constructed a test by tachistoscopically presenting for 1/25 s photographs of very intense facial expressions.[33,34] Prior research had established that these expressions were easily recognized, with high agreement across cultures, when they were viewed for 10 seconds. As predicted on the basis of our observations that micro expressions appear in subjects when they are lying, accuracy on this tachistoscopic test was correlated with accuracy in identifying from videotapes which of 10 women were lying or telling the truth about their emotions ($r = 0.27$, $P < 0.02$). (We presume the correlation is not higher, because not all the women showed micro expressions).

In a second study we constructed a different test of the ability to identify facial expressions.[35] A different set of facial expressions that elicit high agreement across cultures[36] was shown tachistoscopically. Again, we found micro recognition accuracy correlated with deception judgment accuracy ($r = 0.34$, $P < 0.04$).

A potential limitation of testing the ability to recognize micro expressions with a tachistoscopic presentation of facial expressions is that, unlike real life, there is no preceding or following expression. To remedy this problem I produced a new test, which I called the Brief Affect Recognition Test (BART), in which a neutral image of a person is shown, followed by an emotional expression for 1/15 s, followed by the neutral image of that person once again. No afterimage lingers, as the neutral face follows immediately. Photographs of Caucasian and Japanese intense expressions, the JACFEE set, were used. Frank used 24 items from BART and found that accuracy on it correlated with accuracy in judging videos in which 18 people lied or told the truth about their beliefs on a controversial social issue.[37] This was so for both Australians ($n = 104$, $r = 0.19$, $P < 0.05$) and for Americans ($n = 34$, $r = .30$, $P < 0.05$) who took both tests.

Matsumoto et al. used a 56-item version of BART in five experiments.[38] They established that BART is reliable, both in terms of internal consistency and over time. They also found that accuracy was consistently, but modestly, correlated with the Openness score on the Big Five Inventory-54.[39] People who score high on Openness are considered to be more attentive and receptive to the environment and the people around them. Accuracy on BART was also correlated with Extraversion, but on only one of two personality tests (the Eyesenck, not the BFI).

I recently developed a version of BART that is intended to train people to improve accuracy in recognizing micro expressions. This Micro Expression Training Tool (METT) includes feedback about the correct answers, modified faces contrasting the most difficult-to-discriminate emotions, and a pre- and posttest.[40] Frank and I each separately provided this training and, in yet-to-be-published studies, obtained a very large increase in accuracy with less than one hour of training. Thus, it appears that while most people are not attuned to the recognition of micro expressions, most can learn to become sensitive to them. We do not yet know how long improvement gained through training is maintained.

ASYMMETRY IN EXPRESSION

Through serendipity we first found that spontaneous emotional expressions are more symmetrical than those made deliberately.[41]

> We noted in Sackeim, Gur and Saucy's report[42] about emotions being expressed more intensely on the left side of the face, that this effect was evident for all but the happy faces they evaluated. We had supplied Sackeim et al. with the faces and knew that only the happy ones were expressions of felt emotion, having occurred spontaneously as we joked with the models. We had produced all the other by asking our models to deliberately move a specified set of facial action units. ... We reasoned that deliberately made facial expressions, such as false smiles, would require more cortical involvement and thereby be more likely to show asymmetry because of cerebral specialization, than uncontrolled, spontaneous, felt emotional expressions. Searching the literature on facial asymmetry we found support for this hypothesis in Lynn and Lynn's[43, 44] reports that asymmetries were rare for spontaneous smiles [p. 246].[45]

Ekman, Hager, and Friesen verified this difference in symmetry.[45] In one study they found that when children were asked to imitate facial movements, they produced asymmetrical facial actions; while the spontaneous smiles they showed during the task were symmetrical. The symmetry of the expressions shown by adults watching pleasant and unpleasant films was consistent with the children's results. Their smiles in response to watching an amusing film were nearly always (96%) symmetrical. Their expressions that included facial actions associated with negative emotions shown when watching unpleasant films were also for the most part symmetrical (75%).

Hager and Ekman extended the earlier findings by comparing the facial actions shown in response to a very loud noise (startle) with deliberately performed actions, and with a smile made in response to an amusing event.[46] Spontaneous smiles were more symmetrical than requested smiles. The action of the orbicularis oculi, pars lateralis (the sign of genuine enjoyment identified by Duchenne described earlier) was also more symmetrical when it accompanied a spontaneous smile as compared to when it was deliberately performed. Stretching the lips horizontally (AU 20) was more symmetrical when it occurred in response to the loud noise than when it was deliberately performed.[d]

---

[d]They had intended to compare the spontaneous reaction to the startling noise with a simulated startle, but when subjects simulated a startle they performed very different actions than those that had been shown spontaneously. They had also intended to compare spontaneous emotional reactions with posed emotions, but there were too few spontaneous actions to allow the comparison. When facial actions were asymmetrical, the side of the face in which the facial movement was stronger varied muscle by muscle, unrelated to the branch of the facial nerve that activates each muscle.

HOW LONG AN EXPRESSION LASTS

Ekman and Friesen found that spontaneous expressions usually lasted between 2/3 of a second and 4 seconds.[41] Their observation was limited to spontaneous smiles shown when subjects had watched pleasant films. Hess and Kleck replicated this observation, finding a difference in duration between spontaneous smiles and deliberately posed smiling.[47]

Frank *et al.* further confirmed this difference in duration, examining Duchenne smiles and non-Duchenne smiles shown in a sample of people watching a pleasant film and in a sample of people who described their feelings as they watched a pleasant film.[31] They found that there was less variability in the duration of Duchenne smiling and that most such smiles lasted, as predicted, between ½ and 4 seconds.[e]

SMOOTH EXPRESSIONS

Ekman and Friesen observed another difference in timing between spontaneous and deliberate expressions.[41] In deliberate expressions the onset is often abrupt, the apex (moments of maximum contraction) held too long, and the offset (the period from the apex to the disappearance of the expression) is either abrupt or in other ways appears irregular rather than smooth. Frank *et al.* confirmed these observations by contrasting the timing of Duchenne smiles and non-Duchenne smiles shown in subjects watching an amusing film alone and in subjects talking about their feelings as they watched an amusing film.[31]

CONCLUSION

There is no single source within demeanor that is completely trustworthy, impervious to efforts to disguise; nor is there a source that should be ignored because it is completely untrustworthy. Darwin rightly noted how easily "… words may be falsified." It is easy not only to falsify what is said but also to conceal information from speech; yet we have found repeatedly in studies with our experimental materials and in examining real-life cases that words themselves provide important clues that a person may be lying. It would be a mistake *not* to scrutinize very carefully what people say. Some of the verbal clues are topic specific—that is, are useful if they are not part of the person's usual behavioral repertoire but instead appear only when a specific topic is

---

[e]In the solitary condition the average smile was longer, but this was due to two outliers who produced very long smiles. Without those two subjects the findings conformed to the prediction.

discussed. Hesitations, changes in emphasis, speech errors, indirect or distancing language (e.g., "that woman") are all topic-specific clues. Other clues, such as slips of the tongue, implausible statements, contradictions between what is said at different times, and statements that can be incontrovertibly contradicted by other facts, stand on their own. Taking into account not only what a person says, but also the sound of the voice, the expression on the face, gesture, and posture is of critical importance.

Although I have not said much about them in this report, gestural slips—the equivalent of slips of the tongue—do occur in some people and are valuable sources of concealed information.^{f} Because these are typically brief, involving only a fragment of the total gesture, most people do not see them unless they are alerted to the phenomenon. Even then, they miss gestural slips unless they know the vocabulary of gestures—what Efron and we (adopting Efron's terminology) called *emblems*.[14,48] Emblems are culture specific, just as language is, with emblems in one language group totally missing in another or having a different meaning in another language setting.

Micro facial expressions are a very useful sign of concealed emotions. They can be seen in real time with training. (The MicroExpression Training Tool[40] accomplishes this in a short time.) Some people we have found already see them without being trained, but there are not many such people. Much work remains to be done, such as to determine how long the effect of training lasts and whether or when refresher courses are needed. Even without that evidence, it would be wise, in my judgment, for those interviewing people in situations where emotions might be concealed to learn to detect these expressions. Elsewhere I have considered how to use the information revealed by micro expressions in the workplace, friendship, and family life.[49] In situations in which distinguishing lies from truthful statements is the focus, great care must be taken not to make either of two mistakes. First, the absence of micro expressions, like the absence of gestural slips, does not prove a person is truthful; not all liars show such signs.

The second mistake is to presume that concealed emotion is evidence that a person is lying about the topic of interest to the interviewer. We need to be careful to avoid what I have called Othello's error.[10] He mistakenly assumed that Desdemona's expression of fear was the reaction of a woman caught in betrayal. He failed to understand that emotions do not tell you their cause. The fear of being disbelieved looks the same as the fear of being caught. In real-life lies that I have studied people suspected of crimes sometimes show micro expressions of anger. Only through further questioning is it possible to determine whether the concealed anger is the result of being wrongfully under suspicion or whether it is anger toward the interviewer for trying to catch

---

^{f}I have described how gestures may act like slips of the tongue, revealing concealed information, in my book *Telling Lies*.[10] In further research we have confirmed these findings through studying other subjects in other kinds of lies.

the suspect in a misdeed. Lying about the topic of interest should be the last, not the first, explanation of why a micro expression has occurred.

Although the bulk of the findings I have described in this chapter pertain to smiling, my expectation that findings apply to other emotional expressions has been supported by those studies that have examined other expressions. Apart from micro expressions, there are seven characteristics that will be of help in distinguishing voluntary from involuntary facial expressions:

(1) *Morphology.* This is best documented for enjoyment; but the absence of any of the reliable movements should raise questions about whether the expression is voluntary rather than involuntary, and the presence of the reliable actions should suggest that an expression is genuine.

(2) *Symmetry.* While tedious to measure, and not likely to be detectable in real time, asymmetry is a mark that the expression is deliberate.

(3) *Duration.* Very brief (<½ s) and very long (>5 s) duration of expression should occur more often with deliberate than spontaneous expressions.

(4) *Speed of onset.* Although this varies with social circumstances, the onset of a deliberate expression will more often be abrupt than that of a spontaneous expression.

(5) *Apex overlap.* In those expressions in which there are multiple independent facial actions, it is likely that the apexes of the actions will overlap if the expression is spontaneous. There has been no research on this suggestion.

(6) *Ballistic trajectory.* The expression will appear smooth over its trajectory, without a stepped or jagged offset, if it is spontaneous.

(7) *Cohesion.* The expression will fit with what is being said simultaneously.

REFERENCES

1. DARWIN, C. 1998. The Expression of the Emotions in Man and Animals, 3rd edit. Introduction, afterwords, and commentaries by Paul Ekman. Harper Collins. London (US edit.: Oxford University Press. New York).
2. EKMAN, P. & W.V. FRIESEN. 1974. Detecting deception from body or face. J. Pers. Soc. Psychol. **29:** 288–298.
3. EKMAN, P., M. O'SULLIVAN, W.V. FRIESEN & K.R. SCHERER. 1991 Face, voice and body in detecting deception. J. Nonverb. Behav. 15: 125–135.
4. KAHN, E.A. 1966. On facial expression. Clin. Neurosurgery **12:** 9–22
5. MEIHLKE, A. 1973. Surgery of the Facial Nerve. Saunders. Philadelphia.
6. MYERS, R.E. 1976. Comparative neurology of vocalization and speech: proof of a dichotomy. Ann. N.Y. Acad. Sci. **280:** 745–757.
7. TSCHIASSNY, K. 1953. Eight syndromes of facial paralysis and their significance in locating the lesion. Ann. Otol. Rhinol. Laryngol. **62:** 677–691.

8. EKMAN, P., G. ROPER & J.C . HAGER. 1980. Deliberate facial movement. Child Dev. **51:** 886–891.
9. EKMAN, P. & W.V. FRIESEN. 1969. Nonverbal leakage and clues to deception. Psychiatry **32:** 88–105.
10. EKMAN, P. 2001. Telling Lies: Clues to Deceit in the Marketplace, Marriage, and Politics, 3rd edit. W.W. Norton. New York.
11. EKMAN, P., W.V. FRIESEN & S.S. TOMKINS. 1971. Facial Affect Scoring Technique: a first validity study. Semiotica **3:** 37–58.
12. EKMAN, P. & W.V. FRIESEN. 1978. Facial Action Coding System: a technique for the measurement of facial movement, Consulting Psychologists Press. Palo Alto, CA.
13. EKMAN, P., W.V. FRIESEN & J.C. HAGER. 2002. The Facial Action Coding System. Research Nexus eBook. Salt Lake City, UT
14. EKMAN, P. & W.V. FRIESEN. 1969. The repertoire of nonverbal behavior: categories, origins, usage, and coding. Semiotica **1:** 49– 98.
15. EKMAN, P., W.V. FRIESEN & M. O'SULLIVAN. 1988. Smiles when lying. J. Pers. Soc. Psychol. **54:** 414–420.
16. FRANK, M.G. & P. EKMAN. 1997. The ability to detect deceit generalizes across different types of high-stake lies. J. Pers. Soc. Psychol. **72:** 1429–1439.
17. DUCHENNE DE BOLOGNE, G.-B. 1862. Mécanisme de la Physionomie Humaine. Jules Renouard Libraire. Paris.
18. DUCHENNE DE BOULOGNE, G.B. 1990. The Mechanism of Human Facial Expression. A. Cuthbertson, Trans. & Ed. Cambridge Universitiy Press. New York.
19. EKMAN, P., R.J. DAVIDSON & W.V. FRIESEN. 1990. Emotional expression and brain physiology II: the Duchenne smile. J. Pers. Soc. Psychol. **58:** 342–353.
20. BIRDWHISTELL, R.L. 1970. Kinesics and context. University of Pennsylvania Press. Philadelphia.
21. BRUNER, J.S. & R. TAGUIRI. 1954. The perception of people. *In* Handbook of Social Psychology, Vol. 2. G. Lindzey, Ed.: 634–654. Addison-Wesley. Reading, MA.
22. KRAUT, R.E. & R.E. JOHNSTON. 1979. Social and emotional messages of smiling: an ethological approach J. Pers. Soc. Psychol. **37:** 1529–1553.
23. LANDIS, C. 1924. Studies of emotional reactions: II. general behavior and facial expression. J. Comp. Psychol. **4:** 447–509.
24. SMITH, W.J. 1985. Consistency and change in communication. *In* The Development of Expressive Behavior. G. Zivin, Ed.: 51–75. Academic Press. Orlando, FL.
25. EKMAN, P., Ed. 1982. Emotion in the Human Face, 2nd edit. Cambridge University Press. New York.
26. FRIDLUND, A.J. 1991. Sociality of solitary smiling: potentiation by an implicit audience. J. Pers. Soc. Psychol. **60:** 229–240.
27. EKMAN, P. W.V. FRIESEN & S. ANCOLI. 1980. Facial signs of emotional experience. J. Pers. Soc. Psychol. **39:** 1125–1134.
28. FOX, N.A. & R.J. DAVIDSON. 1988. Patterns of brain electrical activity during facial signs of emotion in 10-month-old infants. Dev. Psychol. **24:** 233–240.
29. EKMAN, P. & R.J. DAVIDSON. 1993. Voluntary smiling changes regional brain activity. Psychol. Sci. **4:** 342–345.
30. EKMAN, P. & E.L. ROSENBERG, EDS. 1997. What the Face Reveals: Basic and Applied Studies of Spontaneous Expression Using the Facial Action Coding System (FACS). Oxford University Press. New York.

31. FRANK. M.G., P. EKMAN & W.V. FRIESEN. 1993. Behavioral markers and recognizability of the smile of enjoyment. J. Pers. Soc. Psychol. **64:** 83–93.
32. DAVIDSON, R.J., P. EKMAN, C. SARON, *et al.* 1990. Emotional expression and brain physiology I: approach/withdrawal and cerebral asymmetry. J. Pers. Soc. Psychol. **58:** 330–341.
33. EKMAN, P. & W.V. FRIESEN. 1974. Nonverbal behavior and psychopathology. *In* The Psychology of Depression: Contemporary Theory and Research. R.J. Friedman & M.N. Katz, Eds.: 203–232. J. Winston. Washington, DC.
34. EKMAN, P. & W.V. FRIESEN. 1976. Pictures of Facial Affect. Consulting Psychologists Press. Palo Alto, CA.
35. EKMAN, P. & M. O'SULLIVAN. 1991. Who can catch a liar. Am. Psychol. **46:** 913–920.
36. MATSUMOTO, D.R. & P. EKMAN. 1988. Japanese and Caucasian Facial Expressions of Emotions and Neutral Faces. University of California, San Francisco. Available from author.
37. FRANK, M.G. 2002. Decoding deception and emotion by Australians and Americans. In press.
38. MATSUMOTO, D., J. LEROUX, C. WILSON-COHN, *et al.* 2000. A new test to measure emotion recognition ability: Matsumoto and Ekman's Japanese and Caucasian Brief Affect Recognition Test (JACBART). J. Nonverb. Behav. **24:** 179–209.
39. JOHN, O. 1989. The BFI-54. Unpublished test, Institute of Personality and Social Research, Department of Psychology, Universitiy of California, Berkeley.
40. EKMAN, P. 2002. MicroExpression Training Tool (METT). University of California, San Francisco. Available from www.emotionsrevealed.com.
41. EKMAN, P. & W.V. FRIESEN. 1982. Felt, false and miserable smiles. J. Nonverb. Behav. **6:** 238–252.
42. SACKEIM, H.A., R.C. GUR & M.C. SAUCY. 1978. Emotions are expressed more intensely on the left side of the face. Science **202:** 434–436.
43. LYNN, J.G. & D.R. LYNN. 1938. Face-hand laterality in relation to personality. J. Abnorm. Soc. Psychol. **33:** 291–322.
44. LYNN, J.G. & D.R. LYNN. 1943. Smile and hand dominance in relation to basic modes of adaptation. J. Abnorm. Soc. Psychol. **38:** 250–276.
45. EKMAN, P., J.C. HAGER & W.V. FRIESEN. 1981. The symmetry of emotional and deliberate facial actions. Psychophysiology **18:** 101–106.
46. HAGER, J.C. & P. EKMAN. 1985. The asymmetry of facial actions is inconsistent with models of hemispheric specialization. Psychophysiology **22:** 307–318.
47. HESS, U. & R.E. KLECK. 1990. Differentiating emotion elicited and deliberately emotional facial expressions. Eur. J. Soc. Psychol. **20:** 369–385.
48. EFRON, D. 1941. Gesture and Environment. King's Crown. New York.
49. EKMAN, P. 2003. Emotions Revealed. Times Books. New York.
50. HAGGARD, E.A. & K.S. ISAACS. 1996. Micromomentary facial expressions as indicators of ego mechanisms in psychotherapy. *In* Methods of Research in Psychotherapy. L.A. Gottschalk & A.H. Auerback, Eds.: 154–165. Appleton Century Crofts. New York.
51. EKMAN, P. 1982. Methods for measuring facial action. *In* Handbook of Methods in Nonverbal Behavior Research. K.R. Scherer & P. Ekman, Eds.: 45–135. Cambridge University Press. New York.

Expression and the Course of Life

Studies of Emotion, Personality, and Psychopathology from a Social-Functional Perspective

DACHER KELTNER

Department of Psychology, University of California, Berkeley, Berkeley, California 94720, USA

ABSTRACT: In this paper I discuss how expressive behavior relates to personality and psychopathology, integrating recent findins from my laboratory and the insights of Charles Darwin on this topic. In the first part of the paper I challenge the view, in part espoused by Darwin, that humans are equipped to convey only a limited number of emotions with nonverbal behavior. Our lab has documented displays for several emotions, including embarrassment, love, desire, compassion, gratitude, and awe, to name just a few states that previously were thought not to possess a distinct display. I then present an argument for how individual differences in emotion, although fleeting, shape the social environment. This argument focuses on the functions of nonverbal display: to provide information to others, to evoke responses, and to serve as incentives of preceding or ensuing social behavior. This reasoning sets the stage for the study of the relationships between personality, psychopathology, and expressive behavior, to which I turn in the final part of the paper. Here I show that basic personality traits (e.g., extraversion, agreeableness) and psychological disorders (e.g., externalizing disorder in children, autism) have expressive signatures that shape social interactions and environments in profound ways that might perpetuate and transmit the trait or disorder.

KEYWORDS: facial expression; personality; psychopathology; emotion; social interaction; course of life

> *In every asylum we find examples of absolutely*
> *unmotived fear, anger, melancholy, or conceit;*
> *and others of equally unmotived apathy*
> *which persists in spite of the best outward*
> *reasons why it should give way.*
>
> —WILLIAM JAMES, 1890

Address for correspondence Dacher Keltner, Ph.D., Department of Psychology, University of California, Berkeley, 3210 Tolman Hall, Berkeley, CA 94720-1650. Voice: 510-642-5368; fax: 510-642-5293.
keltner@socrates. berkeley.edu

Ann. N.Y. Acad. Sci. 1000: 222–243 (2003). © 2003 New York Academy of Sciences.
doi: 10.1196/annals.1280.011

Does facial expression tell us about personality and psychopathology? William James thought so, as suggested by the quotation above. So did Charles Darwin.[1] Darwin observed, "The insane ought to be studied, as they are liable to the strongest passions" (p.20).[1] In the Victorian England of Darwin's time, the unregulated emotions of the insane provided rich examples of the universal expressions that he sought and so successfully described. In a more tacit fashion, Darwin's accounts of the expressive behavior of the insane intimated the importance of emotional expression in social life—a theme central to this chapter.

In Darwin's eyes there were pathological excesses of expressed emotion. For example, in several places, quoted below, Darwin described what appear to be individuals suffering from depression:

> In one of these (a case of hypochondria), a widow, aged 51, fancied that she had lost all her viscera, and that her whole body was empty. She wore an expression of great distress and beat her semi-closed hands rhythmically together for hours. The grief muscles were permanently contracted and the upper eyelids arched. This condition lasted for months, then she recovered, and her countenance resumed its natural expression [p. 184].[1]

> Nothing is more characteristic of simple melancholia, even in the male sex, than a tendency to weep on the slightest occasion, or from no cause [p. 157].[1]

> The depression of the corners (of the mouth) may often be seen ... with the melancholic insane, and was well exhibited in ... patients with a strong tendency to suicide [p. 191].[1]

Here we encounter remarkable possibilities: facial expressions of sadness (i.e., "grief muscles") lasting for extended periods of times, perhaps even months; weeping for no reason; expressive behavior revealing depressed states of mind and the predilection to suicide.

Darwin also took note of individuals whose absence of emotion was equally revealing of the individual's mental condition. He noted that "idiots" rarely blush (p. 311),[1] no doubt a sign of their inability to abide by societal norms and morals. Elsewhere Darwin wrote: "Many idiots are morose, passionate, restless, in a painful state of mind, or utterly stolid, and these never laugh [p. 196]." In these cases, the relative absence of expression—blushing or laughing—is just as dysfunctional, and a sign of the individual's inability to participate in normal life.

Underlying these astute observations is the notion that a person's functioning in life is revealed in specific patterns of expressive behavior, in telling cues to a person's state of mind and character. What evidence is there for this provocative thesis? As with many of Darwin's prescient observations, the answers offered by empirical science have only recently begun to emerge. In this article, I consider some of those answers by reviewing recent findings concerning individual differences in facial expression. At stake are several significant opportunities for researchers, which I first discuss. I then turn to a social-functional account of emotions, which argues that emotions evolved to promote and maintain important relationships. Within this perspective, emotional expression coordinates social interactions and should therefore be an important contributor to the individual's adjustment and functioning. With this reasoning as backdrop, I then review four kinds of evidence that indicate that facial expression is revealing of the life course, the life that the individual has led and is likely to continue leading.

BENEFITS TO THE STUDY OF INDIVIDUAL
DIFFERENCES IN EXPRESSION

It is only in the last 20 years that empirical science has begun to address systematically individual differences in expressive behavior. The reasons for this are several. Reliable methods for measuring facial expression, most notably the Facial Action Coding System (FACS),[2] were developed only quite recently. It is somewhat counterintuitive, if not methodologically ill advised (and counter to principles of statistical aggregation), to expect brief observations of facial behavior to predict cumulative life outcomes. The constructs themselves—facial expression, personality traits, and psychological disorders—are different in important ways: emotion refers to that which is transient, specific, situationally specific; personality traits and disorders refer to what are stable, broad, cross-situationally consistent, and idiosyncratic. The notion that certain facial muscle actions would be telling of individual character might have struck some psychologists as perilously close to phrenology. Some social scientists have argued that facial expression provide little coherent information about an individual's emotion, intentions, and dispositions (for review of these and contrary views see Keltner & Ekman[3]).

Yet the benefits of studying the relations between expression and individual differences in personality, or psychopathology, are significant—if not essential—to certain inquiries in the field of emotion. The study of individual differences, in this case in expression and personality, is one method for gathering evidence relevant to functional claims about emotion.[4] For example, in a later section we shall see that people who display little embarrassment or inappropriately timed embarrassment have pronounced difficulties abiding by social norms and morals. This kind of finding is consistent with the notion that one function of embarrassment is to motivate the adherence to social norms and morals.[5] Studies linking individual variation in facial expression to specific outcomes, therefore, lend credence to claims about the particular functions of an emotion.

For those guided by more applied or clinical concerns, studies of individual differences in facial expression are equally informative. Careful analysis of the emotional dynamics of different disorders can help refine the characterization and classification of disorders. For example, it has long been believed that schizophrenia is marked by the relative absence of facial expression. Researchers have only recently sought to empirically test these observations, initially offered by Bleuler and Kraeplin. Kring and colleagues have documented that schizophrenia patients show fewer facial expressions of positive and negative emotions in response to emotionally evocative material when compared to nonpatients, but report comparable experiences of emotion.[6] Interventions that help patients better match their feelings with their outward displays may therefore have positive effects on interpersonal adjustment. To the extent that there prove to be fairly specific expressive markers of a particular disorder—for example, reduced embarrassment with autism[7]—researchers might be better able to identity individuals prone to the disorder earlier in development. Most generally then, studies of emotional expression and psychological disorder will help refine the classification, understanding, and treatment of individuals with different disorders. These gains made by studying individual differences in expression are brought into clearer focus by a social-functional account of emotion.

A SOCIAL-FUNCTIONAL APPROACH TO EMOTION

Humans are profoundly social. We raise offspring, gather resources, mete out justice, work, play, and celebrate in relationships. Our well-being depends on the quality of those relationships more so than on material success.[8] Human relationships are complex and highly differentiated, with their own rules, morals, modes of allocation, accompanying cognitive processes, and functions.[9]

Within the field of emotion, there is a certain irony. Many empirical studies have focused on the intrapersonal processes related to emotion, including emotion-related appraisal,[10] the structure of emotional experience,[11] the effects of emotion upon reasoning,[12] and emotion-specific central and autonomic nervous system physiology.[13] At the same time, there is an increasing consensus that emotions were designed—by evolution or social construction, depending on one's theoretical persuasion—to solve certain problems of human social life.[10,14–18] This view holds that emotions are elicited by problems and opportunities within important social relationships: for example, slights to one's reputation trigger anger or shame, the distress of vulnerable individuals triggers compassion, cues of beauty or sexual receptivity trigger romantic love or desire. Emotions, once elicited, trigger patterns of cognition and action that prompt the individual to avert or reduce the problems or take advantage of the opportunities within ongoing interactions.[12,19]

TABLE 1 presents a social-functional analysis of some emotions.[16,17,20] In TABLE 1, I identity three broad classes of problems and opportunities related

TABLE 1. Taxonomy of problems and the functional systems and emotions that solve them

Problem	Functional systems	Emotions	Specific functions
Problems of physical survival			
Predation	fight-flight	fear	avoidance of threat to self
		rage	removal of threat to self
Disease	food selection	disgust	avoid microbes/ parasites
Problems of reproduction			
Finding a mate	attachment	desire	increase sexual contact
		romantic love	commit to long-term bond
		sadness	replace loss of mate
Keeping mate	mate protection	jealousy	protect mate from rivals
Protecting vulnerable children	caregiving	filial love	increase filial bond
		sympathy	reduce distress of vulnerable individuals
Problems of group governance			
Cooperation and defection	reciprocal altruism	guilt	repair own transgression
		moral anger	motivate other to repair transgression
		gratitude	reward cooperative bond
		envy	reduce unfair differences in equality
Group organization	dominance-submissiveness	shame and embarrassment	pacify likely aggressor
		contempt	reduce status of other
		awe	endow other with status

to human reproduction and survival, and functions that specific emotions serve related to these problems.

Certain emotions help solve the *problems of physical survival*, including avoiding death by predation, violence, and disease. Fear helps individuals avoid death by predation or other physical attacks, in part through amygdala-based automatic processing of sensory information[21] and activity of the hypothalamic-pituitary-adrenocortical axis, which readies the organism for fight or flight. Prototypical fear can be seen as the heart of a system that includes a variety of cognitive and behavioral mechanisms that make it more effective—for example, vicarious learning and the preparedness of animal phobias.[22]

Disgust—along with its simpler precursor, distaste—can similarly be seen at the heart of the "food-selection" system,[23] which helps humans choose a balanced and safe diet. In humans, food rejections are not based primarily on the sensory properties of the object, but rather on a knowledge of what it is or what it has touched.[24] The food selection system is further expanded by the addition of learning mechanisms, such as one-trial learning for nausea-inducing foods;[25] and by cultural mechanisms, such as cuisine, which marks prepared foods with a reassuringly familiar blend of spices or flavors.[26]

Evolutionary and attachment theorists have speculated on how a variety of emotions solve the *problems of reproduction*, which include procreation and the raising of offspring to the age of reproduction. Romantic love and desire facilitate the identification, establishment, and maintenance of reproductive relations. These emotions involve appraisals, perceptions, and experiences that are sensitive to cues related to potential mate value. These include beauty, fertility, chastity, social status, and character;[27] expressive behaviors that signal interest and commitment,[28,29] and evoke desire and love; and hormonal and autonomic responses that facilitate sexual behavior.[29]

Other emotions are sensitive to threats or disruptions to reproductive relationships. Sadness follows the loss of important bonds and helps individuals establish new bonds (for an analysis of grief, see Lazarus[10]). Jealousy relates to mate protection, and is triggered by cues that signal potential threats to the relationship, such as possible sexual or emotional involvement of the mate with others.[27] Jealousy motivates possessive and threat behaviors that discourage competitors and prevent sexual opportunities for the mate.[30] And caregiving-related emotions of parental and child love and sympathy facilitate protective relations between parent and offspring,[31,32] which are especially important for mammalian neonates, who are dependent and vulnerable to predation for much longer periods of time than nonmammalian species.

Finally, emotions help solve *problems related to group governance and allocation of resources and work*.[33] To avoid the problems of cheating and to encourage cooperation, in particular among nonkin, humans reciprocate cooperative and noncooperative acts.[34] Reciprocity is a universal social norm and is evident in gift giving, eye-for-an-eye punishment, *quid-pro-quo* behavior in other species,[35] and the "tit-for-tat" strategy.[36] Several emotions signal when reciprocity has been violated and motivate reparative behavior.[28,34,35,37] Guilt occurs following violations of reciprocity and is expressed in apologetic, remedial behavior that reestablishes reciprocity.[38,39] Moral anger motivates the punishment of individuals who have violated rules of reciprocity. Gratitude for altruistic acts is a reward for adherence to the contract of reciprocity.[34] Envy motivates individuals to derogate others whose favorable status is unjustified, thus preserving equal relations.[9]

Humans must also solve the *problem of group organization*. Status hierarchies provide heuristic solutions to the problems of distributing resources, such as mates, food, and social attention, and the labor required of collective endeavors.[9,40,41] The establishment, maintenance, and preservation of status hierarchies is accomplished in part by emotions related to dominance and submission.[17,42] Embarrassment and shame appease dominant individuals and signal submissiveness,[5,43] whereas contempt is defined by feelings of superiority and dominance vis-à-vis inferior others. Awe tends to be associated with the experience of being in the presence of an entity greater than the self[44] and thereby endows higher-status individuals with respect and authority.

EXPRESSION AND THE COORDINATION OF SOCIAL INTERACTION

Many of the aforementioned problems arise in brief, rapidly changing, interdependent social interactions: a threatening figure approaches one's offspring; in a group of young adults a potential romantic partner shows slight signs of interest; within a group a subordinate member intimates at the inappropriate status of a higher-status individual. These kinds of events arise quickly and present opportunities and problems related to important relationships, such as romantic bonds or social hierarchies. According to social-functional accounts of emotion,[45] emotional expression coordinates social interactions in ways that meet these problems and opportunities, maintaining the stability of social bonds. Facial expressions do this through their informative, evocative, and incentive functions.[46]

First, emotional experience and expression are sources of information about the social world—the informative function. Emotion displays convey information about the sender's emotions, intentions, and relationship with the target.[47] Emotion displays convey information about the environment external to the relationship as well, allowing individuals to coordinate their responses to outside opportunities or threats.[48,49]

Second, emotion displays have evocative functions, eliciting complementary or matching emotions from relationship partners.[46,50] For example, photographed facial displays of anger enhance fear conditioning in observers, even when the photographs are not consciously perceived.[51,52] Several studies have also shown that expressions of distress evoke compassion or sympathy in observers.[53]

Finally, emotion displays provide incentives for desired social behavior.[46] Displays of positive emotion are often used by parents to reward desired behaviors in children, thus increasing the probability of those behaviors in the future.[54] Laughter from interaction partners also rewards desirable social behavior in adults.[55]

Starting from a social functional analysis has helped guide the discovery of how expressions shape interactions. This approach has also led to the discovery of displays of emotions not considered in a first wave of research on expression, which focused on anger, contempt, disgust, fear, happiness, sadness, and surprise.[47] Embarrassment is marked by a sequence of gaze aversion, controlled smile, head turn (which exposes the neck), and occasional face touch (in other studies, just the face touch is sufficient to communicate embarrassment),[56] whereas shame is displayed in a coordinated sequence of downward gaze and head movements lasting 1 to 5 seconds.[43,57,58] Unpublished studies are finding a distinct display of pride, as evident in postural expansion and upwards head and gaze movements.[59] At least three self-conscious emotions appear to have distinct displays.

In the realm of positive emotions, the momentary experience of love is expressed in a coherent pattern of smiling, mutual gaze, affiliative hand gestures, open posture, and forward leans.[29] Desire is signaled in a variety of lip-related actions, including lip licks, wipes, and tongue protrusions.[29] Laughter and smiling have distinct experiential correlates and social consequences.[60,61] At least five positive states, then—love, desire, amusement, happiness, and interest[62]—have distinct displays. In unpublished research, we have shown that awe and gratitude, in this case posed rather than experienced, have distinct actions.[59] And a display of sympathy—namely oblique eyebrows and concerned gaze—is correlated with increased sympathy, heart rate deceleration, and increased helping behavior; this display is different from that of distress.[53]

A social functional account of emotion, therefore, posits that emotions help individuals form and maintain relationships that are essential to the survival and well-being of individuals, relationships, and groups. Emotional expression, in particular, coordinates moment-by-moment interactions between individuals as they respond to the challenges and opportunities that make or break social bonds. Facial expressions signal commitment to romantic partners, appease observers, and prompt well-timed forgiveness; they promote reciprocity. This perspective has led to the study of previously ignored emotions, such as love[29] and awe,[44] and to the discovery of new displays. And this perspective sheds light on the significance of individual differences in emotion.

INDIVIDUAL DIFFERENCES IN EMOTION AND THE SHAPING OF THE LIFE CONTEXT

One of the lasting insights of the study of individual differences is that all situations are not created equal. More concretely, people, as a function of their personality or psychological disorder, create the situations in which they act.[63] Individuals selectively attend to certain features of complex situations, thus endowing contexts with particular, idiosyncratic meaning. Individuals evoke responses in others, thus shaping the social meaning of the situation. In this fashion, across situations individuals will tend to respond and act in a similar fashion, thus expressing their underlying traits and dispositions in a stable fashion. And across the life course, individuals will create certain motifs, themes, and relationship patterns that reveal the particular facets of individual identity.

Emotion is one important part of the way individuals shape their life context.[64] Current evidence points to two specific processes by which this occurs. First, individual differences in emotion lead individuals to selectively construe situations in different fashions. Each emotion is defined by a certain appraisal theme,[10,65,66] which defines in part how the individual will construe any particular situation. Anxious individuals perceive more threat and risk in situations, whereas anger-prone individuals perceive less risk and threat, as do cheerful individuals.[12]

Second, individuals tend to consistently evoke different responses in others. Individuals will evoke different responses in strangers and intimates, at home and at work, as a function of their tendency to express particular emotions. One implication is that in relationships individuals will tend to converge, or become more similar, in their emotional style. Other people come to take on our emotional tendencies, and we take on theirs.

In an investigation of this latter idea, we explored the emotional similarity of romantic partners, roommates, and strangers.[67] To the extent that individual differences in emotion evoke consistent responses in others, individuals in relationships should come to resemble one another in their emotional style. TABLE 2 reveals that this is true across relationships.

TABLE 2. Emotional convergence in close relationships

Subjects	Time 1	Time 2	Change
Romantic partners			
Positive	.32*	.51*	.23*
Negative	.43*	.61*	.31*
Roommates (together)			
Postive	.19	.47*	.31*
Negative	.05	.38**	.34*
Roommates (separately)			
Positive	.26*		
Negative	.35*		
Random dyads			
Positive	−.05		
Negative	−.24		

*P < 0.05; **P < 0.10.

Specifically, in our first two studies we assessed romantic partners' and roommates' emotional responses to the same stimuli (e.g., emotional conversations, embarrassing tasks) at the beginning and end of an academic year. As one can see, romantic partners and roommates became more similar to one another in their emotional response styles over the course of the year.

These initial findings raised an intriguing question: would this emotional convergence be evident when participants were not in the presence of their romantic partner or roommate? The final set of findings in TABLE 2 answers in the affirmative. In this study roommates watched the same film clips, but in different rooms. Here again we see convergence in emotional style: roommates responded emotionally to the clips in similar fashion, but the responses of randomly paired individuals (whose findings are represented in the final two rows) did not resemble one another. The responses relationship partners evoke and shape in one another generalize to contexts in which they are not with one another.

Through these selective and evocative processes, individuals create life contexts and cumulative life outcomes. Facial expression, therefore, should be particularly revealing. More specifically, facial expressions reflect different experiences,[68] patterns of appraisal,[69] and patterns of autonomic nervous system activity.[13] In this fashion, facial expression reveals how the individual selectively interprets and reacts to important life events. Facial expression should also reveal the responses the individual evokes in others and, by implication, patterns of relating to others. Although fleeting and often beyond control, facial expressions appear to be measurable signs of the course of life; indeed, they are windows into the human soul.

My own research has explored ramifications of this general thesis in four different ways. First, I have looked at significant life events that have enduring, if not life-transforming, effects upon the individual. In particular, with George Bonanno I have studied individual variation in emotional expression in response to bereavement, which has profound effects upon social functioning and well-being. Here I have tested specific hypotheses derived from emotion research about how expression reflects individuals' adaptive responses to these events.

In a second line of research I have looked at how expression reflects patterns of adjustment in enduring personal relationships. Again, the reasoning is similar: facial expressions, I have argued, contribute to the stability and well-being of interpersonal bonds. In my own research I have tested specific hypotheses relating displays of romantic love to commitment-enhancing processes within heterosexual bonds.

A third line of evidence pertains to the core of Darwin's original interest, summarized earlier—the connection between facial expression and mental health and disorder. I have focused on embarrassment, a social-moral emotion that reflects the individual's commitment to norms and morals. The evidence indicates that individuals who display little or inappropriate embarrassment have serious difficulties with abiding by the rules that contribute to effective social functioning.

Finally, I have asked whether expression is revealing of the course of life, of how people change and develop, and of the relationships they lead.

EXPRESSION AS THE REGISTER OF
SIGNIFICANT LIFE EVENTS

How might facial expressions relate to individual adjustment in response to one of life's most devastating losses—the early death of a spouse? Traditional bereavement theories offer clear predictions. These theories, based on Freudian notions of "working through" the emotional pain of loss, hypothesize that recovery depends on the expression of negative emotions, such as anger and sadness. The expression of positive emotion, from this perspective, indicates denial and impedes grief resolution. Social-functional accounts of emotion, in contrast, suggest that negative emotional expression may bring about problematic outcomes, whereas positive emotional expression may facilitate the adaptive response to stress.

We pitted these contrasting hypotheses against one another in a longitudinal study of midlife conjugal bereavement.[70] Bereaved adults' facial expressions were coded using Ekman and Friesen's Facial Action Coding System[2] as they talked for six minutes in highly moving and emotional ways about their recently deceased spouse. We related measures of participants' facial expressions of emotions to a well-validated measure of grief severity, gathered in independent interviews at 6, 14, and 25 months postloss. Contrary to widespread assumptions, measures of participants' facial expressions of negative emotion—in particular, anger—predicted *increased* grief severity at 14 and 25 months postloss. Measures of laughter and smiling, in contrast, predicted *reduced* grief over time. Importantly, facial expressions predicted long-term adjustment independent of initial grief and the tendency to report high levels of distress.

These findings raised an intriguing question. Why would laughing while talking about the deceased partner relate to increased personal adjustment? Recent theorizing about the functions of positive emotion points to possible answers.[71] Specifically, positive emotions are believed to accompany the "undoing" of distress, or what we will call *dissociation* from the distress of stressful events, and to enhance social bonds. Clearly, dissociation from distress and enhanced bonds would help the bereaved individual adjust to a profoundly changed life following the loss of a spouse.

To assess these putative functions of positive emotion, we divided our bereaved participants into two groups: those who showed Duchenne laughter, which involves the action of the oribiclaris oculi muscle[47,72] and those who did not. We then compared the two groups on three measures: (1) a well-

TABLE 3. Qualities of bereavement for laughers and nonlaughers

Quality	Laughers	Nonlaughers
Verbal-autonomic dissociation	−0.60	0.43
Satisfaction with spouse	114.10	102.06
Ambivalence in current relation	3.05	3.49
Positive reaction from strangers	0.78	0.34

validated index of emotional dissociation (the discrepancy between self-reports of distress and autonomic reactivity gathered during the bereavement interview); (2) their ambivalence towards a current significant other; and (3) the responses they evoked in strangers, who viewed videotapes of the participants with no sound. Consistent with theorizing about positive emotion, bereaved individuals who laughed while talking about their deceased spouse showed a pattern of dissociation from distress, reported better relations with a current significant other, and evoked more positive responses in strangers (see TABLE 3). Laughers and nonlaughers did not differ in their self-rated personality or in the nature of their spouse's death (e.g., its unexpectedness or financial impact), which might have accounted for variation in the outcome measures of interest.

EXPRESSION AND INTERPERSONAL RELATIONSHIPS

Facial expressions, I argued earlier, coordinate social interactions by providing information to others, evoking responses, and serving as incentives for social behavior. Indeed, facial expressions are essential elements of interactions, such as attachment processes, flirtation, status rituals, and appeasement, that are crucial to human relationships.[50] Individual differences in facial expressions of emotion, therefore, should relate to different levels of adjustment in interpersonal relationships.

Researchers have examined the contribution of emotional expression to problems in interpersonal adjustment. For example, Field and colleagues have shown that mothers with depression express little positive emotion, and that this relative lack of expression is linked with increased anxiety, distress, and disengagement in the child.[73] It is easy to imagine how the mother's lack of positive emotion, a hallmark of depression, contributes to the anxious, disengaged bond between mother and child in this case. More generally, this emotional disturbance in depression is inexorably linked to the well-documented difficulties depressed individuals have in interpersonal relationships.

In studies that perhaps best illustrate the theme of this section—how expression indexes the quality of interpersonal bonds—John Gottman and

Robert Levenson have studied extensively the emotional dynamics of romantic partners. In their work romantic partners visit the laboratory after having not seen each other for the past 24 hours and engage in a variety of conversations about the very substance of intimate bonds—the events of the day, issues of conflict, and so on. Two kinds of expressive style are particularly toxic to romantic bonds: partners' expressions of contempt and wives' expressions of disgust during conversations about conflict predict relationship dissatisfaction and dissolution.[74]

Motivated by a social-functional account of emotion, we asked whether positive emotional behaviors predict commitment and satisfaction in romantic bonds.[29] Following ethological studies of humans and nonhumans, we coded the affiliative and sexual cues displayed by romantic partners as they talked together about a recent positive event. Romantic partners' affiliative cues, which included Duchenne smiles, forward leans, head nods, and open hand gestures, uniquely correlated with self-reports of love. Sexual cues, including lip licks, lip wipes, and tongue protrusions, uniquely correlated with self-reports of desire. This preliminary evidence suggests that there are displays of love and desire.

We then asked whether these facial signs predict different relationship qualities within intimate bonds. We had hypothesized that romantic love serves a commitment function, motivating long-term commitment to a romantic partner. Consistent with this thesis, across two different samples, affiliation cues and self-reports of love gathered from one brief context (when partners were talking about a recent positive event) predicted self-reports of increased commitment, shared goals, playful teasing, constructive conflict resolution, and increased relationship satisfaction. We had hypothesized that desire serves a reproduction function, motivating sexual behavior. Consistent with this thesis, measures of sexual cues and self-reports of desire in one context predicted increased sexual satisfaction.

Taken together, these findings indicate that one can judge the health and disposition of intimate relationships from brief observations of expressive behavior. One can discern whether the relationship will last, its degree of commitment, and its sexual content.

EXPRESSION AND PSYCHOLOGICAL DISORDERS

Thus far we have seen that expressive behavior predicts responses to significant life events and the quality of interpersonal relationships. In light of these findings, one would expect expressive behavior to be related to psychological disorders in a rather specific fashion.

Here there is more relevant evidence, and it suggests that different disorders are likely to be associated with different emotion profiles. We have already seen that schizophrenia is associated with relatively normal levels of experienced emotion but reduced expressive behavior. Select evidence indicates that depressed individuals tend to display less positive emotion.[73] Socially anxious individuals tend to report more fear and to display anxiety-like behaviors.[75] Clearly, this is a fruitful line of inquiry.

In my own research I have been interested in the particular disorders associated with deficits in the self-conscious emotions. It is widely claimed that individuals who are less inclined towards self-conscious emotions, such as embarrassment, shame, or guilt, are more prone to antisocial behavior. The rationale is rather simple: self-conscious emotions motivate the adherence to social norms and restorative interactions that follow norm violations. Individuals who experience and display little self-conscious emotion, by implication, should be more inclined to violate social norms and less likely to restore social relations following norm violations (e.g., in interpersonal conflict). Variants of this hypothesis were advanced long ago by Charles Darwin and Erving Goffman and are embedded in cultural conceptions of the "shameless" individual.

In a first test of this hypothesis about the regulatory function of self-conscious emotion, we coded the facial expressions, again using Ekman and Friesen's Facial Action Coding System, that young boys displayed while taking a brief interactive IQ test.[76] We then related these measures of facial expression to teacher ratings of the boys' levels of externalizing disorder—defined by aggression and delinquent behavior—and internalizing disorder—defined by anxiety, withdrawal, and somatic complaints. The IQ test produced frequent embarrassment, anger, and fear, as the boys made intellectual mistakes in front of an authority figure (one wonders what the effects of those emotions were on performance). As seen in FIGURE 1, the young boys who were most prone to antisocial behavior, the externalizers, displayed the least embarrassment (and the most anger), lending credence to the claim that embarrassment motivates socially normative behavior. Externalizing and internalizing disorders also appear to have different emotional cores.

In similarly motivated research, Beer and colleagues have looked at the self-conscious emotion of individuals with damage to the orbitofrontal region of the frontal lobes.[77] This brain region, which rests behind the eye orbits (i.e., Brodmann's areas 11, 12, 14, and 47), seems particularly involved in the regulation of social behavior. Damage to the orbitofrontal region of the frontal lobes does not impair language, memory, or sensory processing; but it does appear to disrupt social regulation.

Orbitofrontal patients have been observed to greet strangers by kissing on the cheek and hugging,[78] engage in uncontrolled and tasteless social behavior such as inappropriate joking,[79] and make disclosures to a stranger in an inappropriately intimate fashion.[77]

In the study of interest, orbitofrontal patients and age-matched controls engaged in several tasks that generated self-conscious emotion. Two are of in-

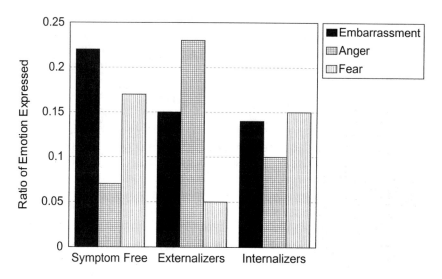

FIGURE 1. Emotional expression and childhood psychopathology.

terest here. First, the subjects teased strangers (notably, two attractive young women), which allowed for the opportunity of inappropriate social behavior. Second, they were presented with slides of photographs of the basic emotions (anger, disgust, fear, happiness, sadness, and surprise) and the self-conscious emotions with known displays (embarrassment and shame) and asked to indicate the emotion being displayed in the photo.

As expected, our orbitofrontal patients clearly had difficulties with regulating their social behavior in the teasing task. They teased in overly forward ways that were not qualified by subtle apologies and paralinguistic acts that mitigate the provocativeness of the tease (e.g., hesitations). Turning to self-reports of emotion, both patients and controls found the teasing amusing; in fact that was the strongest emotion they reported feeling. They differed, however, in their experience of self-conscious emotion. Patients reported greater pride and reduced embarrassment compared to the controls, even though they teased in a more inappropriate fashion. These patients showed inappropriate self-conscious emotion—increased pride and reduced embarrassment—when engaging in socially inappropriate behavior. One interesting possibility is that this tendency towards inappropriate self-conscious emotion might actually reinforce rather than correct inappropriate social behavior.

In the emotion recognition task, we see another side to the deficit in self-conscious emotion associated with orbitofrontal damage. Specially, orbitofrontal patients and controls were equally capable of recognizing the "basic" facial expressions of anger, disgust, fear, happiness, surprise, and sadness. Where they differed was in their recognition of self-conscious emotions: the patients, as one might expect, were not as reliable in labeling the displays of self-conscious emotion. They had trouble making accurate appraisals of others' self-conscious emotions. Together these findings suggest that self-conscious emotions and their underlying appraisal processes are important for the adaptive regulation of social behavior.

EXPRESSION AND THE COURSE OF LIFE

Thus far we have seen that individual variation in facial expressions of emotion predicts responses to significant events, the quality of interpersonal bonds, and particular psychological disorders. With the exception of the bereavement study, the studies that supported these claims were snapshot studies of an individual's life. Brief periods of expressive behavior were shown to relate to contemporaneous measures of relationship quality and psychological functioning.

I have argued, however, that facial expressions should reveal the course of an individual's life.[46,64] Facial expressions reveal how individuals selectively interpret and create situations, and evoke responses in others. In these ways, individual differences in facial expression should relate to the consistent expression of personality traits, stable relationship patterns, and cumulative life outcomes that collectively define the course of life.

To examine these issues, we conducted what seems on the surface to be an improbable study.[80] From women's college yearbook photos, we coded the intensity of the smile in 110 women using the Facial Action Coding System. Our coding of the smile was based on the action of the zygomatic major muscle and the orbicularis oculi muscle. We then related this measure of positive expression to measures of personality, relationships, and personal well-being gathered over the next 40 years.

Our predictions derived from recent theory that holds that positive emotions build personal resources by fostering creative thinking, the readiness to take advantage of opportunities, the strengthening of social bonds, and the "undoing" of negative emotions. In support of these claims, positive emotional expression in the yearbook related positively to the personality traits of affiliation and competence, which reflect good interpersonal and cognitive skills, respectively; and negatively with negative emotionality, in both young and middle adulthood (see TABLE 4). Positive emotional expression also predicted increases in competence and decreases in negative emotionality between ages 21 and 27 and again from ages 43 to 52. Over time, women who expressed more positive emotion in their yearbook pictures became more organized, mentally focused, and achievement oriented, and less susceptible to repeated and prolonged experiences of negative affect.

Turning to the quality of the spousal relationship, those women who displayed more positive emotion in their yearbook pictures were more likely to

TABLE 4. Correlations between positive expression (positivity) and personality and life outcomes controlling for attractiveness and social desirability

	Positivity	Positivity/ Attractive	Positivity/Social Desirability
Self-report			
Negativity (21)	−.38*	−.40*	−.32*
Negativity (27)	−.21*	−.21*	−.21**
Negativity (43)	−.23*	−.23*	−.18**
Negativity (52)	−.27*	−.29*	−.28*
Affiliation (21)	.33*	.32*	.28*
Affiliation (43)	.18**	.18**	.16
Competence (27)	.19**	.20**	.16
Competence (43)	.20**	.24*	.15
Competence (52)	.29*	.31*	.26*
Life outcomes			
Married at 27	.19*	.18**	.16
Marital satisfaction (52)	.20**	.16	.18
Well-being			
Age 21	.20*	.20*	.11
Age 27	.25*	.26*	.23*
Age 43	.18**	.19*	.12
Age 52	.27*	.28*	.24*

*$P < 0.05$; **$P < 0.10$.

be married by age 27, less likely to remain single into middle adulthood, and more likely to have satisfying marriages 30 years later. These findings correspond with those of researchers who have documented how momentary displays of positive emotion help married couples deal more effectively with conflict in their relationships.[81] Positive emotional expression in the yearbook also predicted high scores on measures of well-being at ages 21, 27, 43, and 52. Across young and middle adulthood, women prone to expressing positive emotions experience fewer psychological and physical difficulties, have better relations with others, and generally feel more satisfied with their lives. Importantly, almost all of these findings remained significant when we controlled for the physical attractiveness of the women and their tendency to offer socially desirable responses.

Complementary evidence has been documented in studies of the lives of anger-prone individuals. Caspi, Elder, and Bem found that the tendency to express uncontrolled anger in early childhood (as assessed by parental reports of frequent, severe temper tantrums) later related to the broader trait of ill-temperedness, which showed considerable stability across the life span.[82] Furthermore, this childhood expressive tendency predicted negative life outcomes, including lower educational attainment, lower-status jobs, lower military rank, erratic work patterns, and divorce. The tendency to express intense anger creates a hostile social environment that brings about the stable expression of trait hostility and a pattern of negative life outcomes in work and family.

Taken together, these findings reveal how even the briefest observations of expressive behavior—the millisecond exposure required of photography—can reveal information about the continuity of personality and important life outcomes over the course of life. These studies work, I believe, because expressive behaviors such as smiles or temper tantrums are, indeed, such powerful displays.

CONCLUSIONS

In this essay, I hope to have argued that at their very core emotions are social, they motivate thoughts and actions that are crucial to humans' most important relationships within the context of spontaneous interactions.[17,83] In making this point, I hope to have challenged two notions that have implicitly guided the field of emotion.

The first is that there are a limited number of emotions, anywhere from 7 to 12. A social-functional account of emotion has opened up the field and led researchers to consider a variety of emotions, from compassion to gratitude, that are vital to the functioning of relationships.

The second has to do with the duration of emotions. Emotions have long been viewed as brief phenomena, with little to say about more enduring properties of human nature, such as long-term relationships, personality traits, or psychological disorders. Emotional expressions are, indeed, brief; but they reveal how the human mind selectively interprets and reacts to important situations, and the tone and content of the individual's enduring relationships. Although brief and fleeting, facial expressions of emotion are signs of the course of life.

REFERENCES

1. DARWIN, C. 1872. The Expression of the Emotions in Man and Animals. John Murray. London.
2. EKMAN, P. & W.V. FRIESEN. 1978. Facial Action Coding System: A Technique for the Measurement of Facial Movement. Consulting Psychologists Press. Palo Alto, CA.
3. KELTNER, D. & P. EKMAN. 2000. Facial expression of emotion. In Handbook of Emotion. M. Lewis & J. Haviland-Jones, Eds.: 236–249. Guilford Press. New York.

4. KELTNER, D. & J.J. GROSS. 1999. Functional accounts of emotion. Cognit. Emotion **13:** 467–480.
5. MILLER, R.S. & M.R. LEARY. 1992. Social sources and interactive functions of emotion: the case of embarrassment. *In* Emotion and Social Behavior. M. Clark, Ed.: 202–221. Sage. Beverly Hills, CA.
6. KRING, A.M., S.L. KERR, D.A. SMITH & J.M. NEALE. 1993. Flat affect in schizophrenia does not reflect diminished subjective experience of emotion. J. Abnorm. Psychol. **102:** 507–517.
7. HEEREY, E.A., D. KELTNER & L.M. CAPPS. Making sense of self-conscious emotion: linking theory of mind and emotion in children with autism. Emotion. In press.
8. MYERS, D.G. 2000. The American Paradox. Yale University Press. New Haven, CT.
9. FISKE, A.P. 1992. The four elementary forms of sociality. Framework for a unified theory of social relations. Psychol. Rev. **99:** 689–723.
10. LAZARUS, R.S. 1991. Emotion and Adaptation. Oxford University Press. New York.
11. RUSSELL, J.A. 1994. Is there universal recognition of emotion from facial expression? A review of cross-cultural studies. Psychol. Bull. **115:** 102–141.
12. LERNER, J. & D. KELTNER. 2001. Fear, anger, and risk. J. Pers. Soc. Psychol. **81:** 146–159.
13. LEVENSON, R.W., P. EKMAN & W.V. FRIESEN. 1990. Voluntary facial action generates emotion-specific autonomic nervous system activity. Psychophysiology **27:** 363–384.
14. EKMAN, P. 1992. An argument for basic emotions. Cognit. Emotion **6:** 169–200.
15. FRIJDA, N.H. & B. MESQUITA. 1994. The social roles and functions of emotions. *In* Emotion and Culture: Empirical Studies of Mutual Influences. S. Kitayama & H. Marcus, Eds.: 51–87. American Psychological Association. Washington, DC.
16. KELTNER, D. & J. HAIDT. 1999. Social functions of emotions at multiple levels of analysis. Cognit. Emotion **13:** 505–522.
17. KELTNER, D. & J. HAIDT. 2001. Social functions of emotions. *In* Emotions: Current Issues and Future Directions. T. Mayne & G. Bonanno, Eds.: 192–213. Guilford Press. New York.
18. TOOBY, J. & L. COSMIDES. 1990. The past explains the present: emotional adaptations and the structure of ancestral environments. Ethol. Sociobiol. **11:** 375–424.
19. FRIJDA, N.H. 1986. The Emotions. Cambridge University Press. Cambridge.
20. SHIOTA, M., D. KELTNER, B. CAMPOS & M. HERTENSTEIN. Positive emotion and the regulation of interpersonal relationships. *In* Emotion Regulation. P. Phillipot & R. Feldman, Eds. Erlbaum. Mahwah, NJ. In press.
21. LEDOUX, J. 1996. The Emotional Brain. Simon & Schuster. New York.
22. MINEKA, S. & M. COOK. 1993. Mechanisms involved in the observational conditioning of fear. J. Exp. Psychol. **122:** 23–38.
23. ROZIN, P. 1976. The selection of food by rats, humans, and other animals. *In* Advances in the Study of Behavior: 21–76. Academic Press. New York.
24. ROZIN, P. & A. FALLON. 1987. A perspective on disgust. Psychol. Rev. **94:** 23–41.
25. SELIGMAN, M.E.P. 1971. Phobias and preparedness. Behav. Ther. **2:** 307–320.

26. ROZIN, P. 1996. Towards a psychology of food and eating: from motivation to module to model to marker, morality, meaning, and metaphor. Curr. Dir. Psychol. Sci. **5:** 18–24.
27. BUSS. D. 1992. Male preference mechanisms: consequences for partner choice and intrasexual competition. *In* The Adapted Mind. J.H. Barkow, L. Cosmides & J. Tooby, Eds.: 267–288. Oxford University Press. New York.
28. FRANK, R.H. 1988. Passions within Reason. Norton. New York.
29. GONZAGA, G.C., D. KELTNER, E.A. LONDAHL & M.D. SMITH. 2001. Love and the commitment problem in romantic relations and friendship. J. Pers. Soc. Psychol. **81:** 247–262.
30. WILSON, M.I. & M. DALY. 1996. Male sexual proprietariness and violence against wives. Curr. Dir. Psychol. Sci. **5:** 2–6.
31. BOWLBY, J. 1969. Attachment. Basic Books. New York.
32. MIKULINCER, M. & P.R. SHAVER. The attachment behavioral system in adulthood: activation, psychodynamcs, and interpersonal processes. *In* Advances in Experimental Social Psychology. M.P. Zanna, Ed. In press.
33. FISKE, A.P. 1991. Structures of Social Life. Free Press. New York.
34. TRIVERS, R.L. 1971. The evolution of reciprocal altruism. Quart. Rev. Biol. **46:** 35–57.
35. DE WAAL, F.B.M. 1996. Good Natured. Harvard University Press. Cambridge, MA.
36. AXELROD, R. 1984. The Evolution of Cooperation. Basic Books. New York.
37. NESSE, R. 1990. Evolutionary explanations of emotions. Hum. Nat. **1:** 261–289.
38. KELTNER, D. 1996. Facial expressions of emotion and personality. *In* Handbook of Emotion, Aging, and the Lifecourse. C. Malatesta-Magai & S.H. McFadden, Eds.: 385–402. Academic Press. New York.
39. TANGNEY, J.P., R.S. MILLER, L. FLICKER & D.H. BARLOW. 1996. Are shame, guilt, and embarrassment distinct emotions? J. Pers. Soc. Psychol. **70:** 1256–1269.
40. DE WAAL, F.B.M. 1986. The integration of dominance and social bonding in primates. Quart. Rev. Biol. **61:** 459–479.
41. DE WAAL, F.B.M. 1988. The reconciled hierarchy. *In* Social Fabrics of the Mind. M.R.A. Chance, Ed.: 105–136. Erlbaum. Hillsdale, NJ.
42. OHMAN, A. 1986. Face the beast and fear the face: animal and social fears as prototypes for evolutionary analysis of emotion. Psychophysiology **23:** 123–145.
43. KELTNER, D. & B.N. BUSWELL. 1997. Embarrassment: its distinct form and appeasement functions. Psychol. Bull. **122:** 250–270.
44. KELTNER, D. & J. HAIDT. 2003. Approaching awe: the moral, aesthetic, and spiritual emotions. Cognit. Emotion 17: 297–314.
45. BARRETT, K.C. & J.J. CAMPOS. 1987. Perspectives on emotional development II: a functionalist approach to emotions. *In* Handbook of Infant Development, 2nd edit. J.D. Osofsky, Ed: 555–578. Wiley-Interscience. New York.
46. KELTNER, D. & A.M. KRING. 1998. Emotion, social function, and psychopathology. Rev. Gen. Psychol. **2:** 320–342.
47. EKMAN, P. 1993. Facial expression and emotion. Am. Psychol. **48:** 384–392.
48. KLINNERT, M., J. CAMPOS, J. SORCE, *et al.* 1983. Emotions as behavior regulators: social referencing in infants. *In* Emotion Theory, Research, and Experience, Vol. 2.: Emotions in Early Development. R. Plutchik & H. Kellerman, Eds.: 57–68. Academic Press. New York.

49. SORCE, J.F. & R.N. EMDE. 1981. Mother's presence is not enough: the effect of emotional availability on infant exploration. Dev. Psychol. **17:** 37–45.
50. EIBL-EIBESFELDT, I. 1989. Human Ethology. Aldine de Gruyter Press. New York.
51. OHMAN, A. & U. DIMBERG. 1978. Facial expressions as conditioned stimuli for electrodermal responses: a case of "preparedness"? J. Pers. Soc. Psychol. **36:** 1251–1258.
52. ESTEVES, F., U. DIMBERG & A. OHMAN. 1994. Automatically elicited fear: conditioned skin conductance responses to masked facial expressions. Cognit. Emotion **8:** 393–413.
53. EISENBERG, N., R.A. FABES, P.A. MILLER, et al. 1989. Relation of sympathy and distress to prosocial behavior: a multimethod study. J. Pers. Soc. Psychol. **57:** 55–66.
54. TRONICK, E.Z. 1989. Emotions and emotional communication in infants. Am. Psychol. **44:** 112–119.
55. OWREN, M.J. & J.-A. BACHOROWSKI. 2001. The evolution of emotional expression: a "selfish gene" account of smiling in early hominids and humans. In Emotion: Current Issues and Future Development. T. Mayne & G.A. Bonanno, Eds.: 152–191. Guilford Press. New York.
56. HAIDT, J. & D. KELTNER. 1999. Culture and facial expression: open-ended methods find more expressions and a gradient of recognition. Cognit. Emotion **13:** 225–266.
57. KELTNER, D. 1995. The signs of appeasement: evidence for the distinct displays of embarrassment, amusement, and shame. J. Pers. Soc. Psychol. **68:** 441–454.
58. KELTNER, D. & L.A. HARKER. 1998. The forms and functions of the nonverbal display of shame. In Interpersonal Approaches to Shame. P. Gilbert & B. Andrews, Eds.: 78–98. Oxford University Press. Oxford.
59. CAMPOS, B., M. SHIOTA, D. KELTNER & G.C. GONZAGA. 2002. The Distinct Positive Emotions. Unpublished manuscript.
60. KELTNER, D. & G.A. BONANNO. 1997. A study of laughter and dissociation: the distinct correlates of laughter and smiling during bereavement. J. Pers. Soc. Psychol. **73:** 687–702.
61. RUCH, W. 1993. Exhilaration and humor. In Handbook of Emotions. M. Lewis & J. Haviland, Eds.: 605–616. Guilford. New York.
62. REEVE, J. 1993. The face of interest. Motiv. Emot. **17:** 353–375.
63. BUSS, D. 1987. Selection, evocation, and manipulation. J. Pers. Soc. Psychol. **53:** 1214–1221.
64. MALATESTA, C.Z. 1990. The role of emotions in the development and organization of personality. In Nebraska Symposium on Motivation, Vol. 36: Socioemotional Development. R.A. Thompson, Ed.: 1–56. University of Nebraska Press. Lincoln, NE.
65. KELTNER, D., P.C. ELLSWORTH & K. EDWARDS. 1993. Beyond simple pessimism: effects of sadness and anger on social perception. J. Pers. Soc. Psychol. **64:** 740–752.
66. SMITH, C. & P. ELLSWORTH. 1985. Patterns of cognitive appraisal in emotion. J. Pers. Soc. Psychol. **48:** 813–838.
67. ANDERSON, C., D. KELTNER & O.P. JOHN. 2003. Emotional convergence between people over time. J. Pers. Soc. Psychol. **84:** 1054–1068.
68. EKMAN, P. & E. ROSENBERG. 1997. What the Face Reveals. Oxford University Press. New York.

69. BONANNO, G.A. & D. KELTNER. The coherence of facial expressions of emotion. Cognit. Emotion. In press.
70. BONANNO, G.A. & D. KELTNER. 1997. Facial expressions of emotion and the course of conjugal bereavement. J. Abnorm. Psychol. **106:** 126–137.
71. FREDRICKSON, B.L. 1998. What good are positive emotions? Rev. Gen. Psychol. **2:** 300–319.
72. FRANK, M., P. EKMAN & W.V. FRIESEN. 1993. Behavioral markers and recognizability of the smile of enjoyment. J. Pers. Soc. Psychol. **64:** 83–93.
73. FIELD, T. 1995. Infants of depressed mothers. Infant Behav. Dev. **18:** 1–13.
74. GOTTMAN, J.M. & R.W. LEVENSON. 1992. Marital processes predictive of later dissolution: behavior, physiology, and health. J. Pers. Soc. Psychol. **63:** 221–233.
75. MARCUS, D.K & J.R. WILSON. 1996. Interpersonal perception of social anxiety: a social relations analysis. J. Soc. Clin. Psychol. **15:** 471–487.
76. KELTNER, D., T. MOFFITT & M. STOUTHAMER-LOEBER. 1995. Facial expressions of emotion and psychopathology in adolescent boys. J. Abnorm. Psychol. **104:** 644–652.
77. BEER, J., E.A. HEEREY, D. KELTNER, *et al.* 2003. The regulatory function of self-conscious emotion: insights from patients with orbitofrontal damage. J. Pers. Soc. Psychol. **85:** 594–604.
78. ROLLS, E.T., J. HORNAK, D. WADE & J. MCGRATH. 1994. Emotion-related learning in patients with social and emotional changes associated with frontal lobe damage. J. Neurol. Neurosurg. Psychiatry **57:** 1518–1524.
79. STUSS, D.T. & D.F. BENSON. 1984. Neuropsychological studies of the frontal lobes. Psychol. Bull. **95:** 3–28.
80. HARKER, L.A. & D. KELTNER. 2001. Expressions of positive emotion in women's college yearbook pictures and their relationship to personality and life outcomes across adulthood. J. Pers. Soc. Psychol. **80:** 112–124.
81. GOTTMAN, J.M., J. COAN, S. CARRERE & C. SWANSON. 1998. Predicting marital happiness and stability from newlywed interactions. J. Marriage Fam. **60:** 5–22.
82. CASPI, A., G. ELDER & D.J. BEM. 1987. Moving against the world: life-course patterns of explosive children. Dev. Psychol. **23:** 308–313.
83. EKMAN, P. 1992. An argument for basic emotions. Cognit. Emotion **6:** 169–200.

Sounds of Emotion

Production and Perception of Affect-Related Vocal Acoustics

JO-ANNE BACHOROWSKI[a] AND MICHAEL J. OWREN[b]

[a]*Department of Psychology, Vanderbilt University, Nashville, Tennessee 37203, USA*

[b]*Department of Psychology, Cornell University, Ithaca, New York 14853, USA*

ABSTRACT: In his writing Darwin emphasized direct veridical links between vocal acoustics and vocalizer emotional state. Yet he also recognized that acoustics influence the emotional state of listeners. This duality—that particular vocal expressions are likely linked to particular internal states, yet may specifically function to influence others—lies at the heart of contemporary efforts aimed at understanding affect-related vocal acoustics. That work has focused most on speech acoustics and laughter, where the most common approach has been to argue that these signals reflect the occurrence of discrete emotional states in the vocalizer. An alternative view is that the underlying states can be better characterized using a small number of continuous dimensions such as arousal (or activation) and a valenced dimension such as pleasantness. A brief review of the evidence suggests, however, that neither approach is correct. Data from speech-related research provides little support for a discrete-emotions view, with emotion-related aspects of the acoustics seeming more to reflect to vocalizer arousal. However, links to a corresponding emotional valence dimension have also been difficult to demonstrate, suggesting a need for interpretations outside this traditional dichotomy. We therefore suggest a different perspective in which the primary function of signaling is not to express signaler emotion, but rather to impact listener affect and thereby influence the behavior of these individuals. In this view, it is not expected that nuances of signaler states will be highly correlated with particular features of the sounds produced, but rather that vocalizers will be using acoustics that readily affect listener arousal and emotion. Attributions concerning signaler states thus become a secondary outcome, reflecting inferences that listeners base on their own affective responses to the sounds, their past experience with such signals, and the context in which signaling is occurring. This approach has found recent support in laughter research, with the bigger picture being that the sounds of emotion—be they carried in

Address for correspondence: Dr. Jo-Anne Bachorowski, Department of Psychology, Wilson Hall, Vanderbilt University, Nashville, TN 37203. Voice: 615-343-5915; fax: 615-343-8449.
j.a.bachorowski@vanderbilt.edu

Ann. N.Y. Acad. Sci. 1000: 244–265 (2003). © 2003 New York Academy of Sciences.
doi: 10.1196/annals.1280.012

speech, laughter, or other species-typical signals—are not informative, veridical beacons on vocalizer states so much as tools of social influence used to capitalize on listener sensitivities.

KEYWORDS: emotion; speech; laughter; affect induction; vocal acoustics; expression of emotion

SOUNDS OF EMOTION: PRODUCTION AND PERCEPTION OF AFFECT-RELATED VOCAL ACOUSTICS

The idea that vocal acoustics are imbued with cues to vocalizer emotional state has a long history in human inquiry. For instance, Cicero and Aristotle suggested that each emotion is associated with a distinctive tone of voice[1,2]—a view also espoused by one of the leading contemporary theories of vocal expression. However, it was arguably Darwin[3] who provided the first comprehensive description of the sounds associated with emotion.

Darwin adopted an explicitly comparative perspective, examining emotion-related vocal signals in a variety of species that included nonhuman primates, ruminants, domestic dogs and cats, and humans. In each case, his rich descriptions led him to conclude that both these and other affective expressions are veridical, meaning that there is a direct correspondence between particular signaler states and the communicative display produced. Thus, Darwin treated emotion-related signaling as an inherently honest indicator of internal state. However, he also made two important observations that suggest a different perspective, one that is central to the arguments we will make here. The first was that vocal signals can induce emotional responses in listeners—for example, when courting males use calls that "charm or excite the female" during mating season.[3] The second was then going on to say that these vocal signals become associated with the "anticipation of the strongest possible pleasure which animals are capable of feeling."[3] Putting aside the more contemporary issue of whether terms like charm, excite, and pleasure should be reserved for human experience, the critical ideas are that signalers can use species-typical sounds to influence listener affect, and that individually distinctive aspects of these signals come to elicit learned emotional responses in recipients that hear them in association with affect-inducing events.

Those ideas lie at the heart of a recently developed "affect-induction" view of vocal signaling, which originated as a functional account of nonhuman primate calling.[4-6] This perspective may also have broad applicability to affect-related vocal signaling in humans,[7] which we will highlight by briskly reviewing both theory and empirical evidence concerning emotional communication in the acoustics of speech and laughter, the two most prominent vocalizations in our species. Arguments concerning human laughter are actually the best developed at this juncture, but important commonalities are also evident in speech acoustics.

EMOTION-RELATED VOCAL ACOUSTICS

Speech sounds are replete with "indexical" or "personal" cues, meaning nonlinguistic aspects of the signals that provide acoustic correlates of talker sex, individual identity, age, and emotional state. Indexical cues are likely provided in nonlinguistic vocalizations such as laughter as well. In each case, the source-filter model of speech production[8,9] has been central to selecting the acoustic measurements to make.[10–13] In this model, vocal acoustics are treated as a linear combination of an underlying energy source and filtering effects traceable to the resonances of the pharyngeal, oral, and nasal cavities that make up the supralaryngeal vocal tract. While the source energy is noisy for some speech sounds, those of greatest interest are those in which quasi-periodic vocal-fold vibration produces "voiced" phonemes such as vowels. The rate of vibration is referred to as the "fundamental frequency" (F_0) of these kinds of "phonated" sounds, and is primary in their perceived pitch. The acoustic properties typically emphasized in searching for cues to vocalizer emotional state include F_0 and F_0 variability—with the latter including both overall F_0 range and moment-to-moment perturbations occurring as the vocal folds rapidly open and close. The amplitude or perceived loudness of vocal signals has also been shown to be important, particularly when listeners infer vocalizer emotional state from speech.

Supralaryngeal resonances[14,15] have also been examined, with the frequency of these "formants" being of particular interest. Formant filtering exerts a global shaping effect on the frequency content of voiced sounds, producing prominent energy bands at resonance locations and weakening source energy elsewhere in the frequency spectrum. Close tracking of formant changes has the potential to reveal the effects of momentary emotional states as they occur, although there has to date been little practical realization of this promise. However, global frequency characteristics of emotion-laden voiced speech sounds have been characterized by calculating a long-term average spectrum (LTAS),[16] which typically involves computing mean energy occurring across the frequency range over a duration of 30 seconds or more. As a result, while it is quick and robust, the LTAS does not reflect sound production as it is occurring. In other words, it does not track acoustic cues resulting from fleeting affective experiences, where brief duration is to many a necessary, defining feature of the occurrence of emotion in the first place.

VOCAL EXPRESSION OF EMOTION IN SPEECH

The best-known theoretical position regarding vocal expression of emotion in speech is that discrete affective states experienced by the vocalizer should be reflected in specific patterns of acoustic cues in the speech being produced.[17,18] This view will be referred to as the "cue-configuration" perspective, and is best exemplified by the work of Scherer and colleagues.[12,13,19] These researchers argue further that emotion-specific acoustic cues occur subsequent to the outcomes of a vocalizer's affective appraisal processes and associated physiological changes in vocal-production anatomy. There are other views as well, however, with the principal contrasting perspective being that emotional cues in speech acoustics reflect continuous activation and valence dimensions rather than discrete emotional states. A relatively common suggestion is, for instance, that emotion-related acoustic effects are traceable to two orthogonal underlying dimensions of arousal and pleasure.[20–24] While there has been lively debate among the advocates of these two positions,[17,19] few, if any, empirical studies have been conducted to compare them directly.

Such testing is, in fact, difficult to engineer, and most studies have therefore examined smaller sets of predictions derived from one or the other of the two perspectives. One very influential example is the work of Banse and Scherer,[19] who tested vocalizations produced by 12 professional actors who were asked to portray each of 14 different emotions. This study is especially notable in that it examined a large number of emotions and acoustic features in the speech that was recorded. One key outcome was that of the 29 acoustic properties measured, F_0 and mean acoustic amplitude were found to show the strongest connections to the emotions being portrayed. We consider these findings to be particularly important because regardless of theoretical position, researchers widely agree that these features are most likely to index talker arousal rather than any specifically valenced state. Other acoustic measures also showed significant statistical links to particular emotional portrayals, but accounted for much smaller proportions of the variance involved. For example, examining the distribution of energy across 18 frequency bands extracted from LTAS analyses, the researchers found that on average each acted emotion accounted for only 10% of the variance in each band.

Overall, Banse and Scherer were able to demonstrate classification accuracies of roughly 40% when using an empirically derived subset of 16 of their acoustic measures to distinguish among the various emotions being portrayed. Results varied somewhat, depending on the particular statistical model used, but the variations were consistently relatively modest. On the one hand, this limited classification success might be expected, based on findings about other kinds of indexical cueing in speech. Speech segments can, for instance, be similarly difficult to sort by talker identity.[20] On the other hand, Banse and Scherer had already carefully screened their recordings before attempting statistical classification—only 224 "high-quality" portrayals from among the 1324 samples actually recorded were used in these tests. As a result, even the relatively modest level of classification success reported in this study may have been inflated. When Banse and Scherer then examined 40 hypothesized links between emotion and vocal acoustics,[12] 23 of the predictions were supported, the evidence was tenuous in 6 other cases, and there were 11 instances in which results showed statistically significant deviations from the expected magnitude and/or direction of effect.

Other studies have produced a similar mix of supportive and contrary outcomes,[25,26] suggesting a need for further theoretical work and possible alternative approaches.[23,25,27] In addition, however, we suggest that the use of acted rather than natural stimuli, as well as carefully screened rather than representative samples, may both have important unintended consequences in studies of this kind. The obvious problem with using sounds recorded from actors is that these portrayals do not necessarily correspond to naturally produced vocal expressions of emotion. Validation work could, of course, be performed, but so far has not been. There is also evidence from natural emotion-inducing circumstances suggesting that individual variability in vocalizer acoustics can be substantial.[28] In other words, the careful analysis of acoustic cues to acted emotion conducted by Banse and Scherer[19] and others may be providing more information about emblematic portrayals of affective states than about naturally occurring cueing.

This problem can only be exacerbated by working with a select, nonrepresentative subset of the samples in question. In Banse and Scherer's work, selection was based largely on quality evaluations made by 12 professional acting students, who found some individual actors much more convincing in their portrayals than others and overall tended to favor female over male actors. One result was, for example, that a given actor contributed a single sample to the final set of 224, while others were represented by as many as 47 utterances. These results have been mirrored in other studies, with researchers reporting similar sex and individual differences in the "quality" of production.[18,25,26,29–31] Here again, the issue becomes whether the results of such studies can be taken at face value when the utterances being classified are not representative of the full range of variation observed in the original data set.

Comparing Discrete and Dimensional Approaches

Overall, the most reliable empirical outcomes in testing the acoustics of emotional speech have been arousal related. Numerous studies have shown, for example, that anger and joy are each associated with both increased F_0 and higher amplitude in the sounds produced. Even advocates of cue-configuration perspectives agree that these have been the most prominent effects, whether in studies based on acted emotions or in studies using more natural emotional speech events.[13,17] Overall, associations between valence and vocal acoustics are significantly less clear-cut than are analogous links between internal states and external signals in facial expression of emotion studies.[32]

This point was brought home in Bachorowski and Owren's study[33] of vocal acoustics in 120 naïve participants who were individually recorded as they performed a lexical-decision task. As part of the task, each participant uttered a stock phrase just after receiving affect-inducing success or failure feedback, and the results were then interpreted using the source-filter model outlined earlier.[12,33] The three most prominent acoustic changes from baseline to on-task performance were F_0-related and were taken to reflect simple increases in vocalizer arousal. Valence-related differences were also sought, but emerged only as possible effects reflected in more complex interactions among variables such as talker sex, the relative proportion of positive and negative feedback each participant received, and these individuals' trait differences in emotional intensity. A more exacting comparison was conducted with recordings made of 24 naïve participants who each described the thoughts and feelings evoked by affect-inducing slides.[34] Findings here were consistent with those obtained using the lexical-decision task—namely, that acoustic outcomes were strongly associated with self-reported arousal, to a lesser extent with valence; and that vocal acoustics also reflected trait differences in each participant's emotional-intensity rating. Further analyses tested whether acoustic outcomes could be linked to discrete emotional states, but statistical outcomes were by and large nonsignificant.

Two conclusions that can be drawn from this work are, first, that arousal plays a noticeably more important role in shaping speech acoustics than does valence; and second, that ready links to discrete emotional states are difficult to demonstrate. The latter issue could not be directly examined in Bachorowski and Owren's[33] work because participant affect was not measured during the course of the task. When it was tested in the subsequent work with affect-inducing slides, outcomes were similar to those reported in other studies in which arousal and valence effects can be at least indirectly compared.[18,29,35–42]

It would be premature to conclude, however, that the acoustics of emotional speech only reflect arousal or can be fully accounted for by a dimensional approach alone. Any such conclusion must be preceded by tests of alternative predictions derived from the two perspectives within the same empirical framework. As noted, we know of no direct comparisons that, if undertaken, might also be valuable in facilitating a rapprochement between the two perspectives. As Tassinary and Cacioppo[43] have suggested in the context of facial expressions of emotion, affective intensity level may be a determining factor in whether discrete or valenced effects are observed. One possibility is that arousal might account for the lion's share of variance in vocal expression of emotion at both low and high intensity levels.[44,45] At intermediate intensity levels, however, valenced effects or even evidence of cue configuration may emerge.

The strongest conclusion to draw at this point may simply be that the acoustics of emotional speech are influenced by a variety of factors, not all of which are neatly aligned with the polarized theoretical positions that have been most important in the field to date. The data suggest that arousal and valence effects, however construed, are not sufficient to account for the available data concerning vocal emotion effects on the production side. Other important factors appear to include talker sex and emotional traits, strategic shaping of vocal acoustics that a talker might show in pursuit of social goals, and the particular social context in which the speech is being produced.[46] Nonetheless, as we turn to the perceptual side, it is the acoustic cues most reliably associated with vocalizer arousal that again emerge as being the most important.

VOCAL PERCEPTION OF EMOTION FROM SPEECH

Theoretical approaches and empirical outcomes associated with perception of emotion from speech acoustics generally parallel those we have reviewed for production. Specifically, some researchers adopt a cue-configuration perspective, whereas others emphasize a dimensional view. When listeners are asked to identify the intended emotion in utterances produced by actors, accuracy is about 55–60%.[17] Similar outcomes and confusions are observed across different cultures and language groups, although error rates also reflect the degree of disparity between vocalizer and listener language.[47,48]

On average, listeners do best in identifying anger, fear, and sadness. Performance is usually poor for disgust, presumably because this state is typically conveyed via vocal emblems or exclamations. Results for positive emotions have varied, but in an interesting and potentially informative way. Accuracy can be quite high when listeners are given only one positive response option, such as the word "happiness."[25,49] However, correct responses drop significantly when additional positively toned options such as "elation," "contentment," or "interest" are included.[19] A similar effect may be at work for the identification of sadness, which is often the only low-arousal option included among the negative descriptors used in emotion-perception studies. Overall, perceptual accuracy is reduced when the stimuli presented have been filtered or presented in noise that masks semantic content, but not by a large degree.[49,50]

The standard strategy has been to use a forced-choice identification paradigm in which listeners select the one emotion word that best describes the affect being conveyed. Stimulus sets usually include only a small number of talkers and emotions, and are often selected to include presumably prototypical instances of the emotions in question. For example, the 224 of 1344 original samples that Banse and Scherer[19] used in acoustic analysis were also the ones presented to listeners for identification. Similarly, Leinonen and colleagues[18] tested 120 of 480 original samples, Scherer et al.[25,47] in various experiments used either 10 or 30 of 80 total recordings, and Sobin and Alpert[26] presented only 152 of the 620 recordings they had made. As noted earlier for classification based on acoustic features, the typical strategy of using acted emotional samples and then testing only a screened subset should necessarily produce at least some evidence of differentiated perception of emotion. Data provided by Scherer et al.[25] speak directly to this point. These researchers conducted four perception studies, in which listeners in the first experiment heard all the stimuli and participants in subsequent studies heard only those that had proved most identifiable. Naturally, the latter three experiments produced higher performance than that with the unscreened sample, regardless of the emotion being tested.

Other factors also affect listener accuracy, with forced-choice procedures, for example, producing better performance than free-choice tests.[24,49] Sobin and Alpert[26] further found that the strictness of participant criteria for using a particular emotion label can vary considerably; and Scherer et al.[25] have demonstrated that the particular kind of participant used in a study can be important—in their case reporting that college students and community volunteers show different accuracy rates and error patterns. A last methodological issue of note is that stimulus duration can play a critical role. For instance, Cauldwell[51] found that listeners reported hearing anger being expressed in words presented in isolation, but not when the same words were embedded in carrier phrases. This effect occurred even when the participants were exposed to the full-length versions before hearing the words in isolation. Cauldwell's answer to the rhetorical question "Where did the anger go?" was that the emotion was never present in the first place. He suggested, instead, that perception of anger and possibly other emotions can be an artifact of the particular testing method used.

Overall, there is relatively good agreement among listeners when rating the valence and arousal of vocal stimuli. Pereira,[38,52] for example, had listeners rate vocal samples of various discrete emotions using dimensional scales. By far the strongest associations between the ratings and vocal acoustics were arousal related, with F_0 and amplitude playing primary roles. The importance of these features was corroborated in a study by Streeter et al.,[28] whose participants evaluated talker stress levels from speech. Here, the listeners reported that vocalizers were stressed when hearing significant variation in talker F_0 and amplitude, and otherwise usually failed to perceive stress.

The link between speech acoustics and perceived valence is generally weaker, which again parallels outcomes observed on the production side. Ladd et al.,[45] for example, systematically varied several acoustic parameters as listeners rated vocalizer affect and attitude. Here a central finding was that listeners did not show categorical response patterns in attributing these states, but rather perceived vocalizer arousal to vary continuously in accordance with similarly continuous changes in F_0. While other valence-related studies have similarly emphasized these sorts of source-related cues, Pittam and colleagues[39] have notably used LTAS measurements to argue that spectral features of sounds may also shape listener perception of arousal and pleasure.

Once again, however, direct comparisons of the cue-configuration and dimensional perspectives within the same study are scarce. Work by Breitenstein and colleagues[53] may come the closest, as these researchers included an "activity" dimension in testing whether manipulating the acoustics of synthetic stimuli could alter perception of discrete-emotion categories. They found listener response patterns to be more directly associated with discrete effects than with the activity ratings. The results are, nonetheless, difficult to interpret, as it is not clear how the activity construct was explained to listeners, and neither arousal nor valence were directly assessed. Other outcomes have put dimensional and discrete accounts on a more equal footing,[35,54] including, for example, the pattern of misidentifications occurring when participants are asked to identify vocalizer state within a discrete-emotions paradigm. Resulting confusion matrices have shown that errors are most likely to occur for emotions that are similar in arousal[24,38] and between similarly valenced members of emotion "families."[19,45,53]

There are thus at least two points to consider when contrasting the discrete and dimensional approaches based on perceptual evidence. The first is that listener accuracy is intermediate, averaging about 55% across a number of studies. Many investigators have argued that this result shows that vocalizer affect is, in fact, associated with discrete patterns of acoustic cues and that listeners perceive these effects.[17,19] However, we suggest the opposite—significantly better performance might be expected given that the samples typically used have been produced by actors and then screened by experimenters. Both factors are likely to strongly decrease acoustic variability relative to naturally occurring emotional speech, and thereby to artificially inflate listener scores. To us, an outcome of 55% correct seems quite modest if invariant cues are, in fact, present in the stimuli, with even that figure likely to be a significant overestimate of how listeners would perform under more natural circumstances.

A second point to consider is, therefore, the extent to which invariant acoustic cues are actually present in naturally occurring speech, given that attribution of emotion also importantly reflects perceptual processes, inferential capabilities, or even simple biases that listeners bring to the situation. For example, listeners have been shown to disproportionately weight particular acoustic cues, whether reliably covarying with vocalizer state or not.[17,28] Given the prominence of this sort of "stereotyping" in many automatic evaluations of personal characteristics in others,[55,56] it would arguably not be surprising to find that listener inferences concerning vocalizer affect from acoustics alone are simply not very accurate. Under more natural circumstances, however, a listener would be hearing the speech within a much richer social context and often from familiar vocalizers. Both factors could significantly boost the accuracy of attribution, with listeners having both general knowledge of the emotional states a vocalizer is most likely experiencing under a given set of circumstances, and specific experience with the potentially idiosyncratic cues provided by a particular familiar talker.[20,24]

From a methodological point of view, it therefore becomes critical to explicitly separate these factors, recognizing that listener psychological processes may be equally important to, or even more important than, veridical vocalizer cueing in shaping perceived emotional states. This possibility is elaborated in the next section, which shifts the focus from hypothesized links between emotional states and vocalizer acoustics to the effects that sounds have on listener affect. While compatible with various aspects of both dimensional- and discrete-emotions views, this perspective suggests that emotion-related cueing by vocalizers is actually a secondary outcome of the communication process. The primary function of emotional vocal acoustics is, instead, proposed to be to influence the listener's state and behavior.

AN AFFECT-INDUCTION ACCOUNT OF VOCAL SIGNALING

A central theme of the foregoing review is that in previous work on emotion-related aspects of vocal signals, researchers have generally expected to uncover veridical links between vocalizer affect, associated vocal acoustics, and listener perception. From this perspective, the function of emotion-related signaling is for the vocalizer to specifically inform listeners that particular affective states are being experienced. Of course, simply informing listeners about such states is not beneficial per se—it must be the effect that signaling has on subsequent listener behavior that has shaped the signaling process over evolutionary time.[57,58] It therefore becomes important that there is no guarantee that listeners will behave in ways that benefit vocalizers who are providing veridical cues to internal state. That observation, in turn, suggests that the most fundamental selection pressure acting on signalers must be to modulate others' behavior in ways that are beneficial to themselves. This logic leads to a different way of thinking about affect-related acoustics—namely, that their function is not so much to inform, but to influence. Here we suggest that such influence can occur via the impact of signal acoustics on the emotional systems of listeners, thereby shaping the way these individuals behave towards vocalizers. After describing this perspective, we will specifically apply it to the case of human laughter, a seemingly ubiquitous affect-related vocal signal.

Affect-Induction through Sound

Everyday experience shows that auditory stimuli can induce emotion-related responses in listeners. Sounds as varied as those of doors opening and closing, sirens wailing, and thunderstorms booming can all elicit attention, arousal, and valenced responses. Laughter and infant crying are two examples of potent, affect-inducing auditory signals, but even speech acoustics can produce emotion in listeners.[35,59,60] More broadly, Bradley and Lang[61] showed that responses to an array of environmental and human sounds can be organized along arousal and pleasure dimensions. Moreover, cardiac and electrodermal responses to these sounds were largely consistent with those that earlier studies had shown to occur when similar affective responses were induced using visual stimuli.[62]

The fact that sounds themselves can induce affect has played little in work on production and perception of vocal expression of emotion. Instead, both the discrete-emotions and dimensional approaches appear to approach the problem from a representational standpoint[63]—in the sense that affect-related meaning is "encoded" by vocalizers and subsequently "decoded" by listeners. Emotional expressions are thus a kind of code that vocalizers can use to represent their emotional states, which seems at least implicitly to be a linguistically inspired interpretation.

The "affect-induction" model has been proposed as an alternative to this sort of perspective. Originally developed in the context of nonhuman primate vocalizations,[4–6] this approach may also have broad applicability to human affective signaling.[7] Rather than viewing emotional communication as a process of information encoding and decoding, the model argues that the primary function of nonlinguistic vocal signals is to influence listeners' affect and thereby also modulate their behavior. Whereas representational accounts of communication implicitly implicate rather sophisticated, but typically undescribed, processes of information encoding and decoding, the affect-induction approach argues that vocal signals "work" because they can influence listeners at much lower levels of neural organization by eliciting emotional responses. The effects can be "direct," meaning that signal acoustics themselves have an impact, or "indirect," meaning that listeners experience a learned affective response to sounds as a result of previous experience. For the former, impact depends on the signal energy itself, meaning that aspects such as variability, amplitude, duration, and overall salience are of primary importance. In the latter case, learning arises through social interactions and depends specifically on instances in which individually distinctive sounds produced by particular vocalizers are repeatedly paired with affects experienced by the listener.

Differences between the affect-induction and representational perspectives might be best explained in the context of the similarities that exist between them. There are, for example, at least two important points of contact, the first being that both approaches assume an association between the signaler's internal state and the signal produced. The representational approach argues that the function of signaling is, then, to allow the recipient to infer that this particular state is occurring in the other individual. This view therefore predicts that signals should be strongly associated with differentiated signaler states. The affect-induction approach instead proposes that the vocalizer's internal state is important in the mechanistic underpinnings of signal production, but that the function of signaling is to induce emotion in the listener. As a result, signal features need not be strongly linked to vocalizer states, as it may benefit the signaler to induce similar responses in the listener across a variety of situations. Conversely, a diverse set of acoustic properties in sounds produced in a given situation might serve a common function in modulating listener arousal and valenced emotion. This approach predicts the occurrence of observable relationships between signaler state and physical signal, but predicts that they will be probabilistic in nature.

A second point of contact is that listeners are likely to be able to draw inferences about vocalizer states or likely upcoming behaviors. From a representational perspective, such inferences are part and parcel of why communication signals evolve—signal recipients are receiving encoded information about signaler state and act on that content. The affect-induction approach, in contrast, views listener inference as a secondary outcome of the vocalizing behavior that has evolved first and foremost because it benefits the signaler to exert these influences on listener affect and behavior—no matter what the mechanism is by which that impact occurs. Substantial variability in vocalizing behavior is thus to be expected. However, there will be probabilistic patterning involved, which listeners will inevitably benefit from attending to and learning about, to the extent that they themselves benefit from drawing inferences about vocalizer states and likely behavior.

While emotion-related signals do not have representational value in this view, they are still "meaningful" in the sense that listeners infer their significance based on a host of factors, which can include the acoustic attributes of the sound, the listener's affective state and familiarity with the sound, and the overarching context in which the sounds have occurred.[23,64,65] A corollary is that affective responses to highly similar sounds may be quite variable. For example, hearing a high-pitched shriek might be pleasurable when one is attending a party, but strongly negative when one is walking down a dark, isolated street. In both cases, the acoustics of a loud shriek are likely to elicit orientation, increase listener arousal, and thereby exacerbate whatever affective state the listener is already experiencing—positive and negative, respectively, in these two situations. In addition, if the sound has distinctive acoustic features that have previously been paired with either positive or negative affect in the listener, the sound will also activate corresponding conditioned responses. Finally, the sound can have a larger, likely more complex, inferred significance in a given context—for instance, if the shriek "means" that someone has had too much to drink and should be driven home.

While thus fundamentally different from representational approaches to emotional expression, the affect-induction perspective, nonetheless, has parallels with Scherer's "appeal" and "pull" functions of vocal expression of emotion,[17,63,66] as well as with the construct of "emotion contagion." Hatfield and colleagues'[67] notion of "primitive" emotional contagion is particularly relevant in that this process was described as either unconditioned or conditioned, and occurring outside the realm of conscious awareness. However, the affect-induction perspective takes the mechanism a step farther than the notions of "appeal," "pull," or "contagion" by specifically emphasizing links between the acoustics of vocal expressions of emotion and low-level neural responses in listeners.

Emotional Expressions as Social Tools

A larger implication of the approach we are describing is that emotional expressions function most importantly as nonconscious strategies of social influence, whether facial or vocal in nature.[68,69] Rather than informing per se, both kinds of signals are said to sway or shape perceiver affect and subsequent behavior or attitude toward the signaler. Any "information value" the signal has thus represents a combination of inferences the perceiver may be able to draw, given the context at hand, previous general experience with such signals, and the unique history of interaction shared by the individuals involved.[5,65] The affect-induction approach is thus compatible with research strategies in which affective states are induced using visual or auditory stimuli, and subsequently measured via self-report, psychophysiological assessment, and the like. Quite often, an additional component of such investigations is to have viewers or listeners make inferences about the affect-inducing stimuli they saw or heard. Explanatory slants on the inferential findings are often that perceiver affective state came about by virtue of the interpretative stance. We argue, instead, for a more balanced approach in which bottom-up influences of signals on affective processes are given more weight.

An Affect-Induction Approach to Laughter

Although Darwin thought of laughter as "purposeless" and "meaningless,"[3] a number of his ideas about this signal are compatible with current thinking about why humans laugh. While specifically thinking that the laughter produced by children was invariably associated with joy, Darwin found the laughter of adults more puzzling: "Something incongruous or unaccountable, exciting surprise and some sense of superiority in the laugher, who must be in a happy frame of mind, seems to be the commonest cause."[3] Here, Darwin was touching on several rather contemporary themes, including that laughter is linked not only to positive emotions, but also to feelings of derision and dominance, as well as to humor-eliciting perception of incongruity in events or actions.

There is certainly no shortage of hypotheses concerning the associations between laughter and affect-related states on the part of vocalizers. Other researchers have, for instance, joined Darwin in connecting laughter to positive valence in laughers, including happiness and joy.[70–72] Additional hypotheses have focused on humor perception and tension release,[73–77] masking negative states such as anger and anxiety,[3] signaling self-deprecation,[78] marking attention,[78] indicating appeasement or submission,[78–83] providing cues to individuality,[74] facilitating group cohesion,[81] signifying sexual interest,[83,84] and signaling fitness to prospective mates.[85] Laughter has thus been proposed to function in both cognitive and emotional capacities, with the latter including both positively and negatively valenced affective states.

One can only marvel at how a single vocal signal could be so functionally diverse, especially as some have held it to be a highly stereotyped vocalization.[83,86,87] Most approaches to laughter have at least tacitly adopted a representational stance in which laugh acoustics themselves are considered to provide information about vocal state, with listeners being held to make inferences about that state from signal acoustics (and perhaps contextual cues). The implication is therefore that laugh acoustics should vary in accordance with affective state. To our knowledge, there are no data that specifically test this hypothesis.

The available data do, in fact, show that laugh acoustics are remarkably variable.[83,88] However, this variability actually poses a challenge for representational perspectives in that it occurs both within and among laughers reporting similar arousal and positive-affect states.[7,89] Laughs in the Bachorowski et al.[88] study were recorded from 97 individuals as they watched humorous film clips either alone or with a same- or other-sex friend or stranger. The results of detailed acoustic analyses revealed that laughs can be reliably grouped into voiced and unvoiced (noisy) versions, with the latter being further separable into grunt- and snort-like categories. There was striking variability in a number of F_0-related measures in voiced sounds, suggesting that many of the sounds should have significant, direct impact on listener arousal and affect. Specifically, both males and females could produce laughter with very high mean and maximum F_0s, as well as considerable variability or F_0 modulation both within single laugh sounds and across bouts of laughter. A sizeable proportion of laughs also had evidence of acoustic irregularities (so-called nonlinear phenomena), which we suspect are especially potent in tweaking listener response systems.

Other analyses[89] showed that laugh acoustics did not vary as a function of self-reported affect, which is then inconsistent with a representational view of these sounds. These acoustics were, however, associated with the sex and familiarity of the laugher's social partner in the testing situation.[83,90] So, for instance, males laughed the most and produced a high proportion of laughs likely to have potent direct effects on listeners when the laugher was paired with a friend—especially a male friend. Females, on the other hand, were on average more likely to produce such sounds in the company of a male. While a careful accounting of the interactions between laugher sex and social context is beyond the scope of this chapter, Owren and Bachorowski[7,91] provide a detailed interpretation of these results. The gist is that both males and females produce more direct-effect laughs when it would benefit them to elicit arousal and affect in listeners, while refraining from using such sounds when inducing arousal in listeners would likely only exacerbate negatively toned emotional states in these individuals.

As on the production side, perceptual responses to laughter have also not received much systematic empirical attention. Nevertheless, the data that are available do show that laugh acoustics elicit affective responses in listeners and can have a modulating effect on a social partner's attitude toward the vocalizer. As a first step toward testing hypotheses about direct effects that laugh sounds may exert on listener states, Bachorowski and Owren[92] had listeners rate a sample of voiced and unvoiced laughs. Outcomes were remarkably consistent, regardless of whether listeners rated their own affect in response to hearing a laugh, the likely affective response other listeners would experience, or three affect-related attributes of the laugher. Voiced laughs were given significantly more positive evaluations than were unvoiced laughs, supporting the idea that the acoustic properties of the former (e.g., high mean F_0, marked F_0 modulation, and high amplitude) activate listeners in a direct fashion. More recent work has shown that unvoiced laughs heard in isolation during the course of perceptual testing can actually elicit slightly negative affect in listeners.[93] Grammer and Eibl-Eibesfeldt[83] and Keltner and Bonanno[94] have shown, further, that voicing can be correlated with listener interest in the laugher: males reported more interest in females they had just met if those testing partners produced a larger number of voiced, but not unvoiced, laughs during a 10-min interval.

Other research has begun to focus on indirect or learned effects. Here the expectation is that learned emotional responses should accrue in listeners experiencing positive affect as laughers are able to repeatedly produce individually distinctive sounds in close temporal association with the occurrence of those states. Bachorowski et al.[88] achieved moderate success in statistical classification of both the voiced and unvoiced laughs of individual vocalizers, providing preliminary evidence that laughs are, in fact, individually distinctive. Initial behavioral support was obtained in finding that laughter is far more likely to show coincident occurrence between friends than strangers,[95] and that this temporal linkage is more frequent for voiced than for unvoiced laughs.[96]

These studies are just the beginning, however, with much remaining to be learned about laughter, particularly including the functional importance of unvoiced versions. Laughter is clearly an inherently social event,[97] and we further suggest it is used in a strategic, albeit nonconscious, fashion. That view has been extensively elaborated elsewhere, with the bigger picture being that laughter, like smiling, likely evolved to facilitate formation and maintenance of positively toned relationships as a mechanism facilitating cooperative behavior among genetically unrelated individuals.[98] In the current context, the most important point to note is that there are some telling commonalities that may connect the major findings emerging from studies of emotional communication through speech acoustics and laughter.

CONCLUSIONS: EMOTIONAL SPEECH, LAUGHTER, AFFECT-INDUCTION, AND DARWIN

In our evaluation, the empirical evidence reviewed in this chapter is more compatible with an affect-induction perspective than one that views emotion-related signaling as an inherently representational event. For example, while the data concerning production and perception of emotion-related acoustic cueing in speech are methodologically far from ideal, they provide strong evidence that F_0- and amplitude-related features play the most central role. While there is little or no indication that variation in these characteristics is linked to either discrete emotional states or valenced affect in vocalizers, their impact on listener perception and attribution of emotion is clear.

There is little doubt that the vocalizers themselves are experiencing valenced emotions, and those may even be discretely differentiated states. However, the acoustic effects occurring in association with those emotional experiences are ambiguous at best if they are seen specifically as cues designed to communicate those states. Even for laughter, it is not clear that the sounds produced are unambiguously linked to particular emotions. While clearly associated with positive states and pleasant situations, laughter can also be linked to an evident variety of other states and circumstances. In contrast, there is nothing ambiguous about the effects that laughter can have on listeners, where at least F_0 has again been clearly shown to be an important mediator of that impact (tests of amplitude have not yet been performed). For both speech and laughter, then, it has been easy to demonstrate that these very basic acoustic parameters have general and robust effects on listener states and evaluations.

Those observations do not in and of themselves definitively demonstrate that the affect-induction view is to be preferred, particularly as much of the work conducted on human vocal expression of emotion has assumed, rather than tested, the proposition that representational signaling is involved. However, it is also noteworthy that this research has failed to provide compelling evidence of unique links between vocalizer states, speech acoustics, and listener decoding of affective information. The acoustic features are instead relatively undifferentiated, with listeners showing highly constrained and context-dependent judgments about emotional "content." Our alternative interpretation is, therefore, that these inferences are grounded in the listeners' own arousal and valence responses to signal acoustics, richly interpreted in the context of other information available about the vocalizer and the circumstances under which the signal is being evaluated. Affective communication thus becomes a process of attributing emotion to vocalizers, rather than one of recovering encoded information.

Outcomes have been similar for laughter, where there is evidence of significant acoustic variability occurring even within similarly toned, positive circumstances. In the face of this variety, listeners have been found to respond much more consistently to basic acoustic features of laughter rather than as if decoding information about the situation in which the sounds were originally produced. Much more extensive data are, of course, needed for both emotional speech and laughter, where it is particularly important to record these signals under controlled but naturalistic circumstances. Here, the critical comparisons are between vocalizer affect and acoustic features of associated sounds on the one hand, and between those vocalizations and listener ability to infer signaler states on the other. The more traditional, representational approach predicts an unambiguous connection between affect and acoustics, which thereby allows accurate listener inferences. In contrast, the affect-induction view predicts that vocal acoustics will strongly shape listener attribution, but that the link between signaler emotions and vocal behavior will be moderate—hence allowing comparably modest accuracy in inferring those states.

In making these proposals, it is edifying to find them so clearly foreshadowed in Darwin's writing. His observations concerning emotion-related signaling were not only cogent and pertinent, they also highlighted the major issues that continue to lie at the heart of contemporary work in this area. His thoughts on veridical signaling were, without a doubt, better developed than his nascent analysis of the effects that signals can have on receiver affective systems, but ideas about the latter are also plainly present. Darwin appears not to have recognized the potential contradiction in positing both representational and affect-induction effects, and therefore did not discuss how one might resolve this discrepancy. His observations would likely have been equally sage on this score, and we think it a fitting tribute to Darwin to end by noting that this duality found in his writing and thinking remains a central problem for the modern study of emotional expression as well.

ACKNOWLEDGMENTS

We thank Moria Smoski for her significant contributions to the laughter work described here. Funds for various portions of the work described here came from NIMH B/START, NSF POWRE; from Vanderbilt University Discovery awards to Jo-Anne Bachorowski; from the Positive Psychology Network to Moria Smoski; and from Cornell University to Michael J. Owren.

REFERENCES

1. CICERO, M.T. 2001. De Oratore. Oxford University Press. New York.
2. ARISTOTLE. 1995. Treatise on Rhetoric. T. Buckley, Trans. Prometheus. Amherst, NY.

3. DARWIN, C. 1998. The Expression of the Emotions in Man and Animals, 3rd edit. Harper Collins. London. (US edit.: Oxford University Press. New York.)
4. OWREN, M.J. & D. RENDALL. 1997. An affect-conditioning model of nonhuman primate signaling. *In* Perspectives in Ethology, Vol. 12: Communication. D.H. Owings, M.D. Beecher & N.S. Thompson, Eds.: 299–346. Plenum. New York.
5. OWREN, M.J. & D. RENDALL. 2001. Sound on the rebound: bringing form and function back to the forefront in understanding nonhuman primate vocal signaling. Evol. Anthropol. **10:** 58–71.
6. RENDALL, D. & M.J. OWREN. 2002. Animal vocal communication: say what? *In* The Cognitive Animal. M. Bekoff, C. Allen & G. Burghardt, Eds.: 307–314. MIT Press. Cambridge, MA.
7. OWREN, M.J., D. RENDALL & J.-A. BACHOROWSKI. Nonlinguistic vocal communication. *In* Primate Psychology: Bridging the Gap between the Mind and Behavior of Human and Nonhuman Primates. D. Maestripieri, Ed. Harvard University Press. Cambridge, MA. In press.
8. FANT, G. 1960. Acoustic theory of speech production. 's-Gravenhage. Mouton.
9. STEVENS, K.N. 2000. Acoustic Phonetics. MIT Press. Cambridge, MA.
10. OWREN, M.J. & R.H. BERNACKI. 1998. Applying linear predictive coding (LPC) to frequency-spectrum analysis of animal acoustic signals. *In* Animal Acoustic Communication: Sound Analysis and Research Methods. S.L. Hopp, M.J. Owren & C.S. Evans, Eds.: 129–161. Springer-Verlag. New York.
11. SCHERER, K.R. 1982. Methods of research on vocal communication: paradigms and parameters. *In* Handbook of Nonverbal Behavior Research. K.R. Scherer & P. Ekman, Eds.: 136–198. Cambridge University Press. Cambridge.
12. SCHERER, K.R. 1986. Vocal affect expression: a review and model for future research. Psychol. Bull. **99:** 143–165.
13. SCHERER, K.R. 1989. Vocal measurement of emotion. *In* Emotion: Theory, Research, and Experience, Vol. 4. The Measurement of Emotions. R. Plutchik & H. Kellerman, Eds.: 233–259. Academic Press. New York.
14. JOHNSON, K. 1997. Acoustic and Auditory Phonetics. Blackwell. Cambridge.
15. LIEBERMAN, P. & S.E. BLUMSTEIN. 1988. Speech physiology, speech perception, and acoustic phonetics. Cambridge University Press. Cambridge.
16. PITTAM, J. & K.R. SCHERER. 1993. Vocal expression and communication of emotion. *In* Handbook of Emotions. M. Lewis & J.M. Haviland, Eds.: 185–197. Guilford. New York.
17. JOHNSTONE, T. & K.R. SCHERER. 2000. Vocal communication of emotion. *In* Handbook of Emotions. M. Lewis & J. Haviland, Eds.: 220–235. Guilford. New York.
18. LEINONEN, L., T. HILTUNEN, I. LINNANKOSKI & M.-L. LAAKSO. 1997. Expression of emotional-motivational connotations with a one-word utterance. J. Acoust. Soc. Am. **102:** 1853–1863.
19. BANSE, R. & K.R. SCHERER. 1996. Acoustic profiles in vocal emotion expression. J. Personal. Soc. Psychol. **70:** 614–636.
20. BACHOROWSKI, J.-A. & M.J. OWREN. 1999. Acoustic correlates of talker sex and individual talker identity are present in a short vowel segment produced in running speech. J. Acoust. Soc. Am. **106:** 1054–1063.
21. COWIE, R. 2000. Describing the emotional states expressed in speech. Proceedings of the International Speech Communication Association Workshop on Speech and Emotion. pp. 11–18. Textflow. Belfast.

22. FRICK, R.W. 1985. Communicating emotion: the role of prosodic features. Psychol. Bull. **97:** 412–429.
23. KAPPAS, A., U. HESS & K.R. SCHERER. 1991. Voice and emotion. *In* Fundamentals of Nonverbal Behavior. B. Rime & R. Feldman, Eds.: 200–238. Cambridge University Press. Cambridge.
24. PAKOSZ, M. 1983. Attitudinal judgments in intonation: some evidence for a theory. J. Psycholinguist. Res. **12:** 311–326.
25. SCHERER, K.R., R. BANSE, H.G. WALLBOTT & T. GOLDBECK. 1991. Vocal cues in emotion encoding and decoding. Motivat. Emotion **15:** 123–148.
26. SOBIN, C. & M. ALPERT. 1999. Emotion in speech: the acoustic attributes of fear, anger, sadness, and joy. J. Psycholinguist. Res. **28:** 347–365.
27. KAPPAS, A. & U. HESS. 1995. Nonverbal aspects of oral communication. *In* Aspects of Oral Communication. D.U.M. Quasthoff, Ed.: 169–180. De Gruyter. Berlin.
28. STREETER, L.A., N.H. MACDONALD, W. APPLE, *et al.* 1983. Acoustic and perceptual indicators of emotional stress. J. Acoust. Soc. Am. **73:** 1354–1360.
29. PELL, M.D. 2001. Influence of emotion and focus location on prosody in matched statements and questions. J. Acoust. Soc. Am. **109:** 1668–1680.
30. SCHRÖDER, M. 2000. Experimental study of affect bursts. *In* Proceedings of the International Speech Communication Association Workshop on Speech and Emotion: 132–135. Textflow. Belfast.
31. WALLBOTT, H.G. & K.R. SCHERER. 1986. Cues and channels in emotion recognition. J. Pers. Soc. Psychol. **51:** 690–699.
32. RUSSELL, J.A., BACHOROWSKI, J.-A. & J.-M. FERNANDEZ-DOLS. 2003. Facial and vocal expressions of emotion. Ann. Rev. Psychol. **54:** 329–349.
33. BACHOROWSKI, J.-A. & M.J. OWREN. 1995. Vocal expression of emotion: acoustic properties of speech are associated with emotional intensity and context. Psychol. Sci. **6:** 219–224.
34. BACHOROWSKI, J.-A. & M.J. OWREN. 1996. Vocal expression of emotion is associated with vocal fold vibration and vocal tract resonance. Psychophysiology **33:** S20.
35. HATFIELD, E., C.K. HSEE, J. COSTELLO, *et al.* 1995. The impact of vocal feedback on emotional experience and expression. J. Soc. Behav. Pers. **10:** 293–312.
36. MILLOT, J.-L. & G. BRAND. 2001. Effects of pleasant and unpleasant ambient odors on human voice pitch. Neurosci. Lett. **297:** 61–63.
37. PAESCHKE, A. & W.F. SENDLMEIER. 2000. Prosodic characteristics of emotional speech. Measurements of fundamental frequency movements. *In* Proceedings of the International Speech Communication Association Workshop on Speech and Emotion: 75–80. Textflow. Belfast.
38. PEREIRA, C. 2000. Dimensions of emotional meaning in speech. *In* Proceedings of the International Speech Communication Association Workshop on Speech and Emotion: 25–28. Textflow. Belfast.
39. PITTAM, J., C. GALLOIS & V. CALLAN. 1990. The long-term spectrum and perceived emotion. Speech Commun. **9:** 177–187.
40. PROTOPAPAS, A. & P. LIEBERMAN. 1997. Fundamental frequency of phonation and perceived emotional stress. J. Acoust. Soc. Am. **101:** 2267–2277.
41. TOLKMITT, F.J. & K.R. SCHERER. 1986. Effects of experimentally induced stress on vocal parameters. J. Exp. Psychol. Hum. Percept. Perform. **12:** 302–313.

42. TROUVAIN, J. & W.J. BARRY. 2000. The prosody of excitement in horse race commentaries. *In* Proceedings of the International Speech Communication Association Workshop on Speech and Emotion: 86–91. Textflow. Belfast.

43. TASSINARY, L.G. & J.T. CACIOPPO. 1992. Unobservable facial actions and emotion. Psychol. Sci. **3:** 28–33.

44. SCHERER, K.R., D.R. LADD & K.E.A. SILVERMAN. 1984. Vocal cues to speaker affect: testing two models. J. Acoust. Soc. Am. **76:** 1346–1356.

45. LADD, D.R., K.E.A. SILVERMAN, F. TOLKMITT, *et al.* 1985. Evidence for the independence of intonation contour type, voice quality, and F_0 range in signaling speaker affect. J. Acoust. Soc. Am. **78:** 435–444.

46. BACHOROWSKI, J.-A. 1999. Vocal expression and perception of emotion. Curr. Dir. Psychol. Sci. **8:** 53–57.

47. SCHERER, K.R., R. BANSE & H.G. WALLBOTT. 2001. Emotion inferences from vocal expression correlate across languages and cultures. J. Cross-Cultural Psychol. **32:** 76–92.

48. TICKLE, A. 2000. English and Japanese speakers' emotion vocalisation and recognition: a comparison highlighting vowel quality. *In* Proceedings of the International Speech Communication Association Workshop on Speech and Emotion: 104–109. Textflow. Belfast.

49. JOHNSON, W.F., R.N. EMDE, K.R. SCHERER & M.D. KLINNERT. 1986. Recognition of emotion from vocal cues. Arch. Gen. Psychiatry **43:** 280–283.

50. TARTTER, V.C. & D. BRAUN. 1994. Hearing smiles and frowns in normal and whisper registers. J. Acoust. Soc. Am. **96:** 2101–2107.

51. CAULDWELL, R.T. 2000. Where did the anger go? The role of context in interpreting emotion in speech. *In* Proceedings of the International Speech Communication Association Workshop on Speech and Emotion: 127–131. Textflow. Belfast.

52. GREEN, R.S. & N. CLIFF. 1975. Multidimensional comparisons of structures of vocally and facially expressed emotion. Percept. Psychophysics **17:** 429–438.

53. BREITENSTEIN, C., D. VAN LANCKER & I. DAUM. 2001. The contribution of speech rate and pitch variation to the perception of vocal emotions in a German and an American sample. Cognit. Emotion **15:** 57–79.

54. SCHERER, K.R. & J.S. OSHINSKY. 1977. Cue utilization in emotion attribution from auditory stimuli. Motiv. Emotion **1:** 331–346.

55. BANAJI, M.R. & C.D. HARDIN. 1996. Automatic stereotyping. Psychol. Sci. **7:** 136–141.

56. KAWAKAMI, K., H. YOUNG & J.F. DOVIDIO. 2002. Automatic stereotyping: category, trait, and behavioral activations. Pers. Soc. Psychol. Bull. **28:** 3–15.

57. DAWKINS, R. 1989. The Selfish Gene. Oxford University Press. Oxford.

58. DAWKINS, R. & J.R. KREBS. 1978. Animal signals: information or manipulation? *In* Behavioral Ecology: An Evolutionary Approach. J.R. Krebs & N.B. Davies, Eds.: 282–309. Blackwell Scientific. London.

59. NEUMANN, R. & F. STRACK. 2000. "Mood contagion:" The automatic transfer of mood between persons. J. Pers. Soc. Psychol. **79:** 211–223.

60. SIEGMAN, A.W. & S. BOYLE. 1993. Voices of fear and anxiety and sadness and depression: the effects of speech rate and loudness on fear and anxiety and sadness and depression. J. Abnorm. Psychol. **102:** 430–437.

61. BRADLEY, M.M. & P.J. LANG. 2000. Affective reactions to acoustic stimuli. Psychophysiology **37:** 204–215.

62. LANG, P.J., M.K. GREENWALD, M.M. BRADLEY & A.O. HAMM. 1993. Looking at pictures: affective, facial, visceral, and behavioral reactions. Psychophysiology **30:** 261–273.
63. SCHERER, K.R. 1988. On the symbolic functions of vocal affect expression. J. Lang. Soc. Psychol. **7:** 79–100.
64. BACHOROWSKI, J.-A. & M.J. OWREN. 2002. The role of vocal acoustics in emotional intelligence. *In* The Wisdom of Feelings: Processes Underlying Emotional Intelligence. L.F. Barrett & P. Salovey, Eds.: 11–36. Guilford. New York.
65. HESS, U. & G. KIROUAC. 2000. Emotion expression in groups. *In* Handbook of Emotions. M. Lewis & J. Haviland-Jones, Eds.: 368–381. Guilford. New York.
66. SCHERER, K.R. 1992. Vocal affect expression as symptom, symbol, and appeal. *In* Nonverbal Vocal Communication: Comparative and Developmental Approaches. H. Papoušek, U. Jürgens & M. Papoušek, Eds.: 43–60. Cambridge University Press. Cambridge.
67. HATFIELD, E., J.T. CACIOPPO & R.L. RAPSON. 1992. Primitive emotional contagion. *In* Emotion and Social Behavior. M.S. Clark, Ed.: 151–177. Sage. London.
68. BARGH, J.A. & T.L. CHARTRAND. 1999. The unbearable automaticity of being. Am. Psychol. **54:** 462–479.
69. ZAJONC, R.B. 1980. Feeling and thinking: preferences need no inferences. Am. Psychol. **35:** 151–175.
70. MCCOMAS, H.C. 1923. The origin of laughter. Psychol. Rev. **30:** 45–56.
71. NWOKAH, E.E., P. DAVIES, A. ISLAM, *et al.* 1993. Vocal affect in three-year-olds: a quantitative acoustic analysis of child laughter. J. Acoust. Soc. Am. **94:** 3076–3090.
72. VAN HOOFF, J.A.R.A.M. 1972. A comparative approach to the phylogeny of laughter and smiling. *In* Non-verbal Communication. R.A. Hinde, Ed.: 209–241. Cambridge University Press. Cambridge.
73. APTE, M.L. 1985. Humor and Laughter: An Anthropological Approach. Cornell University Press. Ithaca, NY.
74. BLACK, D.W. 1984. Laughter. J. Am. Med. Assoc. **252:** 2995–2998.
75. EDMONSON, M.S. 1987. Notes on laughter. Anthropol. Linguist. **29:** 23–34.
76. SROUFE, L.A. & E. WATERS. 1976. The ontogenesis of smiling and laughter: a perspective on the organization of development in infancy. Psychol. Rev. **83:** 173–189.
77. WEISFELD, G.E. 1993. The adaptive value of humor and laughter. Ethol. Sociobiol. **14:** 141–169.
78. GLENN, P.J. 1991/1992. Current speaker initiation of two-party shared laughter. Res. Lang. Soc. Interact. **25:** 139–162.
79. MARTIN, G.N. & C.D. GRAY. 1996. The effect of audience laughter on men's and women's response to humor. J. Soc. Psychol. **136:** 221–231.
80. ADAMS, R.M. & B. KIRKEVOLD. 1978. Looking, smiling, laughing, and moving in restaurants: sex and age differences. Environ. Psychol. Nonverbal Behav. **3:** 117–121.
81. DEACON, T.W. 1997. The Symbolic Species. Norton. New York.
82. DOVIDIO, J.F., C.E. BROWN, K. HELTMAN, *et al.* 1988. Power displays between women and men in discussions of gender-linked tasks: a multichannel study. J. Pers. Soc. Psychol. **55:** 580–587.

83. GRAMMER, K. & I. EIBL-EIBESFELDT. 1990. The ritualization of laughter. *In* Naturlichkeit der Sprache und der Kultur: Acta Colloquii. W. Koch, Ed.: 192–214. Brockmeyer. Bochum, Germany.
84. GRAMMER, K. 1990. Strangers meet: laughter and nonverbal signs of interest in opposite-sex encounters. J. Nonverbal Behav. **14:** 209–236.
85. DUNBAR, R.I.M. 1996. Grooming, Gossip, and the Evolution of Language. Faber and Faber. London.
86. PROVINE, R.R. 1993. Laughter punctuates speech: linguistic, social and gender contexts of laughter. Ethology **95:** 291–298.
87. PROVINE, R. R. & Y.L. YONG. 1991. Laughter: a stereotyped human vocalization. Ethology **89:** 115–124.
88. BACHOROWSKI, J.-A., M.J. SMOSKI & M.J. OWREN. 2001. The acoustic features of human laughter. J. Acoust. Soc. Am. **110:** 1581–1597.
89. BACHOROWSKI, J.-A., M.J. SMOSKI, A.J. TOMARKEN & M.J. OWREN. Laugh Rate and Acoustics Are Associated with Social Context. Manuscript under review.
90. DEVEREAUX, P.G. & G.P. GINSBURG. 2001. Sociality effects on the production of laughter. J. Gen. Psychol. **128:** 227–240.
91. OWREN, M.J. & J.-A. BACHOROWSKI. 2003. Reconsidering the evolution of nonlinguistic communication: the case of laughter. J. Nonverbal Behav. In press.
92. BACHOROWSKI, J.-A. & M.J. OWREN. 2001. Not all laughs are alike: voiced but not unvoiced laughter readily elicits positive affect. Psychol. Sci. **12:** 252–257.
93. OWREN, M.J., N. TRIVEDI, A. SCHULMAN & J.-A. BACHOROWSKI. 2003. Laughter produced in positive circumstances can elicit both positive and negative responses in listeners. An implicit association test (IAT) with auditory stimuli: listener evaluations of human laughter. Manuscript under revision.
94. KELTNER, D. & G. BONANNO. 1997. A study of laughter and dissociation: distinct correlates of laughter and smiling during bereavement. J. Pers. Soc. Psychol. **73:** 687–702.
95. SMOSKI, M.J. & J.-A. BACHOROWSKI. Antiphonal laughter between friends and strangers. Cognit. Emotion. **17:** 327–340.
96. SMOSKI, M.J. & J.-A. BACHOROWSKI. 2003. Antiphonal laughter in developing friendships. Ann. N.Y. Acad. Sci. **1000:** this volume.
97. PROVINE, R.R. & K.R. FISCHER. 1989. Laughing, smiling, and talking: relation to sleeping and social context in humans. Ethology **83:** 295–305.
98. OWREN, M.J. & J.-A. BACHOROWSKI. 2001. The evolution of emotional expression: a "selfish-gene" account of smiling and laughter in early hominids and humans. *In* Emotions: Current Issues and Future Development. T. Mayne & G.A. Bonanno, Eds.: 152–191. Guilford. New York.

Expression

Panel Discussion

PAUL EKMAN, *Moderator*

QUESTION: This is a question for Paul Ekman. I wonder if you could bring us up to date on your thinking about certain autonomic phenomena that impact the face—for example, the flush and the blush, pupillary dilatation, and other changes in facial appearance brought about by the autonomic nervous system that have a bearing on the issue of the deception.

PAUL EKMAN (*University of California–San Francisco, San Francisco, CA*): Darwin had a lot to say about blushing—why we blush, about the fact that children blush more than adults, that females blush more than males, that there are families of blushers where everybody blushes, and that there are large numbers of people who don't show any apparent blushes. Richie Davidson and I did a joint study with Bob Zjonc about twenty years ago, in which Bob got facial temperature measures. But the findings never saw the light of day. So that was the only study I know of where there were simultaneous measures of brain activity, facial muscular activity, and thermal changes in the face. There is lots of new technology that allows measuring changes in facial temperature from a distance. Mark Frank and I have just begun a study obtaining both facial expression measures and thermal measures of the face during deception.

QUESTION: In the same vein, you've written about the relative merits of autonomic versus facial indicators of deception, and I wondered if you could bring us up to date on your thinking on that topic.

EKMAN: Well, I'm one of the authors of the recent National Research Council report on the scientific validity of the polygraph in national security applications. In a nutshell our finding is that there is virtually no scientific evidence of validity in this application. That isn't because autonomic measures aren't useful; it's because the research that has been done has been very limited. It has been poorly designed and has little relevance. Building on the work that I've done with Bob Levenson and other work by Bob, I think it would be sensible to combine autonomic measures with facial and vocal measures. To my knowledge, there's been only one such study in the last 35 years, and it had a very small sample, so we couldn't conclude much. But if you start using autonomic measures to look at the occurrence of specific emotions, which I know raises the hackles of at least some people—but

Ann. N.Y. Acad. Sci. 1000: 266–278 (2003). © 2003 New York Academy of Sciences.
doi: 10.1196/annals.1280.013

we think there is some pretty good evidence for that—then I think you could start to improve the accuracy of predictions. Another issue in lie detection is that if you're getting up into the 90's with your predicted accuracy, which we do by using behavioral measures, you start wondering about a ceiling effect limiting the usefulness of additional measures. One more issue: if you're thinking about catching spies, for example, you're up against a base rate problem. Probably fewer than one person in 5,000 who apply to the CIA have the intention of spying, so if you guess "no spy" you're going to be right 99.999% of the time. So clearly, you've got to use other kinds of measures to deal with low base rate phenomena. It's the same with people walking into airports; the low base rate phenomena pose an enormous problem. I'm much more comfortable working with criminal incidents in which, typically, among a group of five suspects one is likely to be the culprit.

DACHER KELTNER (*University of California–Berkeley, Berkeley, CA*): As Paul Ekman said, Darwin had a lot of really interesting things to say about the blush. He talked about how it was the product of directing your attention towards certain parts of the body, which is an interesting hypothesis in light of his being a Victorian. There's a lot of blushing in Victorian literature and culture. He didn't think blushing was a signal. I think that's an open question. Don Shearn at Colorado College has done really neat studies of the blush. What we've learned by measuring facial temperature and blood flow to the cheeks, I think, is actually a very important finding in that blushing is different from an anxiety response. So, it's part of the autonomic nervous system that differs from fear and anxiety. That's very important. He's done more recent work on the empathic blush where he has people singing the Star Spangled Banner while being videotaped. That's odious enough. And then you come back and watch your performance on videotape, with your friend. And that produces a blush response, but now you've found that the blush response gets bigger, the bigger audience. And if you're a friend, you blush when your friend blushes. Contagious emotion is a wildly interesting topic.

EKMAN: I have to add one more thing, which is that people with very dark skins blush, but you can't see it. Now, we don't have emotion signals that we know of that are observable only in some races. And if we all came out of Africa, as people believe, it raises some really interesting questions about whether the blush really did evolve as a signal. It's certainly an interesting phenomenon, and probably occurs only in some people; and certainly it's visible only in some races.

QUESTION: Dr. Keltner, I want to hear more about the study you described of Mills's students. You've got the data that the nature of the smile in the yearbook photo has all this predictive value. What's causing what? Is it in the college student's ability to make a credible, nice smile? What do you think is the underlying mechanism?

KELTNER: Well, with those kinds of longitudinal studies, as opposed to manipulation studies, it's harder to get at causalities. I think that's why those controls we looked at inform us about the causalities. I think the Duchenne smile is a signal of positive affect and sort of an affinitive gesture towards betters. I think smiling and laughter does a couple of really important things, as Bob Levenson has shown with Barbara Fredrickson. It reduces the physiology of distress, so it helps in that fashion. And then it has social effects. So, that's what I think the process or mechanism is. These are not attractiveness effects. Physical attractiveness has a whole set of effects similar to positive emotions, better relationships, and so forth. It's not that. It's not what you alluded to, which is just the social desirability tendency of the women to be able to perform on the spot. So I think there's an emotion effect that occurs in the moment, which then accumulates over time. No one has really studied what I'm talking about, which is, in these longitudinal studies, how we affect the life context in the moment. So that's where I put my money.

QUESTION: Are any of the women who participated in these studies still alive?

KELTNER: Yes, most of them are.

QUESTION: So you could actually go and test them and find out whether they can voluntarily make a Duchenne smile?

KELTNER: Maybe there are a small percentage who can; or maybe they can't do it at all, and they can rule that out.

RICHARD J. DAVIDSON (*University of Wisconsin–Madison, Madison, WI*): Yes, that's a good idea. If I can just follow up on this point. I assume that these are all photographs that were taken by a human photographer in the room. One question is whether you predicted that you would get the same effects if this were an automated system, where there's no human interaction between the individual being photographed and the camera. One hypothesis is that there's a mini-interaction between the photographer and the individual being photographed, a student, which is actually reflected in this smile.

KELTNER: That's a very subtle idea I hadn't thought about. Most people think about the artificiality of having your photograph taken by a photographer, but Richie Davidson is highlighting a different idea, which is that this is actually a social exchange, in which photographers make jokes and make you laugh. And it's those women who can capitalize on that exchange.

DAVIDSON: Photographers differ in how they do these things. Some get behind a camera; some cover their head with a black cloth. You could find out how he took those photographs—was it a social occasion, or not?

FRANS B.M. DE WAALS (*Emory University, Atlanta, GA*): First of all, about the blush: very briefly, Darwin made a very good point, saying that the blush is probably the only human expression that doesn't exist in primates. I was intrigued by that. First of all, I was intrigued from a cultural perspective, because all this smiling in photographs is so American. There are countries where you can photograph 100 people in a row, and they will never smile. I wonder what that means. First of all, there's a cultural question: does it mean that in other countries people are never happy, in their marriages or something? The second question I have is how happy they are, how they feel. Maybe people who smile a lot have a tendency to delude themselves. But do their marriages actually last longer? So the proof is in the pudding, so to speak. You need to investigate whether they actually stay married a longer time in these so-called happy marriages. So those are the two questions that I have. By the way, this is asked by somebody from Holland, the happiest country in the world.

KELTNER: Yes, Americans do have a pathological tendency to smile a lot in photographs. I would expect these kinds of results gathered outside of the context of our yearbook study would work; I think the smiling does have universal effects upon physiology and social relationships. I just have to find the context in which one could reliably observe variation in smiling behavior. I got really excited about the prospect: I think this opens up a lot of methodological opportunities in terms of looking at family lineage and photographs from different generations. I started looking at photographs from different generations, and Paul Ekman would probably agree that people did not smile for photographs until a certain point in history. So that torpedoed that opportunity. We need to have observer reports, so we have somebody else reporting upon the person; I think that would in part reduce the concern about purely self-reported data. So I agree: we would like to look at the longevity of the relationship, see how that works out.

ROBERT W. LEVENSON (*University of California–Berkeley, Berkeley, CA*): It's one of the things that seems to come out in all of your presentations, in some of these anecdotes about emotional virtuosos—the one percent of people who can detect deception; the people who have wonderful smiles in youth and then lead wonderful lives; the people who modulate their voices in remarkably effective ways, and thus their friends are happy to be around them; or they can have their friends enter mood states that are really beneficial. It sounds something like athletic or musical ability, like the coordination of a dancer that comes to few people early in life, without which it's hard to create a virtuoso. Or maybe it's something that comes out of people growing up. I expect it's both. I was wondering about your perspectives. How optimistic are you about the notion reflected in *How to Raise an Emotionally Intelligent Child*, the subtitle of a book by a friend and colleague? How optimistic are you that you can really learn to be more effective in the use of these emotional signals, that you can turn around people's emotional lives?

JO-ANNE BACHAROWSKI (*Vanderbilt University, Nashville, TN*): I think we're in a different place with the evolution of laughter and smiling, actually. We know that there are voluntary and involuntary pathways that can subserve smile production, but not for laughter. The neurological evidence is that most of the laughter that we get where we now are in evolutionary history is spontaneous or involuntary. We can try to fake a laugh, perhaps, and grunt in affirmation in a social circumstance. But for the most part, we don't seem to have any voluntary control over that. And so the people who produce these just amazingly wonderful laughs that make everyone around them laugh and make a party wonderful (and they go on to have happy marriages and all that kind of stuff)—part of what's driving that may be their own emotional organization. But part of what makes that sound seem so musical and affect-inducing to the people who hear it is just their inherent anatomy. And I think that's one of the places where we need to think differently about what's happening with the voice than about what happens with facial expressions; because they are not equally subject to control. That's in part why it is so difficult to find true emotional speech. But at least I've talked about the face more.

KELTNER: I think that's a great question and speaks to a dangerous implication about the culture and literature on emotion, which has to do with the voluntary and involuntary nature of emotional expression. I believe it; I think it's true; I think it's erroneous to assume that we can't build up certain emotional tendencies through other kinds of practices and habits. I'm reading a book on reverence by a Texas philosopher that I'd recommend to all. He writes that one can encourage reverence, one can treat it as a habit that can be learned. I was talking with Richie Davidson last night about his thinking about emotions and emotional expressions like laughter or compassionate gratitude. It's a matter of skills. I think the field has underestimated the capacity to build up virtuosity in emotion; I think that's a really important line of inquiry.

EKMAN: Danny Goleman's bestseller *Emotional Intelligence* says you can. The book doesn't present evidence for it, but makes the promise, which is what I think made it a bestseller. But you have to distinguish between recognizing the emotional signals and improving your life. Some people would think the more you know about how others are feeling, the worse your own life will be. That depends on what kind of a job you have, who you're living with, and the other circumstances of your life. You also have to distinguish between skills in interpreting and expressing. I do think it's much more likely—in fact, I do have some evidence—that I can teach people to read emotions better (see www.emotionsrevealed.com); but I also believe it's much harder to train expression than to train recognition and interpretation. Having done so much work in lying, I would not want to run a school for liars. I haven't tried to teach people to be better deceivers or to be more honest. We certainly need a little more of the latter; we've got plenty of the former.

DAVIDSON: I would like to comment on Bob Levenson's question too, it's just irresistible; it's an important question: I think that we have not given emotional skills training a chance. We have impoverished processes in this culture to train emotion in a systematic way. People go to the gym for an hour a day, train their bodies, and see effects pretty rapidly. There are studies of musical training that show that, started early in life, it systematically shapes the plasticity of the brain in certain specific ways. I just don't think there is a shred of evidence by which to evaluate the impact of certain kinds of emotional skills training, particularly such training that begins very early in life. One of the wonderful things that modern neuroscience has taught us is how plastic the brain is, particularly during this critical period. And so I think it's a tremendously important question for our culture, and it needs to be given a serious evaluation.

LAURA L. CARSTENSEN (*Stanford University, Stanford, CA*): Clearly it is emotional input early on in life that has these kinds of lasting brain effects. I wanted to ask Jo-Anne Bacharowski a question, but really the whole panel as well: when do you decide that something is probably not functional, but rather an artifact of a system that is functional? For instance, nervousness in a void may not have any function at all but may be there because of the biological foundation; the same thing may be true of the blush. What would have caused that if we evolved most of our human history in Africa?

BACHAROWSKI: I think that part of what happens is if you have a person who's anxious and is laughing, the impact on listeners can still be the same—unless the sound is so off that it's off-putting to the audience; unless it's too anxious, and the audience isn't going to go there. But if the person is laughing through their anxiety, it may disarm the audience and cause them to behave positively towards that person. We really have to work that out. One of the things that I'm really excited about doing is finding out whether there are, in fact, differences in the acoustics of laughter when people are being teased or being the teasers. I'm using one of the paradigms that Dacher Keltner's used. I am looking at anxious laughter and derisive laughter in response to humor and seeing whether those sounds really do differ, whether listeners really pick up on the differences in those sounds. It's an open question right now. We already know that we've got tons of variability in the sound itself, even when everybody's happy. So can we get even more variability than that when people are in these different affective states? The answer to your question is I really don't know yet, because I don't know whether we even have it in the sounds themselves.

EKMAN: To the first remark you made: more than 50 years ago Daniel G. Friedman did a dissertation with Paul Scott in which he took two breeds of dogs; every day he handled half of the dogs in each breed for about 30 minutes and then looked at the dogs later in their adult life. The breed effect was as great as the handling effect. Both exist. So there is plasticity, but there are constraints; it's an empirical question.

QUESTION: I have a question for Jo-Anne Bacharowski that is both practical and theoretical. In your talk you opposed as alternative explanations one based on meaning, information, and another based on affect. As a practical measure how would you ever be able to rule out one of those; aren't they both always going to be present in some sense? For example, even in something that is as meaning laden as language, I'm sure that our understanding of words is always going to be inextricably bound up with an emotional valence that we give those words. Even in something like fundamental frequency adjustment that seems to induce certain affective states in listeners, there will be listeners who will incorporate something that we would call "meaning." Do you really want to oppose those as either/or, or is the idea to carve out which is playing a primary and which a secondary role?

BACHAROWSKI: There's an amazing amount of speculation about why we laugh. We just don't have enough data to answer the question that you're asking. Right now I actually do want to pit those as contrasting views, but I know it's unlikely that the data will come out as cleanly. The point I want to stress is that there's inherent information that we can accrue upon seeing something and upon hearing something; but the laughs that we produce are not a code. Instead, it's the sound properties themselves that are doing something to the listeners ear. We have a general, evolved sense to respond positively to laughter, and we have a general sense that laughter's associated with a positive state; so it's easy to make that inference. I want to stress for the time being that meaning is not in the sounds themselves but comes from hearing the sounds produced by a particular person in a particular overarching context. So even though the sound produced might be the same, I'm going to have a different interpretation of a female tittering with a same-aged female friend than of that same female in conversation with the dean of her college. I'd come away with different inferences about her state despite the same sound. The point is that until we have more information, I want to keep sound and meaning separate; but it's probably not going to be as clean-cut as that.

LEVENSON: One of the distinctions that Darwin makes, and that many of the speakers have followed him in making, is that between an internal state and its external expression. But it seems to me that much of what Darwin actually says, and certainly much of what's been said in this conference, points to something very different—the intimacy between, for example, emotion and facial expression, emotion and vocalization. I think that autonomic activity also isn't so clearly internal either, but rather is a function of action, readiness, and facial expression, among other things. My concern is that by continuing to use this kind of internal or external language, we may be belying the very sophisticated analysis, complex correlations, and causal relationships that come from all this interest in analysis.

KELTNER: I would agree with that assessment if I understand you correctly: you're calling into question the distinction between the internal and external sides of expression. I really see them as working in parallel. I think one of the really nice statements on that idea is that of Robert Frank, an economist, who wrote *Passions within Reason*, in which he argued that a lot of emotions such as love, gratitude, compassion, and the like, are really social commitments. Paul Ekman has written about this as well—that in a way we work backwards from external display; knowing that a person feels a particular emotion such as love or sympathy tells us about a social commitment. So I see the two working together.

QUESTION: I've been so excited by this whole presentation of this session because everybody is coordinated into one unit, but what has fascinated me is the absence of the body below the neck [laughter]. I was fascinated by hearing the words, by seeing the faces, but I did not see the talking by the fingers, by the hands, by the movement, poise, and pattern of the people that were moving, sitting, or shifting. It's very difficult to have a sense of humor if you've got your hands fixed behind you by the police [laughter]. It's difficult to have a sense of humor if you hold your hands tight behind your back because automatically your voice gets harder, and it's difficult to laugh. I want to ask if there is any further matter going on with the body as a gestalt when you are communicating with your voice and your face.

EKMAN: During my first 10 or 15 years as a researcher, until I met Sylvan Tompkins, I worked just on body movement; almost all of my early publications are on it. Nobody was interested, I must say. The pioneering work was done here in New York by David Efron, an Argentinean anthropologist, a student of France Boaz, who worked on gestures. Efron distinguished what he called *emblems* or *symbolic gestures*—movements like this (shows an A-OK gesture). As Darwin pointed out, these are social conventions. They are socially learned and culture specific. We mapped them in five cultures, then stopped because nobody would publish our findings. One could write a dictionary of emblems. They are the only body language. We have also found, rather remarkably, that if you know the emblems of the group you're dealing with, there are emblematic slips just as there are verbal slips, slips of the tongue. One of the things we teach people in police work is to be very attentive to emblems and pay attention to when they occur.

Then there are speech illustrator movements. Efron distinguished eight different ways you can do this. He pointed out, for example, that Lithuanian Jews use what he called *idiographic illustrators*, which, in his words, "beat the mental locomotion." They are like conducting a symphony. Turn off the sound, and you have no idea what they're saying. Sicilians draw pictures and trace out actions with their hands. Turn off the sound, and you can still get the content. But those differences between Sicilians and Lithuanian Jews, Efron showed, will generally disappear within a generation.

There are also bodily movements that we called *self-manipulative movements*. These cause others to mistakenly believe you are lying. We warn people not to be misled by the fact that a person may be playing with his hands or a prop, or scratching his face. This has nothing to do with lying or truthfulness; it's a different system.

There are other approaches that aren't looking in this formalistic way, but are looking at the flow, or quality, of movement. These are people who primarily come out of dance. It doesn't appear that these body movements are as direct a signal source for emotion, in humans at least, as the face and voice. That's why we couldn't have found someone able to give a scientific talk on the body movements of emotion.

QUESTION: Related to the person who just raised a question in connection with the area of the human being below the neck, some of Selma Freiburg's research was on infants who were born blind; those children, as is well known, lose the typical morphology of the social smile, and that loss results in very clear grief reactions on the part of the parent. It certainly causes disruption in social communication of the parent. Selma Freiburg discovered that the blind baby very often smiled with his hands. There was a manifestation of social communication, particularly evident in the finger patterning. When the parents had their attention drawn to their blind infant's finger patterning, they felt ebullient the way we do when we see the social smile. So the question is very germane; we can smile with parts of our body other than our face.

QUESTION: I would like to submit that I think we have a great deal of emotional training in our society, and it's called "the entertainment industry." We spend more money on entertainment than we do on food, and I think the purpose of it is to give people practice at emoting. That's mostly what they're doing in the movie theaters. My question to you is, why do you think we like to go to movies and have bad emotions? I mean we go to tragedies, we watch "The God Father," and Al Pacino wants his brother killed. We come out of it, and we say, "That was a great movie." Do you know what is it that draws us toward our bad emotions in a controlled setting? Why do we want to have bad emotions? Why don't we only go to things that are uplifting, and comic?

EKMAN: Aristotle wrote about experiencing pity and fear in theatrical experiences. There's a wonderful Charles Addams drawing depicting an audience in a theatre, a legitimate theater or a movie theater; everyone in the audience is crying except for one ghoulish fellow who's grinning. Clearly we seek emotional experiences in the theater, enjoyable emotions and emotions that traditionally are considered to be unenjoyable or negative. People seek to experience these emotions, and not just in theaters. I don't think there are any bad or negative emotions. There are bad emotional experiences, but emotions are not like our appendices, which we'd be better off without. They are the primary motives; they give the juice and energy to life. But there are ways of enacting emotions that can be harmful to you or others. In movies, you get a chance to vicariously experience emotions. I believe there is evidence that we learn emotional skills and ways of dealing with conflict from movies, but for most movies you wouldn't want your kids to learn those particular skills. "The Cosby Show," on the other hand, had lots of proactive skill training, but that's very different from "The Sopranos." "The Sopranos" is better than most TV shows and movies because, atypically in the mass media, it shows the negative consequences of violence. I think we go to the theater or watch TV or movies to exercise our emotions in a safe way and unwittingly learn skills.

QUESTION: My question has to do with something that Darwin of course observed—the closeness of laughter to tears. We laugh to tears. Darwin talked about the same physiological mechanics being used for laughing and crying. What do you have to say about that? There's also a second part to my question, for Frans de Waals, which is about the distress signals from primate babies, as compared to human babies. Primate babies live so close to their mothers—on their bodies—I know not all the time, but much more than in the so-called advanced human cultures. We don't carry our babies around in Western European culture. I wonder if the incidence of distress signals is lower or if they cry. From my observation of nature films, it appears that they make distress sounds; but they don't weep.

DE WAAL: I think the overlap between laughter and crying is fascinating. I don't think we know much more than Darwin about what he was speculating about. What we've learned is that the same brain system subserves the production of both of those sounds. There are particular parts of the brain stem that course through the midpart of the brain's limbic system and newer cortex and that drive both crying and laughter. These are the same parts of the brain that are largely involved in nonhuman primate vocal production. Such is the degree of similarity between the brains of human and nonhuman primates that I think this speaks to the phylogenic roots of the laughing and crying vocalizations. I don't have a good way of explaining why sometimes we cry when we're laughing and vice versa. This is not a scientific term, but for me it's like emotional cross-talk; you've got highly similar systems involved, and the laugher/cryer is so aroused or engaged at that moment that they actually have trouble modulating between the two systems. That's just a hypothesis; I don't know that anyone has a real answer to that.

DAVIDSON: Just to make one comment: the brain lesion data on laughing and crying subsequent to brain damage does strongly suggest that there are different brain systems, not the same, for laughing and crying; we can talk about that later.

DE WAAL: As far as distress signals of infants and juveniles are concerned, there's a very interesting book on cultural differences in how close babies are to their moms called *Our Babies, Ourselves*, by Meredith Small. In chimpanzees, of course, and in all the great apes the baby is nursed for four years, sometimes five years, so it's very close to the mom, always on the mom. You might think that distress signals would be less common or less important, but actually they are very important. They're often very small when the babies are small; they're not yelling like crazy because there's no need for that, the mother is so close to them. They make little sounds of discomfort when they're not sitting right or want a drink or something like that. Once there was a deaf female in a zoo whose babies always died because she did not respond to these very small but important sounds; at some point we began to take her babies away. If you sit on a baby, it makes a sound and you correct the behavior. She was not able to do that. These little sounds of discomfort are extremely important for the interaction between mother and offspring. At later ages, when the weaning starts, you wouldn't believe how loud they can call, these juveniles; temper tantrums of juvenile apes are incredible. They go on for 10 minutes, they scream and yell and roll around on the floor until their mom pays attention; as soon as she pays attention, they snap out of it. That abrupt turning off of emotions makes you think it's all manipulation; there's interesting literature on animal offspring manipulating adults. So distress sounds in nonhuman primates are very important, but we notice them less because the infants are usually on the mother and have no need to cry out loudly.

QUESTION: I have two questions; the first is for Dr. Bachorowski. You said that it's very difficult, but you use only about 20% of the data.

BACHAROWSKI: I think people have pushed really hard for evidence of acoustic cue differentiation. I think that's grown out of a history in the facial expression literature. It's easier to find differentiation on the face than it is in the voice, so you want to give it your best shot and go ahead and get the samples that are most likely to show it to you. I think it's wrongheaded at this point to keep on pushing that strategy; we haven't found overwhelming evidence for it, and maybe that's telling us that we need to adopt a different strategy.

QUESTION: The other question is for the panel. It was predicated by something in Richie Davidson's research. Has anyone looked at imaging while using a social contagion paradigm or an affect-induction paradigm to see what does go on in the brain in terms of what regions are activated or what circuits are activated. We're just starting to look at that with laughter, but there's a real growing literature about looking at emotional faces that I think others can speak more to.

DAVIDSON: There's a huge literature. We'll talk about that later.

QUESTION: I come to this meeting from a little different perspective from many of you. I'm a psychotherapist, and I'm doing long-term psychotherapy and individual and group sessions. In the middle phase of therapy, one of the major indicators that change is really taking place and being integrated is a change in the characteristic facial expression. I wonder if you would comment on that from your end.

DAVIDSON: Would you elaborate on that a bit? What do you see that tells you that change is taking place?

QUESTION: Well, I think probably the most noticeable thing is with people whose facial expressions are very tight and pulled in; as the inner conflicts begin to be resolved, their face becomes more open and therefore more inviting; then they get different kinds of reactions from other people. There are others whose expressions are very loose, often inappropriately so; they tighten up and become more appropriate, which then brings about different kinds of reactions in others.

EKMAN: I think there would be a benefit to looking in a complex fashion at the overall muscle tonus of the face, not during facial movement, but the face in repose—for example, when listening. You might find relationships to personality and long-term states. But to the best of my knowledge no one's done it; it's unexplored at this time.

QUESTION: What about changes during psychotherapy?

EKMAN: There's a lot of research on how expression, not muscle tonus, changes. Some of it's in a book I edited called *What the Face Reveals*. Before, I was talking about specifically measuring subvisible electrical muscle tonus as an index of personality or changes in overall mood. I don't know of such work over the course of psychotherapy.

QUESTION: I'm interested in the distinction between voluntary and involuntary facial muscular movement and appreciate its use in determining whether a particular facial expression may be deceptive. But I noticed that you characterized remembering a happy moment as in a certain sense cheating, and that makes me reflect a little bit. It seems that all of us are often able to change our mood by invoking, whether through a memory or some other means, a different mood. Clearly that's an intentional change in emotional state and may actually affect some of those muscular movements. So aren't we just stating that some muscles may have functions such as leg muscles that are engaged in locomotion and aren't necessarily related specifically to emotions, and other muscular movements are more tightly connected to the internal emotional system?

EKMAN: I was actually trying to make a joke when I said that was cheating. If you retrieve a memory, you're voluntarily choosing to use an involuntary path: if I decide I'm going to see a Rocky movie, I'm using a particular form of entertainment to set off an involuntary set of emotions.. But the muscles of the face are not dedicated just to emotion. They're used in a variety of ways. Even within the same regions of the face, some of the muscles are for most people very difficult to deliberately activate, and some of them everybody can deliberately activate; so there is this difference. Some movements most people can't deliberately make, yet those movements occur with emotions spontaneously generated either because of someone's action or a memory or imagination or something read in the newspaper. There are many different ways of accessing involuntary emotional changes.

QUESTION: Do traits, personality traits, affective style, or even psychiatric disease get written in the face by the sheer exercise of certain muscles and wrinkling of the face in a certain way?

KELTNER: If you have taken a static photograph of somebody, would you see that person's personality? I think you would. All the research that I presented today attests to that possibility—how warm and competent you are is reflected in the smile.

EKMAN: I'm dubious about that. I don't think that we are all Dorian Gray's, that every emotional experience and how we react to it and our style over life etches permanent changes into our face that are more and more apparent as we age. I'm a little more than agnostic about that.

Emotional Expression in Speech and Music

Evidence of Cross-Modal Similarities

PATRIK N. JUSLIN AND PETRI LAUKKA

Department of Psychology, Uppsala University, SE-751 42 Uppsala, Sweden

KEYWORDS: emotion; expression; speech; music performance; nonverbal communication

Questions about music and emotions have occupied humans since antiquity.[1] However, scientific progress in the area has been slowed by a reluctance to adopt evolutionary approaches. Music is typically regarded as a cultural artifact. Yet, music performance is, like other forms of human behavior, constrained by evolved mechanisms. What would an evolutionary approach to music entail? In Darwin's pioneering work[2] we find some preliminaries for such an approach. Darwin recognized that music has the power to induce strong emotions (p. 216), as is evident from such behaviors as crying. He also noted that music often produces "a peculiar effect...the thrill or slight shiver which runs down the backbone and limbs of many persons when they are powerfully affected by music." This phenomenon has been the focus of much interest in modern research.[3] The most original aspect of Darwin's thinking was the idea that music originally served to attract sexual partners, a notion that has recently been revived.[4] However, this sexual selection theory of the origins of music is controversial, because of weak empirical support.

More fruitful, perhaps, are Darwin's suggestions regarding the relationship between speech and music. Darwin hypothesized that our human ancestors "uttered musical tones before they had acquired the power of articulate speech" (p. 92). Moreover, he noted that "when the voice is used under any strong emotion, it tends to assume...a musical character" (ibid). Like Herbert Spencer,[5] Darwin was inclined to explain the origins of vocal expression (i.e.,

Address for correspondence: Patrik N. Juslin, Department of Psychology, Uppsala University, Box 1225, SE-751 42 Uppsala, Sweden.

Patrik.Juslin@psyk.uu.se

Ann. N.Y. Acad. Sci. 1000: 279–282 (2003). © 2003 New York Academy of Sciences.

doi: 10.1196/annals.1280.025

the nonverbal aspects of speech) in terms of physiological principles: emotions influence physiological processes, which, in turn, influence the acoustic characteristics of speech and singing (though Darwin was slightly reluctant to apply the idea to music). Following Darwin, many theorists have speculated about a close relationship between vocal expression of emotions and musical expression of emotions,[6] but evidence bearing on this relationship has been lacking. The purpose of the present study is to review studies in both domains in order to examine whether the two communication channels really express emotions in similar ways.[7]

We adopted an evolutionary perspective in this review, according to which musicians are able to communicate specific emotions to listeners by using a nonverbal code that derives from vocal expression of emotions. We hypothesized that vocal expression is an evolved mechanism[8] based upon innate and universal affect programs[9] that develop early and are fine-tuned by prenatal experiences. On the basis of this approach, we predicted that:

(a) communication of emotions is cross-culturally accurate in vocal expression and music performance,

(b) the ability to decode basic emotions develops early in ontogeny, and

(c) similar patterns of emotion-specific acoustic cues are used to communicate emotions in both communication channels.

We used two criteria for inclusion of studies in the review. First, we included only studies of nonverbal aspects of speech or specific performances of pieces of music. Second, we included only studies that investigated the communication of discrete emotions. The studies included were gathered using the internet-based scientific databases PsychINFO, Medline, LLBA, Ingenta, and RILM Abstracts of Music Literature. All together, 104 studies of vocal expression and 41 studies of music performance were located in the literature search. The results were reviewed in terms of five general categories of emotion (i.e., anger, fear, happiness, sadness, and tenderness), because these were the only five emotions for which there was enough evidence in both vocal expression and music performance.

The main findings can be summarized as follows. First, a meta-analysis of communication accuracy indicated that communication of emotions may reach an accuracy well above chance in both vocal and musical expression (mean $P_c = 0.70$ in a forced-choice task with five emotions), at least for basic emotions. Such high accuracy has been found even in studies that did not preselect effective stimuli.[10] Second, vocal expression of emotions is cross-culturally accurate, although the accuracy is somewhat lower than for within-cultural vocal expression (we lack cross-cultural data for music). Third, the ability to decode emotion from vocal and musical expression develops in early childhood (at the latest). Fourth, music performance involves mainly the same emotion-specific patterns of acoustic cues as does vocal expression. The cue-patterns are consistent with Scherer's predictions, which presume a correspondence between emotion-specific physiological changes and voice production.[11] Finally, the review indicated some gaps in the literature that need to be filled by further research (e.g., with regard to the measurement of certain cues).

There is currently a debate about whether vocal expression of emotions involves discrete categories and emotion-specific patterns of acoustic cues, or only emotion dimensions such as arousal and valence.[12] Earlier reviews, featuring a smaller selection of studies, have left this question open. This is the most extensive review of vocal expression of emotions to date, and it provides strong evidence of emotion-specific patterns of acoustic cues in vocal expression—not only for those studies that use emotion portrayals. This, along with the fact that communication of basic emotions is cross-culturally accurate, strongly supports a discrete emotions approach to vocal expression. Failure to obtain emotion-specific patterns of acoustic cues in certain previous studies can largely be explained in terms of methodological problems.[7,10]

The findings presented here are consistent with the evolutionary perspective on emotional expression, and support Darwin's idea of an intimate relationship between speech and music. In effect, the present results could help to explain why music is perceived as expressive of emotion. Music is expressive in part because it presents emotion-specific patterns of acoustic cues that are similar to those in vocal expression. We submit that continued cross-modal research will provide further insights about the expressive aspects of vocal expression and music performance, insights that would be difficult to obtain from studying the two domains in separation.

ACKNOWLEDGMENTS

This is partly a summary of an previous article (see ref. 7). The research was supported by The Bank of Sweden Tercentenary Foundation through a grant to Patrik Juslin.

REFERENCES

1. JUSLIN, P.N. & J.A. SLOBODA, Eds. 2001. Music and Emotion: Theory and Research. Oxford University Press. New York.
2. DARWIN, C. 1998. The Expression of the Emotions in Man and Animals, 3rd edit. Harper-Collins. London. (US edit.: Oxford University Press. New York.)
3. GOLDSTEIN, A. 1980. Thrills in response to music and other stimuli. Physiol. Psychol. **8:** 126–129.
4. MILLER, G. 2000. Evolution of human music through sexual selection. *In* The Origins of Music. N. Wallin, B. Merker & S. Brown, Eds.: 329–360. MIT Press. Cambridge, MA.

 5. SPENCER, H. 1857. The origin and function of music. Fraser's Magazine **56:** 396–408.
 6. SCHERER, K.R. 1995. Expression of emotion in voice and music. J. Voice **9:** 235–248.
 7. JUSLIN, P.N. & P. LAUKKA. 2003. Communication of emotions in vocal expression and music performance: different channels, same code? Psychol. Bull. **129:** 770–814.
 8. PLOOG, D. 1992. The evolution of vocal communication. *In* Nonverbal Vocal Communication: Comparative and Developmental Approaches. H. Papoušek, U. Jürgens & M. Papoušek, Eds.: 6–30. Cambridge University Press. Cambridge.
 9. EKMAN, P. 1992. An argument for basic emotions. Cogn. Emotion **6:** 169–200.
10. JUSLIN, P.N. & P. LAUKKA. 2001. Impact of intended emotion intensity on decoding accuracy and cue utilization in vocal expression of emotion. Emotion **1:** 381–412.
11. SCHERER, K.R. 1986. Vocal affect expression: a review and a model for future research. Psychol. Bull. **99:** 143–165.
12. BACHOROWSKI, J.-A. 1999. Vocal expression and perception of emotion. Curr. Directions Psychol. Sci. **8:** 53–57.

Categorical Perception of Emotion in Vocal Expression

PETRI LAUKKA

Department of Psychology, Uppsala University, SE-751 42 Uppsala, Sweden

KEYWORDS: emotion; vocal expression; categorical perception; speech synthesis

Categorical perception (CP) occurs when continuous sensory stimulation is sorted out by the brain into discrete categories. One effect of this is that equal-sized physical differences between stimuli are perceived as smaller or larger depending on whether the stimuli are perceived as belonging to the same category or to different categories.[1] Several studies have investigated CP of facial emotion expressions by creating continua of interpolated (morphed) pictures of facial affect, from one expression to another, that differ by equal physical amounts.[2–5] Evidence of CP is generally assessed in two stages. First, subjects should identify the morphed expressions as belonging to two distinct sections separated by a category boundary even though the expression information is linearly manipulated. Second, it should be easier for subjects to discriminate between two stimuli that are perceived as expressing different emotions than between two stimuli that express the same emotion, even though the physical differences are identical.

Darwin discussed both vocal and facial expression of emotion in his classic treatise,[6] and though less empirical research has since focused on vocal expression, there has recently been increased activity in the field. Recent reviews show that listeners can accurately recognize vocal expressions of discrete emotions, and that emotion-specific patterns of acoustic cues are used to communicate emotions.[7–8] However, there is little knowledge about the perceptual representation of vocal expression of emotion. Currently a debate is going on about whether vocal expressions are perceived as varying continuously along underlying dimensions, or as belonging to qualitatively discrete emotion categories. The issue of CP of vocal expressions is of great

Address for correspondence: Petri Laukka, Department of Psychology, Uppsala University, Box 1225, SE-751 42 Uppsala, Sweden.

petri.laukka@psyk.uu.se

Ann. N.Y. Acad. Sci. 1000: 283–287 (2003). © 2003 New York Academy of Sciences.
doi: 10.1196/annals.1280.026

conceptual relevance, because evidence of CP would be hard to reconcile with a dimensional model, but would fit well within a discrete emotions framework.

In order to investigate CP of emotion in vocal expression, six continua (anger-fear, anger-sadness, fear-happiness, fear-sadness, happiness-anger, and happiness-sadness) of vocal expressions were created using concatenative speech synthesis. Each continuum consisted of a series of vocal expressions differing by constant physical amounts, from one emotional expression to another, using prototype expressions from a previous study.[9] Each syllable of the prototype expressions was acoustically analyzed, and then fundamental frequency, temporal cues, and sound level were manipulated by linear interpolation between the values measured from the respective prototype expression. The manipulations were done using Praat speech analysis software.[10] Five morphed and two prototype expressions were created for each continuum (proportions 100:0, 90:10, 70:30, 50:50, 30:70, 10:90, and 0:100).

Thirty-four subjects first discriminated between pairs of expressions in a sequential discrimination (ABX) task, in which stimuli A, B, and X were presented sequentially and the subjects had to decide whether X was the same as A or B. The pairs to be compared consisted of all combinations for each emotion continuum that differed by 20%: for example, the 90% morph (90% emotion A and 10% emotion B) vs. the 70% morph (70% emotion A and 30% emotion B), the 70% morph vs. the 50% morph, the 50% morph vs. the 30% morph, and the 30% morph vs. the 10% morph. The order of presentation was randomized within and across emotion continua, and the subjects received four trials of each stimulus pair representing all possible orders of presentation (ABA, ABB, BAA, and BAB). The same subjects then identified the emotion of each expression in a forced-choice task. Each expression was presented three times, and the order of presentation was randomized within each emotion continuum. The alternatives that the subjects had to choose among were the same as the two end-emotions of the continuum to which respective expression belonged.

Results from the identification task show that each emotion continuum was perceived as two distinct sections separated by a category boundary (FIG. 1). The results from the discrimination task were assessed using two different approaches. First, using a subject-by-subject method,[3] two measures of discrimination performance were calculated for each subject: (a) a "peak" value—the mean discrimination accuracy for the expression pair that crosses the identification category boundary (i.e., contains the 50% identification point), and (b) a "nonpeak" value—the mean discrimination accuracy for the remaining pairs (FIG. 2). A repeated-measures analysis of variance, with discrimination performance (two levels: peak and nonpeak) and continua (6 levels) as within-subject factors, was conducted on the discrimination performance values. There were significant main effects of discrimination performance [$F(1, 33) = 24.34$, $P < 0.0001$] and continua [$F(5, 165) = 10.49$,

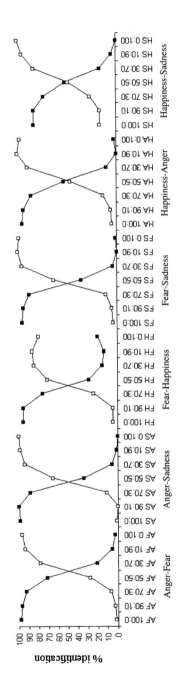

FIGURE 1. Results from the forced-choice identification task in terms of percent identification for the different emotion continua.

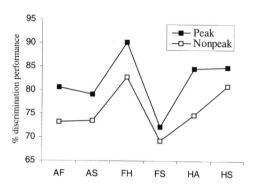

FIGURE 2. Results from the ABX discrimination task in terms of percent correct peak and nonpeak discrimination for the different emotion continua.

$P < 0.0001$], but the interaction was not significant [$F(5, 165) = 0.55$, n.s.]. Across all continua, peak pairs were easier to discriminate (mean accuracy = 0.82, SD = 0.12) than nonpeak pairs (mean accuracy = 0.76, SD = 0.12). Also, discrimination of peak pairs was more accurate than discrimination of nonpeak pairs for all continua (FIG. 2). *Post hoc* multiple comparisons (Fisher's *LSD*) showed significant differences between peak and nonpeak for the anger-fear, fear-happiness, and happiness-anger continua (*P*'s < 0.05), but not for the other continua.

Second, subjects' discrimination performance was predicted from their identification rates, and these predictions were compared with the observed discrimination results.[11] The fit between predicted and observed performance was assessed by correlating predicted and observed scores, and converting this to a *t*-value.[5] This showed a significant correlation of predicted and observed performance ($r = 0.42$, $t = 2.17$, *df* 22, $P < 0.05$). These results suggest that vocal expressions of emotions are recognized by their fit to discrete categories, at least for some emotion continua, and are consistent with results from studies of facial expression of emotion. It can be argued that CP of vocal emotion expressions is an ability that has evolved in order to facilitate the rapid classification of states in others that can motivate behavior.[7] This ability clearly has adaptive significance and thus would be supported by evolutionary mechanisms.

REFERENCES

1. HARNAD, S., Ed. 1987. Categorical Perception. The Groundwork of Cognition. Cambridge University Press. New York.

2. ETCOFF, N.L. & J.J. MAGEE. 1992. Categorical perception of facial expressions. Cognition **44:** 227–240.

3. DE GELDER, B., J-P. TEUNISSE & P.J. BENSON. 1997. Categorical perception of facial expressions: categories and their internal structure. Cogn. Emotion **11:** 1–23.

4. CALDER, A.J. *et al.* 1996. Categorical perception of morphed facial expressions. Vis. Cogn. **3:** 81–117.

5. YOUNG, A.W. *et al.* 1997. Facial expression megamix: tests of dimensional and category accounts of emotion recognition. Cognition **63:** 271–313.

6. DARWIN, C. 1872. The expression of the emotions in man and animals. John Murray. London.

7. JUSLIN, P.N. & P. LAUKKA. 2003. Communication of emotions in vocal expression and music performance: different channels, same code? Psychol. Bull. **129:** 770–814.

8. JOHNSTONE, T. & K.R. SCHERER. 2000. Vocal communication of emotion. *In* Handbook of Emotions. M. Lewis & J.M. Haviland-Jones, Eds.: 220–235. Guilford Press. New York.

9. JUSLIN, P.N. & P. LAUKKA. 2001. Impact of intended emotion intensity on cue utilization and decoding accuracy in vocal expression of emotion. Emotion **1:** 381–412.

10. BOERSMA, P. & D. WEENINK. 2001. Praat 4.0.4 [computer software]. Institute of Phonetic Sciences, University of Amsterdam. Amsterdam.

11. LIBERMAN, A.M. *et al.* 1957. The discrimination of speech sounds within and across phoneme boundaries. J. Exp. Psychol. **54:** 358–368.

Acoustic Analyses Support Subjective Judgments of Vocal Emotion

MARILEE MONNOT,[a,b] DIANA ORBELO,[c] LUCIANA RICCARDO,[a] SEEMA SIKKA,[d] AND ELLIOTT ROSS[a,b]

[a]Department of Neurology, [c]Department of Communication Sciences, [d]College of Medicine, University of Oklahoma Health Sciences Center, Oklahoma City, Oklahoma 73104, USA

[b]Affective Communication Research Laboratory at Veterans Affairs Medical Center, Oklahoma City, Oklahoma 73104, USA

ABSTRACT: Subjective human judgments of emotion in speech have been considered to be less reliable than acoustic analyses in scientific studies, but acoustic analyses have had limited ability to detect subtle vocal nuances that give useful social information about human intent and meaning to discourse partners. Two *post hoc* analyses were undertaken to determine if results from acoustic analyses of vocalizations were related to subjective judgments of vocal affect (affective prosody). Acoustic analyses of fundamental frequency (F_0) and subjective judgments of emotional content of vocal productions from two studies underwent statistical analyses: Study 1—vocal repetition of sentences using 6 basic emotions in 24 detoxified alcoholics and 15 controls; study 2—quality/quantity of "motherese" speech directed to 52 infants in Cambridge, England. Ratings of emotion indicators for both studies were done by female researchers of different ages and cultural/language backgrounds. In both studies, acoustic analyses of F_0 elements in utterances accounted for approximately 50% of the effect when modeling subjective emotion accuracy and emotion intensity ratings, using linear regression analyses. Acoustic analyses of F_0 are positively associated with subjective judgments of emotion indicators, and speakers who cannot vary F_0 are unable to convey emotion accurately to communication partners. Yet acoustic analyses are limited in comparison to the exquisite complexity of the human auditory and cognitive systems. Subjective judgments of emotional meaning in speech can be a reliable variable in scientific inquiry and can be used for more complex, subtle studies of speech communication and intentionality than acoustic analyses.

KEYWORDS: acoustic analyses; affective prosody; subjective judgment; vocal emotion

Address for correspondence: Marilee Monnot, Department of Neurology, University of Oklahoma Health Sciences Center, Oklahoma City, OK 73104. Voice: 405-271-4113; fax: 405-271-5723.

marilee-monnot@ouhsc.edu

Ann. N.Y. Acad. Sci. 1000: 288–292 (2003). © 2003 New York Academy of Sciences.
doi: 10.1196/annals.1280.027

BACKGROUND AND METHODS

Social perceptions and judgments of emotion are ubiquitous and are deemed important to human survival,[1] but "subjective" judgments of emotion were considered to be less reliable in scientific studies than "objective" acoustic analyses during the 20th century. This bias resulted in work showing that vocal manipulation of fundamental frequency (F_0), in nontone languages such as English, is the most salient acoustic element of affect.[2–5] In addition, acoustic analyses have been used for at least three decades in research regarding emotion in the voice, especially in support of attempts to produce synthesized speech with appropriate emotion.[6,7] However, acoustic studies that have attempted to definitively distinguish one emotion from another have had limited success and only partial success in detecting subtle vocal nuances that give useful information about human intent and meaning to discourse partners.[8–11] Therefore, it appears that human judgments of vocal affect identity, quality, and/or intensity are superior to acoustic analyses. To test this hypothesis, *post hoc* analyses of two studies were undertaken to determine how acoustic analyses of vocal productions were related to subjective judgments of vocal affect (affective prosody). Judgments of emotion identity accuracy and emotion intensity of human utterances were rated by a variety of female researchers of different ages (> 50 years and < 35 years) and diverse cultural/language backgrounds (American, English, Asian Indian, and South American). Acoustic analyses were completed using a PM Pitch Analyzer (Voice Identification, Inc.), interfaced with a computer programmed to extract F_0 in hertz (Hz) from each utterance. The extracted information was displayed as traces on a cathode ray tube. The F_0 was accessed every 10 milliseconds (ms) by the computer through a parallel interface. After removal of stray data points resulting from ambient noise and other sampling errors, the digitized F_0 and intensity curves for each utterance were analyzed in terms of four acoustic parameters that were designed previously to quantify global qualities of affective prosody (mean, variability, slope, and attack rate of fundamental frequency). Before the parameters were calculated, the F_0 data were transformed into a coefficient of variation percentage.[2] All statistical studies were conducted using JMP Version 4 Statistical Discovery software.[12]

Study 1 assessed the ability of 24 detoxified alcoholics and 15 control subjects from a prior study[13–15] to accurately repeat 36 exemplars of a sentence from the Aprosodia Battery.[16] Each sentence used one of six emotional tones (happy, sad, angry, bored, surprised, neutral) and two locations of stress (beginning and end of sentence). Raters had to determine which of the six emotions the alcoholic was trying to imitate. The total number of correct responses for the four raters was compared to acoustic analyses of F_0 from the alcoholic's vocal repetitions. Study 2 used data from a prior study of quality/quantity of motherese or infant-directed (ID) speech from 52 mothers to their infants in Cambridge, England.[17] Recordings from each mother were approximately one hour in length, with dozens of utterances. Raters categorized motherese into four levels of affective intensity (Prosody Mean) based on comparison to adult-directed (AD) speech, which has no motherese prosodic variations: Low ID, Average ID, and Exaggerated ID. They also placed each mother's utterance into one of 12 categories of pragmatic statements signaling her communication intent. For instance, Child-Centered% category reflects the infant's activities and is the category used most often when addressing infants, while Declarative% is the category adults use most often when addressing each other. Prosody Mean and Child-Centered% are inextricably intertwined and correlated in each speech act [$r = 0.42$, $P < 0.0001$], but can be rated separately by experienced researchers. *Post hoc* acoustic analyses were conducted of mothers' recorded speech in the same manner as Study 1, using 10 seconds of each of the four intensity levels and the corresponding semantic categories, per mother.

RESULTS AND DISCUSSION

In both studies, acoustic analyses of F_0 elements in subject utterances were positively associated with subjective emotion identity and intensity ratings, using linear regression analyses. In Study 1, mean F_0 of the detoxified alcoholics' utterances and the accuracy of subjective ratings of emotion category in these utterances showed a significant association [$Fratio = 24.58$, $P < 0.0001$, R^2Adjusted $= 0.52$]. Inter-rater reliability of subjective judgments was positively correlated ($r = 0.83$, $P < 0.003$) for four raters. The regression analysis showed that as the mean F_0 decreased, raters' accuracy declined. This result indicates how important F_0 manipulation is in vocal affect communication. In Study 2, subjective ratings from the original study of the two components of infant-directed speech, Prosody Mean and Child-Centered%, were compared to *post hoc* acoustic analyses of mothers' utterances. Standard Least Squares multiple regression analyses showed that affect intensity (Prosody Mean) was predicted by Child-Centered%, F_0attack, F_0variability, and F_0slope of mothers' speech [$R^2 = 0.53$, $P < 0.017$]. Also, Child-Centered% was predicted by Prosody Mean and mean F_0 of mothers' speech [$R^2 = 0.54$, $P < 0.001$]. Inter-rater reliability of subjective judgments was positively correlated for two raters; Child-Centered% was $r = 0.92$, $P < 0.0001$, and Prosody Mean was $r = 0.71$, $P < 0.02$.

These results indicate that different elements of F_0 are involved in the variation or manipulation of affective prosody and emotion communication during speech. In fact, speech without F_0, such as whispering, is almost devoid of cues that enable the listener to detect emotion. However, these statistical analyses also reveal that acoustic analyses of F_0 elements account for only half of the effect in attempts to model emotion identity accuracy and emotion intensity in speech, whereas inter-rater reliability measures show considerable agreement on judgment of emotion identity and intensity. Therefore, subjective judgments of emotional meanings in vocalizations can be a reliable variable in scientific inquiry. Carefully controlled studies using human judgment can be employed for more complex, subtle assessments of emotion identification, pragmatic speech intentionality, and interpersonal communication than can acoustic analyses, which have more limited uses.

ACKNOWLEDGMENT

The authors wish to thank Helen Pleasant of Cambridge University for her assistance with sentence category ratings for interrater reliability studies and for the large amount of time she spent on this project.

REFERENCES

1. SCHERER, K.R. 1995. Expression of emotion in voice and music. J. Voice **9**(3): 235–248.
2. ROSS, E.D., J.A. EDMONDSON & G.B. SEIBERT. 1986. The effect of affect on various acoustic measures of prosody in tone and non-tone languages: a comparison based on computer analysis of voice. J. Phonetics **14:** 283–302.
3. ROSS, E.D. *et al.* 1987. Acoustic analysis of affective prosody during right-sided Wada test: a within-subjects verification of the right hemisphere's role in language. Brain Lang. **33:** 128–145.
4. ROSS, E.D. *et al.* 1992. Affective exploitation of tone in Taiwanese: an acoustical study of "tone latitude." J. Phonetics **20:** 441–456.
5. SCHERER, K.R. & J.S. OSHINSKY. 1977. Cue utilization in emotion attributes from auditory stimuli. Motiv. Emotion **1:** 331–346.
6. SCHERER, K.R. 1979. Acoustic concomitants of emotional dimensions: judging affect from synthesized tone sequences. *In* Non-verbal Communication, 2nd edit. S. Weitz, Ed.: 249–253. Oxford University Press. New York.
7. MURRAY, I.R. & J.L. ARNOTT. 1993. Toward the simulation of emotion in synthetic speech: a review of the literature on human vocal emotion. J. Acoust. Soc. Am. **93**(2): 1097–1108.
8. BANSE, R. & K.R. SCHERER. 1996. Acoustic profiles in vocal emotion expression. J. Pers. Soc. Psychol. **70**(3): 614–636.
9. WHITESIDE, S.P. 1999. Note on voice and perturbation measures in simulated vocal emotions. Percept. Mot. Skills **88**(3 Pt. 2): 1219–1222.
10. WHITESIDE, S.P. 1999. Acoustic characteristics of vocal emotions simulated by actors. Percept. Mot. Skills. **89**(3 Pt. 2): 1195–1208.
11. SOBIN, C. & M. ALPERT. 1999. Emotion in speech: the acoustic attributes of fear, anger, sadness, and joy. J. Psycholinguist. Res. **28**(4): 347–365.
12. SAS INSTITUTE. 2000. JMP Statistical Discovery Software. SAS Institute, Inc. Cary, NC.

13. MONNOT, M. *et al.* 2001. Abnormal emotional perception in alcoholics: deficits in comprehension of affective prosody. Alcohol. Clin. Exp. Res. **25**(3): 362–369.
14. MONNOT, M., D. ORBELO & E.D. ROSS. 2001. Affective prosodic production in alcoholics. Presented at Social Cognitive Neuroscience Symposium. University of California, Los Angeles.
15. MONNOT, M. *et al.* 2002. Neurological basis of deficits in affective prosody comprehension among alcoholics and fetal alcohol exposed adults. J. Neuropsychol. Clin. Neurosci. **14**(3): 321–328.
16. ROSS, E.D., R.D. THOMPSON & J. YENKOSKY. 1997. Lateralization of affective prosody in brain and the callosal integration of hemispheric language functions. Brain Lang. **56**: 27–54.
17. MONNOT, M. 1999. Function of infant-directed speech. Hum. Nat. Interdisc. Biosoc. Perspect. **10**(4): 415–443.

Pleasure, the Common Currency of Emotions

J. MARTIN RAMIREZ[a] AND MICHEL CABANAC[b]

[a]*Department of Psychobiology and Institute for Biofunctional Studies, Universidad Complutense, Madrid, Spain*

[b]*Département de Physiologie, Université Laval, Québec, Canada*

KEYWORDS: emotion; cognition; pleasure; anger; experience; expression

The old controversy on whether emotion is independent of cognition[1,2] or dependent on it[3,4] has now advanced considerably. The solution fundamentally depends on how one defines both terms, emotion and cognition. Most authors would agree that emotion could be elicited in the absence of conscious cognition mediation. But, if "cognitive" is taken in a broad sense including basic sensory information processing, virtually all agree that some cognitive processing is required for most, if not all, emotions.[5] And even if emotion—at least in its broadest meaning, including feelings, mood, and temperament—can be elicited with minimal cognitive prerequisites, via noncognitive routes,[6] the cognitive appraisal is putatively necessary for its elicitation.[7]

Physiologically, there is a two-way interaction between emotion and cognition made possible by the bidirectional connections existent between the main anatomical structures subserving both of them, the amygdala and the neocortex,[8] and by the distribution of neuropeptides in their circuits.[9]

As a follow-up to a definition of sensation as a four-dimensional experience (quality, intensity, hedonicity, and duration),[10] and accepting that sensation is the origin of all consciousness, that model should apply to all forms of mental experience,[11] including emotion, which is just a special case of consciousness: if emotion takes place in consciousness, it should also possess those four dimensions. Actually, Cabanac[12] proposes that *emotion is any mental experience with high intensity and high hedonic content*, expanding on a thesis that motivational states can be compared to each other by a common currency, which would be pleasure.

Address for correspondence: Dr. J. Martin Ramirez, P.O. Box 2, 28792 Miraflores (Madrid), Spain. Voice: 34 918 444 695; fax: 34 913 943 069.
mramirez@med.ucm.es

Ann. N.Y. Acad. Sci. 1000: 293–295 (2003). © 2003 New York Academy of Sciences.
doi: 10.1196/annals.1280.028

This conception, which facilitates the understanding of emotions, can be reached by introspective intuition, but direct evidence of its validity can also be tested by deduction, based on experimental results, such as those obtained by our research group, which described verbal analysis of the mental experience and the expression of anger in different cultures[13,14] and the relationship between aggression, impulsiveness, and hedonicity.[15] We recognize that all these elements possess a strongly hedonic dimension, either positive or negative.

Generalizing our findings to other emotions, it may be concluded that hedonicity would be the dimension of consciousness that motivates the subject towards useful behaviors. This contention matches with Damasio's[16,17] observation that impairment of emotional process in patients undermines their capacity to make decisions: this is what one would expect to find when the hedonic dimension is severed. The lack of pleasure thus impairs emotion.

Consequently, pleasure/displeasure is the common currency for accessing behavior in response to the various emotions; no emotion is hedonically indifferent. The hedonic dimension is what pathognomonically defines emotion.[12,18] Pleasure thus makes emotion a motivating experience.

ACKNOWLEDGMENTS

This work was supported by the Spanish Ministry of Science and Technology (BS2001/1224) and by the Spanish Interministerial Commission for Science and Technology (CICYT) (PR 111/01).

REFERENCES

1. CANNON, W.B. 1927. The James-Lange theory of emotions: a critical examination and an alternation. Am. J. Psychol. **39:** 106–124.
2. LAZARUS, R.S. 1982. Thoughts on the relations between emotion and cognition. Am. Psychol. **37:** 1019–1024.
3. JAMES, W. 1890. The Principles of Psychology. Dover Publications. New York.
4. ZAJONC, R.B. 1984. On the primacy of affect. Am. Psychol. **39:** 117–123.
5. DAVIDSON, R.J. & P. EKMAN. 1994. Afterword: what are the minimal cognitive prerequisites for emotion? *In* The Nature of Emotion. P. Ekman & R.J. Davidson, Eds.: 232–234. Oxford University Press. New York.
6. IZARD, C.E. 1994. Cognition is one of four types of emotion activating systems. *In* The Nature of Emotion. P. Ekman & R.J. Davidson, Eds.: 230–207. Oxford University Press. New York.
7. FRIDJA, N.H. 1994. Emotions require cognitions, even if simple ones. *In* The Nature of Emotion. P. Ekman & R.J. Davidson, Eds.: 197–202. Oxford University Press. New York.

8. LeDoux, J. 1996. The Emotional Brain. The Mysterious Underpinnings of Emotional Life. Simon & Schuster. New York.
9. Paksepp, J. 1986. The anatomy of emotions. *In* Emotion: Theory, Research, and Experience. R. Plutchik & H. Kellerman, Eds.: 91–124. Academic Press. Orlando, FL.
10. Cabanac, M. 1979. Sensory pleasure. Quarterly Rev. Biol. **54:** 1–29.
11. Cabanac, M. 1996. On the origin of consciousness, a postulate and its corollary. Neurosci. Biobehav. Rev. **20:** 33–40.
12. Cabanac, M. 2002, What is emotion? Behav. Processes **60:** 69 –83.
13. Ramirez, J.M., T. Fujihara, S. van Goozen & C. Santisteban. 2001. Anger proneness in Japanese and Spanish students. *In* Cross-cultural Approaches to Aggression and Reconciliation. J. Martin Ramirez & Deborah R. Richardson, Eds.: 87–97. NovaScience. Huntington, NY.
14. Ramirez, J.M., C. Santisteban, T. Fujihara & S. van Goozen. 2002. Differences between experience of anger and readiness to angry action (a study of Japanese and Spanish students). Aggressive Behav. **28:** 429–438.
15. Ramirez, J.M., M.C. Bonniot-Cabanac & M. Cabanac. 2003. Impulsive aggression and pleasure. A study with people of different ages. *In* Human Aggression: A Multifaceted Phenomenon. J.M. Ramirez, Ed.: 449–472. Centreur. Madrid.
16. Damasio, A.R. 1994. Descartes' Error. Putnam. New York.
17. Damasio, A.R. 2003. Looking for Spinoza: Joy, Sorrow and the Human Brain. Harcourt Trade Publishers. New York.
18. Rolls, E.T. 1994. A theory of emotion and consciousness, and its application to understanding the neural basis of emotion. *In* The Cognitive Neurosciences. M.S. Gazzaniga, Ed.: 1091–1105. MIT Press. Boston.

The Faces of Positive Emotion

Prototype Displays of Awe, Amusement, and Pride

MICHELLE N. SHIOTA,[a] BELINDA CAMPOS,[b] AND DACHER KELTNER[a]

[a]Institute for Personality and Social Research, University of California–Berkeley, Berkeley, California 94720-5050, USA

[b]Department of Psychology, University of California–Los Angeles, Los Angeles, California 90095-1563, USA

KEYWORDS: emotion; affect; facial expression; amusement; awe; pride; positive emotion

INTRODUCTION

Although several theorists posit the existence of multiple discrete positive emotion states,[1-4] much empirical research on the nature and consequences of emotion considers only one: happiness.[5-8] Studies of the facial display of emotion have documented universally recognized expressions of sadness, anger, fear, and other negative emotions, but have not differentiated among positive emotions.[6] The Duchenne smile, which includes contraction of the orbicularis oculi as well as the zygomaticus major, is generally considered the sole reliable expression of positive affect.

The goal of this study was to establish the features of facial and upper-body displays participants associate with the experience of distinct positive emotions. Although the full data set explores displays of 17 positive and negative emotions, only the data regarding awe, amusement, and pride displays are discussed here.

Address for correspondence: Michelle N. Shiota, Institute for Personality and Social Research, University of California–Berkeley, Berkeley, California 94720-5050. Voice: 650-346-5726; fax: 510-643-9334.

lshiota@socrates.berkeley.edu.

Ann. N.Y. Acad. Sci. 1000: 296–299 (2003). © 2003 New York Academy of Sciences.
doi: 10.1196/annals.1280.029

METHODS

Participants. Forty male and 32 female undergraduates at a large West Coast university participated: 36 were Asian; 4, African-American; and 10, Latino.

Procedure. Participants were seated at a table and presented with a series of index cards, each naming an emotion. For each emotion, participants were asked to recall and describe a time when they felt that emotion, and then to show how they would express that emotion to another person nonverbally. Participants were videotaped (upper body and face) throughout the session.

Data Analysis. A research assistant recorded the start time for each emotion pose, when a distinct pose could be identified. A FACS-certified coder then coded the ensuing display, using all FACS action units supplemented by 22 head, upper body, and respiratory actions. Frequencies of each action unit (AU) for each emotion were then calculated to establish "prototype" displays.

Hypotheses

Awe is indicated by raised head and eyes, widened eyes, slightly raised inner eyebrows (AUs 1, 5, 53, 63).[9]

Amusement is indicated by drop-jaw Duchenne smile (AUs 6, 12, 26/27), or "play face."[10]

Pride is indicated by Duchenne smile with compressed lips (AUs 6, 12, 24), back straight, shoulders back.[9]

RESULTS AND DISCUSSION

Overall findings supported the three hypotheses regarding expected prototype displays of awe, amusement, and pride. Specifically:

(1) Displays of *awe* frequently included raised inner eyebrow (AU 1, 78%), widened eyes (AU 5, 61%), and an open, slightly drop-jawed mouth (AU 26 or 27, 80%). A slight forward jutting of the head (AU 57, 27%) and visible inhalation (27%) were also common elements of the posed displays. In earlier work we have defined awe as the emotion experienced during cognitive accommodation, or schema formation, which requires intense intake and processing of information.[11] Widened eyes and forward head movement may facilitate this process. The drop-jaw mouth and deep inhalation observed in some participants may promote reduction of physiological arousal, which can interfere with complex cognitive processing.[12] It is noticeable that few participants smiled in their pose (AU 12, only 23%; AU 6, only 10%).

(2) Displays of *amusement* rarely included eyebrow movement, and typically consisted of a drop-jaw Duchenne smile as predicted (AU 6, 85%; AU 12, 95%; AU 26 or 27, 68%). Nearly half of posed displays also included a "head bounce," or repeated up-and-down bobble, even when participants were not laughing (only 36% visibly laughed). A head tilt (AU 55 or 56, 34%) was also a common element. In earlier work we have defined amusement, or humor, as the emotion experienced during a cognitive shift in the contemplation of some target[11]—an experience that may be a mental form of play. If amusement is derived from our rough-and-tumble play instincts, the dropped jaw and neck display that accompanies the head tilt may indicate that one's intentions are not threatening, although one's behavior may include aggressive elements (as in the case of teasing).[13]

(3) Displays of *pride* typically included a mild Duchenne smile with compressed lips (AU 6, 70%; AU 12, 79%; AU 24, 60%), as well as a straightening of the back (55%) and pulling back of the shoulders to expose the chest (45%). A slight head lift was also frequently observed (AU 53, 38%). We have defined pride as the emotion felt when one succeeds at a socially valued endeavor, and the display of pride may have the function of increasing status within the group.[11] The latter three elements of the prototypical pride display all have the effect of making one appear literally larger —and by implication more powerful. The compressed lips may signify control or determination. The mildness of the smile is striking compared with the broad grin of amusement, and likely reflects the difference in the social messages of the two feelings. One striking, yet theoretically consistent, finding is that women in this sample were more likely than men to shrug during the display (Chi-squared = 3.36, d.f. = 1, $P < 0.10$), thereby concealing or negating the upper-body display of pride.

In follow-up research, we plan to determine whether these and other prototypical positive emotion displays can be recognized reliably by judges, using both Western and non-Western samples.

REFERENCES

1. EKMAN, P. 1994. All emotions are basic. *In* The Nature of Emotion. P. Ekman & R. J. Davidson, Eds.: 15–19. Oxford University Press. New York.
2. FREDRICKSON, B.L. 1998. What good are positive emotions? Rev. Gen. Psychol. **2:** 300–319.
3. IZARD, C. E. 1977. Human Emotions. Plenum Press. New York.
4. LAZARUS, R.S. 1991. Goal congruent (positive) and problematic emotions. *In* Emotion and Adaptation. R.S. Lazarus, Ed. Oxford University Press. New York.
5. DAVIDSON, R.J. 1993. The neuropsychology of emotion and affective style. *In* Handbook of Emotions. M. Lewis & J. M. Haviland, Eds.: 143–154. Guilford. New York.

6. EKMAN, P. *et al.* 1987. Universals and cultural differences in the judgments of facial expressions of emotion. J. Pers. Soc. Psychol. **53:** 712–717.
7. ISEN, A.M., P.M. NIEDENTHAL & N. CANTOR. 1992. An influence of positive affect on social categorization. Motiv. Emotion **16:** 65–78.
8. LEVENSON, R.W. *et al.* 1992. Emotion and autonomic nervous system activity in the Minangkabau of West Sumatra. J. Pers. Soc. Psychol. **62:** 972–988.
9. DARWIN, C. 1998. The Expression of the Emotions in Man and Animals, 3rd edit. P. Ekman, Ed. Harper Collins. London. (US edit.: Oxford University Press. New York).
10. SARRA, S. & E. OTTA. 2001. Different types of smiles and laughter in pre-school children. Psychol. Rep. **89:** 547–558.
11. SHIOTA, M.N. *et al.* 2003. Positive emotion and the regulation of interpersonal relationships. *In* The Regulation of Emotion. P. Philippot & R.S. Feldman, Eds. Lawrence Erlbaum. Mahwah, NJ. In press.
12. LEVENSON, R.W. & A.M. RUEF. 1992. Empathy: a physiological substrate. J. Pers. Soc. Psychol. **63:** 234–246.
13. KELTNER, D. *et al.* 1998. Teasing in hierarchical and intimate relations. J. Pers. Soc. Psychol. **75:** 1231–1247.

Antiphonal Laughter in Developing Friendships

MORIA J. SMOSKI AND JO-ANNE BACHOROWSKI

Department of Psychology, Vanderbilt University, Nashville, Tennessee 37203, USA

KEYWORDS: laughter; interpersonal interactions

Darwin described man as "a social animal," and laughter is a decidedly social signal. Although we do laugh alone, laughter is as much as 30 times more likely to occur in the presence of another person than alone.[1] Not all social partners are equal when it comes to the facilitation of laughter, however. Our previous work has shown that both the sex and familiarity of a social partner influence the amount of laughter produced. Specifically, males produce the most laughter when paired with a friend of either sex, whereas females generally produce the most laughter when paired with a male, regardless of familiarity.[2]

In addition to moderating the overall rate of laugh production, social context influences the temporal pattern of laugh production. Antiphonal laughter, in which a laugh is produced concurrently or shortly after the laugh of a social partner, is also dependent on the sex and familiarity of a social partner. In a previous study, we audiorecorded 74 pairs of participants as they played games together. Dyads were composed of either same- or mixed-sex friends or strangers. Across all pairings, friends laughed together more than strangers. Among mixed-sex pairs, females produced more antiphonal laughter than males did.[3]

The results of that study showed that the temporal pattern of laugh production is affected by the familiarity and sex of a social partner. However, the additional influence of acoustic properties on antiphonal laugh production was not measured. Certain laugh acoustics have been found to differentially affect listener arousal and affect.[4] Specifically, laughter that is "voiced" has been

Address for correspondence: Moria J. Smoski, Department of Psychology, Vanderbilt University, Nashville, TN 37203. Voice: 615-343-4229; fax: 615-343-8449.

m.smoski@vanderbilt.edu

j.a.bachorowski@vanderbilt.edu; voice: 615-343-5915; fax: 615-343-8449.

Ann. N.Y. Acad. Sci. 1000: 300–303 (2003). © 2003 New York Academy of Sciences.
doi: 10.1196/annals.1280.030

shown to promote more positive affect than "unvoiced" laughter. Voiced laughs are quasiperiodic, and are thus perceived to have pitch. Unvoiced laughs are aperiodic, and perceived as grunt-like or snort-like. The present study examined whether voiced laughter facilitates antiphonal laugh production, much as it facilitates positive affect on the part of a listener. The development of antiphonal laughter over time was also of interest. To assess the point at which friends begin to use antiphonal laughter more than strangers, we tested new friends and randomly assigned strangers over the first three months of acquaintanceship.

METHODS

Participants included 36 male and 36 female first-year college students. Participants were assigned to same- or mixed-sex friend or stranger dyads, with 6 dyads per condition. Those in the "friend" condition were hallmates who had known each other for at most 3 weeks before the first session. Mean participant age was 18.1 years, and the sample was primarily white (79% white, 11% black, 4% Asian, 3% Hispanic, 1% multiracial; 1% declined to answer). Data were collected in two waves over the course of two years.

Participants attended three sessions, each one month apart. In each session, dyads played games designed to promote laugh production (e.g., played Pictionary with Play-doh; read each other spam haiku). Participants were audio recorded using head-worn microphones. Each session lasted approximately 9 min, for a total of 27 min of interactions analyzed for each dyad. After each session, participants completed the McGill Friendship Questionnaire (MFQ) as an index of friendship strength.

Laugh onsets and cessations were coded based on sound and spectral properties. A laugh was considered antiphonal if its onset occurred during or within one second following a partner laugh. Sequential analysis techniques were used to determine the aggregate degree of temporal association between partner laughs. Yule's Q was used as the sequential analysis statistic.

RESULTS

As measured by the MFQ, friends rated their friendship as stronger than strangers did following all three sessions. A sex × familiarity × time repeated-measures ANOVA of MFQ scores revealed that scores increased over time, $F(2,136) = 5.82$, $P = 0.002$. A sex × time interaction showed that males' scores increased at a higher rate than female scores, $F(2,136) = 3.54$, $P = 0.03$.

Laughs were coded as being either voiced or unvoiced. Averaged across sessions, antiphonal laughter followed voiced laughter more often than unvoiced laughter, t(71) = 9.28, P < 0.001. Both voiced and unvoiced laughs were combined to assess change in antiphonal laughter over time. An omnibus sex × familiarity × dyad sex × time repeated-measures ANOVA was performed. A familiarity × dyad sex interaction revealed that same-sex friends laugh together more than same-sex strangers, but mixed-sex pairs do not differ by familiarity, F(1,64) = 4.73, P = 0.03. In addition, there was a trend for a sex × familiarity × time interaction, F(2,128) = 2.81, P = 0.06. Among same-sex male dyads, friends and strangers did not differ in their use of antiphonal laughter in the first session, but friends laughed together more than strangers by session 3. Among same-sex female dyads, friends laughed together more than strangers across all sessions (see FIG. 1). Among mixed-sex

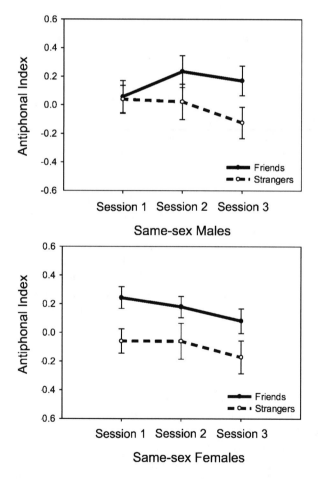

FIGURE 1. Changes in the use of antiphonal laughter in friends and strangers over time.

dyads, antiphonal laughter did not consistently differ by familiarity or sex over time.

DISCUSSION

The use of antiphonal laughter develops early in friendship. Female friends begin laughing antiphonally within 3 weeks of forming a friendship, and male friends begin using antiphonal laughter within 1.5 months. These sex differences may reflect stronger intrasex competition among males. Results for mixed-sex pairs are more puzzling and merit further investigation. The acoustic properties of a social partner's laugh also influence the production of antiphonal laughter, with laughs most strongly associated with the induction of positive affect also showing the greatest facilitation of antiphonal laughter.

REFERENCES

1. PROVINE, R.P. & K.R. FISCHER. 1989. Laughing, smiling, and talking: relation to sleeping and social context in humans. Ethology **83:** 295–305.
2. BACHOROWSKI, J.-A., M.J. SMOSKI, A.J. OWREN & M.J. OWREN. Laugh rate and acoustics are associated with social context. Manuscript under revision.
3. SMOSKI, M.J. & J.-A. BACHOROWSKI. 2003. Antiphonal laughter between friends and strangers. Cogn. Emotion. **17:** 327–340.
4. BACHOROWSKI, J.-A. & M.J. OWREN. 2001. Not all laughs are alike: voiced but not unvoiced laughter readily elicits positive affect. Psychol. Sci. **12:** 252–257.

Darwin's View

Self-Evaluative Emotions as Context-Specific Emotions

MARGARET W. SULLIVAN,[a] DAVID S. BENNETT,[b] AND
MICHAEL LEWIS[a]

[a]Institute for the Study of Child Development, Robert Wood Johnson Medical
School, New Brunswick, New Jersey 08903-0019, USA

[b]Eastern Psychiatric Institute, Drexel University College of Medicine,
Philadelphia, Pennsylvania 19119, USA

KEYWORDS: self-conscious emotions; self-evaluation; self-evaluative
emotions; shame; pride; embarrassment; anger; sadness; maltreatment;
physical abuse; neglect; sex differences

Darwin[1] first proposed that perceiving how others perceive us provides the basis for self-conscious emotions. For him, self-conscious emotions were undifferentiated emotions that involved a motivation to avoid the painful gaze of others. They were expressed as context-specific action patterns including head lowering, wavering or averted eyes, and blushing, which he observed in his three-year-old son.

To study self-conscious emotions, we observe young children succeeding and failing at simple tasks. FIGURE 1 summarizes the results of our studies. Self-conscious emotions first emerge between 2½ and 3 years, following the emergence of self-recognition.[2] There are two main classes of these emotions: early-emerging self-conscious emotions that include exposure embarrassment and other emotions requiring self-awareness and general social comparisons; and later-emerging self-conscious evaluative emotions. These later emotions—evaluative embarrassment, pride, shame, and guilt—require awareness of standards, rules, and goals, in addition to the earlier cognitive skills.[3,4] FIGURE 2 shows how self-evaluative emotions vary with success and failure in preschool-aged children, whereas primary emotions do not.

Address for correspondence: Michael Lewis, Institute for the Study of Child Development, 97 Paterson Street, New Brunswick, NJ 08903-0019. Voice: 732-235-7700; fax: 732-235-6189.
lewis@umdnj.edu.

Ann. N.Y. Acad. Sci. 1000: 304–308 (2003). © 2003 New York Academy of Sciences.
doi: 10.1196/annals.1280.031

A child's social history, especially its parenting, may also affect self-conscious emotions. We hypothesized that maltreated children show different amounts of evaluative emotions than control children of the same age and sex. Our sample is 180 4- to 7-year-old children, 86 (48%) of whom were maltreated as determined by Child Protective Service (CPS) records. The sample is 65% African American and 10% Hispanic. All children were en-

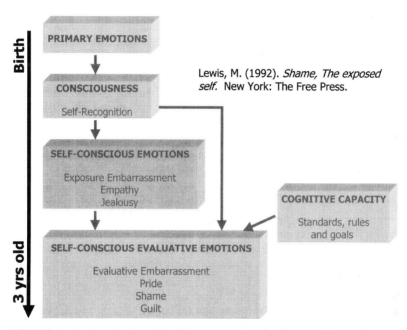

FIGURE 1. A theoretical model of the emergence of self-conscious emotions.

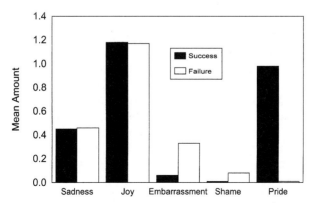

FIGURE 2. Preschooler's emotional expressions by success and failure.

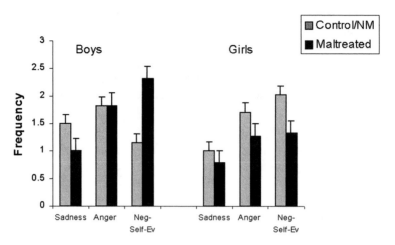

FIGURE 3. Response to failure in boys and girls as a function of maltreatment.

rolled in publicly funded preschool or kindergarten. Their status was determined from review of CPS records after assessment. Fifty-six children were neglected and 25 were physically abused. Five children with both forms of maltreatment were excluded from further analyses.

A female examiner administered eight tasks to children requiring completion of each before a "timer" rang. Half of the tasks were easy; half were difficult. The examiner manipulated the timer so that all children had exactly the same experience. She rang the timer before completion of half of the tasks to produce four failure experiences. She rang the bell 5 sec after the child finished the other half of the tasks to produce four success experiences. Face, body, and vocal behavior were videotaped and scored for 15 sec following the bell in the failure context and 15 sec following task completion in the success context. Primary as well as self-conscious emotions were scored because anger may be related to shame, especially in boys, while sadness may be related to depression, especially in girls. Average frequencies were computed for each emotion across failure and success conditions. Shame and evaluative embarrassment were collapsed to yield the frequency of negative self-evaluative emotions.

FIGURE 3 shows that maltreatment resulted in sex differences in emotions in response to failure. Maltreated boys showed more negative self-evaluative emotion than control boys ($P < 0.05$). Maltreated girls showed less negative evaluative emotion than control girls ($P < 0.08$). There were no significant differences in anger and sadness by maltreatment for either sex.

FIGURE 4 shows children's emotions following success. As expected, there were no differences in enjoyment. There was significantly less pride in maltreated children compared to controls ($P < 0.05$) and no differences by sex.

There was greater exposure embarrassment in maltreated boys compared to control boys ($P < 0.05$). Maltreated and control girls showed no difference.

FIGURE 5 shows anger, sadness, and the evaluative emotions broken down by two types of maltreatment: physical abuse and neglect. Anger was greater on average in physically abused boys compared to the other two groups of boys. Conversely, anger was less in physically abused and neglected girls compared to control girls. Neglected boys showed significantly less sadness than other boys ($P < 0.01$). Physically abused girls showed the least of all

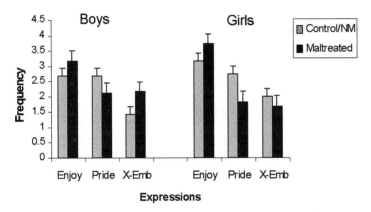

FIGURE 4. Response to success in boys and girls as a function of maltreatment.

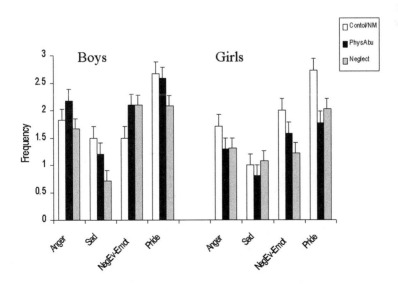

FIGURE 5. Differences in emotions of boys and girls by form of maltreatment.

girls. Negative self-evaluative emotion was greater in maltreated boys regardless of the form of maltreatment ($P < 0.01$). In girls, negative self-evaluative emotion was less in maltreated girls than control girls, with neglected girls showing the least of all groups ($P < 0.03$). For pride, neglected boys showed significantly less pride ($P < 0.05$). Among girls, both neglected and abused showed less pride than control girls, with physically abused girls showing the least of all groups ($P < 0.05$).

Boys and girls who are maltreated respond to success and failure differently. Girls, regardless of the type of maltreatment show significantly less negative evaluative emotion and pride than control girls. For boys, the type of maltreatment affects emotional responses to success and failure. Neglected boys show significantly less pride than controls and physically abused boys, whereas physically abused boys show more anger.

REFERENCES

1. DARWIN, C. 1969. The Expression of Emotions in Animals and Man. University of Illinois Press. Chicago.
2. LEWIS, M., M.W. SULLIVAN, C. STANGER & M. WEISS. 1989. Self-development and self-conscious emotions. Child Dev. 25: 439–443.
3. LEWIS, M. 1992. Shame: The Exposed Self. The Free Press. New York.
4. LEWIS, M. & D. RAMSAY. 2002. Cortisol response to embarrassment, shame, and pride. Child Dev. 73: 1034–1045.

Personality Traits and Sex Differences in Emotion Recognition among African Americans and Caucasians

ANTONIO TERRACCIANO, MARCELLUS MERRITT,
ALAN B. ZONDERMAN, AND MICHELE K. EVANS

*National Institute on Aging, National Institutes of Health,
Baltimore, Maryland, 21224, USA*

KEYWORDS: emotion recognition; personality traits; sex differences; cross-cultural; openness

INTRODUCTION

This study investigated the role of personality traits and sex differences in emotion recognition. In several studies using samples with mostly young Caucasian and Asian students, Matsumoto et al.[1] found strong evidence that recognition of emotional expression in faces was related to openness to experience and, to a lesser extent, conscientiousness. Openness is one of the major dimensions of the five-factor model[2] (FFM) of personality that might play an important role in the recognition of emotion. Open individuals tend to be intellectually curious, imaginative, and sensitive to aesthetics and inner feelings. The present study seeks to replicate Matsumoto et al. and extend the findings to an older African American and an older Caucasian sample. Furthermore, this study tests whether the relation between personality traits and emotion recognition can be replicated with a purely verbal task. Finally, the hypothesis that women tend to be better than men in decoding facial expressions of emotion will be tested.

Address for correspondence: Antonio Terracciano, National Institute on Aging, NIH, Department of Health and Human Services, 5600 Nathan Shock Dr., Baltimore, MD 21224. Voice: 410-558-8358; fax: 410-558-8108.

TerraccianoA@grc.nia.nih.gov

Ann. N.Y. Acad. Sci. 1000: 309–312 (2003). © 2003 New York Academy of Sciences.
doi: 10.1196/annals.1280.032

METHOD

The African American sample was composed of 106 individuals (51 males, 55 females; aged 21 to 92; mean age 52.6 years) participating in NIA's Healthy Aging in Nationally Diverse Longitudinal Samples study (HANDLS). The HANDLS participants live in a low–socioeconomic status neighborhood and have an average of 12 years of education. The second sample was composed of 46 individuals (24 males, 22 females; aged 22 to 87; mean age 66.1) participating in the Baltimore Longitudinal Study of Aging. This sample, composed of 38 Caucasians, 5 Asians or Pacific Islanders, and 3 Hispanics, had a higher socioeconomic status and an average of 16 years of education.

Two subtasks of the perception of affect task (PAT) were used.[3] The faces subtask requires participants to recognize which of six emotions (happiness, sadness, anger, fear, disgust, and surprise) or neutral expression is portrayed in pictures of Caucasian faces. The sentences subtask requires the recognition of emotional content from sentences. The same basic emotions were depicted in vignettes. To assess the major dimensions of the FFM, the NEO Five-Factor Inventory was used with the African American sample, and the Revised NEO Personality Inventory[4] was used with the Caucasian sample.

RESULTS AND DISCUSSION

The proportion of correct responses for faces and sentences tasks are given in TABLE 1. The performance of the African American sample was significantly worse than the performance of the mostly Caucasian sample on the faces task [$t(150) = -5.00$, $P < 0.01$, $d = .94$]. The lower score of the African Americans might be caused by the use of Caucasian faces. However, a similarly low score was obtained with the sentences task [$t(150) = -4.62$, $p < 0.01$, $d = .90$], and the correlation between the two subtasks was .61 and .42, respectively, for the African American and Caucasian sample. ANCOVA analyses were performed to control for the effect of education. Although education predicted performance ($P < 0.01$), the differences between groups remained significant ($P < 0.01$). These results suggest that ethnicity, cultural, or individual factors are more likely to explain differences in performance between these samples.

As shown in TABLE 1, openness to experience was the only dimension of the FFM to be significantly correlated with the ability to recognize emotions from facial expressions and sentences in both the African American and Caucasian samples. Further analyses at the level of specific emotions suggest that the correlations with personality traits are not task or emotion specific, but reflect a general ability to recognize emotions.

TABLE 1. Mean proportion correct in emotion recognition tasks and correlations with personality traits

	African American ($n = 106$)		Caucasian ($n = 46$)	
	Faces	Sentences	Faces	Sentences
Mean (SD)	.74 (.17)	.74 (.17)	.86 (.11)	.86 (.09)
Neuroticism	.06	.01	−.17	−.03
Extroversion	.10	.14	.03	−.04
Openness	.24**	.28**	.30*	.25*
Agreeableness	.05	.10	.12	−.14
Conscientiousness	−.13	−.06	.14	.08

$*P < 0.05$; $**P < 0.01$ (one-tailed).

With the faces task, no sex difference was found for the African American sample [$t(104) = 0.07$, $P > 0.05$, $d = .01$], but women scored significantly higher than men in the Caucasian sample [$t(44) = -3.08$, $P < 0.01$, $d = .92$]. With the sentences task, no sex difference was found in the African American sample [$t(104) = 0.51$, $P > 0.05$, $d = .10$], but women showed a trend toward scoring higher than men in the Caucasian sample [$t(44) = -1.81$, $P = 0.08$, $d = .54$]. These contrasts in the pattern of sex differences are consistent with the study of sex differences in personality traits[5] and emotions[6] across cultures, and suggest that factors such as race or socioeconomic status might moderate the relation between sex and emotion recognition.

CONCLUSION

This study showed evidence for the role of individual and cultural factors in emotion recognition. At the individual level, this study lends support to the notion that openness to experience is important for affective processing. The consistency of results using verbal and nonverbal stimuli suggests that openness to experience is related to basic processing, possibly universal. This interpretation is also supported by the fact that the Matsumoto *et al.* and the present study use judges from different races, cultural backgrounds, and age groups. The advantage in emotion recognition of individuals with higher scores on openness is consistent with a study[7] that found openness to be inversely related to a measure of alexithymia, a cognitive-affective construct that includes difficulty in identifying and expressing feelings. Openness has also been related to variation in the structure of self-rated affect.[8] Finally, women performed better than men in the Caucasian sample, but not in the African American sample. This contrast in the pattern of sex differences highlights the importance of cultural factors.

REFERENCES

1. MATSUMOTO, D., J. LEROUX, C. WILSON-COHN, *et al.* 2000. A new test to measure emotion recognition ability: Matsumoto and Ekman's Japanese and Caucasian Brief Affect Recognition Test (JACBART). J. Nonverbal Behav. **24:** 179–209.
2. MCCRAE, R.R. & O.P. JOHN. 1992. An introduction to the 5-Factor Model and its applications. J. Pers. **60:** 175–215.
3. LANE, R.D., L. SECHREST, R. REIDEL, *et al.* 1996. Impaired verbal and nonverbal emotion recognition in alexithymia. Psychosom. Med. **58:** 203–210.
4. COSTA, P.T., JR. & R.R. MCCRAE. 1992. Professional manual of the Revised NEO Personality Inventory (NEO-PI-R) and NEO Five-Factor Inventory (NEO-FFI). Psychological Assessment Resources, Inc. Odessa, FL.
5. COSTA, P.T., JR., A. TERRACCIANO & R.R. MCCRAE. 2001. Gender differences in personality traits across cultures: robust and surprising findings. J. Pers. Soc. Psychol. **81:** 322–331.
6. FISCHER, A.H. & A.S.R. MANSTEAD. 2000. The relation between gender and emotions in different cultures. *In* Gender and Emotions: Social Psychological Perspectives. A.H. Fischer, Ed.: 71–94. Cambridge University Press. Cambridge.
7. LUMINET, O., R.M. BAGBY, H. WAGNER, *et al.* 1999. Relation between alexithymia and the five-factor model of personality: a facet-level analysis. J. Pers. Assess. **73:** 345–358.
8. TERRACCIANO, A., R.R. MCCRAE, D. HAGEMANN, *et al.* 2003. Individual difference variables, affective differentiation, and the structure of affect. J. Pers. **71:** 669–704.

Does Pride Have a Recognizable Expression?

JESSICA L. TRACY AND RICHARD W. ROBINS

Department of Psychology, University of California–Davis, Davis, California 95616-8686, USA

KEYWORDS: pride; expression; emotion

In 1872, Darwin speculated that emotion expressions in humans and animals are evolved products of natural selection. He argued that a number of emotion expressions are universal, and he wrote, "Of all the … complex emotions, pride, perhaps, is the most plainly expressed. A proud man exhibits his sense of superiority over others by holding his head and body erect … and makes himself appear as large as possible" (p. 263).[1]

Although contemporary emotion researchers have supported Darwin's general speculation by identifying discrete, universally recognized facial expressions for a small set of "basic" emotions (e.g., ref. 2), they have not found a distinct nonverbal expression for pride. In fact, because happiness is the only positively valenced emotion thought to have a discrete, nonverbal expression, researchers have concluded that all positive emotions share the same expression.[3,4] The finding that pride has a unique, identifiable expression would challenge this assumption, suggest that pride meets a central criterion for biologically based emotions, and imply that pride may have evolved to serve a particular communicative function—possibly to convey success and thereby promote status and dominance.

In this paper, we summarize findings from five studies that test whether pride has a distinct, recognizable, behaviorally visible expression (see FIG. 1; also see ref. 5). In Study 1, 56 judges viewed photographs of male and female targets posing expressions of happiness, pride, and surprise and were asked to identify the emotion expressed in each photo. Judges chose from the following options: "happiness," "pride," "surprise," and "no emotion." The re-

Address for correspondence: Jessica L. Tracy, University of California, Department of Psychology, Davis, CA 95616-8686. Voice: 530-754-8299; fax: 530-752-2087.

jltracy@ucdavis.edu

Ann. N.Y. Acad. Sci. 1000: 313–315 (2003). © 2003 New York Academy of Sciences.
doi: 10.1196/annals.1280.033

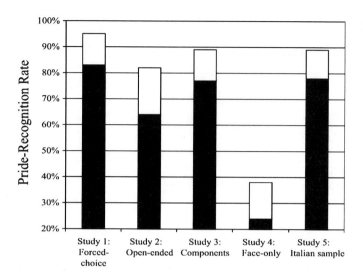

FIGURE 1. Pride recognition rates for studies 1–5. The *black bars* show mean recognition rates across pride photos; the *white bars* show recognition rates for the best pride photo. Studies 1, 3, 4, and 5 used a forced-choice response format (judges were given 4 response options in Study 1 and 8 response options in Studies 3–5). Recognition rates in Studies 1, 2, 3, and 5 are comparable to those found for basic emotions in the present research and in previous studies.

sults show that judges agreed on a pride expression and could distinguish pride from both happiness and surprise.

In Study 2, 96 judges responded to the photos using an open-ended response format. This design addresses a potential critique of Study 1—namely, that the forced-choice response format may constrain judges' response options and thereby inflate recognition rates.[6] A set of coders rated the extent to which each open-ended response was prototypical of pride. Results showed that responses to the pride photos were classified as prototypical of pride at frequencies that were greater than chance and comparable to those found in previous open-ended studies of basic emotions.[7]

In Study 3 ($N = 178$), we manipulated several facial and bodily features to more precisely determine the components of the pride expression. Results showed that the pride expression includes a small smile, head tilted slightly back, arms either raised above the head or hands placed on the hips, and a visibly expanded posture.

In Study 4, 85 judges viewed photos cropped to include only the face. Pride recognition was below chance for all face-only photos, suggesting that, unlike basic emotions, the pride expression includes more than the face.

Finally, in Study 5, 28 judges who were born, raised, and living in Italy viewed the photos. Pride recognition rates were comparable to recognition rates for United States judges, suggesting that the pride expression generalizes at least across Western cultures.

In summary, these studies show that pride has a recognizable nonverbal expression, which can be distinguished from expressions of other positive emotions and can be identified using forced-choice and open-ended response formats. The expression is recognized equally well by men and women and by American and Italian judges. These findings imply that pride can be added to the pantheon of emotions that have discrete behavioral expressions, that pride might have evolved to serve communicative functions, that nonverbal expressions of emotion are not restricted to the face, and that it might be possible to assess pride from nonverbal behaviors.

REFERENCES

1. DARWIN, C. 1872. The Expression of the Emotions in Man and Animals, 3rd edit. P. Ekman, Ed. Harper Collins. London. (US edit.: Oxford University Press. New York).
2. EKMAN, P., E.R. SORENSON & W.V. FRIESEN. 1969. Pan-cultural elements in facial displays of emotion. Science 164: 86–88.
3. EKMAN, P. 1992. An argument for basic emotions. Cognit. Emotion **6:** 169–200.
4. FREDRICKSON, B.L. & C. BRANIGAN. 2001. Positive emotions. *In* Emotions: Current Issues and Future Directions. T.J. Mayne & G.A. Bonanno, Eds.: 123–151. Guilford Press. New York.
5. TRACY, J.L. & R.W. ROBINS. Show your pride: evidence for a discrete emotion expression. Psychol. Sci. In press.
6. RUSSELL, J.A. 1994. Is there universal recognition of emotion from facial expressions? A review of the cross-cultural studies. Psychol. Bull. **115:** 102–141.
7. BOUCHER, J.D. & G.E. CARLSON. 1980. Recognition of facial expression in three cultures. J. Cross-Cult. Psychol. **11:** 263–280.

Darwin and the Neural Bases of Emotion and Affective Style

RICHARD J. DAVIDSON

Laboratory for Affective Neuroscience, W.M. Keck Laboratory for Functional Brain Imaging and Behavior, University of Wisconsin, Madison, Wisconsin 53706, USA

ABSTRACT: This article presents an overview of ways to think about the brain and emotion and consider the role of evolution and expression in shaping the neural circuitry of affective processing. Issues pertaining to whether there are separate unique neural modules hard-wired for emotion processing or whether affective processing uses more generalized circuitry are considered. Relations between affect and cognition—specifically, memory—are examined from the perspective of overlapping neural systems. The role of individual differences in neural function in affective style are discussed, and the concepts of affective chronometry, or the time course of emotional responding and emotion regulation, are introduced. Finally, the extent to which certain emotional traits can be viewed as trainable skills is considered, and the relevance of work on neural plasticity to the skill framework is addressed. Data from a variety of sources using different types of measures is brought to bear on these questions, including neuroimaging and psychophysiological measures, studies of individuals of different ages ranging from early childhood to old age, studies of nonhuman primates, and observations of patients with localized brain damage. Emotions are viewed as varying in both type and dimension. Honoring brain circuitry in parsing the domain of affects will result in distinctions and differentiations that are not currently incorporated in traditional classification schemes.

KEYWORDS: Darwin; emotion; affective processing; affective style; emotion regulation

Darwin's *Expression of Emotion in Man and Animals*[1] contained the seeds that have since blossomed into what now is generally called *affective neuroscience*. Darwin was extraordinarily prescient in his observations and predictions about the nervous system and emotion, though it has taken more than 100 years to witness the embryonic development of a neuroscience of emotion. The reasons for the long period of development are numerous and

Address for correspondence: Richard J. Davidson, Laboratory for Affective Neuroscience, University of Wisconsin, Department of Psychology, 1202 West Johnson Street, Madison, WI 53706. Phone: 608-262-8972; fax: 608-265-2875.

rjdavids@facstaff.wisc.edu

Ann. N.Y. Acad. Sci. 1000: 316–336 (2003). © 2003 New York Academy of Sciences.
doi: 10.1196/annals.1280.014

complex, but they are in part a function of the paucity of methods for interrogating the intact nervous system for much of the 20th century. The advent of neuroimaging has changed the landscape and has contributed, among other recent trends, to the rapid acceleration of knowledge in affective neuroscience. This essay will review some promising new developments in our understanding of the neural basis of emotion and individual differences in emotional reactivity and emotion regulation subsumed under the rubric of affective style. Throughout this review, suggestions made by Darwin in his classic 1872 monograph will be highlighted, and I will attempt to illustrate how they have come to be studied in contemporary affective neuroscience. I will mostly use examples from recent work in my laboratory but will also selectively refer to work of others where relevant.

Darwin's third principle is the "direct action of the excited nervous system on the body, independently of the will…" It is in this principle that Darwin declares his psychophysiological position and expresses his conjecture that much of the neural signaling about emotion from the brain to the body bypasses the will and is thus often nonconscious. Modern research in affective neuroscience has delineated circuitry that includes both cortical and subcortical territories implicated in different components of affective processing. Most investigators in this area now include at least the following brain regions in the circuitry that participates in most emotion: prefrontal cortex (PFC; multiple territories of the PFC are implicated and will be discussed below); amygdala; anterior cingulate; hippocampus; and insula. In several recent publications, I have discussed the functional contributions of each of these brain regions to affective processing.[2–4] In this essay, emphasis will be given to the prefrontal cortex and amygdala. An important challenge for modern research in affective neuroscience is anticipated by Darwin's intuition that most of our emotions are inextricably entwined with their expression. The dominant methods of affective neuroscience, at both the animal and human levels, most often precludes the natural full-blown expression of the emotions. Thus the data that we have are necessarily constrained and rarely include epochs of very intense emotion. Nevertheless, some consistent trends have emerged and will be highlighted below.

FUNCTIONAL NEUROANATOMY OF AFFECTIVE PROCESSING: PREFRONTAL CORTEX AND AMYGDALA

Prefrontal Cortex

Although the prefrontal cortex is often considered to be the province of higher cognitive control, it has also consistently been linked to various features of affective processing (see, e.g., ref. 5 for an early preview). Miller and

Cohen[6] have recently outlined a comprehensive theory of prefrontal function based upon nonhuman primate anatomical and neurophysiological studies, human neuroimaging findings, and computational modeling. The core feature of their model holds that the PFC maintains the representation of goals and the means to achieve them. Particularly in situations that are ambiguous, the PFC sends bias signals to other areas of the brain to facilitate the expression of task-appropriate responses in the face of competition with potentially stronger alternatives. In the affective domain, we often confront situations in which the arousal of emotion is inconsistent with other goals that have already been instantiated. For example, the availability of an immediate reward may provide a potent response alternative that may not be in the best service of the overall goals of the person. In such a case, the PFC is required to produce a bias signal to other brain regions that guide behavior toward the acquisition of a more adaptive goal, which in this case would entail delay of gratification. Affect-guided planning and anticipation that involves the experience of emotion associated with an anticipated outcome is the hallmark of adaptive, emotion-based decision making. Patients with lesions to certain zones of the PFC, particularly the ventromedial PFC, have been shown to exhibit profoundly impaired decision making.[7] Affect-guided anticipation is most often accomplished in situations that are heavily laden with competition from potentially stronger alternatives. In such cases in particular, we would expect PFC activation to occur. Certain disorders of emotional processing such as depression may be caused by abnormalities of affect-guided anticipation. For example, the failure to anticipate positive incentives and direct behavior toward the acquisition of appetitive goals are symptoms of depression that may arise from abnormalities in the circuitry that implements positive affect-guided anticipation. Our laboratory has contributed extensively to the literature on asymmetries in PFC function associated with approach- and withdrawal-related emotion and mood.[4,8] In this context, we suggest that left-sided PFC regions are particularly involved in approach-related, appetitive goals. The instantiation of such goals, particularly in the face of strong alternative responses, requires left-sided PFC activation; and hypoactivation in these circuits has been linked to depression. Right-sided PFC regions, alternatively, are hypothesized to be particularly important in behavioral inhibition and vigilant attention that often accompanies certain aversive emotional states and traits. Whether right-sided PFC activation is a core feature underlying withdrawal behavior in general, or behavioral inhibition and vigilant attention more specifically, is a question to which we still do not have an adequate answer. The prototype of the behavioral inhibition process, which we have hypothesized to be subserved by specific right PFC mechanisms, has recently been captured in several neuroimaging studies that involve variants of a go/no-go task, where a dominant response set is established to respond quickly, except for those trials in which a cue to inhibit the response is presented. Two recent studies using event-related functional

MRI (fMRI) have found a lateralized focus of activation in the right lateral PFC (inferior frontal sulcus) to cues that signaled response inhibition that were presented in the context of other stimuli toward which a strong approach set was established.[9,10] This is the same region of right lateral PFC that has been found to be activated in a number of neuroimaging studies in which withdrawal-related negative affect has been elicited.[4]

Depressed individuals with hypoactivation in certain regions of the PFC may be deficient in the instantiation of goal-directed behavior and in the overriding of more automatic responses that may involve the preservation of negative affect and dysfunctional attitudes. Such deficits would be expected to be unmasked in situations where decision making is ambiguous and where the maintenance of goal-directed behavior is required in the face of potentially strong alternative responses. As we will argue below, when the strong alternative responses involve affect, which they often do, the ventromedial PFC is particularly implicated.

Recent neuroimaging and electrophysiological studies suggest that the orbital and ventral frontal cortex in particular may be especially important for the representation of rewards and punishments, and different sectors within this cortex may emphasize reward versus punishment.[11–12] In particular, a left-sided medial region of the orbitofrontal cortex (OFC) appears particularly responsive to rewards, while a lateral right-sided region appears particularly responsive to punishments.[12] Kawasaki and colleagues[11] recorded from single units in the right ventral PFC of patients with implanted depth electrodes for presurgical planning. They found these neurons in healthy tissue to exhibit short-latency responses to aversive visual stimuli. Such studies provide important clues regarding the circuitry that might be most relevant to understanding differences among individuals in affective style. For example, there are individual differences in responsivity to rewards versus punishments that can be probed behaviorally using signal detection methods.[13,14] Most normal individuals exhibit systematic modification of response bias to monetary reward, but some do not. Those who do not showed elevated depressed mood. We would also predict that left medial OFC would be hyporesponsive to manipulations of reward in such individuals, while right lateral OFC to punishment would either be normal or perhaps accentuated.

AMYGDALA

Although a link between amygdala activity and negative affect has been a prevalent view in the literature, particularly when examined in response to exteroceptive aversive stimuli,[15] recent findings from invasive animal studies and human lesion and functional neuroimaging studies are converging on a broader view that regards the amygdala's role in negative affect as a special case of its more general role in directing attention to affectively salient stimuli and issuing a call for further processing of stimuli that have major significance for the individual. Extant evidence is consistent with the argument that the amygdala is critical for recruiting and coordinating cortical arousal and vigilant attention for optimizing sensory and perceptual processing of stimuli associated with underdetermined contingencies, such as novel, "surprising," or "ambiguous" stimuli (see also refs. 16–18). Most stimuli in this class may be conceptualized as having an aversive valence since we tend to have a negativity bias in the face of uncertainty.[19]

The role of the amygdala in the activation of cortex for further processing of salient stimuli may be most apparent in the visual system. Darwin commented in several places in *Expression* on the importance of the visual modality for both identifying prey and avoiding danger. A number of recent studies have found that when visual emotional stimuli are compared with visual nonemotional stimuli that are matched to basic visual characteristics, the visual cortex is more activated in response to the emotional compared with the nonemotional stimuli (see refs. 20,21). We and others have speculated that the increase in activation in visual cortex in response to emotional stimuli may be a function of back projections from the amygdala to primary visual cortex. Amaral and his colleagues[22] have identified pathways in the macaque brain that connect the basolateral region of the amygdala all the way down to V1 in primary visual cortex. This provides a mechanism whereby visual information processing can be modulated by affect-related signals from the amygdala.

Both structural and functional differences in the amygdala have been reported in disorders of emotion, particularly depression. Structurally, several recent studies reported an association between enlargement of amygdala volume and depression. This association has been found in depressed patients with bipolar disorder[23,24] as well as temporal lobe epilepsy (TLE).[25,26] In a recent study, Mervaala *et al.*[27] observed significant asymmetry in amygdalar volumes (right smaller than left) in patients with major depressive disorder (MDD) but not the controls. In TLE patients with dysthymia, left amygdala volume was positively correlated with depression severity, as assessed with the Beck Depression Inventory.[25] Although these findings depict a relation between increased amygdalar volume and depression, it is important to stress that (a) the causal relations between the two entities are still unknown, and (b) some inconsistencies among studies are present. Indeed, some studies reported either *decreased* bilateral volume in the amygdala core nuclei[28] or null findings.[29–31] Although the reasons are still unclear, it is interesting to note that two null findings were found in geriatric depression.[30,31]

Functionally, abnormal elevations of resting rCBF or glucose metabolism in the amygdala have been reported in depression during both wakefulness[32] and sleep.[33,34] In an FDG-PET study, Ho *et al.*[33] reported increased absolute cerebral glucose metabolic in several brain regions, particularly the amygdala (+44%), in 10 unmedicated men with unipolar depression during non-REM sleep period. Further, in his recent review, Drevets[35] reports data from five consecutive studies in which increased rCBF or glucose metabolism has been consistently replicated in depressives with familial MDD or melancholic features. In a postmortem study, 5-HT2 receptor density was significantly increased in the amygdala of depressive patients committing suicide.[36] Abnormally increased amygdalar activation has also recently been reported in bipolar depression[37] and anxiety disorders, which often show a high degree of comorbidity with depression.[38–44] Further establishing a link between depression and amygdalar activation, two studies have reported a positive correlation between amygdalar activation and depression severity or dispositional negative affect in patients with MDD.[32,45] After pharmacologically induced remission from depression, amygdalar activation has been observed to decrease to normative values.[46] In familial pure depressive disease, however, increased (left) amygdalar activation persists during the remitted phases,[32] suggesting that at least in some subtypes of depression amygdalar dysfunction may be trait-like. Interestingly, remitted MDD patients showing symptom relapse as a consequence of serotonin depletion showed increased amygdalar activation *prior* to the depletion compared to those who will not relapse.[47] Finally, in one of the first fMRI studies using an activation paradigm, Yurgelun-Todd *et al.*[48] reported higher left amygdalar activation for bipolar patients than controls in response to fearful faces.

In light of the pivotal role of the amygdala in recruiting and coordinating vigilant behavior toward stimuli with underdetermined contingencies, hyperactivation of the amygdala in major depression may bias initial evaluation of and response to incoming information. Although still speculative, this mechanism may rely on norepinephrine, which (a) is oftentimes abnormally elevated in depression,[49] (b) is involved in amygdala-mediated emotional learning,[50] and (c) is affected by glucocorticoid secretion, which is often elevated in MDD.[51] Thus, these findings may explain cognitive biases towards aversive or emotionally arousing information observed in depression.

Increased amygdalar activation in depression may also represent a possible biological substrate for anxiety, which is often comorbid with depression. In this respect, elevated levels of glucocortocoid hormones—which characterize at least some subgroups of patients with depression—may be especially relevant, since elevated glucocorticoid hormones have been shown to be associated with increased corticotropin-releasing hormone (CRH) in the amygdala. Increased CRH availability may increase anxiety, fear, and expectation for adversity.[52]

In light of evidence suggesting a link between amygdalar activation on the one hand and memory consolidation and acquisition of long-term declarative knowledge about emotionally salient information on the other hand, the observations of dysfunctionally increased amygdalar activation in major depression are intriguing. As recently pointed out by Drevets *et al.*,[46] tonically *increased* amygdalar activation during depressive episodes may favor the emergence of rumination based on increased availability of emotionally negative memories. Although still untested, it is possible that these aberrant processes may rely on dysfunctional interactions between the amygdala, the PFC, and the anterior cingulate cortex (ACC). Notably, structural abnormalities have been reported in territories of the PFC intimately connected with the ACC.[53,54] Recent functional imaging data implicate abnormalities in ACC function in depression.[21,55] ACC dysfunction, in particular, may lead to a decreased capability of monitoring potential conflict between memory-based ruminative processes and sensory information coming from the environment.

AFFECTIVE STYLE

Darwin admonished his readers to pay attention to individual differences. For example, early in *Expression* Darwin noted "...the insane ought to be studied, for they are liable to the strongest passions, and give uncontrollable vent to them" (p. 13).[1] He also underscored the importance of developmental differences in emotional reactivity for similar reasons. In this section, I will review one modern approach to the study of individual differences in emotional reactivity and emotion regulation, subsumed under the term *affective style*. This corpus of work includes the study of both normal individual variation as well as pathological extremes of such variation. The study of affective style has proceeded in individuals throughout the life span.

In several recent publications, I have suggested that the term affective style be used to denote a broad range of individual differences in different parameters of emotional reactivity. Davidson[56,57] has defined affective style as valence-specific features of emotional reactivity and affective responding. Specific parameters of affective style can be objectively measured including: (a) the threshold to respond; (b) the magnitude of the response; (c) the rise time to the peak of the response; (d) the recovery function of the response; (e) the duration of the response. The last three parameters all refer to different aspects of affective chronometry or the time course of emotional responding. We have proposed that time course variables are particularly germane to understanding individual differences that may reflect vulnerability to psychopathology since certain forms of mood and anxiety disorders may be specifically associated with either a failure to turn off a response sufficiently quickly and/or an abnormally early onset of the response that may then result in a bypassing of normal regulatory constraints. The specific parameters of affective style described above all jointly govern in a complex fashion the dispositional mood and other reportable characteristics that reflect affective style. In this section, data from my laboratory pertaining to relations between individual difference in both prefrontal and amygdala function and their relation to measures that reflect affective style will be summarized.

In both infants[58] and adults[59] there are large individual differences in baseline electrophysiological measures of prefrontal activation, and such individual variation is associated with differences in aspects of affective reactivity. In infants, Davidson and Fox[58] reported that 10-month babies who cried in response to maternal separation were more likely to have less left- and greater right-sided prefrontal activation during a preceding resting baseline compared with those infants who did not cry in response to this challenge. In adults, we first noted that the phasic influence of positive and negative emotion elicitors (e.g., film clips) on measures of prefrontal activation asymmetry appeared to be superimposed upon more tonic individual differences in the direction and absolute magnitude of asymmetry.[59]

During our initial explorations of this phenomenon, we needed to determine if baseline electrophysiological measures of prefrontal asymmetry were reliable and stable over time and thus could be used as a trait-like measure. Tomarken et al.[60] recorded baseline brain electrical activity from 90 normal subjects on two occasions separated by approximately three weeks. At each testing session, brain activity was recorded during eight 1-minute trials, four with eyes open and four with eyes closed, presented in counterbalanced order. The data were visually scored to remove artifact and then Fourier-transformed. Our focus was on power in the alpha band (8–13 Hz), though we extracted power in all frequency bands (see refs. 61 and 62 for methodological discussion). We computed coefficient alpha as a measure of internal consistency reliability from the data for each session. The coefficient alphas were quite high, with all values exceeding .85, indicating that the electrophysiological measures of asymmetric activation indeed showed excellent internal consistency reliability. The test-retest reliability was adequate, with intraclass correlations ranging from .65 to .75, depending upon the specific sites and methods of analysis. The major conclusion from this study was the demonstration that measures of activation asymmetry based upon power in the alpha band from prefrontal scalp electrodes showed both high internal consistency reliability and acceptable test-retest reliability to be considered a trait-like index. Similar findings have recently been obtained by Hagemann et al.[63]

On the basis of our prior data and theory, we reasoned that extreme left and extreme right frontally activated subjects would show systematic differences in dispositional positive and negative affect. We administered the trait version of the Positive and Negative Affect Scales (PANAS)[64] to examine this question and found that the left frontally activated subjects reported more positive and less negative affect than their right frontally activated counterparts.[60] More recently with Sutton[65] we showed that scores on a self-report measure designed to operationalize Gray's concepts of Behavioral Inhibition and Behavioral Activation (the BIS/BAS scales)[66] were even more strongly predicted by electrophysiological measures of prefrontal asymmetry than were scores on the PANAS scales. Subjects with greater left-sided prefrontal activation reported more relative BAS-to-BIS activity compared with subjects exhibiting more right-sided prefrontal activation. Independently, Harmon-Jones and Allen[67] published findings that were consistent with Sutton and Davidson;[65] but see Hagemann et al.[68] and Davidson[69] for complications associated with attempts to replicate these basic findings.

We also hypothesized that our measures of prefrontal asymmetry would predict reactivity to experimental elicitors of emotion. The model that we have developed over the past several years (see refs. 56 and 70-72 for background) features individual differences in prefrontal activation asymmetry as a reflection of a diathesis that modulates reactivity to emotionally significant events. According to this model, individuals who differ in prefrontal asymmetry should respond differently to an elicitor of positive or negative emotion, even when baseline mood is partialled out. We[73,74] performed an experiment to examine this question. We presented short film clips designed to elicit positive or negative emotion. Brain electrical activity was recorded prior to the presentation of the film clips. Just after the clips were presented, subjects were asked to rate their emotional experience during the preceding film clip. In addition, subjects completed scales that were designed to reflect their mood at baseline. We found that individual differences in prefrontal asymmetry predicted the emotional response to the films even after measures of baseline mood were statistically removed. Those individuals with more left-sided prefrontal activation at baseline reported more positive affect to the positive film clips, and those with more right-sided prefrontal activation reported more negative affect to the negative film clips. These findings support the idea that individual differences in electrophysiological measures of prefrontal activation asymmetry mark some aspect of vulnerability to positive and negative emotion elicitors. The fact that such relations were obtained following the statistical removal of baseline mood indicates that any difference between left and right frontally activated subjects in baseline mood cannot account for the prediction of the film-elicited emotion effects that were observed.

The relation between individual differences in brain electrical measures of prefrontal activation asymmetry and depression is a topic that has received extensive treatment in several recent articles. There has been a failure to replicate[75] our initial findings of decreased left prefrontal activation in depression,[76–78] though there have also been several published independent replications or conceptual replications (e.g., refs. 79 and 80). Moreover, using positron emission tomography, Baxter and colleagues (e.g., ref. 81) have reported decreased activation in regions of left dorsolateral prefrontal cortex that were associated with depression severity (i.e., lower glucose metabolic rate predicted increased severity). Drevets and his colleagues[53] reported decreased activation in the subgenual prefrontal cortex in patients with depression that was more left sided, though the laterality of this finding is equivocal because of its proximity to the midline. Drevets and colleagues[53] also reported a highly significant reduction in gray matter volume in the left subgenual

PFC region. We have interpreted the decrease in left-sided prefrontal activation as a diathesis related to deficits in the approach system and in reward-related responding.[13,14] We also argued that this pattern of left prefrontal hypoactivation would be found only in certain subgroups of mood-disordered patients in light of the heterogeneity of the disorder (see ref. 69 for an extended discussion of both conceptual and methodological issues germane to this area). Most importantly, we have suggested that it is crucial to move beyond descriptive phenomenology and to examine with objective laboratory methods variations in reactivity to emotion elicitors in individuals with this hypothesized diathesis. We have proposed that individuals who display left prefrontal hypoactivation will show specific deficits in reactivity to reward, though the need to consider other components of the circuitry with which the prefrontal cortex is interconnected must be underscored in any effort to understand the neural bases of emotion and its disorders.

In addition to the studies described above using self-report and psychophysiological measures of emotion, we have also examined relations between individual differences in electrophysiological measures of prefrontal asymmetry and other biological indices that in turn have been related to differential reactivity to stressful events. Three recent examples from our laboratory include measures of immune function, cortisol, and corticotropin-releasing hormone. The latter two measures represent key molecules in the activation of a coordinated response to stressful events. Our strategy in each case was to examine relations between individual differences in measures of prefrontal activation asymmetry and these other biological indices. In two separate studies[82,83] we examined relations between the prefrontal activation indices and natural killer (NK) activity since declines in NK activity have been reported in response to stressful, negative events.[84] We predicted that subjects with greater right prefrontal activation would exhibit lower NK activity compared with their left-activated counterparts because the former type of subject has been found to report more dispositional negative affect, to show higher relative BIS activity, and to respond more intensely to negative emotional stimuli. In each of the two studies conducted with independent samples, we found that right frontally activated subjects indeed had lower levels of NK activity compared to their left frontally activated counterparts.[82,83] We also examined the magnitude of change in NK activity in response to stress and found that subjects with greater baseline levels of right prefrontal activation showed the largest-magnitude decline in NK activity compared with other subjects.[83] Very recently, we[85] have extended this work to include measures of *in vivo* immune function. In a sample of 52 subjects between the ages of 57 and 60 years, we measured prefrontal activation asymmetry according to our usual methods. In addition, we administered an influenza vaccine and measured antibody titers in response to the vaccine at several intervals following vaccination. We found that subjects with greater left-sided prefrontal activation at both baseline and in response to a negative affect challenge had greater antibody titers in response to influenza vaccine, suggesting more robust immunity in response to vaccination.

In collaboration with Kalin, our laboratory has been studying similar individual differences in scalp-recorded measures of prefrontal activation asymmetry in rhesus monkeys.[86,87] Recently, we[88] acquired measures of brain electrical activity from a large sample of rhesus monkeys ($N = 50$). EEG measures were obtained during periods of manual restraint. A subsample of 15 of these monkeys was tested on two occasions four months apart. We found that the test-retest correlation for measures of prefrontal asymmetry was .62, suggesting similar stability of this metric in monkey and man. In the group of 50 animals, we also obtained measures of plasma cortisol during the early morning. We hypothesized that if individual differences in prefrontal asymmetry were associated with dispositional affective style, such differences should be correlated with cortisol, since individual differences in baseline cortisol have been related to various aspects of trait-related stressful behavior and psychopathology (see, e.g., ref. 89). We found that animals with right-sided prefrontal activation had higher levels of baseline cortisol than their left frontally activated counterparts (see FIG. 1). As can be seen from the figure, it is the left-activated animals that are particularly low compared with both middle- and right-activated subjects. Moreover, when blood samples were collected two years following our initial testing, animals classified as showing extreme right-sided prefrontal activation at age one year had significantly higher baseline cortisol levels when they were three years of age compared with animals who were classified at age one year as displaying extreme left-sided prefrontal activation. Similar findings were obtained with cerebrospinal fluid levels

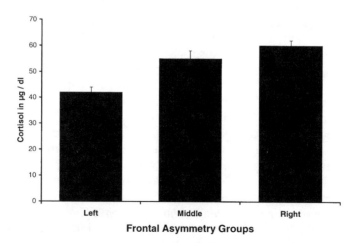

FIGURE 1. Basal morning plasma cortisol from one-year-old rhesus monkeys classified as left ($N = 12$), middle ($N = 16$), or right ($N = 11$) frontally activated based upon electrophysiological measurements. (Reprinted from Kalin *et al.*[88] with permission.)

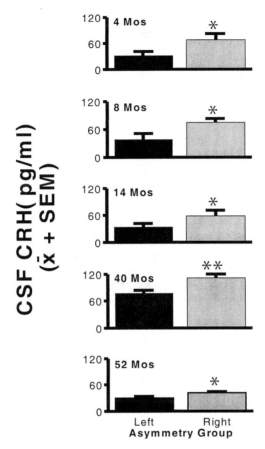

FIGURE 2. Differences between right ($N = 9$) and left prefrontally ($N = 10$) activated animals in cerebrospinal fluid measures of corticotropin-releasing hormone at five different ages. The original classification of the animals as extreme right or left activated was performed on the basis of brain electrical activity data collected when the animals were 13 months of age. (Reprinted from Kalin *et al.*[90] with permission.)

of CRH. Those animals with greater right-sided prefrontal activation showed higher levels of CRH (see Fig. 2).[90] These findings indicate that individual differences in prefrontal asymmetry are present in nonhuman primates and that such differences predict biological measures that are related to affective style.

As noted earlier, there are several regions of the PFC that play important roles in emotion. The OFC has been implicated as a primary region for decoding the affective value of stimuli.[91] Scalp-recorded brain electrical measures are not ideal for detecting activation in these more inferior regions of PFC. In a recent study, we[92] used fMRI to probe the OFC for individual dif-

ferences in a more subtle emotion, one that Darwin suggested was not associated with a specific expression. Darwin noted that "Although the emotion
of love, for instance that of a mother for her infant, is one of the strongest of
which the mind is capable, it can hardly be said to have any proper or peculiar
means of expression…" (pp. 212–213).[1] To investigate individual differences
in love between mother and infant, we brought primiparous mothers into the
laboratory with their infants when the infants were 3–4 months of age. We
photographed the infants and then used these photos in a subsequent scanning
session during which the mothers were presented with pictures of their own
infants and pictures of unrelated infants in a block design. We also had mothers rate their mood in response to seeing each type of photo. We found that
the greater the increase in feelings of love, affection, and warmth that the
mothers reported in response to seeing their own infants (compared with
viewing unrelated infants), the greater the activation of the OFC. We used visual cortex as a control region to establish that the effects were indeed specific to OFC; and although visual cortex showed greater activation to pictures of
own versus other infants, activation in this region was uncorrelated with feelings of love and other positive emotions reported by the mothers. These findings indicate that despite the lack of a unique expressive signal associated
with love, sensitive measures of brain function do indeed reflect this emotion.

   With the advent of neuroimaging, it has become possible to investigate the
relation between individual differences in aspects of amygdala function and
measures of affective style. We have used PET with flourodeoxyglucose
(FDG) as a tracer to investigate relations between individual differences in
glucose metabolism in the amygdala and dispositional negative affect. FDG-
PET is well-suited to capture trait-like effects since the period of active uptake of tracer in the brain is approximately 30 minutes. It is inherently more
reliable than O15 blood-flow measures because the FDG data reflect activity
aggregated over a 30-minute period. We have used resting FDG-PET to examine individual differences in glucose metabolic rate in the amygdala and
its relation to dispositional negative affect in depressed subjects.[45] We acquired a resting FDG PET scan as well as a structural MR scan for each subject. The structural MR scans are used for anatomical localization by
coregistering the two image sets. Thus, for each subject, we used an automated algorithm to fit the MR scan to the PET image. Regions of interest (ROI's)
were then drawn on each subject's MR scan to outline the amygdala in each
hemisphere. These ROI's were drawn on coronal sections of subjects' MR
images, and the ROI's were then automatically transferred to the coregistered
PET images. Glucose metabolism in the left and right amygdala ROI's were
then extracted. The interrater reliability for the extracted glucose metabolic
rate is highly significant, with intraclass correlations between two independent raters $\geq .97$. We found that subjects with greater glucose metabolism in
the right amygdala report greater dispositional negative affect on the PANAS
scale. These findings indicate that individual differences in resting glucose

metabolism in the amygdala are present and that they predict dispositional negative affect among depressed subjects.

In a small sample of 12 normal subjects, we[93] have been able to examine the relation between the magnitude of MR signal change in the amygdala in response to aversive compared with neutral pictures and dispositional negative affect on the PANAS scale. We correlated the average value of the pixels with the maximum Student's t from the left and right amygdala with dispositional negative affect. There was a robust correlation such that increased signal intensity in the right amygdala was associated with higher levels of negative affect. A pixel in the fusiform gyrus that revealed robust activation by the aversive pictures was selected as a control region. We correlated the magnitude of activation in the pixel showing the maximal response in this region to the aversive pictures with dispositional negative affect and found no relation ($P > 0.5$). Moreover, the correlations in the amygdala and fusiform gyrus were found to be significantly different. The findings from the fMRI and PET studies of amygdala function indicate that individual differences in both tonic activation and phasic activation in response to aversive stimuli predict the intensity of dispositional negative affect.

EMOTION REGULATION: A KEY COMPONENT OF AFFECTIVE STYLE

One of the key components of affective style is the capacity to regulate negative emotion and specifically to decrease the duration of negative affect once it arises. We have suggested in several recent articles that the connections between the PFC and amygdala play an important role in this regulatory process.[3,4,56,57] In two recent studies, we[94,95] examined relations between individual differences in prefrontal activation asymmetry and the emotion-modulated startle. In these studies, we presented pictures from the *International Affective Picture System*[96] while acoustic startle probes were presented and the EMG-measured blink response from the orbicularis oculi muscle region was recorded (see ref. 97 for basic methods). Startle probes were presented during the slide exposure as well as at various latencies following the cessation of the pictures, on separate trials. We interpreted startle magnitude during picture exposure as providing an index related to the generation of the emotional response, while startle magnitude following the *cessation* of the pictures was taken to reflect the recovery from emotional challenge. Used in this way, startle probe methods can potentially provide new information on the time course of emotional responding. We expected that individual differences during actual picture presentation would be less pronounced than individual differences following picture presentation since an acute emotional stimulus is likely to pull for a normative response across subjects, while individuals are more likely to differ once the stimulus has terminated. Similarly, we predicted that individual differences in prefrontal asymmetry would account for more variance in predicting magnitude of recovery (i.e., startle magnitude poststimulus) than in predicting startle magnitude during the stimulus. Our findings in both studies were consistent with our predictions and indicated that subjects with greater right-sided prefrontal activation show a larger blink magnitude following the cessation of the negative stimuli, after the variance in blink magnitude *during* the negative stimulus was partialled out. Measures of prefrontal asymmetry did not reliably predict startle magnitude during picture presentation. The findings from this study are consistent with our hypothesis and indicate that individual differences in prefrontal asymmetry are associated with the time course of affective responding, particularly the recovery following emotional challenge. In a related study, we have found that subjects with greater baseline levels of left prefrontal activation are better able to voluntarily suppress negative affect.[98,99] Moreover, in an initial study using fMRI we have demonstrated that when subjects are instructed to voluntarily regulate their negative emotion, reliable changes in amygdala signal MR signal intensity are found.[100]

The findings from these studies indicate that individual differences in prefrontal activation may play an important role in emotion regulation. Individuals who report greater dispositional negative affect and who show increased reactivity to stressful events are more likely to be those individuals who have difficulty regulating negative affect and specifically in modulating the intensity of negative affect once it has been activated.

SUMMARY AND CONCLUSIONS

Darwin was a remarkable observer, and many of his observations presaged important research questions that are now central in affective neuroscience. One of Darwin's great contributions was the comparative study of emotion and his observations of expressive behavior and emotional processes in animals. This work provided an important foundation for the examination of the neural systems underlying emotion in nonhuman species. This corpus of evidence has been crucial in catalyzing the study of the neuroscience of emotion in humans using neuroimaging and related methods. Progress has been rapid over the past decade because of a remarkable convergence between findings at the animal and human levels. Although Darwin implicitly recognized the importance of individual differences in emotion by calling attention to possible sex differences, developmental differences, and differences between normal subjects and patients with psychiatric disorders, he did not systematically treat this issue. As this essay has documented, it is now possible to rigorously interrogate the brain circuitry underlying individual differences in emotional reactivity with neuroimaging. Another topic not addressed by Darwin but that is now central to understanding emotion is the process of emotion regulation. Darwin implicitly acknowledged its importance by suggesting that emotions were less controllable for the "insane." Emotion regulation is likely ubiquitous and overlaps in time with the actual generation of emotion (see ref. 2 for review), making it difficult to isolate and distinguish from emotion per se. However, new paradigms have recently been developed that offer some promise in the study of both automatic and voluntary emotion regulation (see ref. 62), and they illustrate the importance of this construct for understanding individual differences in both normal and pathological emotion.

Darwin's powerful insights and extraordinary observations in *Expression* still stimulate and guide research on emotion, especially work on the neural substrates of emotion. Darwin recognized that emotions, unlike most other psychological processes, are instantiated in both the brain and the body. For him, both the heart and the brain were keys to understanding emotion; future research must be directed to the study of how the heart and brain interact during emotion. Darwin explained that "…when the heart is affected it reacts on the brain…so that under any excitement there will be much mutual action and reaction between these, the two most important organs of the body" (p. 69).[1]

ACKNOWLEDGMENTS

The research reported in this article was generously supported by National Institute of Mental Health Grants MH43454, MH40747, P50-MH52354, and P50-MH61083; by Research Scientist Award K05-MH00875; and by support from the University of Wisconsin. I am deeply indebted to the many students and collaborators associated with the Laboratory for Affective Neuroscience and the W.M. Keck Laboratory for Functional Brain Imaging and Behavior for making this work possible.

REFERENCES

1. DARWIN, C. [1872] 1965. The Expression of Emotion in Man and Animals. University of Chicago Press. Chicago.
2. DAVIDSON, R.J., K.M. PUTNAM & C.L. LARSON. 2000. Dysfunction in the neural circuitry of emotion regulation: a possible prelude to violence. Science **289:** 591–594.
3. DAVIDSON, R.J., *et al.* 2003. Parsing the subcomponents of emotion and disorders of emotion: perspectives from affective neuroscience. *In* Handbook of Affective Science. R.J. Davidson, H.H. Goldsmith & K. Scherer, Eds.: 8–24. Oxford University Press. New York.
4. DAVIDSON, R.J. & W. IRWIN. 1999. The functional neuroanatomy of emotion and affective style. Trends Cogn. Sci. **3:** 11–21.

5. NAUTA, W.H. 1971. The problem of the frontal lobe: a reinterpretation. J. Psychiatr. Res. **8:** 167–187.
6. MILLER, E.K. & J.D. COHEN. 2001. An integrative theory of prefrontal cortex function. Ann. Rev. Neurosci. **24:** 167–202.
7. DAMASIO, A.R. 1994. Descartes' Error: Emotion, Reason, and the Human Brain. Avon Books. New York.
8. DAVIDSON, R.J., J.R. MARSHALL, A.J. TOMARKEN & J.B. HENRIQUES. 2000. While a phobic waits: regional brain electrical and autonomic activity in social phobics during anticipation of public speaking. Biol. Psychiatry **47:** 85–95.
9. GARAVAN, H., T.J. ROSS & E.A. STEIN. 1999. Right hemispheric dominance of inhibitory control: an event-related functional MRI study. Proc. Natl. Acad. Sci. USA **96:** 8301–8306.
10. KONISHI, S. et al. 1999. Common inhibitory mechanism in human inferior prefrontal cortex revealed by event-related functional MRI. Brain **122:** 981–991.
11. KAWASAKI, H. et al. 2000. Single-neuron responses to emotional visual stimuli recorded in human ventral prefrontal cortex. Nat. Neurosci. **4:** 15–16.
12. O'DOHERTY, J. et al. 2001. Abstract reward and punishment representations in the human orbitofrontal cortex. Nat. Neurosci. **4:** 95–102.
13. HENRIQUES, J.B., J.M.GLOWACKI & R.J. DAVIDSON. 1994. Reward fails to alter response bias in depression. J. Abnorm. Psychol. **103:** 460–466.
14. HENRIQUES, J.B. & R.J. DAVIDSON. 2000. Decreased responsiveness to reward in depression. Cogn. Emotion **15:** 711–724.
15. LEDOUX, J.E. 2000. Emotion circuits in the brain. Ann. Rev. Neurosci. **23:** 155–184.
16. DAVIS, M. & P.J. WHALEN. 2001. The amygdala: vigilance and emotion. Mol. Psychiatry **6:** 13–34.
17. HOLLAND, P.C. & M.GALLAGHER. 1999. Amygdala circuitry in attentional and representational processes. Trends Cogn. Sci. **3:** 65–73.
18. WHALEN, P.J. 1998. Fear, vigilance, and ambiguity: initial neuroimaging studies of the human amygdala. Curr. Dir. Psychol. Sci. **7:** 177–187.
19. TAYLOR, S.E. 1991. Asymmetrical effects of positive and negative events: the mobilization-minimization hypothesis. Psychol. Bull. **110:** 67–85.
20. BRADLEY, M.M. et al. 2003. Activation of visual cortex in motivated attention. Behav. Neurosci. **117:** 369–380.
21. DAVIDSON, R.J., W. IRWIN, M.J. ANDERELE & N.H. KALIN. 2003. The neural substrates of affective processing in depressed patients treated with Venlafaxine. Am. J. Psychiatry **160:** 64–75.
22. AMARAL, D.G., et al. 1992. Anatomical organization of the primate amygdaloid complex. In The Amygdala: Neurobiological Aspects of Emotion, Memory and Mental Dysfunction. J.P. Aggleton, Ed.: 1–66. Wiley-Liss, Inc. New York.
23. ALTSHULER, L.L., et al. 1998. Amygdala enlargement in bipolar disorder and hippocampal reduction in schizophrenia: an MRI study demonstrating neuroanatomic specificity. Arch. Gen. Psychiatry **55:** 663–664.
24. STRAKOWSKI, S.M., et al. 1999. Brain magnetic resonance imaging of structural abnormalities in bipolar disorder. Arch. Gen. Psychiatry **56:** 254–260.
25. TEBARTZ VAN ELST, F.G. WOERMANN, L. LEMIEUX & M.R. TRIMBLE. 1999. Amygdala enlargement in dysthymia—a volumetric study of patients with temporal lobe epilepsy. Biol. Psychiatry **46:** 1614–1623.

26. TEBARTZ VAN ELST, F.G. WOERMANN, L. LEMIEUX & M.R. TRIMBLE. 2000. Increased amyglada volumes in female and depressed humans: a quantitative magnetic resonance imaging study. Neurosci. Lett. **281:** 103–106.
27. MERVAALA, E., et al. 2000. Quantitative MRI of the hippocampus and amygdala in severe depression. Psychol. Med. **30:** 117–125.
28. SHELINE, Y.I., M.H. GADO & J.L. PRICE. 1998. Amygdala core nuclei volumes are decreased in recurrent major depression. Neuroreport **9:** 2023–2028.
29. COFFEY, C.E., et al. 1993. Quantitative cerebral anatomy in depression: a controlled magnetic resonance imaging study. Arch. Gen. Psychiatry **50:** 7–16.
30. PANTEL, J., et al. 1997. Quantitative magnetic resonance imaging in geriatric depression and primary degenerative dementia. J. Affect. Disord. **42:** 69–83.
31. ASHTARI, M., et al. 1999. Hippocampal/amygdala volumes in geriatric depression. Psychol. Med. **29:** 629–638.
32. Drevets, W.C., et al. 1992. A functional anatomical study of unipolar depression. J. Neurosci. **12:** 3628–3641.
33. HO, A.P., et al. 1996. Brain glucose metabolism during non-rapid eye movement sleep in major depression. A positron emission tomography study. Arch. Gen. Psychiatry **53:** 645–652.
34. NOFZINGER, E.A., et al. 1999. Changes in forebrain function from waking to REM sleep in depression: preliminary analyses of [18F]FDG PET studies. Psychiatry Res. **91:** 59–78.
35. DREVETS, W.C. 2001. Neuroimaging and neuropathological studies of depression: implications for the cognitive-emotional features of mood disorders. Curr. Opin. Neurobiol. **11:** 240–249.
36. HRDINA, P.D., et al. 1993. 5-HT uptake sites and 5-HT2 receptors in brain of antidepressant-free suicide victims/depressives: increase in 5-HT2 sites in cortex and amygdala. Brain Res. **614:** 37–44.
37. KETTER, T.A., et al. 2001. Effects of mood and subtype on cerebral glucose metabolism in treatment-resistant bipolar disorder. Biol. Psychiatry **49:** 97–109.
38. BIRBAUMER, N., et al. 1998. fMRI reveals amygdala activation to human faces in social phobics. Neuroreport **9:** 1223–1226.
39. LIBERZON, I., et al. 1999. Brain activation in PTSD in response to trauma-related stimuli. Biol. Psychiatry **45:** 817–826.
40. RAUCH, S.L., et al. 1996. A symptom provocation study of posttraumatic stress disorder using positron emission tomography and script-driven imagery. Arch. Gen. Psychiatry **53:** 380–387.
41. RAUCH, S.L., et al. 1996. A symptom provocation study of posttraumatic stress disorder using positron emission tomography and script-driven imagery. Arch. Gen. Psychiatry **53:** 380–387.
42. SCHNEIDER, F., et al. 1999. Subcortical correlates of differential classical conditioning of aversive emotional reactions in social phobia. Biol. Psychiatry **45:** 863–871.
43. SEMPLE, W.E., et al. 2000. Higher brain blood flow at amygdala and lower frontal cortex blood flow in PTSD patients with comorbid cocaine and alcohol abuse compared with normals. Psychiatry **63:** 65–74.
44. SHIN, L.M., et al. 1997. Visual imagery and perception in posttraumatic stress disorder. A positron emission tomographic investigation. Arch. Gen. Psychiatry **54:** 233–241.

45. ABERCROMBIE, H.C., *et al.* 1998. Metabolic rate in the right amygdala predicts negative affect in depressed patients. Neuroreport **9:** 3301–3307.
46. DREVETS, W.C., *et al.* 2001. Amphetamine-induced dopamine release in human ventral striatum correlates with euphoria. Biol. Psychiatry **49:** 81–96.
47. BREMNER, J.D., *et al.* 1997. Positron emission tomography measurement of cerebral metabolic correlates of tryptophan depletion-induced depressive relapse. Arch. Gen. Psychiatry **54:** 364–374.
48. YURGELUN-TODD, D.A., *et al.* 2000. fMRI during affect discrimination in bipolar affective disorder. Bipolar Disord. **2:** 237–248.
49. VEITH, R.C., *et al.* 1994. Sympathetic nervous system activity in major depression: basal and desipramine-induced alterations in plasma norepinephrine kinetics. Arch. Gen. Psychiatry **51:** 411–422.
50. FERRY, B., B. ROOZENDAAL & J.L. MCGAUGH. 1999. Role of norepinephrine in mediating stress hormone regulation of long-term memory storage: a critical involvement of the amygdala. Biol. Psychiatry **46:** 1140–1152.
51. CARROLL, B.J., G.C. CURTIS & J. MENDELS. 1976. Cerebrospinal fluid and plasma free cortisol concentrations in depression. Psychol. Med. **6:** 235–244.
52. SCHULKIN, J. 1994. Melancholic depression and the hormones of adversity: a role for the amygdala. Curr. Dir. Psychol. Sci. **3:** 41–44.
53. DREVETS, W.C., *et al.* 1997. Subgenual prefrontal cortex abnormalities in mood disorders. Nature **386:** 824–827.
54. ONGUR, D., W.C. DREVETS & J.L. PRICE. 1998. Glial reduction in the subgenual prefrontal cortex in mood disorders. Proc. Natl. Acad. Sci. USA **95:** 13290–13295.
55. MAYBERG, H.S., *et al.* 1997. Cingulate function in depression: a potential predictor of treatment response. Neuroreport **8:** 1057–1061.
56. DAVIDSON, R.J. 1998. Affective style and affective disorders: perspectives from affective neuroscience. Cogn. Emotion **12:** 307–320.
57. DAVIDSON, R.J. 2000. Affective style, psychopathology, and resilience: brain mechanisms and plasticity. Am. Psychol. **55:** 1196–1214.
58. DAVIDSON, R.J. & N.A. FOX. 1989. Frontal brain asymmetry predicts infants' response to maternal separation. J. Abnorm. Psychol. **98:** 127–131.
59. DAVIDSON, R.J. & A.J. TOMARKEN. 1989. Laterality and emotion: an electrophysiological approach. *In* Handbook of Neuropsychology, Vol 3. F. Boller & J. Grafman, Eds.: 419–441. Elsevier. Amsterdam.
60. TOMARKEN, A.J., R.J. DAVIDSON, R.E. WHEELER & R.C. DOSS. 1992. Individual differences in anterior brain asymmetry and fundamental dimensions of emotion. J. Pers. Soc. Psychol. **62:** 676–687.
61. DAVIDSON, R.J., J.P. CHAPMAN, L.P. CHAPMAN & J.B. HENRIQUES. 1990. Asymmetrical brain electrical activity discriminates between psychometrically-matched verbal and spatial cognitive tasks. Psychophysiology **27:** 238–543.
62. DAVIDSON, R.J., D.C. JACKSON & N.H. KALIN. 2000. Emotion, plasticity, context, and regulation: perspectives from affective neuroscience. Psychol. Bull. **126:** 890–909.
63. HAGEMANN, D., E. NAUMANN, J.F. THAYER & D. BARTUSSEK. 2002. Does resting electroencephalograph asymmetry reflect a trait? An application of latent state-trait theory. J. Pers. Soc. Psychol. **82:** 619–641.
64. WATSON, D., L.A. CLARK & A. TELLEGEN. 1988. Developmental and validation of brief measures of positive and negative affect: the PANAS scales. J. Pers. Soc. Psychol. **54:** 1063–1070.

65. SUTTON, S.K. & R.J. DAVIDSON. 1997. Prefrontal brain asymmetry: a biological substrate of the behavioral approach and inhibition systems. Psychol. Sci. **8:** 204–210.
66. CARVER, C.S. & T.L. WHITE. 1994. Behavioral inhibition,behavioral activation and affective responses to impending reward and punishment: the BIS/BAS scales. J. Pers. Soc. Psychol. **67:** 319–333.
67. HARMON-JONES, E. & J.J.B. ALLEN. 1997. Behavioral activation sensitivity and resting frontal EEG asymmetry: covariation of putative indicators related to risk for mood disorders. J. Abnorm. Psychol. **106:** 159–163.
68. HAGEMANN, D., *et al.* 1998. Frontal brain asymmetry and affective style: a conceptual replication. Psychophysiology **35:** 372–388.
69. DAVIDSON, R.J. 1998. Anterior electrophysiological asymmetries, emotion and depression: conceptual and methodological conundrums. Psychophysiology **35:** 607–614.
70. DAVIDSON, R.J. 1992. Emotion and affective style: hemispheric substrates. Psychol. Sci. **3:** 39–43.
71. DAVIDSON, R.J. 1994. Complexities in the search for emotion-specific physiology. *In* The Nature of Emotion: Fundamental Questions. P. Ekman & R.J. Davidson, Eds.: 237–242. Oxford University Press. New York.
72. DAVIDSON, R.J. 1995. Cerebral asymmetry, emotion, and affective style. *In* Brain Asymmetry. R. J. Davidson & K. Hugdahl, Eds.: 361–387. MIT Press. Cambridge, MA.
73. WHEELER, R.E., R.J. DAVIDSON, & A.J. TOMARKEN. 1993. Frontal brain asymmetry and emotional reactivity: a biological substrate of affective style. Psychophysiology **30:** 82–89.
74. TOMARKEN, A.J., R.J. DAVIDSON & J.B. HENRIQUES. 1990. Resting frontal activation asymmetry predicts emotional reactivity to film clips. J. Pers. Soc. Psychol. **59:** 791–801.
75. REID, S.A., L.M. DUKE & J.J. ALLEN. 1998. Resting frontal electroencephalographic asymmetry in depression: inconsistencies suggest the need to identify mediating factors. Psychophysiology **35:** 389–404.
76. SCHAFFER, C.E., R.J. DAVIDSON & C. SARON. 1981. Parietal and frontal EEG asymmetry in depressed and non-depressed subjects. Psychophysiology **19:** 345–246.
77. HENRIQUES, J.B. & R.J. DAVIDSON. 1990. Regional brain electrical asymmetries discriminate between previously depressed and healthy control subjects. J. Abnorm. Psychol. **99:** 22–31.
78. HENRIQUES, J.B. & R.J. DAVIDSON. 1991. Left frontal hypoactivation in depression. J. Abnorm. Psychol. **100:** 535–545.
79. ALLEN, J.J., W.G. IACONO, R.A. DEPUE & P. ARBISI. 1993. Regional electroencephalographic asymmetries in bipolar seasonal affective disorder before and after exposure to bright light. Biol. Psychiatry **33:** 642–646.
80. FIELD, T., N.A. FOX, J. PICKENS & T. NAWROCKI. 1995. Relative right frontal EEG activation in 3- to 6-month-old infants of "depressed" mothers. Dev. Psychol. **3:** 358–363.
81. BAXTER, L.R., JR., *et al.* 1989. Reduction of prefrontal cortex glucose metabolism common to three types of depression. Arch. Gen. Psychiatry **46:** 243–250.
82. KANG, D.H., *et al.* 1991. Frontal brain asymmetry and immune function. Behav. Neurosci. **105:** 860–869.

83. DAVIDSON, R.J., C.C. COE, I. DOLSKI & B. DONZELLA. 1999. Individual differences in prefrontal activation asymmetry predict natural killer cell activity at rest and in response to challenge. Brain Behav. Immun. **13:** 93–108.
84. KIECOLT-GLASER, J.K. & R. GLASER. 1981. Stress and immune function in humans. *In* Psychoneuroimmunology. R. Ader, D.L. Felten & N. Cohen Eds.: 849–867. Academic Press. San Diego, CA.
85. ROSENKRANZ, M.A., *et al.* 2003. Affective style and *in vivo* immune response: neurobehavioral mechanisms. Proc. Nat. Acad. Sci. USA **100:** 11148–11152.
86. DAVIDSON, R.J., N.H. KALIN & S.E. SHELTON. 1992. Lateralized effects of diazepam on frontal brain electrical asymmetries in rhesus monkeys. Biol. Psychiatry **32:** 438–451.
87. DAVIDSON, R.J., N.H. KALIN & S.E. SHELTON. 1993. Lateralized response to diazepam predicts temperamental style in rhesus monkeys. Behav. Neurosci. **107:** 1106–1110.
88. KALIN, N.H., C.L. LARSON, S.E. SHELTON & R.J. DAVIDSON. 1998. Asymmetric frontal brain activity, cortisol, and behavior associated with fearful temperament in rhesus monkeys. Behav. Neurosci. **112:** 286–292.
89. GOLD, P.W., F.K. GOODWIN & G.P. CHROUSOS. 1988. Clinical and biochemical manifestations of depression: relation to the neurobiology of stress. N. Engl. J. Med. **314:** 348–353.
90. KALIN, N.H., S.E. SHELTON & R.J. DAVIDSON. 2000. Cerebrospinal fluid corticotropin-releasing hormone levels are elevated in monkeys with patterns of brain activity associated with fearful temperament. Biol. Psychiatry **47:** 579–585.
91. ROLLS, E.T. 1999. The Brain and Emotion. Oxford University Press. New York.
92. NITSCHKE, J.B., *et al.* Orbitofrontal cortex tracks positive mood in mothers viewing pictures of their newborn infants. NeuroImage. In press.
93. IRWIN, W., *et al.* 1998. Relations between human amygdala activation and self-reported dispositional affect. J. Cogn. Neurosci. S109.
94. LARSON, C.L., S.K. SUTTON & R.J. DAVIDSON. 1998. Affective style, frontal EEG asymmetry and the time course of the emotion-modulated startle. Psychophysiology **35:** S52.
95. JACKSON, D.C., *et al.* 2003. Now you feel it, now you don't: frontal brain electrical asymmetry and individual differences in emotion regulation. Psychol. Sci. **14:** 612–617.
96. LANG, P.J., M.M. BRADLEY & B.N. CUTHBERT. 1995. International Affective Picture System (IAPS): technical manual and affective ratings. The Center for Research in Psychophysiology, University of Florida. Gainsville, FL.
97. SUTTON, S.K., *et al.* 1997. Manipulating affective state using extended picture presentation. Psychophysiology **34:** 217–226.
98. JACKSON, D.C., *et al.* 2000. Resting frontal and anterior temporal EEG asymmetry predicts ability to regulate negative emotion. Psychophysiology **37:** 550.
99. JACKSON, D.C., J. MALMSTADT, C.L. LARSON & R.J. DAVIDSON. 2000. Suppression and enhancement of emotional responses to unpleasant pictures. Psychophysiology **37:** 515–522.
100. SCHAEFER, S.M., *et al.* 2002. Modulation of amygdalar activity by the conscious regulation of negative emotion. J. Cogn. Neurosci. **14:** 913–921.

The Amygdala, Social Behavior, and Danger Detection

DAVID G. AMARAL

*Department of Psychiatry and Behavioral Sciences, Center for Neuroscience,
The California National Primate Research Center, and the M.I.N.D. Institute,
University of California–Davis, Davis, California 95616, USA*

ABSTRACT: The amygdala is a distinctive portion of the anterior temporal lobe that has been implicated in a variety of functions including expression of fear, modulation of memory, and mediation of social communication. While work on the rodent amygdala often deals with emotion, much of the research in nonhuman primates and in man deals with its role in the perception of social signals, such as facial expressions, and the maintenance of social position, such as in primate dominance hierarchies. We have established a program of research that has as its major goal the definition of neural systems that underlie species-typical social communication. A first phase of the program was launched on the premise that the amygdala is essential for species-typical social behavior. We sought to examine in more detail the impairments of social behavior that followed discrete, bilateral lesions of the amygdala. We found, however, that mature rhesus monkeys with bilateral lesions of the amygdala not only were capable of species-typical social behavior, but actually engaged in more affiliative social interactions. The lesioned animals also demonstrated a striking lack of fear of normally fear-inducing stimuli such as replicas of snakes. In a second, ongoing series of studies in the infant rhesus monkey, we are examining whether the amygdala is essential for gaining social knowledge during development. Infant animals that receive bilateral lesions of the amygdala at two weeks of age and are raised by their biological mothers demonstrate all expected social behaviors for their ages. These animals, like the adults, demonstrate a lack of fear of objects such as snakes. However, unlike the adults, they demonstrate more fear when placed into novel social situations. The results from these studies are most consistent with the conclusion that the amygdala is not necessary for species-typical social behavior or for gaining social knowledge during development. We hypothesize that the amygdala is a critical component of a system that evaluates the environment for potential dangers. As such, it has a modulatory role on social behavior—that is, it typically inhibits social interaction with novel conspecifics while they are evaluated as potential adversaries. This per-

Address for correspondence: David G. Amaral, Ph.D., The M.I.N.D. Institute, UC Davis, 2825 50th St., Sacramento, CA 95817. Voice: 916-703-0237; 916-703-0225; fax: 916-703-0287.
dgamaral@ucdavis.edu

Ann. N.Y. Acad. Sci. 1000: 337–347 (2003). © 2003 New York Academy of Sciences.
doi: 10.1196/annals.1280.015

spective predicts that hyperactivity of the amygdala would be associated
with increased fear or anxiety and may contribute to disorders such as social phobia.

KEYWORDS: fear; anxiety; monkey; rhesus; lesions; social cognition

INTRODUCTION

Work beginning with the reports of Kluver and Bucy[1] indicated that damage to the amygdala and surrounding temporal lobe regions produced myriad
effects but most prominently decreased emotional reactivity. Aggleton and
colleagues[2] confirmed this with more selective lesions confined to the
amygdala and suggested that it takes near-total, bilateral lesions to achieve
the hypoemotionality described by Kluver and Bucy. The most exhaustive
analysis of the role of the amygdala in emotionality, and fear in particular, has
been carried out in the rodent,[3,4] on which an enormous literature has been
generated. With the notable exception of Kalin and colleagues,[5,6] relatively
little modern work has been carried out in the nonhuman primate on the relationship between the amygdala and emotional behavior. In contrast, there has
been a long, rich literature that relates the nonhuman primate amygdala to social behavior.

Rosvold and colleagues[7] were among the first to explicitly investigate the
role of the amygdala in nonhuman primate social behavior. They took previously unfamiliar macaque monkeys and formed artificial social groups. Once
stable dominance hierarchies had been established, they removed the most
dominant animal and subjected it to a bilateral lesion of the amygdala. The
animal was then returned to the social troop. These high-ranking, previously
aggressive rhesus monkeys fell in the dominance hierarchy and became extremely submissive following the bilateral amygdalectomy. Undoubtedly, the
most extensive analysis of the amygdala and primate social behavior was
conducted by Kling and colleagues.[8-11] These studies were carried out using
free-ranging vervet and rhesus monkeys as well as laboratory-housed animals. In studies carried out in Cayo Santiago (a "monkey island" just off the
coast of Puerto Rico) macaque monkeys were prepared with bilateral damage
of the amygdala and anterior temporal lobe and released back into their natal
social groups. These animals did not reintegrate with other group members,
did not engage in social interactions, and usually remained socially isolated.
In most cases, the amygdala-lesioned monkeys were attacked and died either
from their wounds, from predation, or from malnutrition. When caged,
amygdalectomized stump-tailed macaques were observed in a social group,
they generally displayed a decrease in aggression and a reduction in positive
social behaviors, such as huddling and grooming.[12] The conclusion from this
short introduction is that there is a substantial literature to support the conten-

tion that the amygdala is highly involved in the mediation both of species-typical social behavior as well as emotional responsivity, both within and outside of a social context. We began our program of studies on the neurobiology of primate social behavior with the intention of further specifying the role of the amygdala in macaque monkey social behavior. However, we were also interested in evaluating the effects of amygdala lesions on emotional responsivity in order to compare our studies with those in the literature as well as to calibrate our lesion and behavioral approaches. We have carried out extensive behavioral and physiological analyses of both mature and infant rhesus monkeys following complete, bilateral ibotenic acid lesions of the amygdaloid complex.

WHY STUDY THE EFFECTS OF AMYGDALA LESIONS ON PRIMATE SOCIAL BEHAVIOR?

Given the substantial literature that already exists on the role of the amygdala and social behavior, one might wonder what prompted us to reexamine this topic. There were a number of technical issues related to the previous lesion studies that have proved to be problematic in other areas of neuroscience research. For example, until recently, all lesions in the non-human primate were made using either radio frequency or suction ablation techniques. These destructive techniques suffer from the "fiber of passage" problem since they not only remove or destroy cell bodies in the lesioned nucleus, but also damage axons that travel through the targeted brain area. We know from our neuroanatomical studies that there are pathways from temporal lobe structures such as the entorhinal cortex that pass through the amygdala en route to other brain regions. Thus, it is impossible to determine whether behavioral changes resulting from a destructive lesion of the amygdala are due to the elimination of its neurons and projections or to inadvertent damage to projections that run through it. Moreover, most previous destructive lesions were not completely selective in their targets since they often destroyed neighboring brain regions. Many of the early lesion studies, for example, employed the suction ablation technique, which damaged the surrounding perirhinal cortex en route to the amygdala. The perirhinal cortex plays important roles in high level visual processing and other cognitive functions.[13–15] Consequently, one can reasonably ask whether the changes in social behavior observed in the earlier studies were the result of damage to the amygdala, to the fibers of passage, or to areas adjacent to the amygdala, such as the perirhinal and entorhinal cortices. This question is further complicated by the fact that histological analysis was often not carried out and certainly not carried out in a quantitative fashion.

Finally, earlier studies used behavioral data collection methods that were often subjective and resulted in little actual data that could be analyzed statistically. Often the investigators did not use an established ethogram or catalogue of social behavior. There were no direct comparisons between lesion and control groups; subjects were usually chosen at random from an established social group, and their behavior was recorded before and after the placement of the lesions. The subjects used were often of mixed age and sex, and there was virtually no effort to control for neuroendocrine differences among subjects due to reproductive status or gender. Another behavioral concern is that young male rhesus monkeys typically emigrate from their natal group to another group where they are incorporated in the social system. If a young male attempts to return to its natal group after emigrating, it is typically rebuffed by the group. Therefore, it is not clear whether the animals that received lesions were receiving abuse because of something to do with the lesion or because they were perceived as attempting to rejoin a social group that they had left.

Rather than employing suction ablation or other destructive lesion techniques, we have used the selective neurotoxin ibotenic acid, which is injected stereotaxically into the brain, causing minimal damage to adjacent areas. This toxin has the advantage of destroying only cell bodies and leaving fibers of passage intact.[16] In addition to using the more selective neurotoxin approach, the stereotaxic placement of every lesion was made more accurate by using an individual MRI atlas for each subject. In order to evaluate the lesions, extensive quantitative histological analysis was also performed for each brain. The adult subjects for these studies were male rhesus monkeys who were born and raised in outdoor social enclosures and who were assessed preoperatively to determine social status in their natal groups. To maintain some commonality of social experience, an additional group of "stimulus animals" served as partners for members of all experimental groups for at least some of the social interaction studies. We investigated the effects of these lesions on the responses animals made to inanimate objects as well as on their behaviors in various social contexts. A comprehensive list of social and nonsocial behaviors (the ethogram) was used to assess the behavioral repertoire of all animal groups.[17] The behavioral observers were blind to the lesion status of the animals, and the ethogram allowed the detection of increases or decreases of either affiliative or agonistic behaviors.

THE EFFECTS OF AMYGDALA LESIONS ON EMOTIONAL AND SOCIAL BEHAVIOR IN THE ADULT RHESUS MONKEY

We first evaluated the subjects emotional responsivity to a variety of stimuli including novel objects (Mason *et al.*, in preparation; Amaral *et al.*, in preparation). Some of the objects, such as rubber replicas of snakes or alligators, provoke intense fear responses in normal monkeys. In one such study, the latency to retrieve a food reward (usually a piece of desirable fruit) from in front of the stimulus items was measured. For normal animals, the latency to retrieve the food reward depended on the complexity or fear provoking qualities of the stimulus. With the amygdala-lesioned animals, in contrast, fear-eliciting stimuli such as a snake did not appreciably increase the latency to retrieve the food. The lesioned animals would even tactually explore objects such as snakes that the normal animals never touched. These observations were consistent with findings in the literature based on subjects with destructive lesions that bilateral damage to the amygdala produces a subject that is less fearful and emotionally responsive.

The same animals were then tested in a variety of social situations with either two animals (dyads) or four animals (tetrads) present in a large chain-link enclosure. In a condition that we have called *unconstrained dyads*, either the amygdala-lesioned animals or age-, sex-, and dominance-matched control animals interacted with "stimulus monkeys" (two males and two females). In another test of dyadic social interaction (the round-robin format) each of the experimental animals interacted with each of the other 11 experimental animals (in the first study) for one 20-minute episode. The results from both tests of dyadic interaction were striking and consistent. Rather than exhibiting social apathy or social awkwardness, the amygdala-lesioned monkeys generated qualitatively similar types of social interactions and responded to social gestures from the stimulus animals in an entirely species-typical manner. In fact, the amygdala-lesioned animals actually generated significantly greater amounts of affiliative social behavior towards the stimulus monkeys or the other experimental monkeys. On closer analysis, it appeared that the most striking alteration in behavior was at the early stages of social interaction. While the control animals were initially reluctant to interact with the stimulus monkeys, the amygdala animals initiated affiliative social behavior almost immediately. The lesioned monkeys appeared to be socially uninhibited in that they did not go through the normal period of evaluation of the social partner before engaging in social interactions. These results were completely at odds with our hypothesis that the amygdala is essential for normal social behavior. A detailed description of the dyadic social interaction studies has been published.[18]

Thus, contrary to our original premise, it appears that monkeys with extensive bilateral lesions of the amygdala can interpret and generate social gestures and, in fact, they initiate more affiliative social interactions than normal controls. They are clearly not critically impaired in carrying out social behavior. It appears that the lesions have produced a socially uninhibited monkey since their normal reluctance to engage a novel animal appears to have been clearly diminished if not eliminated.

Based on the apparent lack of fear that these monkeys demonstrate to inanimate objects and the uninhibited social interaction in the dyad studies, we have hypothesized that a primary role of the amygdala is to evaluate the environment for potential dangers. Without a functioning amygdala, macaque monkeys do not evaluate other novel conspecifics as potential dangers, and whatever system(s) are involved in mediating social interactions are freed of the inhibitory influence of the amygdala. This, of course, could lead to devastating consequences in a more challenging environment. We would expect that the amygdala-lesioned animals, for example, would approach a predator as eagerly as they approach a novel conspecific.

THE EFFECTS OF NEONATAL LESIONS OF THE AMYGDALA ON THE DEVELOPMENT OF SOCIAL BEHAVIOR

Even though the amygdala may not be necessary for generating social behavior in the adult, it is possible that it might be essential during development for learning appropriate social behaviors. There is an analogous situation in the literature on the hippocampal formation and memory. The hippocampal formation is clearly essential for the establishment of long-term episodic memories. Yet, amnesic patients, such as H.M. or R.B., who have marked bilateral damage to the hippocampal formation, can retrieve memories stored prior to the hippocampal damage. One interpretation of these findings is that declarative memories cannot be stored solely in the hippocampal formation; they must also be stored in other brain regions.[19]

In order to investigate the role of the amygdala in the development of social knowledge, we are conducting a series of studies in which the amygdala is lesioned bilaterally in rhesus monkeys at two weeks of age.[20] This is at a time when infant macaque monkeys are mainly found in ventral contact with their mothers, and there is virtually no play or other types of social interactions with other animals. One issue that was a concern in designing these studies was how the infants were raised following their neurosurgical procedure. The issue is of enormous significance in interpreting any behavioral pathology in animals that have received brain manipulations. It is now becoming increasingly clear that when nonhuman primates are reared other than by their mother or by an adoptive mother, a variety of aberrant behaviors are observed. Sackett[21] has described some of these and demonstrated that extraordinary measures are needed in order to partially mitigate the deleterious effects of nursery rearing on psychosocial behavior. This laboratory has previously provided substantial evidence that pair rearing leads to socioemotional pathologies such as excessive clinging.[22] Early nonmaternal rearing situations also negatively impact an animal's ability to respond to environmental challenges.[23] The early rearing experience of the animal also contributes to success in gaging social status as an adult.[24] Parr and colleagues[25] have also demonstrated that peer-reared rhesus monkeys have higher baseline levels of fear-potentiated startle than mother-reared age-matched controls. This may be taken as an indication of an increased overall anxiety level in these animals. Moreover, compared to maternally reared animals, animals reared in a standard primate center nursery show reduced reciprocal social behaviors, increased agonistic behavior, and high levels of stereotypy.[26] Wallen has also pointed out that the ability to express species-typical sexual behavior "results from hormonally induced predispositions to engage in specific patterns of juvenile behavior whose expression is shaped by the specific social environment experienced by the developing monkey."[27] Rearing conditions have also been shown to have a profound influence on the development of monoaminergic systems,[28] leading these authors to conclude that primate mothers influence the psychobiological development of central nervous system neurotransmitter systems in their infants. Finally, Coe and colleagues[29] have produced overwhelming evidence that rearing in the absence of the mother severely affects several aspects of cellular immunity. For example, nursery-reared monkeys have significantly lower proportions of CD8 cells and lower natural killer cell activity than mother-reared monkeys. Given these behavioral and physiological alterations due to rearing condition, it is difficult to interpret previous lesion studies with infant monkeys. Are the behavioral alterations due to rearing, to the lesion, or to some complex interaction of the two? To circumvent these interpretive problems, we have developed and implemented strategies to allow the postsurgical return of the infant to its biological mother for rearing. Moreover, all mother-infant pairs engaged in daily three-hour-long "play groups" with other mother-infant pairs and an adult male in order to allow the possibility of experiencing and learning normal conspecific social interactions.

An equally vexing problem relates to the fact that once a lesion is made in a developing brain, the remainder of the brain undergoes a morphological and functional reorganization in an attempt to compensate for the loss. Our lesion procedure is as susceptible to this problem as the earlier destructive lesions. Thus, any loss of function is difficult to ascribe to the lesioned region since other brain regions that may be more important to the function may rely on input from the damaged area. For this reason, a negative result—a function thought to be associated with a brain region that is preserved after lesion—is potentially more instructive about what the lesioned brain area does.

In our population of infant animals who received bilateral lesions of the amygdala, we found that the interactions of the lesioned animals with their mothers was similar to that of control animals. Moreover, like adult animals with bilateral amygdala lesions, they showed little fear of normally fear-provoking objects such as rubber snakes. However, they showed increased fear—as indicated by more fear grimaces, more screams, and less social interactions—in novel dyadic social situations. An intriguing, yet unsolved, puzzle with this finding is the elucidation of which brain region is subserving the social fear since the amygdala was entirely eliminated. More germane to this discussion, however, is the finding that the lesioned animals generated substantial social behavior that could not be distinguished from age-matched controls. The quality and quantity of social interactions of the neonatally lesioned animals in a number of social formats has been investigated. While the amygdala-lesioned animals may demonstrate subtle differences in their social interactions, the inescapable conclusion from observations of these animals is that there are none that are markedly impaired in generating species-typical social behaviors such as grooming, play, and facial expressions (Bauman *et al.*, in preparation). If anything, the data appear to indicate that the animals show increased social interest!

Our conclusion from this series of studies is that the amygdala is not necessary for gaining social knowledge and demonstrating normal social behavior. The ability to perceive and produce typical types of social communication appears to be intact in these animals with neonatal lesions. Their behavior, however, has been substantially altered by the lesions. As in the adults, the main consequence of the lesion appears to be a dysregulation of the fear system. However, the outcome is more complex than in the adult. The infant lesioned animals appear to be less fearful of inanimate objects—even those, like snakes, that normally elicit an innate fear response. In this respect, the infants are similar to the adults. However, unlike the adults, the infants appear to be more fearful in novel social situations. But even this is complex since at one and the same time they appear to show increased social interest (as do the adults), but then increased social fear when a novel conspecific shows interest in them.

The infants with bilateral amygdala lesions are being studied in a variety of social contexts. In one of these studies, we have evaluated whether the lesioned animals demonstrate a normal preference for their biological mother over other females with whom they are familiar (Bauman *et al.*, in press). In this experiment, the infant is released into the same large cage that is used for dyadic social testing with the adults, and the mother and another female are randomly placed in the start boxes located at either end of the enclosure. This experiment is conducted just after the normal weaning of the infant, and the amount of time that the infant spends in proximity to the mother versus the other female is recorded. The behaviors that the infant carries out during the two minutes that it is allowed to explore the cage are also recorded. As expected from the literature,[30] control infants demonstrated a strong preference for their mothers, as did infant animals with lesions of the hippocampus. However, the amygdala-lesioned infants did not demonstrate a preference for proximity to their mothers. This result might make one think that the amygdala infants had failed to form a normal attachment with their mothers. However, all other available information, such as the amount of time that the infants spent in ventral contact both in the home cage and in the social play groups indicated that the amygdala infants spent more time with their mothers. The reason for the amygdala-lesioned animals' behavior became clear when we analyzed what else the animals were doing during the two-minute mother preference test. We found that both the control and hippocampal-lesioned animals were producing large numbers of screams and fear grimaces, indicating that they were stressed by exposure to the novel enclosure. The amygdala-lesioned animals, in contrast, demonstrated significantly fewer screams and other indications of stress. We have concluded, therefore, that both the control and hippocampal-lesioned animals perceived the novel enclosure as a fearful environment and sought the comfort of their mothers through proximity. The amygdala-lesioned animals, in contrast, were much less stressed or fearful of the novel enclosure and therefore were less inclined to seek the comfort of their mothers. Thus, the lesion altered not social affiliation but the perception of a fearful environment.

WHAT ARE THE BEHAVIORAL CONSEQUENCES OF BILATERAL LESIONS OF THE AMYGDALA IN HUMAN SUBJECTS?

It is rare to find a human patient that has a selective and complete bilateral lesion of the amygdaloid complex. There are, however, reports of a few patients that have Urbach-Wiethe syndrome, which is a congenital disorder that can lead to cystic lesions of the temporal lobe. Damasio and colleagues have studied such a patient, S.M., who appears to have rather complete damage bilaterally to the amygdala with relatively little involvement of surrounding structures.[31–33] This woman has been married, is raising a family, and has held various jobs. Despite the complete absence of her amygdala, she would appear to have a remarkably normal daily life. She clearly does not demonstrate significant social pathology. She is impaired, however, in her ability to judge facial emotions. While she can reliably interpret happy faces, she has difficulty in seeing fear in a face. Moreover, she is markedly impaired in attributing "trustworthiness" to an individual on the basis of facial appearance. These findings are consistent with the notion that the amygdala is surveying the environment for danger signals, and in S.M. at least some of these signals are not detected.

CONCLUSIONS

Nonhuman primates with bilateral lesions of the amygdala are capable of species-typical social interactions. This is true regardless of whether the lesions are performed near birth or in the mature animal. These findings would suggest that the amygdala is not an essential component of the neural system that mediates social cognition. These animals do demonstrate, however, abnormal fear responses to environmental stimuli. Most of the altered behavior of these animals can be accounted for by the hypothesis that the amygdala plays a primary role in evaluating the environment for potential dangers. Once detected, the amygdala would play an organizing role in mounting an appropriate response to the danger. While this function would have obvious adaptive significance for the preservation of the organism, dysfunction of the amygdala might contribute to psychopathologies such as anxiety disorders and social phobia.

REFERENCES

1. KLUVER, H. & P.C. BUCY. 1938. An analysis of certain effects of bilateral temporal lobectomy in the rhesus monkey, with special reference to "psychic blindness." J. Psychol. **5:** 33–54.
2. AGGLETON, J.P. & R.E. PASSINGHAM. 1981. Syndrome produced by lesions of the amygdala in monkeys (*Macaca mulatta*). J. Comp. Physiol. Psychol. **95:** 961–977.
3. LEDOUX, J.E. 1995. Emotion: clues from the brain. Annu. Rev. Psychol. **46:** 209–235.
4. DAVIS, M. & P.J. WHALEN. 2001. The amygdala: vigilance and emotion. Mol. Psychiatry **6:** 13–34.
5. KALIN, N.H. 1993. The neurobiology of fear. Sci. Am. **268:** 94–101.
6. KALIN, N.H., S.E. SHELTON, R.J. DAVIDSON & A.E. KELLEY. 2001. The primate amygdala mediates acute fear but not the behavioral and physiological components of anxious temperament. J. Neurosci. **21:** 2067–2074.
7. ROSVOLD, H.E., A.F. MIRSKY & K.H. PRIBRAM. 1954. Influence of amygdalectomy on social behavior in monkeys. J. Comp. Physiol. Psychol. **47:** 173–178.
8. DICKS, D., R.E. MYERS & A. KLING. 1968. Uncus and amygdala lesions: effects on social behavior in the free-ranging rhesus monkey. Science **165:** 69–71.
9. KLING, A., J. LANCASTER & J. BENITONE. 1970. Amygdalectomy in the free-ranging vervet (*Cercopithecus aethiops*). J. Psychiatr. Res. **7:** 191–199.
10. KLING, A. 1972. Effects of amygdalectomy on socio-affective behavior in non-human primates. *In* Neurobiology of the Amygdala. B.E. Eleftheriou, Ed.: 511–536. Plenum. New York.
11. KLING, A.S. & L.A. BROTHERS. 1992. The amygdala and social behavior. *In* The Amygdala: Neurobiological Aspects of Emotion, Memory, and Mental Dysfunction: 353–377. Wiley-Liss. New York.
12. KLING, A. & R. CORNELL. 1971. Amygdalectomy and social behavior in the caged stumped-tailed macaque (*Macaca speciosa*). Folia Primat. **14:** 190–208.
13. BUCKLEY, M.J. & D. GAFFAN. 1997. Impairment of visual object-discrimination learning after perirhinal cortex ablation. Behav. Neurosci. **111:** 467–475.
14. MIYASHITA, Y., M. KAMEYAMA, I. HASEGAWA & T. FUKUSHIMA. 1998. Consolidation of visual associative long-term memory in the temporal cortex of primates. Neurobiol. Learn. Mem. **70:** 197–211.
15. ERICKSON, C.A. & R. DESIMONE. 1999. Responses of macaque perirhinal neurons during and after visual stimulus association learning. J. Neurosci. **19:** 10404–10416.
16. JARRARD, L.E. 2002. Use of excitotoxins to lesion the hippocampus: update. Hippocampus **12:** 405–414.

17. CAPITANIO, J.P., S.P. MENDOZA, N.W. LERCHE & W.A. MASON. 1998. Social stress results in altered glucocorticoid regulation and shorter survival in simian acquired immune deficiency syndrome. Proc. Natl. Acad. Sci. USA **95:** 4714–4719.

18. EMERY, N.J., J.P. CAPITANIO, W.A. MASON, et al. 2001. The effects of bilateral lesions of the amygdala on dyadic social interactions in rhesus monkeys (*Macaca mulatta*). Behav. Neurosci. **115:** 515–544.

19. SQUIRE, L.R., B. KNOWLTON & G. MUSEN. 1993. The structure and organization of memory. Annu. Rev. Psychol. **44:** 453–495.

20. PRATHER, M.D., P. LAVENEX, M.L. MAULDIN-JOURDAIN, et al. 2001. Increased social fear and decreased fear of objects in monkeys with neonatal amygdala lesions. Neuroscience **106:** 653–658.

21. SACKETT, G.P., G.C. RUPPENTHAL & A.E. DAVIS. 2002. Survival, growth, health, and reproduction following nursery rearing compared with mother rearing in pigtailed monkeys (*Macaca nemestrina*). Am. J. Primatol. **56:** 165–183.

22. NOVAK, M.F. & G.P. SACKETT. 1997. Pair-rearing infant monkeys (*Macaca nemestrina*) using a "rotating peer" strategy. Am. J. Primatol. **41:** 141–149.

23. SUOMI, S.J. 1991. Early stress and adult emotional reactivity in rhesus monkeys. Ciba Found. Symp. **156:** 171–183; discussion 183–178.

24. BASTIAN, M.L., A.C. SPONBERG, S.J. SUOMI & J.D. HIGLEY. 2003. Long-term effects of infant rearing condition on the acquisition of dominance rank in juvenile and adult rhesus macaques (*Macaca mulatta*). Dev. Psychobiol. **42:** 44–51.

25. PARR, L.A., J.T. WINSLOW & M. DAVIS. 2002. Rearing experience differentially affects somatic and cardiac startle responses in rhesus monkeys (*Macaca mulatta*). Behav. Neurosci. **116:** 378–386.

26. WINSLOW, J.T., P.L. NOBLE, C.K. LYONS, et al. 2003. Rearing effects on cerebrospinal fluid oxytocin concentration and social buffering in rhesus monkeys. Neuropsychopharmacology **28:** 910–918.

27. WALLEN, K. 1996. Nature needs nurture: the interaction of hormonal and social influences on the development of behavioral sex differences in rhesus monkeys. Horm. Behav. **30:** 364–378.

28. CLARKE, A.S., D.R. HEDEKER, M.H. EBERT, et al. 1996. Rearing experience and biogenic amine activity in infant rhesus monkeys. Biol. Psychiatry **40:** 338–352.

29. LUBACH, G.R., C.L. COE & W.B. ERSHLER. 1995. Effects of early rearing environment on immune responses of infant rhesus monkeys. Brain Behav. Immun. **9:** 31–46.

30. BERMAN, C. 1980. Mother-infant relationships among free-ranging rhesus monkeys on Cayo Santiago: a comparison with captive pairs. Anim. Behav. **28:** 860–873.

31. ADOLPHS, R., D. TRANEL, H. DAMASIO & A.R. DAMASIO. 1995. Fear and the human amygdala. J. Neurosci. **15:** 5879–5891.

32. ADOLPHS, R., D. TRANEL & A.R. DAMASIO. 1998. The human amygdala in social judgment. Nature **393:** 470–474.

33. ADOLPHS, R., D. TRANEL, S. HAMANN, et al. 1999. Recognition of facial emotion in nine individuals with bilateral amygdala damage. Neuropsychologia **37:** 1111–1117.

Blood, Sweat, and Fears

The Autonomic Architecture of Emotion

ROBERT W. LEVENSON

Department of Psychology, University of California, Berkeley,
Berkeley, California 94720-1650, USA

ABSTRACT: The autonomic nervous system (ANS) plays a critical role in emotion, providing metabolic support for adaptive action, generating appearance changes with high signal value for conspecifics, and producing visceral sensations that shape subjective emotional experience. In this chapter, I consider several of the most important ways that the ANS is involved in emotion, including: (a) peripheral activation of emotion; (b) autonomic influences on emotional language and the labeling of subjective emotional experience; (c) positive emotion and autonomic soothing; (d) expressive signs of autonomic origin; (e) autonomic substrates of emotional contagion and empathy; and (f) autonomic consequences of emotion regulation. For each, I describe relevant research from our laboratory and discuss implications for an evolutionary account of emotion. In these and many other ways the autonomic architecture of human emotion has evolved not only to move blood and tears in the service of fears, but also to provide us with a rich set of tools that help us communicate and signal the nature of our internal emotional experiences, understand the emotions of others, calm ourselves and others, and give us some modicum of control over harmful and unproductive emotions.

KEYWORDS: emotion; autonomic nervous system; activation of emotion; deactivation of emotion; suppression of emotion; emotion regulation

The autonomic nervous system (ANS) is the body's most critical life support system, regulating a wide range of cardiovascular, gastrointestinal, electrodermal, respiratory, endocrine, and exocrine organs. The primary regulatory functions of the ANS can be organized broadly into three processes: (a) *maintenance* of an optimal "baseline" bodily milieu (i.e., homeostasis); (b) *activation* of bodily systems to support action in response to challenge and opportunity; and (c) *deactivation* of bodily systems when action is no longer

Address for correspondence: Robert W. Levenson, Institute of Personality and Social Research, 4143 Tolman Hall #5050, University of California, Berkeley, Berkeley, California 94720-5050. Voice: 510-642-5050; fax: 510-643-9334.
boblev@socrates.berkeley.edu

Ann. N.Y. Acad. Sci. 1000: 348–366 (2003). © 2003 New York Academy of Sciences.
doi: 10.1196/annals.1280.016

needed. Emotion and the ANS are intricately intertwined—emotions are a major consumer of autonomic resources, and the ANS provides a key to understanding many of the functions of human emotions. Because integration of emotion and the ANS is so important to our survival and reproduction, refinement of the autonomic architecture of emotion and integration of this architecture with other processing and control systems was undoubtedly an important part of human evolution. Despite enormous differences between contemporary and early evolutionary times, the autonomic architecture of emotion is still a remarkably effective and efficient design, which profoundly influences our day-to-day lives. In this chapter, I will discuss five key features of this architecture:

(1) emotional activation: autonomic reactivity and peripheral activation;
(2) language and labeling of subjective emotional experience: the autonomic element;
(3) positive emotion: autonomic soothing;
(4) autonomic expression: signals from the viscera;
(5) emotional contagion and empathy: the autonomic substrate;
(6) emotion regulation: autonomic consequences.

I will not provide a comprehensive review of each of these topics, but rather will draw primarily on work done by my research group to help illustrate the commingling of emotional and autonomic functioning. In keeping with the theme of this volume, whenever possible I will speculate as to the evolutionary forces that may have shaped these interconnections.

EMOTIONAL ACTIVATION: AUTONOMIC REACTIVITY AND PERIPHERAL ACTIVATION

The ANS prepares the body for dealing with a range of internal and external challenges that require coordinated action. Many of these challenges are such that they require a rapid response (e.g., responding to the appearance of a predator) while others require a more gradual, sustained response (e.g., regulating blood flow to maintain core body temperature). There is often a life-and-death quality to ANS activation—failure to adjust can be fatal.

Autonomic Reactivity

Human emotions evolved to deal with situations of great significance to the individual and group in which a rapid, multisystem response is required. I have described this as follows:

> Emotions are short-lived psychological-physiological phenomena that represent efficient modes of adaptation to changing environmental demands. Psychologically, emotions alter attention, shift certain behaviors upward in response

hierarchies, and activate relevant associative networks in memory. Physiologically, emotions rapidly organize the responses of disparate biological systems including facial expression, somatic muscular tonus, voice tone, autonomic nervous system activity, and endocrine activity to produce a bodily milieu that is optimal for effective response. Emotions serve to establish our position vis-à-vis our environment, pulling us toward certain people, objects, actions and ideas, and pushing us away from others. Emotions also serve as a repository for innate and learned influences, possessing certain invariant features, and others that show considerable variation across individuals, groups, and cultures.[1]

I have written previously about my views on the evolution of emotion activation, referring to this as the "core system" in emotion.[2] This core system is thought to have evolved to solve a set of elemental problems[1,3–5] that are fairly common to all species as they interact with their external environment, with conspecifics, and with members of other species.

> The core system has all of the capabilities necessary for processing incoming information continuously and for detecting a small number of prototypical situations that have profound implications for the organism's immediate well-being and long-term survival. Having recognized in the stream of incoming perceptual information the configuration of features that defines one of a small number of prototypical situations, the core system activates an emotion, which is comprised of a set of response tendencies that have been selected by evolution for their high probability of dealing successfully and efficiently with the problems posed by that particular situation.[2]

For humans, the response package spans a number of different systems including perception/attention,[6] gross motor behavior, purposeful behavior,[7] expressive behavior,[8,9] gating of higher mental processes,[10] and physiological support.[11,12]

Among the physiological systems that are activated by emotion, the ANS is particularly important. The ANS must prepare the body for a set of diverse actions that include (but are not limited to) fighting, fleeing, freezing, comforting, bonding, and expelling, each of which requires somewhat different configurations of physiological support.[13] Like a modern factory that subscribes to the "just in time" model of inventory control, the ANS not only has to deliver sufficient quantities of all of the components needed to craft an appropriate response, but also has to deliver them at precisely the right time, and then quickly remove anything that is unused. This daunting task is made all the more difficult by the fact that emotion-eliciting situations are dynamic rather than static; thus, midcourse adjustments in physiological support are the rule rather than the exception.

Peripheral Activation

In the account of emotional activation presented above, the sequence begins with an external or internal stimulus, progresses through a process of

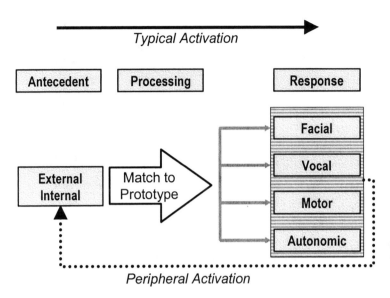

FIGURE 1. Emotional activation sequence begins with an external or internal stimulus, progresses through a process of matching percepts to prototypes, and moves on to the activation of various response systems including the autonomic nervous system; direction of activation is indicated as flowing from left to right.

matching percepts to prototypes, and moves on to the activation of various response systems including the autonomic nervous system. This sequence is depicted in FIGURE 1, with the typical direction of activation indicated as flowing from left to right. However, this is only one of many possible ways that emotion can be activated. In fact, it is becoming increasingly clear that activation can flow from right to left as well, as indicated by the dotted arrow labeled *Peripheral Activation* in the figure. Thus, any of the so-called response systems can become the initiating event for emotional activation. James advanced a particularly cogent version of this notion, stating:

> ...[T]he emotion both begins and ends with what we call its effects or manifestations....[A]ny voluntary arousal of the so-called manifestations of a special emotion ought to give us the emotion itself.[14]

From an evolutionary perspective, if emotion is viewed as highly critical to survival, then an activation system with multiple initiation points would have considerable adaptive advantage.

In a series of studies[15–18] we have used the Directed Facial Action task to examine the capacity of one response system (the face) to initiate the emotion sequence. In this task, subjects are given specific muscle-by-muscle instructions (e.g., "raise your brows," "draw them together," etc.), which, if fol-

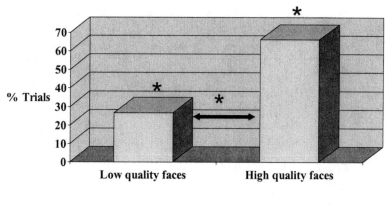

FIGURE 2. Reports of experiencing the emotions displayed on face. The more closely the faces resembled the associated prototypical expression, the greater the likelihood of experiencing the emotion.

lowed correctly, result in the production of a facial configuration that resembles a prototypical emotional expression (anger, disgust, fear, happiness, sadness, or surprise). A "coach," viewing the subject's face on a video monitor, provides coaching as needed to help the subject comply with the instructions (e.g., "raise your brows, but don't bring them together"). Facial configurations are held for 10 seconds, during which time autonomic and somatic nervous system activity is measured. The experimental session is organized into trials, each consisting of a baseline rest period, instructions to produce a nonemotional facial configuration, instructions to produce an emotional facial configuration, and questions concerning thoughts, feelings, and sensations that might have occurred.

The first question to consider is whether these facial actions are sufficient for producing subjective emotional experience. Our findings are shown in FIGURE 2. Subjects reported experiencing the emotion associated with the facial configuration at significantly greater than chance levels (chance was one in six emotions or 16.6%). Importantly, when the configuration most closely matched the prototype, the subject was significantly more likely to report feeling the associated emotion than when the face did not closely match the prototype. In fact, with high-quality faces, subjects reported feeling the associated emotion on over 60% of trials. Those who conduct laboratory studies of emotion will recognize that a 60% hit rate would be very good for any procedure designed to produce particular emotions (e.g., films, slides). This finding[19,20] provides important support for the capacity of the face to initiate subjective emotional experience.

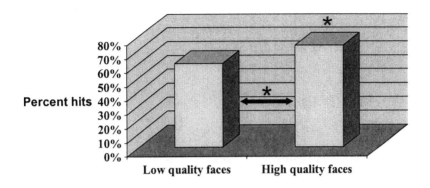

FIGURE 3. The extent to which four common autonomic differences among negative emotions (i.e., faster heart rate in anger versus disgust, fear versus disgust, sadness versus disgust; warmer skin temperature in anger versus fear) are found when emotions are activated using the Directed Facial Action task. As was the case with self-reported emotional experience data described earlier, the more closely faces resembled the associated prototypical expression, the greater the degree of autonomic differentiation among emotions.

Of course, subjective emotional experience is only one part of the picture (a part that is notoriously susceptible to demand characteristics and the like). Does the face have the capacity to activate the autonomic nervous system component as well? Our research[17] suggests that the answer to this question is also yes. FIGURE 3 depicts the findings for the extent to which four common autonomic differences among negative emotions (i.e., faster heart rate in anger versus disgust, fear versus disgust, sadness versus disgust; warmer skin temperature in anger versus fear) are found when emotions are activated using the Directed Facial Action task. As was the case with self-reported emotional experience data described earlier, as faces more closely resembled the associated prototypical expression, the degree of autonomic differentiation among emotions increased. Putting this latter finding in perspective, we found that the degree of autonomic differentiation produced by voluntary facial action was essentially equivalent to that produced by initiating emotion in a more "conventional" way via recalling emotional memories.[21]

These findings that voluntary facial expression can lead to self-reported emotional experience and differentiated autonomic activity provide support for the viability of peripheral activation by the face. We expect that similar activation occurs for involuntary facial expression (e.g., with automatic empathic mimicry of the facial expressions of others). Although it is possible that the face occupies a privileged position among peripheral responses in terms of being able to activate emotion, we think that James[14] is correct and that this capacity is shared with the other peripheral response systems as well.

LANGUAGE AND LABELING OF SUBJECTIVE EMOTIONAL EXPERIENCE: THE AUTONOMIC ELEMENT

We know precious little about subjective emotional experience—what it is and where it comes from. Unlike other emotion response systems (autonomic, motor, vocal, expression), which have been studied in multiple species, subjective emotional experience has been studied almost exclusively in humans. Whether subjective emotional experience exists in other species remains an interesting question (e.g., can dogs feel shame?). Currently, however, human language is the best tool available to us for studying these subjective states. Not surprisingly, the ease of collecting self-report data and their potential richness has made them the most popular measure in research on human emotions. Thus, much of what we know about human emotion rests on a foundation of self-report data. This, however, is clearly a mixed blessing. We know that self-reports of any kind are vulnerable to all sorts of biases (e.g., demand characteristics, social desirability biases). The fragility of emotion self-reports was illustrated quite dramatically four decades ago when Schachter and Singer[22] showed that manipulating the cues in the environment could radically change what participants said they were feeling. Their model of emotion, which underscored the malleability of self-reported subjective experience, is captured in the following quotation:

> ...[G]iven a state of physiological arousal for which an individual has no explanation, he will label this state in terms of the cognitions available to him. ... [B]y manipulating the cognitions,...we can manipulate his feelings in diverse directions.[22]

Schachter and Singer were primarily concerned with understanding the ways that things *outside* of the person influence the labeling of emotional states. Internal sources of emotional experience were seen primarily as sources of "confusion" (i.e., perceptions of unexplained physiological arousal). But we know that it is not *necessary* to observe clowning or threatening others to feel and label emotions such as happiness or anger. Thus, the question remains: What is the stuff of which feelings are made? Based on a number of sources of evidence, it appears that the primary ingredients of our subjective emotional experience are visceral and somatic. In this regard, the phenomenologists' challenge of describing what an emotion "feels" like without reference to bodily changes is instructive. What can we say about the feeling of fear once we eliminate the changes in temperature, tension, breathing, and heart-beating? James illustrates this point very nicely:

> If we fancy some strong emotion, and then try to abstract from our conscious-
> ness of it all the feelings of its characteristic bodily symptoms, we find we have
> nothing left behind...[14]

If our subjective emotional experience is based primarily on our perceptions of autonomic and somatic response systems, then the accuracy of our
self-reports of emotion is going to be linked in part to the accuracy of our visceral perceptions. Research on visceral perceptions clearly indicates that we
are not very accurate at such tasks as tracking our heart beats or estimating our
current autonomic levels.[23,24] But our limited accuracy in these demanding
tasks does not mean that there is no connection between physiological activity
and verbal report. Rather, the very language we use to talk about our emotions
is replete with metaphors that translate the emotional into the physiological.[25]

To evaluate the association between physiology and language, we[26] de-
vised a procedure to assess the connection between autonomic nervous system activity and emotional language. We created verbatim transcripts of 143
unrehearsed 15-minute conversations between spouses about a problem area
in their marriage.[27] These conversations are known to be rich sources of emotion.[16] Working from the transcripts, we located all metaphors that suggested
heat and pressure (e.g., "I'm really burning up," "I'm going to blow my top").
Across the 15-minute conversations, couples used between 0 and 5 of these
metaphors. We correlated the number of metaphors with ANS levels averaged over the 15-minute conversation. Results revealed a striking relationship
between cardiovascular levels and the use of these heat and pressure metaphors: the greater the amount of blood in the fingers, the faster the blood
moved from the heart to the fingers, and the warmer the hand temperature,
the more heat and pressure metaphors the couple used. Thus, there was a clear
association between particular kinds of autonomic (cardiovascular) activity
and the use of metaphors that were suggestive of that activity. Because of the
correlational nature of this study, the direction of causality cannot be determined. Still these findings support the notion that our subjective experience
of emotion (as reflected in the metaphors we use to describe our emotions)
reflects our underlying state of autonomic activation. Similar studies looking
at emotional language in relation to motor, vocal, and facial activity would be
very useful in exploring the breadth and depth of the relationship between the
language of emotion and the internal physiological milieu.

AUTONOMIC EXPRESSION: SIGNALS FROM THE VISCERA

The study of expressive behavior in emotion has focused primarily on the
face and voice. This research has been facilitated greatly by the availability
of tools for precisely quantifying facial expression[28] and for measuring the
acoustic properties of vocalizations.[29] Both of these expressive systems

TABLE 1. Changes in appearance and ANS activity associated with specific emotions

Type	Change	ANS-Mediated Basis	Emotion
Coloration	reddening	vasodilation, increased contractility	anger
	blushing	vasodilation	embarrassment
	blanching	vasoconstriction	fear
Moisture and secretions	sweating, clamminess	sweat glands	fear
	salivating, drooling	salivary glands	disgust
	foaming	salivary glands	anger
	tearing, crying	lacrimal glands	sadness
	lubricating	mucus membranes	sexual arousal
Protrusions	piloerection	muscle fibers at base of hair follicles	fear, anger
	genital erection	vasodilation	sexual arousal
	blood vessels bulging	vasodilation	anger
Appearance of eyes	constriction	pupils	anger
	dilation	pupils	fear
	bulging	eyelid muscles	anger, fear
	drooping lids	eyelid muscles	sexual arousal
	twinkling	lacrimal glands plus contraction of orbicularis oculi	happiness

clearly have high signal value for conspecifics. Although the primary role of the ANS in emotion is usually thought to be providing physiological support for action, many of these autonomic adjustments create appearance changes that have strong signal value. Most prominent are those that produce visible changes in color, moisture, protrusion, and in the appearance of the eyes. In TABLE 1, I have listed some of the these appearance changes along with the likely underlying ANS activity and the emotions they typically signal.

This list, which is intended to be illustrative rather than exhaustive, is indicative of the large number of visible signs of ANS changes in emotion that have developed signal value for conspecifics. To the extent that these visible signs are involuntary and merely reflect the activity of bodily systems, their signal value best fits Darwin's[30] third principal of expression (i.e., direct action of the nervous system). That humans make decisions, plan strategies, and regulate their behavior in response to these signs of underlying autonomic activity in others underscores the utility and value of these signs as indicators of emotional states.

EMOTIONAL CONTAGION AND EMPATHY:
THE AUTONOMIC SUBSTRATE

For social species, there are enormous advantages to having a mechanism by which emotions can be transferred quickly and efficiently across individuals. In humans, emotion contagion serves a number of functions including: (a) alerting, (b) calming, and (c) empathy. In the case of alerting, the emotion induced in an individual who has directly experienced a dangerous situation can be transmitted quickly to others who have not experienced the danger directly. When this works well, the group can be quickly mobilized to attack, defend, or flee. However, if the group response is out of proportion to the original threat, it can lead to inappropriate group behavior such as panic or violence. In the case of calming, signs of positive affect (e.g., smiles, laughter) in the face of potentially dangerous situations can defuse group activation.

Empathic contagion usually operates on a smaller, more intimate scale, with one person coming to know or feel the emotions of another person. Empathy is critical to social bonding and attachment, and, under appropriate conditions, can lead to prosocial, helping behaviors. Because empathy often occurs in dyads, it is quite amenable to laboratory study. For this reason, much of what we know about the role that the ANS plays in emotional contagion comes from studies of empathy. In the typical study, ANS activation in a person who is observing another person's distress is interpreted as indicating that emotion contagion has occurred.[31,32]

In our work on emotional contagion, we have proposed that when the ANS physiology of two people shows "linkage" (i.e., one person's patterns of activation and deactivation across ANS measures mirror those of another person), there is emotional involvement. In our work studying the interactions of married couples, we found that high levels of physiological synchrony between spouses when discussing marital problems were most likely to be found in the most unhappily married couples.[33] We hypothesized that physiological linkage in this instance was an indicator of the high level of contagion and exchange of negative emotions that occur in unhappy marriages. This ebb and flow of negative emotion produces concomitant parallel patterns of ANS activation and deactivation in the spouses.

In later studies, we turned more explicitly to empathic accuracy (i.e., the extent to which one person can know the emotions of another) in strangers. Here we found that higher accuracy in detecting the negative emotions of another person was associated with higher degrees of physiological linkage between the person detecting the emotions and the person whose emotions were being detected.[34] We speculated that this physiological linkage results in part from a process of emotional contagion through which the observers who rate the emotions of others most accurately have emotions that are similar in type and timing to those experienced by the person being observed. A subsequent study suggested that those individuals who are most accurate at rating the emotions of others do in fact show the most facial evidence of emotion.[35] However, questions of whether these signs of emotional contagion are similar in type and timing to those of the person being observed and whether they are the basis of the observed physiological linkage remain untested. In the meantime, the possibility that ANS linkage between individuals is a nonverbal marker of emotional contagion and empathy remains an intriguing possibility that could provide a very useful tool for research in humans and other species.

POSITIVE EMOTION: AUTONOMIC SOOTHING

Evolutionary accounts of emotion often start (and end) with the threat of predators and the survival advantages associated with rapid activation in support of combat or escape. Thus, it is not surprising that "fight" and "flight" have been the dominant metaphors in evolutionary accounts of human emotion. Accordingly, we know a great deal more about the activating aspects of human emotion than we do about its deactivating aspects. This imbalance is quite unfortunate. While human evolution no doubt looked favorably on the ability to activate when danger was present, it also likely favored the ability to calm down when safety was restored. Human emotions are intimately involved in coping with both danger and safety. Analogously, we would expect that emotions would also be involved both in rapidly activating and in rapidly deactivating physiological systems.

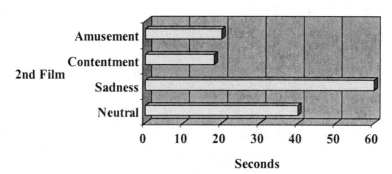

FIGURE 4. Cardiovascular response: time to return to baseline.

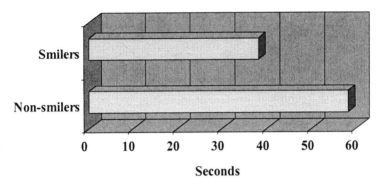

FIGURE 5. Cardiovascular response: time to return to baseline—smilers versus non-smilers.

In thinking about the role that emotions play in efficiently activating physiological systems, "negative" emotions such as fear, anger, and disgust come to mind. These emotions seem to have the capacity to activate physiological systems in ways that provide optimal support for actions such as fleeing, fighting, and expelling.[2,13] In contrast, when considering the role that emotions play in efficiently deactivating physiological systems, "positive" emotions such as amusement, contentment, and happiness come to mind.[36]

To test the role that positive emotions play in deactivating or "undoing" physiological arousal, we[37] conducted two studies, one experimental and one correlational. In the first study, subjects watched a fear-inducing film that was followed immediately by one of four other films (which either induced sadness, amusement, or contentment, or was emotionally neutral). Our dependent measure was the time it took participants to calm down from the cardiovascular arousal caused by the fear-inducing film. The results can be seen in FIGURE 4, which shows that return to the pre-fear film baseline levels was twice as fast when the second film induced positive emotion (either amusement or contentment) as when the second film was emotionally neutral. Moreover, this return to baseline associated with positive emotional films was three times as fast as that associated with a second film that induced a negative emotion (sadness).

In our second study, we explored a situation that we often see in the laboratory and in life—people showing positive affect in situations where we would expect negative emotion. A classic example of this is the laughter that often follows the most shocking moments in a horror film. In accordance with our thinking about positive emotions, these intrusions of positive emotion may be quite functional, taking advantage of their capacity to calm physiology and reduce tension. In our study, we showed participants a very sad film and coded their facial expressions to detect participants who smiled during the film. Dividing the sample into those who smiled and those who did not, we compared the two groups in terms of how long it took for their cardiovascular system to calm down (i.e., return to prefilm baseline levels) once the film had ended. As can be seen in FIGURE 5, those who smiled during the sad film calmed down cardiovascularly almost twice as fast as those who did not smile.

These two studies support the notion that certain positive emotions play an important role in rapidly restoring physiological calm. In these studies, this effect was found for positive emotions such as amusement and contentment and for smiles. I expect that this may hold true for some positive emotions,[38] but not for others (e.g., exhilaration). It is also important to acknowledge that this calming effect is only one of several functions of positive emotions that likely played an important role in their evolution. Positive emotions also are critical in building interpersonal attachments and in shaping and reinforcing the behavior of others. Moreover, they play an important role in creating conditions conducive to expansive thinking and creativity.[39,40]

EMOTION REGULATION: AUTONOMIC CONSEQUENCES

In moments of extraordinary danger where there is scant time for pondering options and planning strategies, we are well served by having a simple emotional system that does a few things exceedingly well, automatically choosing precisely those actions that have the highest likelihood of success, and quickly adjusting bodily systems to create the optimal support for the se-

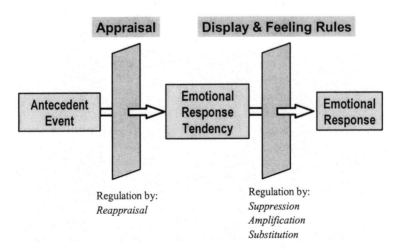

FIGURE 6. Model of emotion and the regulation of emotion. (Reprinted from Levenson[2] with permission.)

lected action.[2] During the human evolutionary period, selection pressures likely worked in favor of this kind of system. As long as our major threats were of the "predators jumping out of trees" variety, this kind of emotion system served us well. In more contemporary times, however, such an automatic system is often not advantageous. Many of the situations that threaten us today are more nuanced, more psychological, and more chronic; and, more often than not, we have to try to deflect our powerful initial emotional tendencies in the service of our own welfare and that of others.

Humans spend a great deal of energy in the service of learning to control their emotions. Training in these skills begins in early childhood; acquired skills are sorely tested by adolescence; and, arguably, we may achieve true expertise in emotion regulation only late in life.[41] Although there are myriad specific strategies for emotional control,[42] most of the time we seem to control our emotions in one of two primary ways: (a) changing the ways we appraise incoming information, and (b) altering the natural transition between *tendencies* to respond in a given way and the *actual* responses we produce. FIGURE 6 portrays a simplified schematic of a model of emotion and emotion regulation that I have presented elsewhere.[2] In this model, the two primary forms of emotional regulation are shown as vertical planes that: (a) early in the process, interrupt the flow between antecedent events and the activation of emotional response tendencies, and (b) later in the process interrupt the flow between emotional response tendencies and the actual emotional response.

Because the ANS response is such an important aspect of "unregulated" emotion, the question is raised as to how various regulation strategies impact this system. In a series of studies, we[43,44] examined the effect of emotional suppression, a variant of the second kind of regulation strategy that involves attempting to reduce the visible signs of emotion. In these studies subjects were shown emotion-eliciting films and asked to "behave so that somebody

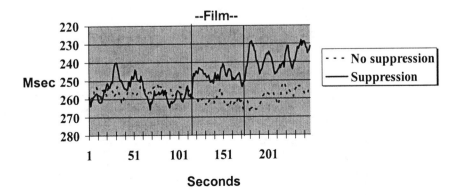

FIGURE 7. Finger pulse transmission time.

watching you would not know that you were feeling anything." We found that for several different emotions participants could dramatically reduce the visible signs of emotion, and that this reduction had little effect on the strength of their self-reported emotional experience. However, this voluntary suppression of emotion produced large increases in the amount of cardiovascular activation compared to controls who merely watched the films. FIGURE 7 illustrates this finding by depicting the aggregated cardiovascular responses of participants who either watched a disgust-eliciting film or watched it and tried to suppress their emotional responses.[43] In this figure, greater cardiovascular activation is indicated by changes in the upward direction. As can readily be seen, the group that suppressed the behavioral signs of emotion had greater cardiovascular activation during the film, and this continued even after the film was over.

We interpreted these cardiovascular changes as indicating that stopping the behavioral manifestations of an emotion once the emotion has been set into motion requires significant levels of effort and this exacts a substantial metabolic cost. But are the costs and benefits of all kinds of emotion regulation the same?

Gross[45] compared the effects of variants of the two primary kinds of emotion regulation when he compared suppression with reappraisal (by asking subjects to "adopt a detached and unemotional attitude ... such ... that you don't feel anything at all"). He found that reappraisal reduces the behavioral manifestations of emotion (but not as completely as suppression did) and reduces the level of subjective emotional experience without exacting the large physiological cost that suppression engenders. FIGURE 8 summarizes the findings from this entire series of studies.

Although reappraisal is not as effective as suppression in eliminating the behavioral signs of emotion, its relatively low metabolic cost underscores its value as a means of controlling emotion. Moreover, reappraisal also has the advantage over suppression in reducing subjective emotional experience

	Face	Subjective experience	Autonomic
Suppression	Large reduction	No change	Large increase
Reappraisal	Reduction	Reduction	No change

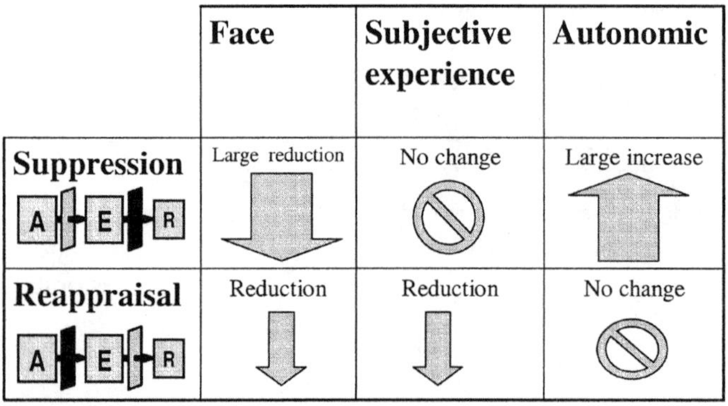

FIGURE 8. Summary of studies of suppression and reappraisal of emotion.

(e.g., when reducing the experience of negative emotions is deemed desirable). Unfortunately, emotion-eliciting events do not always lend themselves to this kind of intervention early in the course of activation—in many situations, the later-acting suppression strategy, with its greater metabolic costs, may be the only option.

THE AUTONOMIC ARCHITECTURE OF EMOTION: FINAL THOUGHTS

In traditional accounts of emotion the ANS does a lot of heavy lifting, creating the physiological milieu necessary to support behavioral action. In this kind of model, if emotion is the stimulus, then ANS activity is the response. In this chapter I have tried to expand this simple model by demonstrating that the role the ANS plays in emotion is far more elaborate and pervasive.

The ANS is intimately involved in our subjective emotional experience, helping us know that we are feeling something, what it is that we are feeling, and how to label the feeling. Growing out of this important contribution to the phenomenology of emotion, autonomic percepts influence the way we describe and talk about our emotions to others. The metaphors we use to enliven and vivify our emotional language are predominately autonomic in origin. In addition to language, we communicate our emotions to others via a universally recognized set of signs and signals. Although facial expressions and vocalizations garner most of the attention in this research area, there is a rich and arguably equally universal set of appearance changes of autonomic origin. These changes give notice to others of what we are feeling in ways that can profoundly influence their actions and feelings.

Continuing in this social/interpersonal vein, emotions are also contagious. We become emotional in the presence of others who are emotional, sometimes as part of group processes of alerting and calming and sometimes in the more intimate realms of interpersonal empathy. In empathy, the ANS plays an important role as a marker of states of shared and interconnected emotion. No doubt this is another area where appearance changes of autonomic origin play an important role in communicating to others that we are feeling things in response to their feelings. Moreover, this autonomic substrate of empathy has the promise of providing us with a nonverbal window onto this elusive phenomenon that could be extremely useful in emotion research.

The ANS is profoundly intertwined in processes of emotional soothing. Certain positive emotions have the capacity to hasten the restoration of ANS equilibrium in the aftermath of ANS activation produced by negative emotions. This kind of tension reduction is enormously reinforcing and no doubt plays an important role in building attachment bonds when relationships are experienced as soothing and emotionally positive.

The ANS provides a way of understanding the impact and costs of the various ways we attempt to regulate our emotions. Strategies that attempt to shut down the behavioral manifestations of emotions after they have gained a full head of steam are very costly in terms of additional ANS activation. In contrast, more preemptive strategies that involve viewing the world in a different, less threatening way may have much the same result without engendering the physiological costs. Historically, emotions have been seen as having profound implications for health and wellness. Although a life replete with chronic, sustained activation of negative emotions will be autonomically costly, it may be even more detrimental to live a life in which negative emotions are chronically suppressed. At the risk of sounding like an evangelist for new-age religion, applying our rational powers in the service of viewing the world in different, less threatening ways; trying to look at things from a broader perspective; considering contextual factors; and being more accepting of the shortcoming of others may have tangible health benefits when they are part of reappraisal strategies of emotion regulation.

In these and many other ways the autonomic architecture of human emotion has evolved not only to move blood and tears in the service of fears, but also to provide us with a rich set of tools that help us communicate and signal the nature of our internal emotional experiences, understand the emotions of others, calm ourselves and others, and give us some modicum of control over harmful and unproductive emotions.

ACKNOWLEDGMENTS

Preparation of this chapter was supported by grants from the National Institute on Aging (AG17766 and AG19724) and the National Institute of Mental Health (MH50841).

REFERENCES

1. LEVENSON, R.W. 1994. Human emotion: a functional view. *In* The Nature of Emotion: Fundamental Questions. P. Ekman & R.J. Davidson, Eds.: 123–126. Oxford. New York.
2. LEVENSON, R.W. 1999. The intrapersonal functions of emotion. Cogn. Emotion **13:** 481–504.
3. EKMAN, P. 1992. An argument for basic emotions. Cogn. Emotion **6:** 169–200.
4. LAZARUS, R.S. 1991. Emotion and Adaptation. Oxford University Press. New York.
5. TOOBY, J. & L. COSMIDES. 1990. The past explains the present: emotional adaptations and the structure of ancestral environments. Ethol. Sociobiol. **11:** 375–424.
6. MATHEWS, A. & B.P. BRADLEY. 1983. Mood and the self-reference bias in recall. Behav. Res. Ther. **21:** 233–239.

7. FRIJDA, N.H. 1986. The Emotions. Cambridge University Press. Cambridge.

8. EKMAN, P. 1984. Expression and the nature of emotion. *In* Approaches to Emotion. K.R. Scherer & P. Ekman, Eds.: 319–343. Erlbaum. Hillsdale, NJ.

9. IZARD, C.E. 1971. The Face of Emotion. Appleton-Century-Crofts. New York.

10. BOWER, G.H. 1981. Mood and memory. Am. Psychol. **36:** 129–148.

11. DAVIDSON, R.J., P. EKMAN, C.D. SARON & J.A. SENULIS. 1990. Approach-withdrawal and cerebral asymmetry: emotional expression and brain physiology I. J. Pers. Soc. Psychol. **58:** 330–341.

12. LEVENSON, R.W. 1992. Autonomic nervous system differences among emotions. Psychol. Sci. **3:** 23–27.

13. LEVENSON, R.W. 2003. Autonomic specificity and emotion. *In* Handbook of Affective Sciences. R.J. Davidson, K.R. Scherer & H.H. Goldsmith, Eds.: 212–224. Oxford University Press. New York.

14. JAMES, W. 1884. What is an emotion? Mind **9:** 188–205.

15. EKMAN, P., R.W. LEVENSON & W.V. FRIESEN. 1983. Autonomic nervous system activity distinguishes among emotions. Science **221:** 1208–1210.

16. CARSTENSEN, L.L., J.M. GOTTMAN & R.W. LEVENSON. 1995. Emotional behavior in long-term marriage. Psychol. Aging **10:** 140–149.

17. LEVENSON, R.W., P. EKMAN & W.V. FRIESEN. 1990. Voluntary facial action generates emotion-specific autonomic nervous system activity. Psychophysiology **27:** 363–384.

18. LEVENSON, R.W., P. EKMAN, K. HEIDER & W.V. FRIESEN. 1992. Emotion and autonomic nervous system activity in the Minangkabau of West Sumatra. J. Pers. Soc. Psychol. **62:** 972–988.

19. DUCLOS, S.E., J.D. LAIRD, E. SCHNEIDER, *et al.* 1989. Emotion-specific effects of facial expressions and postures on emotional experience. J. Pers. Soc. Psychol. **57:** 100–108.

20. LAIRD, J.D. 1974. Self-attribution of emotion: the effects of expressive behavior on the quality of emotional experience. J. Pers. Soc. Psychol. **29:** 475–486.

21. LEVENSON, R.W., L.L. CARSTENSEN, W.V. FRIESEN & P. EKMAN. 1991. Emotion, physiology, and expression in old age. Psychol. Aging **6:** 28–35.

22. SCHACHTER, S. & J.E. SINGER. 1962. Cognitive, social, and physiological determinants of emotional state. Psychol. Rev. **69:** 379–399.

23. KATKIN, E.S., J. BLASCOVICH & S. GOLDBAND. 1981. Empirical assessment of visceral self-perception: individual and sex differences in the acquisition of heart beat discrimination. J. Pers. Soc. Psychol. **40:** 1095–1101.

24. PENNEBAKER, J.W. 1982. The Psychology of Physical Symptoms. Springer-Verlag. New York.

25. LAKOFF, G. 1987. Women, Fire, and Dangerous Things. University of Chicago Press. Chicago.

26. MARCHITELLI, L. & R.W. LEVENSON. 1992. When couples converse: the language and physiology of emotion. Paper presented at the Society for Psychophysiological Research, San Diego, CA.

27. LEVENSON, R.W., L.L. CARSTENSEN & J.M. GOTTMAN. 1994. Influence of age and gender on affect, physiology, and their interrelations: a study of long-term marriages. J. Pers. Soc. Psychol. **67:** 56–68.

28. EKMAN, P. & W.V. FRIESEN. 1978. Facial Action Coding System. Consulting Psychologists Press. Palo Alto, CA.

29. SCHERER, K.R. 1989. Vocal Measurement of Emotion. Academic Press, Inc. San Diego, CA.

30. DARWIN, C. 1872. The Expression of the Emotions in Man and Animals. Murray. London.
31. VAUGHAN, K.B. & J.T. LANZETTA. 1980. Vicarious instigation and conditioning of facial expressive and autonomic responses to a model's expressive display of pain. J. Pers. Soc. Psychol. **38:** 909–923.
32. WIESENFELD, A.R., P.B. WHITMAN & C.Z. MALATESTA. 1984. Individual differences among adult women in sensitivity to infants: evidence in support of an empathy concept. J. Pers. Soc. Psychol. **46:** 118–124.
33. LEVENSON, R.W. & J.M. GOTTMAN. 1983. Marital interaction: physiological linkage and affective exchange. J. Pers. Soc. Psychol. **45:** 587–597.
34. LEVENSON, R.W. & A.M. RUEF. 1992. Empathy: a physiological substrate. J. Pers. Soc. Psychol. **63:** 234–246.
35. SOTO, J., N. POLE, L. MCCARTER & R.W. LEVENSON. 1998. Knowing feelings and feeling feelings: are they connected? Paper presented at the Society for Psychophysiological Research, Denver, CO.
36. LEVENSON, R.W. 1988. Emotion and the autonomic nervous system: a prospectus for research on autonomic specificity. *In* Social Psychophysiology and Emotion: Theory and Clinical Applications. H.L. Wagner, Ed.: 17–42. John Wiley & Sons. Chichester, England.
37. FREDRICKSON, B.L. & R.W. LEVENSON. 1998. Positive emotions speed recovery from the cardiovascular sequelae of negative emotions. Cogn. Emotion **12:** 191–220.
38. KELTNER, D. & J. HAIDT. 2003. Approaching awe, a moral, spiritual, and aesthetic emotion. Cogn. Emotion **17:** 297–314.
39. FREDRICKSON, B.L. 1998. What good are positive emotions? Rev. Gen. Psychol. **2:** 300–319.
40. ISEN, A.M. 1999. Positive Affect. John Wiley. New York.
41. GROSS, J.J. & R.W. LEVENSON. 1997. Hiding feelings: the acute effects of inhibiting negative and positive emotion. J. Abnorm. Psychol. **106:** 95–103.
42. GROSS, J.J. 1998. Antecedent- and response-focused emotion regulation: divergent consequences for experience, expression, and physiology. J. Pers. Soc. Psychol. **74:** 224–237.
43. GROSS, J.J. & R.W. LEVENSON. 1993. Emotional suppression: physiology, self-report, and expressive behavior. J. Pers. Soc. Psychol. **64:** 970–986.
44. GROSS, J.J., L.L. CARSTENSEN, M. PASUPATHI, *et al.* 1997. Emotion and aging: experience, expression, and control. Psychol. Aging **12:** 590–599.
45. GROSS, J.J. 1998. The emerging field of emotion regulation: an integrative review. Rev. Gen. Psychol. **2:** 271–299.

Physiology

Panel Discussion

RICHARD J. DAVIDSON, *Moderator*

QUESTION: I was actually interested in the visual cortex activation that you got for the moms viewing their kids faces. In the negative emotion results, you were talking about the amygdala input to the visual cortex and explaining it that way, but I'm wondering what could lead to that with these positive emotional stimuli?

RICHARD J. DAVIDSON (*University of Wisconisn—Madison, Madison, WI*): Certainly some of the extant data would lead you to propose the same mechanism—that is, that the amygdala is detecting information of salience, particularly critical information of survival value for the organism, and it will then activate other brain regions to alert those systems that additional important incoming information is available. We certainly know from David Amaral's and others' work that the anatomy is such that the amygdala has the connections to recruit those cortical regions; and data suggest that the amygdala is activated not just by negative stimuli, but by positive stimuli as well.

QUESTION: To follow that up with David, in the social interactions your results were focused specifically on fear, and yet we do know that the amygdala can respond to positive affect–inducing events. Would you say that it's positive emotion-eliciting stimuli that are highly salient? Would it be a surprise, which you'd subsequently interpret as positive? Do you have an explanation as to why we can see amygdala activation in response to positive stimuli?

DAVID AMARAL (*University of California–Davis, Davis, CA*): I don't have an explanation for that. There are data that highly positive—for example, erotic—stimuli might activate the amygdala. I think it's an open question at this point; I think more evaluations have to be done. It looks like for our monkeys the predominant response of the amygdala is to noxious or potentially threatening stimuli. For example, in appetitive reward object discrimination, amygdala lesions have no effect whatsoever. So if there is an appetitive component to amygdala function, I think it's a bit more distant or more complex.

Ann. N.Y. Acad. Sci. 1000: 367–374 (2003). © 2003 New York Academy of Sciences.
doi: 10.1196/annals.1280.017

QUESTION: Dr. Amaral, what's your explanation for the fact that the infant monkeys with amygdala lesions showed no fear in groups, but fear in the dyadic testing situation?

AMARAL: I don't have an explanation; I wish I did. Even in that context, while we do see all of the normal species-typical social behaviors, it's not to say that they're interacting exactly the same way as the other two groups. We do see a slight decrease in social interaction—we actually see more time spent on the mother—with the amygdala-lesioned animals. There's something clearly different about these animals from the other animals, and it does affect the quantity, if not quality, of their social interactions. Why they have less fear when they become habituated to the group, I don't know, but that seems to be the observation.

COMMENT: One thing that differs between the dyadic situation and the group situation is that in the group situation they can see other animals interacting with each other, and in the dyadic situation, they can't. That suggests that the experience of watching two individuals interact is important for getting you in the right emotional state, so that you can then interact with others; and it raises the possibility that if you then repeated the snake experiments with the amygdalectomized monkeys and you put them in with two or three other normal animals, all of whom were afraid of the snake, they would quickly learn to be afraid themselves.

ANSWER: That's an interesting experiment; we haven't tried it yet. I think it's possible. But again I'll just remind you that on a daily basis these animals are with their other social cohorts; they're performing essentially normally.

QUESTION: Dr. Levenson, do we have evidence from self-reports within the United States population that we do infer emotions from autonomic physiology? Is that speculation based on the differences that you got?

ROBERT W. LEVENSON (*University of California–Berkeley, Berkeley, CA*): I think the better evidence is from the large international surveys that show that across a range of Western cultures people associate the same set of physical changes with different emotions. That's one line of research. The second relevant line of research is a series of studies that were done in experimental psychophysiology looking at the extent to which people can accurately perceive things like changes in blood pressure. There is also the more casual version of that that Pennebaker did when he was writing his book on physical symptoms or sensations. The message of all of that is people are very interested in their visceral perceptions, and they associate them very clearly with different emotions; but they're not very accurate in making fine judgments. Those are the two things that we know; the rest is all speculation.

QUESTION: Would you expect to find similar patterns in cultures that are more likely to somaticize than not?

ANSWER: That would be a good prediction.

DAVIDSON: Bob, is anyone doing new work with pharmacological blockers to evaluate more experimentally your suggestion that the autonomic feedback is really playing a critical role in the subjective experience? It seems to me that a beautiful way to begin to dissect that is to block that autonomic change. You would certainly have a strong prediction that there should be a corresponding subjective change.

LEVENSON: I'm not aware of anybody who's doing that. It is the obvious study. People have been going the other way, looking at the extent to which the prominence of certain visceral information is associated with the stronger experience of emotion. For example, Katkin's group was looking at a pretty good measure of cardiac contractile force. You probably know that when you become aware of your heart beating, it's really the rate and pressure that you're aware of. We can measure that more directly now. This supports the idea that the stronger, the greater the contractility, everything else held equal, the stronger the report.

DAVIDSON: Although obviously, as you well know, that can all be produced by central changes.

LEVENSON Sure.

DAVIDSON: So it doesn't speak directly to the issue of whether it's the automatic feedback that's driving the subjective experience.

COMMENT: I don't think Bob's taking the position that the only source of subjective experience is feedback from the autonomic nervous system. I'm sure he would agree that there are lots of determinants of expectations, ideas of what social norms are, situations.

AMARAL: In the old Papez circuit, the notion that Papez came up with is that you didn't get conscious appreciation of an emotion until you got up through the anterior cingulate, or anterior thalamus to the cingulate cortex; it was in the cingulate cortex that you were aware of the emotion. You were implying that the decision that an emotion was going to be generated had taken place in the amygdala, although it may not have led to conscious appreciation, and then a whole series of steps took place. Perhaps then there was some pathway where conscious appreciation of emotion was taking place. I wonder how you think about the amygdala in terms of subconscious versus conscious emotion.

DAVIDSON: I think the amygdala can respond and begin to generate autonomic activity prior to any conscious experience of emotion, and I think the conscious experience is probably something that takes place further in the processing stream. I think consciousness is kind of slow and sloppy, so there's a lot of processing that occurs prior to any subjective awareness.

LISA A. PARR (*Emory University, Atlanta, GA*): Since Darwin's third principle deals with direct action of the nervous system and with these physiological changes and feedback that you have all have talked about, I'm just wondering if you can talk about the process of contagion from an evolutionary perspective. It seems to be a really important process whereby animals can unconsciously come to learn about the emotional states of others. Why is this so controversial?

ANSWER: It seems to me there's a lot of value in knowing what conspecifics feel, in being in tune with both their positive and negative feelings. In fact, it's hard to think of a situation in which it wouldn't be enormously helpful for you to have some sense of an emotion that a conspecific is having. Does that have to be conscious? Probably not. So you get into this interesting question of whether or not it's really knowledge about what the other person is feeling. The other person's emotions could become stimuli that could set up either learned or hard-wired responses. I think we're very far away from any critical experiments, certain in humans, that could begin to dissect that.

QUESTION: I think this would probably be a very fruitful way to begin to think about how animals might become emphatic or the evolution of empathy: if you see a stimulus that may produce a hard-wired response and then you become aware of those feelings yourself, the next time you're in that situation you may be more likely to feel that way. Then these stimuli come to have meanings and representations without your actually having to go through the situation or knowing exactly what the consequences are that led up to the event. It seems like a really interesting process. But when you talked about contagion, you said it was somewhat controversial or a little bit dubious that this process actually takes place. Is an autonomic response really necessary for the subjective feeling of emotion?

ANSWER: I think in humans there are other paths to emotional or empathic enlightenment. By one path you can feel what the other person is feeling. I think that's reflected in a kind of autonomic coactivation. By another path we're quite capable of figuring out what another person is feeling; we can be quite analytic. We have a finding from a recently completed dissertation that suggests that in very long–term married couples, husbands over time begin to use a much more cognitive strategy to figure out what their wives are feeling; they don't actually show evidence that they're feeling what their wives are feeling. Their wives continue to have the coactivation pattern.

DAVIDSON: Lots of work has been done on imitation learning of an emotional sort. Learning via observational learning of emotional responses, the situation that Frans mentioned earlier with the snake fear, is a good example of that. There are lots of other examples, both in humans and in an animals of that kind of observational learning. I think one suggestion implied in Bob's work is that some of that learning may be mediated through autonomic reciprocity or coherence, which I think would be very interesting to explore. If you somehow disrupted the autonomic response, you may actually interfere with that kind of emotional, observational learning.

QUESTION: Bob, because of time you really gave very short shrift to your work on empathy, which I think is really fascinating and has so much relevance to our understanding of how people understand each other. I was interested in whether or not you have tested your nonempathic people separately, to verify that they don't do as well as other people on reading either the face or the voice. Also, have you seen whether or not the absence of empathy might possibly be interaction or situation specific—that is, if you present to them a series of people, both males and females in the couples, do they do badly on all of them? In other words, is this really a trait that you were seeing? Last, can we use this as a kind of predictor of who will be good therapists, good interviewers?

LEVENSON: The only thing we really know is that it is trait-like in the sense that it seems to carry over. I think the most we've assessed is four different targets in one person, and it is consistent in that way. We don't know what the consequences of this kind of empathy are.

QUESTION: You were noting that when you assume a certain posture with your face, the emotion tends to follow. I'd like to bring up the converse of that. How about patients with pathological laughter or crying? I have a patient who laughs every time I take his blood pressure. He doesn't just giggle; he laughs a full-throated, full-blown laugh, which makes everyone in the room laugh as well. I ask him, "How are you feeling right now?" He says, "Embarrassed." There's nothing in his autonomic system or physiology that suggests the embarrassed state. He laughs like crazy. How do you describe the mismatch between the physiology going one way and the internal subjective experience going exactly the opposite way?

ANSWER: I suppose the most provocative possibility is that an emotion is designed with redundancies across these different systems—the physiology, the expression, and what not; and when everything is working according to plan and you're seeing an emotion uninhibited, unaffected by the demands of a situation, uninfluenced by pathology, there's a lot of coherence and agreement across these systems. Discoherences reflect an intentional interruption in the flow of emotion, as when you try to cover up what you're feeling. Maybe the essence of emotional pathology is that these disorders—whether they are something as dramatic as pseudobulbar palsy, where you see explosions like you're talking about and they seem to be removed from any contingent stimulating event; or findings like in the schizophrenia literature, where you see patients with blunted facial affect but high levels of internal autonomic response and subjective emotion—are signs that the system has broken down for some reason. What you've described in a patient is a great example of that.

QUESTION: Dr. Levenson, it makes sense that in a more collectivist culture, people would deemphasize their own facial expressions when gauging their emotions. I was wondering if you got cross-cultural differences for disgust. If you did, how you would explain it?

LEVENSON: Yes, in this particular instance where Paul and I did this work together, we had two ways of studying disgust. One was with the facial activation paradigm, and the other was by showing people surgical films. Interestingly enough, we didn't see this dissociation between physiology and self-report for the films. Looking at a surgical procedure produced the same level of report of disgust in this culture as it did in our comparison Western control group. I'm not sure exactly how this is going to play out with your underlying question, but I do think it suggests that the self-reported emotion may be not only culture bound; it may be that within a culture there are situation-related variations. For example, if you see someone in pain undergoing a kind of a gross surgical procedure, whether you say you feel sadness or disgust may be just as cultural bound as whether or not, when your face is looking disgusted but there's no one else in the context, you say that it's disgust. I think there's a real opportunity here for quite situation-specific feeling rules within cultures. This is not a new idea: Hochschild wrote about it a number of years ago, and I think it's pretty well accepted in anthropology and sociology.

QUESTION: As a psychiatrist I was told that two things are actually going on: sympathy, when you have an autonomic response and feel exactly like your patient; and empathy, where you put your yourself in your patient's shoes. Can you please comment on this distinction?

ANSWER: I'm going to take your two and raise you one: I think there are three processes at work here. The first is now called *empathic accuracy*; simply speaking, it's knowing what someone else is feeling. I think it's really useful for therapists to know what their patients are feeling. The second is what we've been talking about: feeling what someone else is feeling. It's debatable whether it's good for nurses, therapists, or even actors to feel what the character is feeling; it depends on what you think. The third thing is being helpful: you know someone's in pain and you're acting in a proactive, helpful way. I think that's probably also pretty useful. Therapists do it, nurses do it. I think the real controversy concerns living somebody else's emotions—whether that does you or the other person any good.

QUESTION: Back in 1993, there was a paper published in the *American Scientist* devoted to defects in the pleasure center using PET scan studies and relating it to things like attention deficit disorder, alcoholic addiction, gambling addiction, and probably drug addiction. One of the questions I have is why they used PET scans when functional MRI's and MRI's were also available and probably in some cases better. Further, with autistic children, the latest controversy is multiple vaccination: how would that affect the amygdala in producing autism?

ANSWER: We're anticipating using PET, we haven't done it yet. We're going to use microPET. The reason we're doing that as opposed to functional imaging is, first, doing functional imaging with a monkey is extremely difficult. There are a couple of places in the world that are trying to do it. It takes a specialized fMRI that has a vertical board, because the animals don't like to lie on their backs. What we're really looking for is the integrated brain activity that takes place while the animal is engaging in a social interaction, so obviously the animal has to be behaving while you're imaging their brain. To do that, you can use PET because you can inject the glucose tracer into the animal before it actually engages in the behavior. Those brain areas that are activated take more of this tracer. You can image that 20 or 30 minutes later, after the animal has been finished the behavior. It really is the only technique for evaluating the functional activation of the monkeys brain when you have them running around doing something. The beauty of microPET is that the resolution is about 1–2 mm. We'll be doing those studies next year.

I'm intrigued by all of the potential causes for autism, and parents are very concerned about the possibility that combined vaccines might be causing autism. My institute has some studies ongoing to see whether there is a link between vaccinations and autism. Interestingly, there was a paper published just last week in the *New England Journal of Medicine* from a longitudinal study done in Denmark, where, as I understand, the medical records of the whole population are much better. There's a large database of all the citizenry. The bottom line is that they looked at kids over the last 20 years who have and have not received the measles, mumps, and rubella combined vaccine. They found that if you received the vaccine, the risk for autism actually was slightly lower than if you didn't. So essentially they found no relationship between the vaccine and autism. Now, of course, there are other vaccines; other research groups are examining these. We don't have a leading hypothesis at the moment. While it's a genetic disorder in part, there's concern that it's a matter of both genetics and some other factor, such as environmental contamination. The number of kids with autism is, I think it's clear, going up. The strategy at my institute is still to cast a pretty broad net on trying to find causes. From this study in Denmark and a couple of others, it's looking like the MMR vaccine cannot be the strongest candidate. It's still conceivable that a subset of kids with autism that has so-called regressive autism might actually have some link to MMR, but I think the evidence at the moment is against a strong link between MMR and autism.

QUESTION: I'm interested in the contagion of emotion between mothers and infants. I don't think anyone has come up with emotional mirror neurons yet, but I was wondering if you, for instance, trained a mother to be afraid of a sound and then played the sound to her infant, would the infant's brain have a contagion of activation along with the mother? Has that been studied?

ANSWER: There has been precious little work that I'm aware of where both the mother and the infant had been recorded simultaneously in interaction. There are pragmatic constraints against doing that, although it's certainly not impossible. But behavioral data is available that suggests that the kind of emotional contagion you're suggesting can occur. I think it's the principal vehicle through which affective skills can be conveyed during sensitive periods of development; and we know from research at the animal level that environmental input during these sensitive periods can set up brain systems in ways that are quite enduring and, in certain cases, persist for life. At the animal level, there is evidence to suggest that these kinds of environmental inputs can actually change gene expression in systems that we've talked about. So I think that it's a wide open area; there's just very little research at the human level that has specifically addressed this issue with regard to neural systems.

Varieties of Emotional Experience during Voluntary Emotional Facial Expressions

JAMES A. COAN AND JOHN J. B. ALLEN

Department of Psychology, University of Arizona,
Tucson, Arizona 85721-0068, USA

KEYWORDS: EEG asymmetry; emotional experience; facial expression

Emotion theorists have argued that emotions are patterns of responses that imply coherence between behavioral, physiological, and phenomenological systems,[1] including coherence between physiology and emotional expression[2] and the modulation of emotional expression and subjective experience by trait physiological dispositions.[3] A physiological measure sensitive to emotion—frontal EEG asymmetry—has been hypothesized to reflect approach and withdrawal propensities,[4] with relatively greater left frontal activity indexing a propensity for approach-related behavior, and relatively less left frontal activity indexing a propensity for withdrawal-related behavior. By this scheme, disgust, fear, and sadness—all thought to be withdrawal-related emotions—should show relatively less left frontal activity; while the putative approach-related emotions of anger and joy should show relatively greater left frontal activity.[5]

Using voluntary posed emotional facial expressions depicting anger, disgust, fear, joy and sadness, this study examined: (1) the coherence between physiological change and subjective reports of emotional experience, and (2) the modulation of subjective reports of emotional experience by resting physiology. The modulation hypothesis states that individuals with relatively greater left frontal activity at rest will be more likely to report approach emotions during this task and less likely to report withdrawal emotions during this task. This hypothesis states that trait levels of CNS activity will be related to

Present address and address for correspondence: James A. Coan, W.M. Keck Center for Functional Brain Imaging and Behavior, Waisman Center, University of Wisconsin, Madison, WI 53705. Voice: 608-265-6602.

jacoan@wisc.edu

John J.B. Allen, Department of Psychology, University of Arizona, Tucson, AZ 85721-0068. Voice: 520-621-4992; fax: 520-621-9306.

jallen@u.arizona.edu

Ann. N.Y. Acad. Sci. 1000: 375–379 (2003). © 2003 New York Academy of Sciences.
doi: 10.1196/annals.1280.034

state changes in emotional experience. The coherence hypothesis states that individuals who are more left frontally active during anger and joy should be more likely to report those emotions, while individuals who are more right frontally active during disgust, fear, and sadness will be more likely to experience those emotions. According to this hypothesis, state levels of CNS activity will be related to state levels of emotional experience. Individual differences in reported dimensions of emotional experience were also examined.

METHOD

Eight minutes of resting EEG was recorded from 30 participants prior to the state emotion task. EEG was additionally recorded while 31 participants performed voluntary facial expressions in a directed facial action (DFA) task: anger (4+5+7+23/24), disgust (9+15), fear (1+2+4+5+15+20), joy (6+12+25) and sadness (1+6+15+17). Faces were held for two one-minute segments. Particular facial movements are here noted using the Facial Action Coding System.[6] EEG alpha asymmetry was calculated using ln(right)–ln(left) alpha (8–13 Hz) at homologous sites, with higher scores indicating greater relative left activity.

Immediately following each two-minute facial expression sequence, participants were asked: (1) While making that face, did you experience any thoughts? (2) While making that face, did you experience any emotions? (3) While making that face, did you experience any sensations? (4) While making that face, did you feel like taking any kind of action, like doing anything? Participants were then asked to rate the intensity of their reported experiences on a scale from 1 (very slight experience) to 7 (extremely intense experience).

RESULTS

Resting EEG Asymmetry and Emotional Experience

Relatively greater left frontal activity at rest predicted an increased likelihood of reporting an experience of anger, joy, disgust, and the average of all five emotions (trait EEG asymmetry by emotion interaction, $F[4,865] = 3.53$, $P < 0.01$), independently of reference scheme (average and linked mastoid) or specific frontal region (F7/8, F3/4, and FTC1/2). Similarly, trait frontal EEG asymmetry differentially predicted emotional intensity ratings (interaction $F[4,865] = 2.38$, $P = 0.05$) as depicted panel A of FIGURE 1, again independently of reference scheme (average and linked mastoid) or specific frontal region (F7/8, F3/4 and FTC1/2).

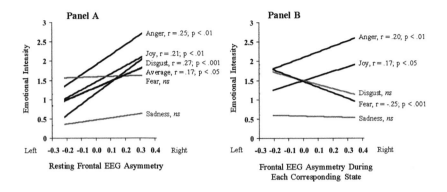

FIGURE 1. Regression lines depicting the relationship between frontal EEG asymmetry and emotional intensity ratings recorded following emotional facial expressions. **Panel A** depicts this relationship for resting frontal EEG asymmetry. **Panel B** depicts this relationship for concomitant-state frontal EEG asymmetry.

State EEG Asymmetry and Emotional Experience

Anger and, marginally, joy were more likely to be reported if their concomitant-state EEG asymmetries involved greater left activity; and fear was more likely to be reported if its concomitant-state EEG asymmetry involved greater right activity (state EEG asymmetry by emotion interaction, $F[4,895] = 8.17$, $P < 0.001$), with results independent of reference scheme or specific frontal region. Similarly, state EEG predicted intensity of subjective emotional experience (interaction $F[4,895] = 6.30$, $P < 0.001$), independent of reference scheme or specific frontal region. As depicted in panel B of FIGURE 1, anger and joy were more intense if their concomitant-state EEG asymmetries involved greater left activity, and fear was more intense if its concomitant-state EEG asymmetry involved greater right activity.

Individual Differences

Bodily sensations played a more prominent role in the experience of fear than in other emotions (emotion by dimension interaction, $\varepsilon = .67$; $F(12,396) = 2.51$, $P < 0.05$, followed up with simple effects). Anger was more likely to be labeled as a specific emotion than disgust ($P < 0.01$), fear ($P < 0.001$), sadness ($P < 0.01$) and, marginally, joy ($P < 0.10$).

Individuals who were high in trait behavioral activation[7] were more likely to report experiencing emotion in terms of action tendencies ($r = .36$; $P < 0.05$), but not other dimensions. Individuals who were high in trait-negative affectivity[8] were more likely to experience emotion in terms of bodily sensations ($r = .32$; $P < 0.07$) and assigned greater intensity ratings to their experiences of fear ($r = .39$; $P < 0.05$) and bodily sensations ($r = .49$; $P < 0.01$).

DISCUSSION

The Modulation Hypothesis

While a form of the modulation hypothesis was clearly supported, results only partially supported the predictions of the approach/withdrawal model of motivation and emotion. Trait-relative left-frontal EEG activity predicted an increased likelihood of any emotional experience, and increased intensity in anger, disgust, and joy. Although consistent with the model's predictions for anger and joy, the approach/withdrawal model would predict that disgust, fear, and sadness should have shown the opposite relationship.

The Coherence Hypothesis

Relatively greater state left frontal EEG activity corresponded with a greater likelihood of reporting approach (anger and joy) emotions, and greater emotional intensity associated with those emotions. Relatively greater state right activity during fear, a withdrawal emotion, corresponded with a greater likelihood of reporting fear experiences, as well as with higher reports of emotional intensity associated with fear. While the same was not true of disgust and sadness, it is striking that both of these withdrawal emotions were correlated with experience and intensity reports in the expected direction. Thus, the evidence for coherence is generally consistent with the approach/withdrawal model of frontal EEG asymmetry and emotion.

Individual Differences

Dimensions of experience (i.e., thoughts, action tendencies, bodily sensations, and emotion-labeling behaviors) vary as a function of specific emotions and individual differences. Fear was more likely than any other emotion except for anger to be experienced normatively in terms of bodily sensations. Individuals high in trait-negative affectivity were more likely to report fear, and reported their experiences of bodily sensations to be more intense, regardless of specific emotion—findings that hold implications for links between emotion and perceptions of physical sensations in mental and physical illness. Finally, those reporting the highest behavioral activation tended to experience all emotions in terms of action tendencies, suggesting they may be most likely to find emotions as motivations to action.

REFERENCES

1. ROSENBERG, E. & P. EKMAN. 1994. Coherence between expressive and experiential systems in emotion. Cognit. Emotion **8:** 201–229.
2. EKMAN, P., R.J. DAVIDSON, & W.V. FRIESEN. 1990. The Duchenne smile: emotional expression and brain physiology II. J. Pers. Soc. Psychol. **58:** 342–353.
3. WHEELER, R.E., R.J. DAVIDSON & A.J. TOMARKEN. 1993. Frontal brain asymmetry and emotional reactivity: a biological substrate of affective style. Psychophysiology **30:** 82–89.
4. DAVIDSON, R.J. 1998. Affective style and affective disorders: perspectives from affective neuroscience. Cognit. Emotion **12:** 307–330.
5. COAN, J.A., J J.B. ALLEN & E. HARMON-JONES. 2001. Voluntary facial expression and hemispheric asymmetry over the frontal cortex. Psychophysiology **38:** 912–925.
6. EKMAN, P. & W.V. FRIESEN. 1978. The Facial Action Coding System. Consulting Psychological Press. Palo Alto, CA.
7. CARVER, C.S. & T.L. WHITE. 1994. Behavioral inhibition, behavioral activation, and affective responses to impending reward and punishment: the BIS/BAS scales. J. Pers. Soc. Psychol. **67:** 319–333.
8. WATSON, D., L.A. CLARK & A. TELLEGEN. 1988. Development and validation of brief measures of positive and negative affect: the PANAS scales. J. Pers. Soc. Psychol. **54:** 1063–1070.

Disgusting Smells Activate Human Anterior Insula and Ventral Striatum

MAIKE HEINING,[a,b] ANDREW W. YOUNG,[c] GLAVKOS IOANNOU,[a]
CHRIS M. ANDREW,[d] MICHAEL J. BRAMMER,[e]
JEFFREY A. GRAY,[a] AND MARY L. PHILLIPS[b]

[a]Department of Psychology, Institute of Psychiatry, Kings College London, London, UK

[b]Section of Neuroscience and Emotion, Division of Psychological Medicine, Institute of Psychiatry and GKT School of Medicine, London, UK

[c]Department of Psychology, University of York, York, UK

[d]Neuroimaging Research Group, Department of Neurology, Institute of Psychiatry, Kings College London, London, UK

[e]Brain Image Analysis Unit, Department of Biostatistics & Computing, Institute of Psychiatry, Kings College London, London, UK

KEYWORDS: Huntington's disease; disgusting smells; anterior insula; ventral striatum

INTRODUCTION

Patients with Huntington's disease, who initially develop lesions in the striatum,[1,2] and a patient with a lesion of the left insula and striatum[3] are impaired in the perception of facial expressions of disgust. Thus these brain structures may be important for the perception of disgust. Several neuroimaging studies have demonstrated activation of the anterior insula and the ventral striatum in response to facial expressions of disgust, supporting this hypothesis.[4] The anterior insula is also involved in gustation and olfaction.[5] Thus it is unclear whether this region is concerned with all smells or whether it includes a region more specifically involved in the analysis of disgusting tastes or odors. To examine this issue we used functional magnetic resonance imaging (fMRI) to determine brain activity during the presentation of (1) disgusting, (2) pleasant, and (3) unpleasant (not disgusting) odors, each compared to fresh air.

Address for correspondence: Maike Heining, P069, Section of Neuroscience & Emotion, Division of Psychological Medicine, Institute of Psychiatry, DeCrespigny Park, London SE5 8AF UK. Voice: +44 20 7848 0365; cell phone: +44 7718 257907; fax: +44 20 7848 0379.
M.Heining@iop.kcl.ac.uk

Ann. N.Y. Acad. Sci. 1000: 380–384 (2003). © 2003 New York Academy of Sciences.
doi: 10.1196/annals.1280.035

METHODS

Two groups of eight healthy volunteers (male, right-handed, nonsmoking) each participated in two 5-min experiments during which they were exposed to disgusting (D) odors and, in addition, to either pleasant (P; group 1) or unpleasant but not disgusting (U; group 2) odors. Fresh air served as a neutral control stimulus. All participants performed normally on the UPSIT[6] and gave informed written consent. Subjects rated the stimuli used during fMRI several days before their arranged scan time to verify appropriate hedonic responses to D, P, and U stimuli. The stimuli used were banana (P), vanilla (P), AR300 (acrid rubbish) (D), SK200 (animal feces) (D), CV900 (cat urine) (U), IBQ (musty) (U) (all supplied by Caravansons, Ltd.). During fMRI the 5-min experiments each consisted of blocks of 30-s ON (odors) and 30-s OFF (fresh air). Two different odors of the same category (D, P, or U) were alternated in each ON phase to prevent habituation. Odors were delivered to a facemask at 1 L per min and extracted by vacuum pump to avoid mingling of odors in the facemask. Subjects kept their eyes closed and breathed normally.

Image Acquisition

In each of 14 near-axial planes (7 mm thick, 0.7-mm gap, in-plane resolution 3 mm) T2*-weighted MR images (TE = 40 ms, TR = 3000 ms, theta = 90°, 100 images/slice) depicting BOLD[7] contrast were acquired over 5 min per experiment on a GE Signa 1.5T Neurovascular system. In the same session, a 43-slice, high-resolution inversion recovery echoplanar image of the whole brain was acquired in the AC-PC plane.

Image Analysis

The data were analyzed using Generic Brain Activation Mapping.[8,9] As we wished to compare directly the intensity of activation in response to D, P, and U odors we chose several clusters of activation within the bilateral insula and ventral striatum. The power of functional response was averaged over each cluster. Statistical comparisons of intensity of activation in each cluster were made for the two experimental conditions (D vs. P and D vs. U) by matched-pairs *t*-tests.

RESULTS

Generic brain activation was demonstrated in the left anterior insula in response to all odors contrasted with air, but in the right anterior insula only in response to disgusting odors (FIG. 1). In group 2, additional activation was demonstrated within the right ventral striatum in response to disgusting odors. In group 1, the comparison of a measure of the mean intensity of activation within the anterior insula and ventral striatum across conditions revealed a significant difference in response to disgusting compared with pleasant odors in the right anterior insula (x = 42, y = 20, z = -2,) at $P = 0.05$. No difference in activation was found in the left anterior insula (x = −31, y =

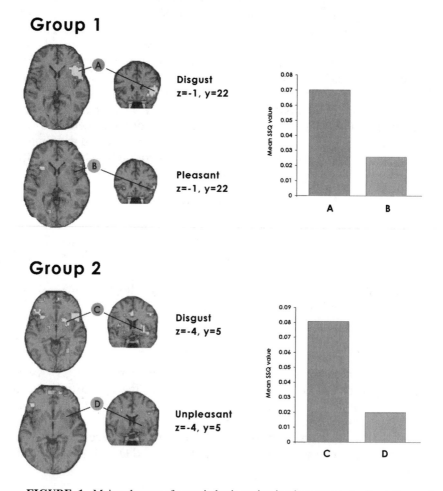

FIGURE 1. Major clusters of generic brain activation in response to disgusting and pleasant (Group 1), and disgusting and unpleasant but not disgusting (Group 2) odors compared with air are demonstrated in axial and coronal brain slices. In group 1, the magnitude of functional response in a cluster within the right anterior insula (x = 42, y = 20, z = −2) was significantly greater ($P = 0.05$) in response to disgusting odors (cluster A) than to pleasant odors (cluster B). In group 2, the magnitude of functional response in a cluster within the right ventral striatum (x = 22, y = 10, z = −7) was significantly greater ($P = 0.01$) (cluster C) in response to disgusting odors than to unpleasant odors (cluster D).

25, z = 4). In group 2, there was a significant difference in BOLD signal change in response to disgusting compared with unpleasant odors in the right ventral striatum (x = 22, y v 10, z = −7) at $P = 0.01$. No statistically significant difference in activation was found in the (a) right or (b) left anterior insula [(a) x = 35, y = 18, z = −2, (b) x = −36, y = 16, z = 4].

DISCUSSION

Disgust is believed to have evolved to provide protection from the risk of contamination and disease. The characteristic facial expression of disgust involves muscles necessary for the avoidance of ingestion of contaminants.[10,11] A close link between systems specialized to react to harmful odors, whether detected directly by the individual or indirectly by way of conspecific facial expression, is likely to have aided survival. Based on the results of previous studies of neural responses to facial expressions of disgust,[4,12] we hypothesized that the anterior insula might be activated by disgusting odors to a significantly greater extent than by pleasant or unpleasant odors. Our results are consistent with this suggestion, but involve unexpected hemispheric lateralization: we demonstrated a significant increase in *right* anterior insula and ventral striatal activation in response to disgusting odors. Left-sided anterior insula activation was demonstrated in response to all odors regardless of valence, reflecting the role of the insula in olfactory perception *per se*.[13]

Our findings demonstrate a specific role of the anterior insula and ventral striatum in the response to disgusting stimuli presented in the olfactory modality. Given previous findings highlighting the importance of these regions in the response also to visual displays of disgust, we propose that the anterior insula and ventral striatum are key components in a system mediating the response to disgusting stimuli irrespective of sensory modality.

REFERENCES

1. GRAY, J.M., *et al.* 1997. Impaired recognition of disgust in Huntington's disease gene carriers. Brain **120:** 2029–2038.
2. SPRENGELMEYER, R., *et al.* 1996. Loss of disgust. Perception of faces and emotions in Huntington's disease. Brain **119:** 1647–1665.
3. CALDER, A.J., *et al.* 2000. Impaired recognition and experience of disgust following brain injury. Nat. Neurosci. **3:** 1077–1078.
4. CALDER, A.J., A.D. LAWRENCE & A.W. YOUNG. 2001. Neuropsychology of fear and loathing. Nat. Rev. Neurosci. **2:** 352–363.
5. SMALL, D.M., *et al.* 1997. Flavor processing: more than the sum of its parts. NeuroReport **8:** 3913-3917.

6. DOTY, R.L., P. SHAMAN & M. DANN. 1984. Development of the University of Pennsylvania Smell Identification Test: a standardized microencapsulated test of olfactory function. Physiol. Behav. **32:** 489-502.

7. OGAWA, S., T.M. LEE & B. BARRERE. 1993. The sensitivity of magnetic resonance image signals of a rat brain to changes in the cerebral venous blood oxygenation. Magn. Reson. Med. **29:** 205–210.

8. BRAMMER, M.J., *et al.* 1997. Generic brain activation mapping in functional magnetic resonance imaging: a nonparametric approach. Magn. Reson. Imaging **15:** 763–770.

9. BULLMORE, E.T., *et al.* 2001. Colored noise and computational inference in neurophysiological (fMRI) time series analysis: resampling methods in time and wavelet domains. Hum. Brain Mapp. **12:** 61–78.

10. DARWIN, C. [1872] 1998. The Expression of the Emotions in Man and Animals. P. Ekman, Ed. Harper Collins. London. [US edit.: Oxford University Press. New York.]

11. ROZIN, P., L. LOWERY & R. EBERT. 1994. Varieties of disgust faces and the structure of disgust. J. Pers. Soc. Psychol. **66:** 870-881.

12. PHILLIPS, M.L., *et al.* 1997. A specific neural substrate for perceiving facial expressions of disgust. Nature **389:** 495-498.

13. ZALD, D.H. & J.V. PARDO. 2000. Functional neuroimaging of the olfactory system in humans. Int. J. Psychophysiol. **36:** 165–181.

Damage to the Right Hippocampal-Amygdala Formation during Early Infancy and Recognition of Fearful Faces

Neuropsychological and fMRI Evidence in Subjects with Temporal Lobe Epilepsy

STEFANO MELETTI,[a] FRANCESCA BENUZZI,[b] PAOLO NICHELLI,[b] AND CARLO ALBERTO TASSINARI[a]

[a] Division of Neurology, Department of Neurosciences, Bellaria Hospital, University of Bologna, Bologna, Italy

[b] Department of Neurosciences, University of Modena and Reggio Emilia, Modena, Italy

KEYWORDS: amygdala; fear; temporal lobe epilepsy; early damage

In the human the processing of facial expressions relies upon a distributed neural network involving the amygdala and strictly connected subcortical and cortical regions, especially the superior temporal sulcus and the orbitofrontal and right frontoparietal cortices.[1–3] Human subjects with bilateral amygdala damage typically fail in recognizing facial expressions and especially fear.[4] Emotional processing, and particularly the recognition of facial expressions of emotions, has not been investigated after unilateral medial temporal lobe damage occurring in childhood. To address this issue we studied the recognition of emotional facial expressions in temporal lobe epilepsy (TLE) subjects. TLE is often associated with childhood febrile convulsions followed by drug-resistant seizures during adolescence, and the amygdala complex may be damaged unilaterally in children and adults with TLE.[5] Recent studies have hypothesized that hippocampal-amygdala atrophy (HAA) might be caused by progressive seizure-induced damage to the medial temporal lobe structures.[6,7] We evaluated patients with symptomatic TLE ($n = 63$; 25 men, 38 women; mean age 35.9 years) and extra-TLE ($n = 33$;

Address for correspondence: Stefano Meletti, Division of Neurology, Bellaria Hospital, University of Bologna, Via Altura no. 2, Bologna 40139, Italy. Voice: 039 051 6225369.
stefano.meletti@neuro.unibo.it

Ann. N.Y. Acad. Sci. 1000: 385–388 (2003). © 2003 New York Academy of Sciences.
doi: 10.1196/annals.1280.036

15 men, 18 women; mean age 33.5 years), comparing their performances with age-matched controls ($n = 50$; 18 men, 32 women; mean age 34 years). Emotion recognition (ER) was examined with a task that required matching a facial expression (photographs from the Ekman & Friesen series[8]) with the name of one of the following basic emotions: happiness, sadness, fear, disgust, and anger. ER was impaired (correct ER < 2SD from controls' mean) in 19 TLE patients: right-sided HAA was evident in 15 subjects; right-sided temporo-polar atrophy was present in four. No patient with left-sided HAA was impaired (0 out of 16). Extra-TLE patients performed as controls. We therefore examined ER in right TLE ($n = 32$) as a function of the age at first seizure (febrile or afebrile). A positive correlation was present (Spearman r = 0.64, $P < 0.01$), indicating that earlier-onset seizures lead to worse recognition. To assess if the recognition of facial expressions was disproportionally impaired for one basic emotional category, patients with right TLE were grouped as follows: early-onset seizures (EOS) and late-onset seizures (LOS) according to the age at the first seizure, setting five years as the critical age. Results showed that right-sided TLE with EOS were selectively impaired in fear recognition (50.5%) with respect to right-sided TLE with LOS (89.0%; Mann-Whitney U test, U = 65; $P < 0.001$) (FIG. 1). Right-sided TLE with EOS were also impaired in the recognition of sadness (72%) and disgust (72%) with respect to controls ($P < 0.01$). On the contrary, right TLE

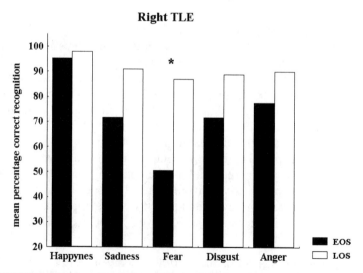

FIGURE 1. Correct recognition of basic facial emotional expressions in epileptic patients with right TLE and early-onset seizures (EOS) versus epileptic patients with right TLE and late-onset seizures (LOS). *$P < 0.001$.

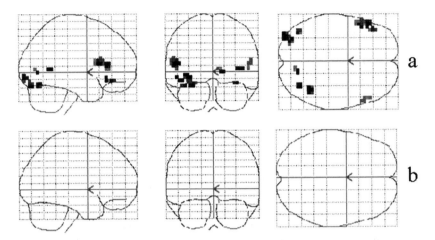

FIGURE 2. Activated regions for fearful compared to neutral facial expressions are shown in glassbrain projections. The statistical threshold is set at $P < 0.001$ (uncorrected) for the maximum pixel and at least four contiguous voxels. (**a**) In controls and late-onset TLE subjects the presentation of fearful expressions evoked activation in the inferior frontal cortex and in the occipito-temporal structures of both sides. (**b**) No activation cluster was found in subjects with right early-onset TLE.

subjects with LOS and controls did not differ in the recognition of any emotional category.

Based on the neuropsychological findings a functional magnetic resonance imaging (fMRI) study was performed to compare the neural network engaged in processing fearful faces in patients with early-onset right medial TLE ($n = 4$), late-onset medial TLE (3 right, 5 left), and control subjects ($n = 14$). A three-condition blocked design was used: presentation of fearful and neutral faces, in which the subjects had to make a gender decision task. In the third condition (control), scrambled faces were used, and the subjects were asked to detect a white square in the center of the picture. Data were acquired using a GE Signa HHS77 system at 1.5 Tesla (TR = 3380 ms; TE = 40 ms) across 16 axial 5-mm slices (64×64 matrix) and analyzed using SPM99. In controls and in patients with late-onset right and left TLE the presentation of fearful compared to neutral expressions evoked activations in the inferior frontal cortex and in the occipito-temporal cortex bilaterally (FIG.2a). On the contrary, in patients with right early-onset TLE no single brain area of activation for processing fearful expressions was found (FIG.2b).

Our study demonstrates that, in subjects with epilepsy, early-onset right-sided medial temporal lobe damage can lead to a selective impairment in the explicit recognition of negative facial expressions, and maximally of fearful ones. This behavioral impairment is functionally mirrored by the lack of a distinctive neural network underlying the processing of fearful facial expressions. Several studies conducted on human subjects showed the presence of a crucial period for the development of emotion-recognition ability between the fifth and the seventh year of age.[9] It has been proposed that the amygdala is part of a system that has evolved for rapid detection of threatening stimuli and social signals such as facial expressions.[10] Our data suggest that integrity of the right amygdala and related limbic structures during early infancy are essential for the processing and appropriate interpretation of social signals conveyed by negative facial expressions later in life.

REFERENCES

1. ADOLPHS, R. 2002. Neural systems for recognizing emotions. Curr. Opinion Neurobiol. **12:** 169–177.
2. MORRIS, J.S., *et al.* 1998. A neuromodulatory role for the human amygdala in processing emotional facial expressions. Brain **121:** 47–57.
3. IIDAKA, T., *et al.* 2001. Neural interaction of the amygdala with the prefrontal and temporal cortices in the processing of facial expressions as revealed by fMRI. J. Cogn. Neurosci. **13:** 1035–1047.
4. ADOLPHS, R., *et al.* 1994. Impaired recognition of emotion in facial expression following bilateral damage of the human amygdala. Nature **372:** 669–672.
5. GLOOR, P. 1992. Role of the amygdala in temporal lobe epilepsy. *In* The Amygdala. Neurobiological Aspects of Emotion, Memory, and Mental Dysfunction. J. Aggleton, Ed.: 507–538. Wyley and Liss. New York.
6. TASCH, E., *et al.* 1999. Neuroimaging evidence of progressive neuronal loss and dysfunction in temporal lobe epilepsy. Ann. Neurol. **45:** 568–576.
7. FUERST, D., *et al.* 2001. Volumetric MRI, pathological, and neuropsychological progression in hippocampal sclerosis. Neurology **57:** 184–188.
8. EKMAN, P. & W.V. FRIESEN. 1976. Pictures of Facial Affect. Consulting Psychologist Press. Palo Alto, CA.
9. TREMBLAY, C., *et al.* 2001. The recognition of adults' and children's facial expressions of emotions. J. Psychol. **121:** 341–350.
10. ROLLS, E.T. 1992. Neurophysiology and functions of the primate amygdala. *In* The Amygdala: Neurobiological Aspects of Emotion, Memory and Mental Dysfunction. J.P. Aggleton, Ed. Wyley-Liss. New York.

The Relationship between EEG Asymmetry and Positive Emotionality in Young Children

STEWART A. SHANKMAN,[a,b] CRAIG E. TENKE,[a] GERARD E. BRUDER,[a]
C. EMILY DURBIN,[a] ELIZABETH P. HAYDEN,[a]
MAUREEN E. BUCKLEY,[a] AND DANIEL N. KLEIN[a]

[a]Department of Psychology, Stony Brook University,
Stony Brook, New York 11794-2500, USA

[b]New York State Psychiatric Institute, New York, New York 10032, USA

KEYWORDS: EEG asymmetry; children; positive emotionality

INTRODUCTION

There is a long clinical tradition of examining the relationship between depression and personality.[1] In the adult literature, low positive emotionality (low PE: listlessness, low enthusiasm) has received much attention as a specific risk factor for depression.[2] In the developmental literature, however, low PE has been largely ignored as a general dimension of temperament, let alone as a risk factor for depression.

The current study is part of a larger project that seeks to test and elaborate the hypothesis that low PE is a precursor of depression. In order to evaluate a nomological network, we selected a series of features to test the validity of the low PE–depression link. The two features we focused on were family history of depression[3] and EEG asymmetries. In this report, we focus on whether low-PE children exhibited EEG asymmetries.

Much of the research on resting EEG asymmetries and depression arises from Davidson's approach-withdrawal model.[4,5] This model hypothesizes that individuals with a "low-approach affective style" (i.e., a decrease in reward-seeking motivation) exhibit a frontal asymmetry due to decreased left frontal activity. Other researchers have focused on posterior regions of the brain—specifically, an asymmetry due to a decrease in right posterior regions

Address for correspondence: Stewart Shankman, Department of Psychology, SUNY Stony Brook, Stony Brook, NY 11794-2500. Voice: 631-632-4099; fax: 631-632-7876.
sshankma@ic.sunysb.edu

Ann. N.Y. Acad. Sci. 1000: 389–392 (2003). © 2003 New York Academy of Sciences.
doi: 10.1196/annals.1280.037

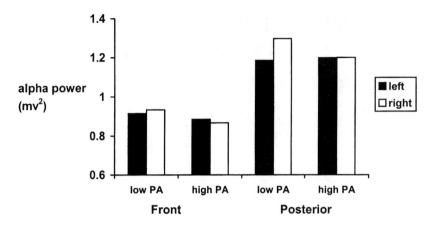

FIGURE 1. EEG asymmetries by region.

of the brain. This asymmetry is hypothesized to reflect a reduced ability in depressed individuals to accurately judge the affective significance of stimuli. The low-PE children in the present study have a reduced response to positive stimuli and may thus exhibit a posterior asymmetry.

METHODS

Subjects

PE was determined by coding behavior during episodes of Laboratory Temperament Assessment Battery (Lab-TAB)[7] at age 3. The children in the top and bottom 25% on PE dimension were followed up at age 5–6. The final sample was 17 high PE children and 11 low PE children, all of whom were right-handed.

EEG Procedure

Six 60-s blocks of EEG were recorded while children either had their eyes open (O) or closed (C) from 6 lateral electrode pairs (F7/F8, F3/F4, T7/T8, C3/C4, P7/P8, P3/P4). Data were segmented into overlapping epochs (2.048 s; overlap 50%), and epochs contaminated by artifact were excluded. Alpha band power (7–12 Hz) was computed using a fast Fourier transform. We focused on this band because of its hypothesized inverse relation with cortical activity. Finally, regional alpha values were computed by pooling electrodes within anterior (F7/F8, F3/F4), central (T7/T8, C3/C4), and posterior (P7/P8, P3/P4) regions of each hemisphere.

RESULTS

ANOVAs yielded a group (low PE vs. high PE) × hemisphere (right vs. left) interaction for the posterior region, [$F (1, 26) = 5.94, P < 0.05$ eta^2 = .19] but not for frontal region, [$F (1, 26) = 2.23, P = 0.15$, eta^2 = .08]. These findings were independent of gender differences. The findings also held when we restricted analyses to the 23 children who were classified as high or low PE at ages 3 and 5 (i.e., the children with stable temperaments).

Finally, we computed asymmetry (log right − log left) indices for both the frontal and posterior regions. Neither of these metrics significantly correlated with temperamental dimensions of negative emotionality (NE: fear, sadness, and anger).

DISCUSSION

Children with low PE exhibited a significant posterior EEG asymmetry compared to high-PE children. These results support the hypothesis that the posterior asymmetry found in depression reflects a deficit in positive emotionality. Taken together with the finding that low PE predicted maternal depression,[3] the present findings suggest that low PE may be a temperamental marker for depression.

Interestingly, EEG asymmetry was specific to the positive emotionality dimension, as it did not correlate with the negative emotionality dimension. This mirrors our other finding that low PE (and not high NE) predicted maternal depression.[3]

The low-PE and high-PE groups did not differ on frontal asymmetry. This may be because the frontal lobes in children are less developed.

REFERENCES

1. KLEIN, D.N., C.E. DURBIN, S.A. SHANKMAN & N.J. SANTIAGO. 2002. Depression and Personality. Handbook of Depression. I.H. Gotlib & C.L. Hammen, Eds. Guilford Press. New York.
2. CLARK, L.A. & D. WATSON. 1991. Tripartite model of anxiety and depression: psychometric evidence and taxonomic implications. J. Abnorm. Psychol. **100:** 316–336.

3. DURBIN, C.E., D.N. KLEIN, E.P. HAYDEN & M.E. BUCKLEY. Temperament and familial risk for mood disorders in preschoolers: a multitrait-multimethod approach. Submitted for publication.
4. DAVIDSON, R.J. 1992. Anterior cerebral asymmetry and the nature of emotion. Brain Cogn. **20:** 125–151.
5. DAVIDSON, R.J. 1998. Affective style and affective disorders: perspectives from affective neuroscience. Cogn. Emotion **12:** 307–330.
6. BRUDER, G.E. 2002. Frontal and parietotemporal asymmetries in depressive disorders: behavioral, electrophysiologic, and neuroimaging findings. *In* The Asymmetrical Brain. R.J. Davidson & K. Hugdahl, Eds.: 719–742. MIT Press. Cambridge, MA.
7. GOLDSMITH, H.H., J. REILLY, K.S. LEMERY, *et al.* 1995. Laboratory Temperament Assessment Battery: Preschool version. Unpublished manuscript.

Facial Expression of Emotion in Human Frontal and Temporal Lobe Epileptic Seizures

CARLO ALBERTO TASSINARI,[a] ELENA GARDELLA,[a]
GUIDO RUBBOLI,[a] STEFANO MELETTI,[a] LILIA VOLPI,[a]
MARCO COSTA,[b] AND PIO ENRICO RICCI-BITTI[b]

[a]Division of Neurology, Bellaria Hospital University of Bologna,
40139 Bologna, Italy

[b]Department of Psychology, University of Bologna, Bologna, Italy

KEYWORDS: temporal lobe epilepsy; facial expression; emotion; frontal lobe epilepsy

While there is evidence of an impaired perception of emotion in verbal and facial expression in epileptic patients with unilateral focal resection of frontal, temporal, or parieto-occipital cortex,[1] there is up to now a lack of research on the encoding aspects of facial expressions during seizure. In this study the video recordings of 146 seizures of 20 patients with temporal lobe epilepsy (12 females and 8 males) and 9 patients with frontal lobe epilepsy (2 females and 7 males) were analyzed using the Facial Action Coding System (FACS). Seizures were recorded in a standard hospital setting. Each video was paired with an EEG recording in order to ascertain the relationship between the clinical manifestations and the ictal discharge. The hypothesis was that, during the seizure, in addition to well-established facial expressions such as the "blank stare" during a "petit mal" absence with impaired consciousness, and the grimaces (unilateral or bilateral jerking and tonic contractions of the facial musculature), the facial displays can show a coherent pattern that is comparable to the facial expressions of emotions as they appear in normal subjects. Coherent patterns of facial expressions of emotions during the ictal event (see FIG. 1) can emerge as a result of the activa-

Address for correspondence: Carlo Alberto Tassinari, M.D., Department of Neurological Sciences, University of Bologna, Bellaria Hospital, V. Altura, 3, 40139 Bologna, Italy. Voice: 0039-051-6225739; fax: 0039-051-6225369.
carlo.tassinari@unibo.it

Ann. N.Y. Acad. Sci. 1000: 393–394 (2003). © 2003 New York Academy of Sciences.
doi: 10.1196/annals.1280.038

FIGURE 1. Facial expressions of happiness (**A**) and fear (**B**), occurring during the seizure and ending with the ictal event itself. (F.A.C.S. by P.E. Ricci-Bitti & M. Costa, Department of Psychology, University of Bologna, Italy.)

tion of selective inborn motor patterns.[2] Further displays of emotional patterns during temporal lobe seizures are recognizable in the ictal laughing, (gelastic seizure), characterized by forced and unmotivated laughter; and the dacrystic seizure, characterized by forced and unmotivated crying.[3] These date confirm a crucial role of the limbic system both in the recognition and expression of emotion.[4]

REFERENCES

1. KOLB, B. & L. TAYLOR. 1981. Affective behavior in patients with localized cortical excisions: role of lesion site and side. Science **214:** 89–91.
2. TASSINARI, C.A., E. GARDELLA, S. MELETTI & G. RUBBOLI. 2003. The neuroethological interpretation of motor behaviors in "nocturnal-hyperkinetic-frontal seizures": emergence of "innate" motor behaviors. *In* Frontal Seizures and Epilepsy in Children. A. Beaumanoir *et al.*, Eds.: 43–48. John Libbey Eurotext. Montrouge, France.
3. MARCHINI, C., D. ROMITO, B. LUCCI & E. DEL ZOTTO. 1994. Fits of weeping as an unusual manifestation of reflex epilepsy induced by speaking: case report. Acta Neurol. Scand. **90:** 218–221.
4. MELETTI, S., F. BENUZZI, G. RUBBOLI, *et al.* 2003. Impaired facial emotion recognition in early-onset right mesial temporal lobe epilepsy. Neurology **60**(3): 426–431.

Buccofacial Apraxia and the Expression of Emotion

JOSHUA DAVID WOOLLEY

Memory and Aging Center and the Department of Neuroscience, University of California–San Francisco, San Francisco, California 94143-1207, USA

KEYWORDS: buccofacial apraxia; emotion; expression; automato-voluntary dissociation

Apraxia is a disorder in executing "learned"[1] or "skilled" movement (excluding explicitly symbolic movements[2]) not accounted for by weakness, incoordination, sensory loss, incomprehension or inattention to commands.[3, 4] In a classic case, the patient carried out commands such as, "show me how you would use a hammer" with his right arm without hesitation.[1] However, when asked to perform the same actions with his left arm, the patient would either do nothing or make an obviously incorrect response. When given real objects, the patient showed no deficits with either arm. The fact that the right arm performed the actions normally rules out the possibility of incomprehension, inattention, or uncooperativeness; while the successful performance of the left arm with real objects rules out the possibility of weakness or incoordination. This particular pattern of deficits is now called *ideomotor apraxia*.

When patients have damage centered in the premotor area of the left frontal lobe, they may exhibit limb apraxia (LA) but may also show apraxia of the face, so-called *buccofacial apraxia* (BFA). These patients cannot pretend or imitate facial movements such as blowing out a match or sucking through a straw, but they usually perform normally when presented with a real match or straw. BFA, while fairly common, has been less studied than limb apraxia and has seldom been related to facial emotion expression.

Care must be taken to separate BFA from automato-voluntary dissociation (AVD) affecting the face. In AVD, corticospinal innervation of the face is im-

Address for correspondence: Joshua David Woolley, Memory and Aging Center, UCSF, 350 Parnassus St., Suite 706, San Francisco, CA 94143-1207. Voice: 415-476-6880; fax: 415-476-4800.

jwoolle@itsa.ucsf.edu

Ann. N.Y. Acad. Sci. 1000: 395–401 (2003). © 2003 New York Academy of Sciences.
doi: 10.1196/annals.1280.039

paired, leading to loss of voluntary control of the face, while "automatic" emotional responses such as crying and smiling, presumably subserved by subcortical pathways, remain intact. This leads to an inability to voluntarily move the face or pose emotional faces while leaving spontaneous emotional facial movements and automatic facial movements intact. Bilateral lesions of the frontal operculum can lead to this syndrome.[5] The separation of neural circuits for voluntary and involuntary control of the face is supported by numerous lines of evidence including the existence of lesions that selectively impair either system and the decreased involuntary emotional facial displays with relative sparing of voluntary facial posing exhibited by patients with Parkinson's disease and other basal ganglia dysfunction.[3,6–9] Furthermore, patients whose severed facial nerves (VII) have been reattached to their accessory nerves (XI) recover voluntary, but not spontaneous, emotional control.[9] Because they fail on tests of praxis, patients with AVD are sometimes labeled as having BFA.[4,10] In contrast to those affected by BFA, AVD patients have paralysis of voluntary facial movement and thus lack any deficit specific to planning complex movement. Therefore, patients with AVD should not be considered apraxic.

To show that a patient has BFA, one must show that (1) the patient is not paralyzed for voluntary movements and (2) the patient has deficits specific to pretending and or imitating movements with the face. Merely observing that the patient cannot perform facial movements to command or imitation but does not exhibit total facial paralysis is insufficient to diagnose BFA, since casual observation cannot separate voluntary from involuntary movements. Asking the patient to perform buccofacial tasks with real objects such as sucking on a straw formally rules out AVD.

Most studies implicate the left frontal operculum and surrounding tissue to be important for BFA (refs. 3, 10–15; but see 16, 17). These areas include the premotor cortex for the face, an area known to be important for planning deliberate facial movement. Raade *et al.* explicitly investigated the relationship between limb apraxia and BFA in patients with single left-sided strokes.[11] While eight subjects exhibited both LA and BFA, three patients had BFA without LA, and three patients had LA without BFA. Furthermore, both the nature of errors and the lesion locations differed significantly between subjects with LA and BFA. The authors conclude that the underlying neural substrates of LA and BFA are at least partially distinct.

The relationship between BFA and emotion has rarely been studied. One study took 27 brain-damaged males and asked them to make 6 facial movements, first with a neutral command followed by an emotional command.[18] The neutral commands included "close one eye" and "put your tongue out," while the corresponding emotional commands were "close one eye like a wink" and "stick your tongue out like you are making a face at me." Commands were presented in a fixed order: 6 neutral commands, then 4 buccofacial tasks, followed by 6 emotional commands. Left brain–damaged patients

(LBD) exhibited BFA; all groups improved with emotional cueing, but the LBD group showed a significantly larger improvement.

The authors accept that their study design did not separate the effects of cueing from task order. However, they claim that the improved response of patients with BFA to emotional cueing is different from apraxic patients' known lack of improvement with repeated trials.[19] They also suggest that since the right hemisphere may have a "special role in emotion processing, it may [be] mediating the facilitation effect."[20] Given more recent evidence showing no particular connection between right or left hemisphere damage with deficits in spontaneous or voluntary expression of emotions,[21,22] this hypothesis seems unlikely. Furthermore, the authors note that context may have provided some sort of general facilitation. This seems probable given that the emotional commands contained within them the neutral commands; replacing "close one eye like a wink" with "wink your eye" would control for patients' possessing more information about the intended movement.

A more serious concern is the questionable relationship between commands such as "close one eye like a wink" and emotion. These commands could be taken as merely descriptive. Winking, for instance, can be considered emotional in the context of flirting and nonemotional in the context of having something caught in your eye. Performance for each item was not reported separately, preventing the evaluation of this hypothesis. These experimental limitations prevent strong conclusions from being drawn from this study, although the data suggest that emotional information can improve apraxic performance.

BFA is usually assessed by asking the patient to make simple single movements. However, most authors do not take into account the actual functional anatomy of the facial musculature when they define "single movements." For example, Mater and Kimura included "upper teeth on lower lip," while De Renzi et al. included "give a 'Bronx cheer' or 'raspberry'" as "single movements."[4,15] However, according to Ekman and Frieson's Facial Action Coding System (FACS, a system whereby all individual movements of the face can be objectively measured), each of these movements includes more than one action unit (AU, the simplest unit of facial movement).[23] Few studies of BFA have directly studied the relationship between patients' ability to make single AUs and to make these "simple movements."

One study of 57 stroke patients addressed the relationship between the ability to imitate 14 single AUs, including items such as raising the inner and outer eyebrows separately, and BFA. Subjects were shown videos of actors posing the various facial movements and were given verbal encouragement such as "you are lowering not raising your eyebrow."[24] Subjects were given three scores for making the movement: (1) absent all other movements, (2) associated with extraneous movements, and (3) associated with other facilitating movements. For all groups (LBN, RBN, and controls) the first two scores were low (20–25% and 30–35%), while the third score was high

(90%). Surprisingly, brain damage had no significant effect on either of the first two scores, while RBN showed a marginal but significant impairment in imitation with facilitation. Furthermore, deficits in AU imitation showed no relationship to BFA or other types of apraxia. However, only four individuals in the entire study showed deficits in imitation. This study suggests that the ability to imitate single facial movements (AUs) is more resistant to focal damage than the ability to pretend or imitate more complex movement combinations that may require learning. The authors conclude that the "control of facial mimic movements might be partly dependent on the pyramidal system, but in addition might have a diffuse and multiple representation in the non-pyramidal system, similarly to what has been proposed[1]... for the central axial and extrinsic eye movements."

If patients with BFA can perform single AUs, then why do they fail on tasks of BFA that require only a single AU? Several of the items in the test of BFA used in this study[24] such as "show how you would kiss someone" and "puff or blow," have corresponding single AUs (AUs 18 and 34, respectively). Unfortunately, this study[24] cannot address this issue since these AUs (18 and 34) were not evaluated during the AU imitation portion of the study. Furthermore, not all of the items on the test of BFA had corresponding AUs, and performance for each item was not reported separately. Further confusing the issue, Borod *et al.* used "pucker your lips like a kiss" for their emotional command 18, whereas the present study of Pizzamiglio *et al.*[24] used "show how you would kiss someone" as one of the items on the test of BFA.

Perhaps the discrepancy in behavioral deficits is due to significant differences in the procedure for eliciting the facial movements. For the test of individual AUs, the patients saw a video and were given verbal encouragement. For the test of BFA, patients were given a verbal command and then, if necessary, shown the proper movement. The verbal encouragement in particular could have given the patients the extra information necessary for successful facial posing. This methodological concern could be addressed by systematically altering the procedures used to elicit identical facial movements. This would allow the exact deficit in BFA and its relation to the ability to make single movements to be ascertained. For example, for the pucker (AU 18), a patient could be asked to "pucker your lips" as a simple anatomical command. Then the patient could be asked to "show how you would kiss someone." This command should activate stored, possibly learned, motor programs. Finally, the patient could be asked to "show how you would suck on a straw" and then given a real straw and asked to repeat the movement. These commands would presumably engage a stored motor program involving tool use. By using this research methodology, the target motor output would be held constant while the method for eliciting the movement is systematically varied. This would allow the specific nature of the deficit in BFA to be investigated (TABLE 1).

TABLE 1. Facial action units

Action Unit	Anatomical Command	Nonemotional Motor Program	Nonemotional Motor Program Utilizing Tools	Emotional Motor Program
1+2	Raise your eyebrows.	Make your forehead wrinkle.		Move your eyebrows as if you are surprised.
4	Lower your eyebrows.	Move your eyebrows as if you are concentrating.		
	Bring your eyebrows together.	Move your eyebrows as if the sun is in your eyes.		Move your eyebrows as if you are angry.
5	Raise your eyelids.			Move your eyelids as if you are surprised.
	Open your eyes wide.			
7	Tighten your eye-lids without closing your eyes.	Move your eyelids as if the sun is in your eyes.		Move your eyelids as if you are angry.
		Squint.		
		Move your eyelids as if you are trying to see something far away.		
9	Wrinkle your nose.	Move your nose as if you have smelled something bad.		Move your nose as if you are disgusted.
12	Pull the corner of your lips up.			Move your lips as if you are happy.
15	Pull the corner of your lips down.			Move your lips as if you are sad.
17	Push your lower lip up.			Pout.
18	Purse your lips.	Show how you would kiss someone.	Show how you would suck through a straw.	
	Pucker your lips.	Show how you would whistle.	Show how you would blow out a match.	
	Make your lips as small as you can in the shape of an "O" and push them slightly forward.			
27+25	Lower your jaw and part your lips.	Pretend to say "Ah."		Move your mouth as if you are surprised.
	Open your mouth.	Yawn as if sleepy.		

The same patients from the Pizzamiglio *et al.* study[24] were asked to pose the six commonly accepted basic emotions, and their attempts were both FACS coded and judged by naïve observers.[21] No differences were found between controls and brain-damaged patients in the appropriateness of their posed facial displays. Furthermore, while no groups showed deficits in posing, roughly half of the LBDs had BFA; no correlation was found between the presence of BFA and the ability to perform facial expression. These data suggest that BFA and emotional face posing do not share a neural substrate.

BFA is a common neurological disorder that affects the ability to make some voluntary movements with the face to command or imitation. Involuntary facial movements such as smiling at a joke or coughing, imitation of individual facial movements, and voluntary emotional facial displays are apparently spared in BFA. The definitions of these categories of facial movements have not always been carefully delineated, and much confusion exists as to how to differentiate among them. A promising avenue of future research is to address the salient features of these categories and how they relate to BFA. While the current data remain incomplete, available evidence suggests that there are at least three distinct neural circuits innervating the face. These include a subcortical circuit subserving spontaneous emotional expression, a presumably multiply represented circuit subserving voluntary emotional expression, and a circuit that contains the left frontal cortical lobe that subserves complex and/or learned movements, which is disrupted in BFA. Knowledge of these separate circuits allows for more precise investigation and classification of patients with facial movement dysfunction and direct testing of this schema. This will allow a deeper understanding of the functional neuroanatomy of the neural circuits innervating the face.

REFERENCES

1. GESCHWIND, N. 1975. Am. Sci. **63**(2): 188–195.
2. HEILMAN, K.M., L.J. ROTHI & E. VALENSTEIN. 1982. Neurology **32**(4): 342–346.
3. ALEXANDER, M.P., E. BAKER, M.A. NAESER, *et al.* 1992. Brain **115** (Pt. 1): 87–107.
4. DE RENZI, E. & L.A. VIGNOLO. 1966. Cortex **2**: 50–73.
5. WELLER, M. 1993. J. Neurol. **240**(4): 199–208.
6. WEDDELL, R.A., C. TREVARTHEN & J.D. MILLER. 1988. Neuropsychologia **26**(3): 373–385.
7. EBLEN, F., M. WELLER & J. DICHGANS. 1992. Eur. Arch. Psychiatry Clin. Neurosci. **242**(2-3): 93–95.
8. GRAFF-RADFORD, N.R., H. DAMASIO, T. YAMADA, *et al.* 1985. Brain **108**(Pt. 2): 485–516.
9. KAHN, E.A. 1964. Clin. Neurosurg. **12**: 9–22.
10. TOGNOLA, G. & L.A. VIGNOLO. 1980. Neuropsychologia **18**(3): 257–272.

11. RAADE, A.S., L.J. ROTHI & K.M. HEILMAN. 1991. Brain Cogn. **16**(2): 130–146.
12. MINTZ, T.R. & A. KERTESZ. 1989. Presented at the meeting of the Canadian Association of Speech-Language Pathologists and Audiologists, Toronto, Ontario.
13. MAESHIMA, S. *et al.* 1997. Brain Inj. **11**(11): 777–782.
14. BROUSSOLLE, E. *et al.* 1996. J. Neurol. Sci. **144**(1-2): 44–58.
15. MATEER, C. & D. KIMURA. 1977. Brain Lang. **4**(2): 262–276.
16. MANI, R.B. & D.N. LEVINE. Arch. Neurol. 1988. **45**(5): 581–584.
17. KRAMER, J.H., D.C. DELIS & T. NAKADA. 1985. Ann. Neurol. **18**(4): 512–514.
18. BOROD, J.C., M.P. LORCH, E. KOFF & M. NICHOLAS. 1987. J. Clin. Exp. Neuropsychol. **9**(2): 155–161.
19. MATEER, C. 1978. Brain Lang. **6**(3): 334–341.
20. BOROD, J.C., E. KOFF, M. PERLMAN LORCH & M. NICHOLAS. 1986. Neuropsychologia **24**(2): 169–180.
21. CALTAGIRONE, C. *et al.* 1989. Cortex **25**(4): 653–663.
22. MAMMUCARI, A. *et al.* 1988. Cortex **24**(4): 521–533.
23. EKMAN, P. & W. FRIESON. 1978. Consulting Psychologist Press. Palo Alto, CA.
24. PIZZAMIGLIO, L., C. CALTAGIRONE, A. MAMMUCARI, *et al.* 1987. Cortex **23**(2): 207–221.

Index of Contributors